The Columbia Guide to
Asian American Literature Since 1945

Columbia Guides to Literature Since 1945

The Columbia Guides to Literature Since 1945

Contents

Acknowledgments

I would like to thank the following individuals who helped make this book possible. James Raimes and James Warren, both formerly of Columbia University Press, guided the progress of the book in its earlier stages, and Juree Sondker, associate editor at CUP, offered timely help in the final stages of its preparation. I also wish to thank the two anonymous reviewers of the book in its manuscript form, from whose reviews I benefited considerably. Leslie Kriesel, Senior Manuscript Editor, is truly an outstanding editor, for whom I have only kudos. In 2002–2003, the State System of Higher Education of Pennsylvania awarded me a Faculty Professional Development Award to support this project, for which I am most grateful. Robert Swanson again demonstrated excellent indexing skills, as he did for my previous book, *Asian American Literary Studies* (Edinburgh University Press, 2005). My wife, Dr. Yufeng Qian, not only supported me throughout the research and writing process but also helped fix many computer problems, and my son, George Ian, showed patience and understanding during the countless hours I spent at the computer. This book is for them all.

Part I
Narrative Overview

The main purpose of this book is to provide a historical overview of the development of major genres of Asian American literature from the end of World War II to the beginning of the twenty-first century. Asian American writers made landmark achievements with some works produced soon after 1945, notably the Chinese American autobiographer Jade Snow Wong's *Fifth Chinese Daughter*, with the war as an ancillary theme, and the Japanese American novelist John Okada's *No-No Boy*, an antiwar and identity-exploring work of political and ethnographic significance. Since the 1960s civil rights movement, Asian American literature has flourished into a diverse, heterogeneous field characterized by a great variety of themes, genres, styles, and ethnic and cultural backgrounds of its writers. This reference guide, encompassing major authors and works in Asian American literature, offers a comprehensive picture of that evolution over the past sixty years (1945–2005) for both the general reader and the specialist, to benefit the teaching and study of one of the fastest-growing fields in American literature.

"Asian American" has been a contested term since its inception in the 1960s. Historically the hyphenated version, "Asian-American," has been used by literary writers and scholars as well as by historians, but in recent decades there has been a tendency to use "Asian-American" as an adjective and "Asian American" as a noun. Maxine Hong Kingston, in "Cultural Mis-readings by American Reviewers," says, "We ought to leave out the hyphen in 'Chinese-American,' because the hyphen gives the word on either side equal weight, as if linking two nouns. It looks as if a Chinese-American has double citizenship, which is impossible in today's world. Without the hyphen, 'Chinese' is an adjective and 'American' a noun; a Chinese American is a type of American" (60). As an adjective, "Chinese" or "Asian" assumes a qualifying role in the expression, giving greater weight to "American" because the noun designates national and geographical affiliations and affirms the citizenship status of the bearer of the label.

"Asian American" has been broadly used to denote Americans of ethnic groups with ancestral roots in or connections to the landmass of Asia. In practice—certainly in the embryonic stages of Asian American studies, beginning with the 1968 students' protest against the absence of "Third World" curricula and faculty at San Francisco State College—"Asian American" designated primarily national origins in the Far Eastern countries of China, Japan, and Korea. In the past decade, the label suddenly found itself limited, if not altogether ineffective, in describing other emerging cultures and literatures produced by writers and artists from South and Southeast Asian countries, such as Bangladesh and Sri Lanka, not to mention the countries that have been linked to the United States as consequences of wars, such as Vietnam, and colonial adventures, such as the Philippines. Indeed, the definition of "Asian America" as both a reality and an imagined construct has been considerably influenced by the geopolitical boundaries of the continent of Asia.

The expansion of the field of Asian American literary production and critical studies in the last quarter of the twentieth century (I am thinking of Kingston's *The Woman Warrior*, published in 1976, as a possible landmark work) has exposed the restrictive functions of the umbrella rubric "Asian American." In the forum "What Do We Need to Teach?" in the June 1993 issue of *American Literature*, Stephen H. Sumida writes: "Whereas in the mid-1970s we could carry all Asian American texts in print to class with one hand, today there are far more texts available than my beginnings of a list here can possibly include" (352). Sumida offered a number of undergraduate and graduate courses at the University of Michigan, including what he then called a "third tier" course on Hawaiian literatures, which he said "tends to be more insistently 'multicultural' than my survey of literary history because Hawaii's literature ranges from native Hawaiian poetry and narrative, to journals of European visitors, to Melville and Twain (and his never published 'novel' of Hawai'i), to poetry and culture of Asian immigrant laborers, to the polyethnic literature whose authors are identified with voicing the 'Local' in Hawai'i today" (353). This practice resembles that of many other scholars and writers—notably writers from Hawai'i—who have adopted the term "Asian/Pacific American" for its broader and more inclusive functions. The many islands of Hawai'i provide not only a bridge of communication between the two continents of Asia and America but also a site for the fusion of Asian, Pacific, and American cultures. The inhabitants of course belong in the Pacific American category and are included in this book. The term "Asian" is thus employed to refer to authors having racial and ethnic origins in the Far East, South and Southeast Asia, and the Hawaiian islands of the Pacific.

"American" has been no less problematic in its multiple functions to designate socio- and geopolitical identities of the land and the people. America remains an important identity marker in the name the United States of America, and therefore citizens of this country are called (and call themselves) Americans, preempting any possibility of Canadians using the same term for self-reference. Craig Tapping, in "South Asia Writes North America," finds it sometimes very difficult to distinguish among Asian writers residing and writing in North America because of the linguistic heritage shared by Canada and the United States, and because of the easy crossing of their national boundaries by migrant writers such as Bharati Mukherjee and Michael Ondaatje, to name only two. Thus, argues Tapping, "Domicile and ethnicity do not alone determine Indo-American or Indo-Canadian identities: geographical, lexical, political, and cultural differences are the signifying tropes of Indo-American ethnic literatures" (287). Ethnic Asians in both the United States and Canada have encountered similar legal discrimination and government-imposed, race-based restrictions in their struggles for acceptance; in both countries, for example, they were forced to resort to legal measures to protect their civil rights as citizens. But it must also be noted, as Brook Thomas convincingly argues in connection with Kingston's *China Men* and the 1898 Supreme Court decision in *United States v. Wong Kim Ark*, that "Laws do not only restrict; they can also generate possibilities" (694).

Asian American literature tentatively began at the end of the nineteenth century, with the two Eaton sisters, Edith (Sui Sin Far) and Winnifred (pseudonym Onoto Watanna), and developed markedly in the second half of the twentieth century, becoming established as a distinct field of literary production. Scholars and teachers have argued eloquently that American literature has become a comparative discipline since the emergence of ethnic literatures such as African American, Native American, Latino/a American, and Asian American, to name only the most obvious. The publication of *Redefining American Literary History* in 1990, among other things, further attests to this view. The editors and contributors of that volume reconsider, and indeed redefine the canon of American literature. Ethnic literatures, both drawing on and diverging from mainstream American literary traditions and establishments, have, however, developed distinctly and separately. Asian American literature—literatures—originates as responses to the cultural, political, existential, and legal experiences of ethnic Asians living in America as immigrants, citizens, and people; North American citizenship, resident status, and experience of authors of Asian racial descent are therefore the principles of inclusion in this guide. Asian writers living in North America but writing exclusively about non-American experiences, despite their immigrant or citizenship status, such as Ha Jin, Nien Cheng, Rohinton Mistry, Raja Rao, and Alberto Florentino are excluded.

Asian American writing, in both its earliest manifestations and contemporary expressions, is informed, and to a considerable degree defined, by Asian Americans' racial past and existential experience in America. Of course there is no such thing as one Asian American group, for Asia subsumes hundreds of ethnicities, of the same or different races. King-Kok Cheung writes, "The term 'Asian American literature' generally describes works by writers of diverse national origins—Chinese, Japanese, Korean, Filipino, East Indian, Pakistani, Vietnamese, Thai, Cambodian, Laotian, and Pacific Islanders" (xv). However, so far no single study has precisely mapped out the boundaries pertaining to "Asian America," and every author or Asian subgroup has their own understanding and definition of this contested term, which comments on the power differentials and power struggles as well as the complexity of identity politics within the heterogeneous groups. This guide aims to reflect the heterogeneity and diversity within the large rubric of Asian American literature and culture.

The heterogeneity of Asian Americans is embodied in their race, ethnicity, class, politics, religion, culture, and sexual orientation. As Lisa Lowe argues in "Heterogeneity, Hybridity, Multiplicity": "From the perspective of the majority culture, Asian Americans may very well be constructed as different from, and other than, Euro-Americans. But from the perspectives of Asian Americans, we are perhaps even more different, more diverse, among ourselves: being men and women at different distances and generations from our 'original' Asian cultures" (27). Geographically, these peoples emigrated from the same continent, and they have shared the same destination, undergone similar historical and legal experiences, reaped similar rewards, and tasted similar culture- and race-related bitterness. They share similar immigration histories and diasporic movements in the United States and Canada; they pursue both material and political ends in coming to America; and they both face the problems and garner the benefits of assimilation and Americanization, which are sometimes synonymous but not always the same.

The more populous Asian subgroups—Chinese and Japanese—share similar patterns of immigration but have experienced historical and legal events unique to their own home country and ethnicity. The Chinese, for example, along with the Irish and others, provided labor for the construction of America's railroads in the mid-nineteenth century; and yet they suffered a great deal from the 1882 Chinese Exclusion Act. This legalized discriminatory practice became a major reference point for a considerable amount of Chinese American writing. The building of the transcontinental railroad and the Chinese Exclusion Act expose governmental racism in its most hypocritical and ironical form: the Asian group that contributed significantly to America's material wealth was subjected to the most race-based persecution. Such humiliating experiences, as well as Chinese Americans' remarkable achievements, are thoughtfully represented in works like Kingston's auto/biographical *China Men* and Frank Chin's novel *Donald Duk*, and in occasional poems in Cathy Song's *Picture Bride*. Together, these works delineate a people who made their mark in American history with sweat and blood and through legal battles.

Japanese Americans, faring only slightly better than their Chinese counterparts during the first four decades of the twentieth century, experienced one of the most humiliating injustices in American history: evacuation and internment by the government after Japan's bombing of Pearl Harbor on December 7, 1941. The Chinese became the heroes and the Japanese the villains, in public perceptions of the two Asian subgroups. However, the internment of the Japanese in essence differs little from the exclusion of the Chinese six decades earlier: both resulted from legalized racism initiated by the national government and enacted at the local level. This experience had crippling effects on Japanese Americans, as is uncompromisingly depicted in John Okada's *No-No Boy*, Joy Kogawa's *Obasan*, and Hisaye Yamamoto's short fiction, most notably "The Legend of Miss Sasagawara" and "A Fire in Fontana." Thus, internment has been the most traumatic event in the history of the Japanese in North America (similar events happened in Canada) and was seared in its collective memory, which runs deep in the writings of many Japanese American authors.

The Philippines and India, different as they are from China and Japan in racial terms, both were colonized lands and have a colonial past, though they were controlled by different countries. In both cases the colonial experience prompted immigration to North America. In more than one way, the immigration history of Filipinos and Indians is about a quest for freedom and liberty. Carlos Bulosan's autobiographical yet universal *America Is in the Heart*, about the Filipino American immigration and assimilation experience, is a classic that limns such a quest. Bharati Mukherjee's *Jasmine* and *Tiger's Daughter* are likewise bicultural works that depict important facets of the South Asian immigration experience. Vietnamese Americans face yet another set of issues as a result of the U.S. military involvement in Vietnam from 1964 to 1973. The Vietnam War and the armed conflicts inside Cambodia under Pol Pot in the 1970s both caused expatriatism and immigration. Tran Van Dinh's *Blue Dragon, White Tiger*, Wendy Law-Yone's *The Coffin Tree*, and Haing Ngor's *A Cambodian Odyssey* all reflect their respective cultures, domestic upheavals, and diasporic hardships and triumphs, and all helped shape twentieth-century Asian America's literary landscape. This guide reviews such works to provide readers with a sense of their historical, political, literary, and ethnic significances.

The Columbia Guide to Asian American Literature Since 1945 represents North American writers with cultural and ethnic origins in the Asian countries of China, Japan, Korea, the Philippines, and Vietnam, and in the South and Southeast Asian countries of Bangladesh, Burma, Cambodia, India, Indonesia, Malaysia, Pakistan, and Sri Lanka. While the majority of North American writers of Asian descent are American, namely, U.S. citizens and nationals, or simply Asian diasporic writers residing in the country, Canadian writers of Asian ancestry constitute a considerable number as well. The shared language of English helps facilitate such an inclusion; more important, Asians—the Chinese and Japanese in particular—have experienced a similar history of negative sentiment on both sides of the border. Some notorious examples include Canada's 1923 Exclusion Act excluding Chinese from immigration; Canadian citizens of Asian descent being denied the right to vote until 1947; and, even prior to the U.S. government's internment of Japanese Americans, Canada's declaration of the Pacific Coast as a strategic military zone from which residents of Japanese descent were removed. These three examples are evidence of a shared history affected and partly defined by ethnicity and race, complicated by the extreme circumstances of World War II on both sides of the Pacific. The two English-speaking countries are therefore included in the monolithic expression "America," which apparently fulfills the reference functions of "North America," which in turn enables "Asian America" to imply the boundaries of "Asian North America."

Asia is generally divisible into three geographical areas: East Asia, South Asia, and Southeast Asia. East Asia, also known as the Far East, includes China, Japan, and Korea, and as many critics and scholars have argued, "Asian America" has come to mainly refer to people from these three originating countries. Indeed, these peoples seem to have produced the most literary works. Authors of South Asian descent, on the other hand, have generally been treated as one group, perhaps unjustifiably, in Asian American anthologies, collections of critical essays, and other similar publishing endeavors. However, as Ketu H. Katrak points out, "Writers from South Asian nations (themselves often invented as nations by the British) encompass a multiplicity of ethnicities, religions, languages, and cultures. Hence the category 'South Asian American' does not indicate a monolithic whole, but rather a collection of differences that are often more compelling and significant than any similarities" (192). Of the South Asian nations, India, Pakistan, and Bangladesh share similarities in ethnicity and culture, certainly before the British partition of India in 1947 and the separation of Pakistan from Bangladesh in 1971.

In the last quarter of the twentieth century no other branch of American literature seems to have experienced such a great revival as Asian American writing, and in the immediate wake of the publication of works such as Kingston's *The Woman Warrior* and Amy Tan's *The Joy Luck Club*, there have appeared a good number of critical studies of individual authors and studies of a general and theoretical nature. However, the first major critical work, Elaine Kim's *Asian American Literature: An Introduction to the Writings and Their Social Context*, did not appear until 1982. In the approximately two decades since then, numerous anthologies of Asian American literature have been published for classroom use; hundreds of articles have been printed in significant journals and books; and dozens of book-length studies of individual authors or groups have been published by major university and commercial presses throughout the country, most notably on the West Coast but also in the Northeast.

To better situate and contextualize this reference guide, I now briefly consider a dozen or so critical and scholarly works in Asian American literary studies. Elaine Kim's *Asian American Literature* is influential because as a groundbreaking work, it first drew the boundaries, however tentative and porous, for an emerging literature. Kim considers Asian American writing generally and Chinese and Japanese American literature particularly; she mentions some Korean and Filipino American authors but takes no note of Vietnamese, Indian, or South Asian American writing. Amy Ling's *Between Worlds: Women Writers of Chinese Ancestry* (1990), as the title indicates, deals with one ethnic group—Chinese Americans, and one gender—women writers such as the Eaton sisters, Lin Tai-yi, Hazel Lin, Diana Chang, Mai-Mai Sze, and Maxine Hong Kingston. A. LaVonne Brown Ruoff and Jerry W. Ward Jr.'s *Redefining American Literary History* (1990) is the first study of its kind that attempts to redefine the canon of American literature from a multiethnic, crosscultural, and comparative perspective, and is useful in the study of U.S. minority literatures; it includes three chapters and a bibliography on Asian American literature.

Shirley Lim and Amy Ling's *Reading the Literatures of Asian America* (1992) is a collection of critical essays that addresses vital issues in literature written by major Asian subgroups. Sau-ling Cynthia Wong's *Reading Asian American Literature: From Necessity to Extravagance*

(1993), called "the first comprehensive book on Asian American literature" since Kim's study, engages topics such as tradition, the practice of reading Asian American literature, and its distinction from mainstream and other minority literatures. King-Kok Cheung's *Articulate Silences: Hisaye Yamamoto, Maxine Hong Kingston, Joy Kogawa*, also published in 1993, is a study of the thematic and rhetorical uses of silence in the fiction of these three Asian North American women novelists. *Racism, Dissent, and Asian Americans from 1850 to the Present* (1993), edited by Philip Foner and Daniel Rosenberg, is an illuminating documentary history of Asian America, especially useful for its historicizing and contextualizing material relevant to the government's treatment of Asian Americans.

Another collection, John Maitino and David Peck's *Teaching American Ethnic Literature* (1996), consists of nineteen essays that deal with four major ethnic literatures; a chapter is devoted to each of five Asian American fiction writers: Bulosan, Kingston, Kogawa, Tan, and Yamamoto. *Immigrant Acts* (1996), by Lisa Lowe, approaches Asian American history and literature from the viewpoints of immigration and citizenship, arguing that the racialized foundations of both the United States as a nation and the development of American capitalism must be understood in the light of Asian immigration. Asian American literature to a great extent reflects the struggles that Asians in America have to endure to gain citizenship and achieve constitutional rights, to be "equal" with members of the mainstream culture. King-Kok Cheung's *An Interethnic Companion to Asian American Literature* (1997), a more comprehensive project consisting of eleven essays alphabetically arranged by national origins, provides useful overviews of literature by Chinese, Filipino, Japanese, Korean, South Asian, and Vietnamese Americans. The second part deals with major political, theoretical, and cultural issues: nationalism and postcolonialism, immigration and diaspora, and gender and identity.

Jinqi Ling's *Narrating Nationalism: Ideology and Form in Asian American Literature* (1998), on the other hand, considers five texts: Okada's *No-No Boy*, Louis Chu's *Eat a Bowl of Tea*, Frank Chin's two plays, *The Chickencoop Chinaman* and *The Year of the Dragon*, and Kingston's *China Men*. Historical and theoretical issues are discussed in the first and final chapters of the book, where the author proposes a reconceptualization of the relationship between the past and the present of post-World War II Asian American literary history. David Leiwei Li's *Imagining the Nation: Asian American Literature and Cultural Consent* (1998), like Lisa Lowe's book, places contemporary Asian American literary production in the context of citizenship, revealing the historical contradiction of a United States caught between the utopian impulses of democratic consent and the residual practice of national inheritance. Li also offers analyses of *The Woman Warrior* and of the polemical views presented in the anthology *Aiiieeeee!*, refuting the controversial "Asian American sensibility" that the editors (Frank Chin et al.) advocate through their choices of works. Li's discussion of "national" and "transnational," "identity" and "difference" not as binary oppositions but as mutually constitutive concepts sheds light on the formative process of Asian American literature. David Palumbo-Liu's *Asian/American: Historical Crossings of a Racial Frontier* (1999), a theory- and issue-oriented study, seeks to read the history of Asian Americans' proximity to the ideal of a white totality as a series of reconfigurations and transgressions of the Asian/American "split."

While the quantity and quality of these publications strongly attest to the intense ongoing interest in the field, until now there has been no guide to post-World War II Asian American literature accessible to both the general reading public and the more specialized audience; therefore, this combination of overviews on major genres, authors, and works, with an A–Z reference section, is a timely effort. This book is meant to be a combined survey and reference work that offers concise information to readers who wish either to obtain a general sense of literary developments or to simply broaden their knowledge of this literature from 1945 to the present. Breadth, comprehensiveness, accuracy, and specificity will be its main characteristics.

* * *

The Columbia Guide to Asian American Literature Since 1945 consists of three main parts: an introductory narrative overview, an A–Z reference section, and a selected bibliography of secondary sources. The overview surveys literary developments in Asian American literature from 1945 to the present. The A–Z reference section—the bulk of the book— deals with six genres, in alphabetical order: anthologies, autobiographies/memoirs, drama, fiction, poetry, and short fiction; each entry (except for anthologies) is followed by bibliographical information on studies of individual authors. The following discussion is keyed to these genres as well. The selected bibliography at the end of the book mainly covers works of a more general nature, such as literary criticism and histories, reference works, and collections of essays.

For coherence and ease of reference, entries on writers are listed alphabetically (only the section on anthologies is arranged chronologically), and when possible, include information on ethnicity or national origin intended to facilitate understanding of the subjects' cultural, racial, intellectual, and biographical background, while providing a chance for comparison between authors with similar backgrounds. Cross-referencing is also used, as many writers tend to engage in several genres. For example, Meena Alexander is primarily considered a poet, but she is also accomplished as a novelist and memoirist, so the main entry on her is found under "Poetry," while her name is also listed under "Fiction" and in "Autobiographies/ Memoirs." An inherently multiethnic project such as this is meant to help the reader grasp the concepts of race, ethnicity, nation, identity, and citizenship in a broad, transnational, and cross-cultural context. Likewise, the approach by genre gives a historical perspective on the evolution of Asian American literature. While this guide cannot offer the analytical or critical depth of specialized studies, it is better able to provide breadth of information on the writers and their works.

Anthologies

Literary anthologies have been such commonly accepted and broadly used instructional tools in college and high school classrooms that not many readers today would consider them hard-won luxuries. This is certainly true of mainstream literary anthologies, but not necessarily of anthologies of literature by minority writers. But what is an anthology? And what is an Asian American anthology? An anthology is generally a collection of selected writings by various authors. This broad definition foregrounds the *collectiveness*—numerous works written by a group of writers compiled in a volume—as well as the *selectiveness* of its contents, which reflects the Greek root meaning of the word for picking flowers: only the good and the spectacular get in. Asian American anthologies, on the other hand, are an approximately three-decade-old phenomenon, and they are mostly collections of selected writings by groups of American authors of Asian descent, often writing in different forms and different time periods, but hardly ever on the same subject; the works are usually multigeneric and sometimes interdisciplinary, the reason that this guide does not qualify "anthologies" with "literary" in the title of that section.

In recent decades, a number of major, influential anthologies of American literature have appeared; among them, the most widely used is probably *The Norton Anthology of American Literature*, and more recently, *The Heath Anthology of American Literature*. While the Heath book is considerably broader in its representation of minority writers and much more experimental with its selection criteria than its Norton cousin, both anthologies understandably retain their editorial focus on mainstream American writers—Caucasian, male, and until recently, female writers of European descent. In the following pages, I compare two recent editions—the fourth and fifth—of volume 2 of *The Norton Anthology of American Literature* to see how Asian American writers are represented, before I turn to two Asian American anthologies published on the cusp of the twenty-first century, Shirley Geok-lin Lim's *Asian-American Anthology* and Victoria Chang's *Asian American Poetry: The Next Generation*.

Under the general editorship of Nina Baym, the first edition of the *Norton Anthology* was published in 1979; the fourth edition came out in 1994. The preface to the fourth edition, much of which was restated in the preface to the fifth edition, opens with an unambiguous editorial statement: "From its inception, a guiding principle of *The Norton Anthology of American Literature* has been to provide a balanced combination of traditional and emergent works" (xxix). And in response to changes in critical interest and classroom need, the editors expanded the fourth edition by adding writings by early European explorers in North America and more writers in every period covered by the anthology. American literature from 1865 to 1914, for example, includes additions of women writers such as Charlotte Perkins Gilman, Kate Chopin, and Mary Austin, as well as Native American and African American writers of the period.

In terms of drama since 1945, the fourth edition adds August Wilson (*Fences*) and David Mamet (*House of Games*), after such familiar playwrights as Eugene O'Neill, Tennessee Williams, and Arthur Miller. Even though the fourth edition appeared eight years after the publication of the Chinese American playwright David Henry Hwang's well-known drama, *M. Butterfly*, Hwang did not make it into this expanded edition. Also noteworthy is the section on American poetry since 1945, where two new poets were added, "the influential early experimentalist George Oppen, and the vibrant and contemporary Li-Young Lee" (xxxi); the latter is a Chinese born in Indonesia and raised in the United States. Cathy Song, a Chinese/Korean American poet, appears before Lee, so the two poets conclude the anthology. In fact, they are the only two Asian American writers lucky or good enough to be represented in this influential volume that sought to balance "traditional and emergent works." Song and Lee are a generation younger than Maxine Hong Kingston and Bharati Mukherjee, both of whom became established writers at least a decade earlier, but neither of whom was included in the fourth edition of the *Norton Anthology*.

The preface also points out, "The editors of this anthology were selected on the basis of their expertise in their individual areas" (xxxii). Arnold Krupat, for example, is a Native American writer and scholar who edited Native American literature for volume 1, and the oratory, songs, and chants, among other things, in volume 2. The presence of a large number of African American writers in both volumes bespeaks the fact that editorial expertise likewise existed in African American literature. The paucity of Asian American writers in the anthology thus suggests that no expert was available to facilitate the editing of Asian

American works, even though Hsu and Palubinskas edited *Asian-American Authors* in 1972, David Hsin-Fu Wand did *Asian-American Heritage* in 1974, and Chin et al. published *Aiiieeeee!* also in 1974, all predating Norton's fourth edition (1994) by approximately two decades! In 1998, when Norton's fifth edition appeared, little changed in terms of coverage of Asian American authors, except for the addition of an excerpt from Kingston's *Tripmaster Monkey: His Fake Book*, even though by then Asian American studies had become an established discipline on many university campuses, and its literature had been taught at almost all universities and colleges in one form or another, whether in an entire course or as a selected text in a course.

The preface to Norton's fifth edition, now signed by Nina Baym, the general editor, recapitulates the contents of its predecessor while laying out a few new features. Baym writes: "From the anthology's inception, three goals have been paramount: first, to present a variety of works rich and substantial enough to enable teachers to build their own courses according to their own ideals . . . ; second, to make the anthology self-sufficient by featuring many works in their entirety and longer selections so that individual authors can be covered in depth; and third, to balance traditional interests with developing critical concerns" (xxix). This balancing effort seems to be a response to new developments in American literature in recent decades. Baym shows an awareness of these: "As every teacher of American literature knows, over the last two decades the American literary canon has become still more extensive and diverse than it was in the mid-seventies" (xxix).

To reflect the expansion of the field and the diversity of writers, Jerome Klinkowitz, a section editor, recasts American prose since 1945 (the starting point of the present guide as well), "to convey five decades of diverse movements in prose, with an emphasis on ethnic diversity and experimental writing" (xxx). As a result, at least twenty-one new writers were added to the fifth edition, including Gerald Vizenor, Ishmael Reed, Toni Morrison, Sandra Cisneros, and Maxine Hong Kingston. The effort to enlarge the canon defined by the Norton anthology and to diversify its offerings resulted in Kingston becoming the third Asian American writer included in the book, after Cathy Song and Li-Young Lee. Kingston is represented by an excerpt from her *Tripmaster Monkey*, not from her widely discussed auto/biographical *The Woman Warrior*. On the other hand, Song and Lee enter the anthology with what appear to be their better-known works: "The White Porch," "Beauty and Sadness," "Lost Sister," "Chinatown," and "Heaven," by Song, seem to reflect her favorite themes—the relationship between art and life, desire, and immigration experience. Lee's poems, "The Gift," "Persimmons," "Eating Alone," "Eating Together," "Mnemonic," and "This Room and Everything in It," all showcase one of his most persistent themes—memories of his father, the only exception being "Persimmons," which questions the authority of a teacher's knowledge about a fruit favored by a particular ethnic group.

Of the approximately 150 writers found in volume 2 of the fifth edition (literature since 1865), spanning 140 years to date, only three are Asian American. All three are, loosely labeled, Chinese Americans (Kingston is Chinese; Song is half Chinese and half Korean; Lee is ethnic Chinese born in Indonesia). The other Asian subgroups that have produced great amounts of literature—Filipino, Indian, and Japanese Americans—are not at all represented. Genre representation is limited as well, to poetry and prose; drama and short fiction by Asian Americans are nowhere to be seen; autobiography/memoir, which has received a great deal of critical and popular attention in the past quarter century, gained no notice either.

While Asian Americans started to produce literary writings as early as the end of the nineteenth century (short story writer Edith Maude Eaton and poet Sadakichi Hartmann come to mind immediately), the first Asian American anthology, *Asian-American Authors*, edited by Kai-yu Hsu and Helen Palubinskas, did not appear until 1972. A second collection, David Hsin-Fu Wand's *Asian-American Heritage*, followed in 1974. However, the anthology that made a more palpable impact across Asian American intellectual communities and that still remains a source of debate and contention is *Aiiieeeee!*, edited by four ambitious young men: Frank Chin, Jeffery Paul Chan, Lawson Fusao Inada, and Shawn Wong. But as many literary scholars have pointed out, *Aiiieeeee!*'s definition of "Asian American" is narrow, limited to only three ethnic groups: Chinese, Filipino, and Japanese Americans, who also had to be American-born and raised to qualify.

Later Asian American anthologies have often hearkened back to *Aiiieeeee!*, regardless of the editors' agreement or lack thereof with the viewpoints of Chin and his group. For example, Shirley Geok-lin Lim, editor of *Asian-American Literature* (2000), recognizes the Asian American sensibility in her introduction: "Influenced by the civil rights movement of the 1960s, the editors of *Aiiieeeee!* looked beyond the melting pot to argue that Asian-American 'sensibility' was an American phenomenon distinctly different from and unrelated to Asian cultural sources" (xix). But in editing her own anthology, Lim rejects the American-born sensibility and takes a more inclusive approach, so "In deliberately placing American-born, migrant, and transnational Asian-American writers together, this anthology seeks to suggest a collective set of new American identities now emerging as Asian American" (xxii). While Chin and his colleagues felt obligated in 1973 to justify making their voices heard by publishing an anthology, Lim, working in 2000, only needed to explain how her anthology is different from her predecessors'. In other words, roughly a quarter century after the publication of *Aiiieeeee!*, Asian American literature has experienced such tremendous growth that it has acquired a disciplinary status, and its anthologies are now common on the academic publishing market and in the university classroom.

The frequent, successive appearances of Asian American anthologies in the 1980s and 1990s suggest the increasing demands for literature produced by Asians in America; they also indicate that Asian American literature continues to diversify and expand in terms of styles, content, and genres. Citing anthologies such as *Breaking Silence*, *The Open Boat*, *Charlie Chan Is Dead*, *Between Worlds*, *The Politics of Life*, and *Unbroken Threads*, Shirley Lim considers them a sign of "the continuous reinvention of Asian-American cultural identity" (xxi). In contrast to Chin et al.'s inclusion of only three ethnic groups, Lim's anthology contains at least ten, which gives a panoramic picture of how the definition and parameters of Asian American literature have evolved and expanded in the last quarter of the twentieth century.

While Lim's book still retains Asian American markers of racial and/or national origins, as seen in the names of the authors included, Victoria Chang's genre-specific anthology, *Asian American Poetry: The Next Generation*, goes a step further to suggest that Asian American poetry in the late twentieth and early twenty-first centuries is more mainstream than ever before, in that the new generation has departed considerably from what Chang calls the first generation of Asian American poets, such as Cathy Song, Li-Young Lee, and Marilyn Chin, to mention only three, in terms of style and subject matter. While the first generation dealt more with "issues of culture, identity, family, politics, ethnicity, and place" (xv), argues Chang, the themes of the new generation, forty years of age and younger, are "more mainstream American, dealing with gay and lesbian lifestyles, voyeurism, and gender. They also write in innovative styles (experimenting with the line, white space, and stanza) and new voices" (xviii). Chang's anthology is generation-specific in that it caters to certain subgroups of readers, for no previous anthology "has specifically showcased the work of the new generation of Asian American poets" (xxvii). The editorial aim is to gather the best work from young, contemporary Asian American poets, so "best" overrides "Asian," for the collection "reflects a shift away from this ideal of a 'recognizable Asian voice' and toward poetry that transcends racial, gender, and cultural boundaries" (xxviii).

Thirty-two years elapsed between the publication of Hsu and Palubinskas's *Asian-American Authors* (1972) and Chang's *Asian American Poetry* (2004), and those years have made a great deal of difference in the development of Asian American literature, from struggling to be heard to choosing to anthologize its best writings. In this period, anthologies have taken a unique role in defining and promoting Asian American literature, and not coincidentally, they have also become the material witnesses of the ups and downs in the evolution and growth of Asian American literature of the past three decades; anthologies like *Our Feet Walk the Sky: Women of the South Asian Diaspora* (1993), edited by Women of South Asian Descent Collective, and Rakesh Ratti's *Lotus of Another Color: An Unfolding of the South Asian Gay and Lesbian Experience* (1993) are examples of new writings from the underrepresented groups.

Autobiographies/Memoirs

While scholars and historians generally consider the short stories of Edith Maude Eaton as the beginning of Asian American literary production, they have not given credit to an even earlier writer, Lee Yan Phou, who published *When I Was a Boy in China* in 1887. Lee's book was an autobiography. Its publication year backdated the origins of Asian American literature by at least a decade. Unless evidence is found—and it is not inconceivable that it may be—that Asian American writings existed before it, *When I Was a Boy in China* is among the earliest. But Lee's work did not arouse any real critical notice from his contemporary audience. For the nearly six decades between Lee's book and Jade Snow Wong's *Fifth Chinese Daughter* (1945), only one Asian American autobiography, Yung Wing's *My Life in China and America* (1909), seems to have been written. In 1953, inspired by Wong's success, Japanese American Monica Sone published an autobiography titled *Nisei Daughter*. Over the subsequent two decades, autobiographies and memoirs by Asian Americans were written, but again they fell on the deaf ears and unseeing eyes of literary critics and historians whose most important professional responsibility was to take care of canonical writings by mainstream American writers of European descent. This situation did not change until 1976, when a very unconventional auto/biography, *The Woman Warrior*, by Maxine Hong Kingston, hit the shelves of bookstores. Since then, autobiographies and memoirs by Americans of Asian ethnicities have mushroomed—*Asian American Autobiographers* alone showcases fifty-nine notables, and even that is a far cry from an exhaustive listing of writers who have engaged in this genre.

The early autobiographies by Asians in America often take on an informant role, targeting an American audience that knew virtually nothing of Asian cultures and peoples, or knew only through hearsay or stories from the few Western missionaries who went to spread the word of the Bible in the East. To learn about Asia through the writing of or direct personal contact with an Asian was rare. Lee's *When I Was a Boy in China* came five years after the passage of the Chinese Exclusion Act in 1882. The book seems to have been written under the obligation the author felt to tell his American readers about his home country. In fact, Lee's autobiographical details focus on his childhood years spent in China. The reader learns that Lee was a privileged child, for his family was able to afford him a private education, even if he was treated harshly or rigidly by his teachers. Lee recollects his school years to underscore differences in educational practices in China and the United States. For example, all his Chinese teachers were male. He also talks about the curriculum that the pupils were forced to study, including *The Great Learning*, *Doctrines of the Mean*, and Confucius's *The Analects*, among other literary classics. In the final analysis, *When I Was a Boy in China* is a comparative book that chronicles an Americanized adult's memories of an inferior childhood in contrast with the upbringing of his American peers.

Another early autobiography, *My Life in China and America*, was written by Yung Wing, one of China's first hundred students dispatched by the government to study in the United States; in fact, Yung was the first Chinese to graduate from an American college, Yale, in 1852. He became a naturalized American citizen but returned to China in the hope of strengthening and modernizing his mother country; he went on to become perhaps the best known of the "first hundred" in modern Chinese history. Yung's autobiography, somewhat similar to Lee's in subject matter, was first published by the New York-based company Holt in 1909, when the author was eighty-one years old. Yung's narrative credits his American education for his achievements: it empowered him as a visionary on a quest for a more prosperous future for China, and it also shaped him as a progressive reformer. But the reforms he championed all ended in failures that necessitated his escape back to the United States.

It was Western education that enlightened Yung about China's political, economic, and social problems and enabled him to see an urgent need for reform in a deeply troubled country with a dim and uncertain future. While Yung emphasizes the benefits of education on a personal level, he makes the larger case that China needs to enlighten its people by educating them. His own education, vis-à-vis a dangerously high percentage of illiteracy in China at the turn of the twentieth century, made him an advocate for the Chinese Educational Mission, which many believe failed and which he considered successful in the long run. Yung's autobiography also delves into other aspects of his life as a Chinese government official, most notably his role as a reformer. While he shies away from failures—both his own and the government's—Yung takes care to drive home an important point: the utility of an education and his own application of it to help his country modernize.

Despite his American citizenship, Yung was not born and raised in the United States, and his autobiography is not strictly a record of his American experience. Like Lee's book, Yung's focuses on China, but it holds a unique place in the literature of Asian America: "the book's status as one of the only Asian American autobiographies from this period makes it of historical significance" (Floyd Cheung 417). As autobiographies are stories of lives set against the backdrop of contemporary events, their historical significance is often implied, if not stated. *My Life in China and America* narrates historical events that mostly occurred in the latter half of the nineteenth century, and the author draws connections between his personal life and his public functions. Later Asian American autobiographers follow a similar narrative approach. Wong's *Fifth Chinese Daughter*, for example, depicts her growth against the background of World War II. Unlike Lee and Yung, though, she was born and raised on American soil, and her childhood years were spent in the enclave of the Chinese community of San Francisco's Chinatown. While Yung avoids the topic of racism, Wong merely, and lightly, cites a couple of instances of racist conduct.

While Yung recognizes the multifaceted superiority of America and sees a need for China to emulate it, Wong learns about China only through her parents, but she cannot help but compare what is Chinese and what is American through examining cultural customs and eating habits. More important, Wong realizes the critical connection between education and success, just as Yung did, but she stresses that education opens the gateway toward assimilation for the ethnic self, which leads to recognition and acceptance by the mainstream culture. But Wong did not pursue an education only to benefit her community and country; she also wanted her Confucian parents to recognize her talents as equal to those of her male siblings (in fact, hers exceeded theirs). Wong fought the Confucian bias against women while carrying out the Confucian doctrine of pleasing the parents by glorifying them through her success. She thus projects contradicting images, as both a traditionalist loyal to her parents and a feminist struggling for her own rights and identity.

The Japanese American protagonist in Monica Sone's *Nisei Daughter* resembles the Chinese daughter in Wong's work: they are both second-generation Americans of Asian descent, and they both inform the reading public of their respective ancestral culture as they know it, though Sone relates an American experience Wong was lucky to have avoided: life in an internment camp. The Japanese American evacuation and internment in various concentration camps is the subject of countless prose narratives produced since the close of World War II. Sone's book first presents a picture of an almost idyllic life in prewar Seattle, Washington, enjoyed by her family and their Japanese community, in stark contrast to her concentration camp life of confinement and humiliation. As in other autobiographies written by the second generation, the relationship between parents and children takes up a great deal of narrative space: generational conflicts and different views on national and cultural identity and on governmental politics are dramatized, and self-acceptance and public recognition of the children's identity are reconciled. Complicated by race-based government decisions, the identity of the ethnic self is frequently cast into doubt; writing an autobiography is therefore a way to assert individual identity and to define a place in society. *Farewell to Manzanar*, by Jeanne Wakatsuki and James Houston, is an even better-known account detailing the internment experience. Though that is the narrative focus, the point is the case the Houstons want to make against racism.

Institutionalized racism in the guise of laws and presidential executive orders is a common motif in works by ethnic and minority writers. *Farewell to Manzanar* is one of many examples that examines a period when the U.S. government used race as a reason to persecute an ethnic group during wartime. In Yung's, Lee's, and Wong's autobiographies, racism does not play a conspicuous role. World War II, involving European and Asian countries, foregrounded the issue when Japan stood on the wrong side of history and the United States singled out Americans of Japanese ancestry for evacuation, but not those of Italian and German ancestry. Awareness of racial inequality escalated as the civil rights movement advanced throughout the 1960s, and as Asian Americans started to follow the example set by African Americans in their persistent struggles for equal rights with their white counterparts. By then, African American literature had become well recognized, though not yet widely studied and taught. Very few people were aware of an Asian American literature, if it existed at all; in fact, the term "Asian American" was just beginning to come into use. It would take a few more years for Asian America to be heard, loudly, through Kingston's *The Woman Warrior*. The book was controversial—loved and hated—but few deny its power as an ethnic writer's articulation of urgent and important issues confronting Asian Americans, particularly Asian American women.

Though indebted to Wong's *Fifth Chinese Daughter*, *The Woman Warrior* does not limn tour guides of Chinatowns. The quiet, tenacious, and loyal image of the fifth Chinese daughter is replaced with a strong, aggressive, and militant character of a female soldier, modeled on the mythical figure Hua Mulan, a young woman who voluntarily took her father's place when he was drafted into the military. Kingston creatively retells the story of Mulan in such a way that the stories of her own girlhood are juxtaposed with those of the woman warrior. The traditional narrative mode of autobiography adopts the first-person singular to recount life stories and related historical events, but *The Woman Warrior* alternates between the first person, the third person, and the omniscient narrator to recount tales of heroism, violence, revenge, racism, and sexism. Very few twentieth-century American autobiographies/ memoirs are so successful at merging voices and collapsing cultures. *The Woman Warrior* has blazed a new path in the genre.

The subjects and styles of Asian American autobiographies written in the last two decades have continued to vary, and their authors continue to diversify in terms of cultural and national origins. The field formerly dominated by Chinese and Japanese American autobiographers has widened to include writers from other Asian subgroups. For example, Phung Thi Le Ly Hayslip, a Vietnamese American, published two critically acclaimed autobiographies: *When Heaven and Earth Changed Places* (1979) and *Child of War, Woman of Peace* (1993). The former narrates the author's early life in Vietnam as well as her return to it after years of residence in the United States. The latter continues to describe episodes of her life lived alternately between Vietnam and America, though it also examines her relationships of all kinds. Sara Suleri, a Pakistani American, wrote *Meatless Days* (1989) to explore the space between the private and the public in which the protagonist's family lives. These three works have departed greatly from the thematically narrow and politically complimentary autobiographies of the late nineteenth and early twentieth centuries. Their authors no longer have to be so concerned about whether or not their writings will be positively received by the mainstream reading public, as their audience is not just the white population that was faced by Yung Wing in the early twentieth century, or even by Jade Snow Wong in the middle of the century. Their overriding concern is that their voice be heard, and in their own words.

Drama

The Japanese-born Japanese/German American Carl Sadakichi Hartmann, better known as a poet who apprenticed with Walt Whitman, wrote a couple of the earliest, if not the earliest, Asian American plays. Having lived in Nagasaki, Japan; Hamburg, Germany; and Paris, France before 1882, Hartmann finally settled down in Philadelphia, where his father sent him to live with relatives at the age of fifteen. While the experience with his uncle's family turned out to be very unfulfilling, Hartmann availed himself of opportunities to meet and work for the famous author of *Leaves of Grass*, who was living in the same city. His encounter with Whitman exposed him to poetry writing; in fact, Whitman not only discussed poetry and other arts with the young man, he also encouraged him to write poems of his own. While working as a journalist, Hartmann expressed his artistic versatility by trying his hand at different genres of literature, including drama. His literary career advanced in the early 1890s while he was a foreign correspondent for McClure Syndicate in Europe, where he became acquainted with literary figures such as Liszt, Swinburne, and Mallarmé. Back in the United States, Hartmann wrote his first play, *Christ* (1893), which caused him both financial and personal problems. Two other plays appeared along with it in a collection called *Buddha, Confucius, Christ: Three Prophetic Plays*, edited by Harry Lawton and George Knox, published by the New York-based Herder & Herder in 1971, nearly eight decades after *Christ* was written. Another play, *A Tragedy in a New York Flat: A Dramatic Episode in Two Scenes*, was privately published in 1896. Even though he was accomplished in various art forms, "Hartmann seemed most interested in drama" (Moser 129). His early prophetic plays, it is easy to see, are cross-cultural and international in scope and theme, a salient feature that has continued in Asian American drama since.

Another early Asian American (Asian Hawaiian) playwright is Ling-ai Li, whose first play, *The Submission of Rose Moy*, was first produced in Hawaii in 1925 and published in 1928, followed by *The Law of Wu Wei* in 1929 and by her adaptation of the Chinese classic drama *The White Serpent* in 1932. *The Submission of Rose Moy* is noteworthy because it deals with themes still popular in contemporary Asian American and other ethnic theater: conflicts between tradition and modernity, different cultural values, feminist ideals and patriarchy, and so on. The test of these conflicts is Rose Moy's tense relationship with her tradition-bound father. The Western emphasis on freedom and the Chinese advocacy of filial obedience collide when the female protagonist decides to become a women's suffrage advocate while her father simply wants her to obey him and marry a wealthy married man. This thematic thread also runs through Li's *The Law of Wu Wei*, in which the male protagonist follows his family's order to fulfill an arranged marriage at the expense of true love. In Hawai'i, where Li was born and educated, women writers of Asian descent were rare in the early decades of the twentieth century. But significantly, the feminist motif that holds a prominent place in Li's plays continues to be important in contemporary Asian American dramas.

Li's plays were all staged in late 1920s Hawai'i and gained no mainland notice. Plays by mainland Asian Americans did not pique any serious critical interest until the early 1970s, when there appeared some conspicuous production of writings by Asian Americans. Frank Chin's *The Chickencoop Chinaman* was first staged at the prestigious American Place Theatre in May 1972. In it, the race factor looms large: characters of Caucasian, Native American, Asian, and African origins all appear on the stage in various capacities. At the core of the interrelated issues and concerned characters are once again the precarious condition of the Asian American family, represented by the father, and the identity of confused and interracial children. Chin's *The Year of the Dragon* premiered at the same theater in May 1974, and was videotaped and broadcast by PBS the following year. This play probes the connectedness of the individual, the family, and the community situated in the dominant culture. While race is not a predominant factor in the lives of the Chinatown characters, die-hard traditions exert a considerable influence upon members of the second generation. Both of Chin's plays received mixed reviews at the time of their performances, but garnered more critical attention two decades later, probably due to their publication in one volume in 1981 by the University of Washington Press, which has published many Asian American titles.

Another play written in this time period is the award-winning *And the Soul Shall Dance* by Wakako Yamauchi. First published as a short story in *Rafu Shimpo* in 1966, *And the Soul Shall Dance* was included in *Aiiieeeee!* in 1974, before it was rewritten for stage production in 1976. Since then the play has enjoyed a good number of productions in major cities, especially on the West Coast. Like Chin's *The Year of the Dragon*, it chronicles family affairs and deals with ways to reconcile the past and the present. A younger playwright, Momoko Iko, who had been interned at the tender age of two, wrote an award-winning play called

Gold Watch, the first act of which was also included in *Aiiieeeee!*. First written as a novel, *Gold Watch* was reworked into a drama and staged in Los Angeles in 1972, the same year Chin's *The Chickencoop Chinaman* premiered in New York. And like Chin's *The Year of the Dragon* and Yamauchi's *And the Soul Shall Dance*, Iko's *Gold Watch* was broadcast on PBS in 1975. So between 1975 and 1977, at least three plays by Asian American authors rose to national prominence. In retrospect, the early-to-mid 1970s was a period of revival for Asian American letters. Besides these plays included in the PBS series of American dramas, at least three Asian American anthologies were produced (*Asian-American Authors*, *Aiiieeeee!*, and *Asian-American Heritage*) between 1972 and 1974. But it would take another dozen years for Asian American playwrights to catch the national spotlight with several heavy-hitting dramatic productions.

By now, playwrights Velina Hasu Houston, Philip Kan Gotanda, and David Henry Hwang are no longer known just within Asian American literary and theatrical circles—they have acquired national, and in the cases of Houston and Hwang, international reputations. Houston is the author of a great number of published and unpublished plays; her well-known pieces include *Tea* and *Asa Ga Kimashita*. *Tea* is "one of the most widely produced Asian American plays in mainstream, Asian American, and college and university theaters" (Uno 193), and was produced at Theatre X in Tokyo, Japan, in 1995. Against the backdrop of World War II, specifically the American occupation of Japan following the war, *Tea* dramatizes the stories of five Japanese women (war brides) married to racially different American husbands. Somewhat in the fashion of Amy Tan's *The Joy Luck Club*, the women reminisce about their past and confront present challenges such as physical abuse, racial discrimination, and war-caused pain. While Houston's play focuses on relationships among women within one ethnic group, Gotanda's *Yankee Dawg You Die* considers the interethnic relationship between two men—a Chinese American and a Japanese American—in their professional world, the entertainment industry. The characters' dialogues and interactions illuminate the evolution of the roles Asian men have played on stage and expose the stereotyping by racism against Asians in general and Asian male actors in particular. Ultimately, then, the play raises issues about representation and self-representation of Asians in America. Gotanda also critiques racism in his other works, where he examines the effects of the Japanese American internment, though he himself did not experience concentration camp life during World War II.

Few contemporary playwrights are as much celebrated and discussed as David Henry Hwang, author of *M. Butterfly*, with which both mainstream and Asian American audiences are familiar, in part due to its adaptation into a movie starring Jeremy Irons and John Lone. The immensely successful play became "the longest-running nonmusical play in Broadway since the production of Peter Shaffer's *Amadeus*" (Kim 128). But *M. Butterfly* did not overshadow all of Hwang's other works. For example, his first play, *FOB*, was written and presented at Stanford in 1979, while Hwang was still in college. By 1980 the play had gained national attention after its premiere at the Public Theater in New York City. *FOB* considers issues related to ethnicity, culture, and national origin, specifically the East-West dynamic, and dramatizes the difficulty and complexity of immigration and Americanization, experiences that affect all immigrant families and their communities—a topic that a great number of ethnic and immigrant writers explore not only in drama but also in other genres.

With the widening of the field of literary production, more writers arrived on the scene with new plays in the 1990s. Vietnamese American lé thi diem thúy, for example, wrote

Mua He Do/Red Fiery Summer (1995) and *the bodies between us* (2002). The former presents contrasting lifestyles of a Vietnamese family in wartime Vietnam and postwar Southern California, and the latter focuses on the father/daughter relationship. Diana Son, a Korean American of lé thi diem thúy's generation, wrote interesting plays such as *R.A.W. ('Cause I'm a Woman)* and *Stop Kiss*, among others. *R.A.W.* deals with Asian American women's experience of being stereotyped and their subversive responses; *Stop Kiss* explores lesbian issues and sexual identity. The examples of these two playwrights suggest that Asian American dramatists are seeking more creative ways to express themselves and are experimenting more with styles and subject matter.

Fiction

Diana Chang, author of *Frontiers of Love* (1956), is considered the first American-born Chinese to publish a novel in the United States (Roh-Spaulding 38), although there had been novels written by Eurasians in America since the end of the nineteenth century. Winnifred Eaton (Onoto Watanna) published *Miss Numé of Japan* in 1899, followed by many other novels between 1901 and 1925. Korean-born Younghill Kang published an autobiographical novel, *The Grass Roof*, in 1931; the book is largely critical of his home country of Korea and complimentary of the new land of America. Adet Lin (daughter of the Chinese writer Lin Yutang), more positive about her ancestral country, published a novel in 1943, *Flame from the Rock,* that depicts the eventful life of a nurse during the Sino-Japanese war in the early 1940s. More critical of the United States is the novel *Westward to Chungking,* by Helena Kuo, published in New York in 1944, in the heat of the Pacific War that involved China, Japan, and the United States. Even though the novel is China-centered, it touches upon issues affecting Japanese and Chinese Americans, such as racism and the Japanese American internment. Another writer publishing prose narratives in the mid-1940s was Mai-Mai Sze, whose *Silent Children* came out in 1948. Diana Chang's *Frontiers of Love*, about the lives of three Eurasians living in Shanghai, China, was published a year before Okada's *No-No Boy* (1957), a decade after Wong's *Fifth Chinese Daughter,* and about eight decades after the first Asian American poems and autobiographies appeared. Another noteworthy novel published in 1957 was C. Y. Lee's *The Flower Drum Song,* a story about father–son relationships in San Francisco's Chinatown.

The 1950s witnessed the publications of numerous novels by writers of a variety of ethnic and racial backgrounds. The Indian Canadian writer and educator Balachandra Rajan, for example, was born in Burma but has lived and worked in India, the United States, and Canada, where he makes his permanent residence. While fulfilling academic responsibilities and writing scholarly works, he wrote and published two novels, *The Dark Dancer* in 1958 and *Too Long in the West* in 1961, in which he explores the agonizing partition of India as well as traditional Indian culture represented by arranged marriage. The partition as a historical and political narrative and its psychological effects on resident and diasporic Indians are prominent themes in some Indian American stories and novels. Arranged marriage, likewise, has been an important concern of Indian Canadian/American prose narratives. *The Dark Dancer*, exploring this cultural issue, predates Chitra Banerjee Divakaruni's short story collection *Arranged Marriage* by almost four decades.

Asian American writers continued to produce a steady stream of novels in the 1960s. Louis Hing Chu published *Eat a Bowl of Tea* in 1961; hardly known during its author's lifetime, it is a classic today. Chu was not American born, but he was educated in New Jersey and New York, spending many years in New York's Chinatown, which he came to know so well that he centered his novel around it. Like Wong's *Fifth Chinese Daughter*, *Eat a Bowl of Tea* portrays the lives and residents of Chinatown, though the two books differ considerably in that Wong's focuses on the self in San Francisco's Chinatown, while Chu's offers fictional accounts of Chinatown life in New York City. It is considered a classic today in part because Chu refuses to exoticize and negativize his characters; in fact, he subverts the stereotypes of Chinese Americans and Chinatowns as portrayed in works like Pardee Lowe's *Father and Glorious Descendants* and Lin Yutang's *Chinatown Family*, in which an East-West comparison of cultural values and customs almost always favors the West. The Korean American novelist Richard E. Kim produced the majority of his works in the 1960s, including his two novels, *The Martyred* and *The Innocent*. Also writing in these years and continuing to publish throughout the 1980s was Bienvenido Santos, who lived alternately in the Philippines and the United States, though the great majority of his works were published in the former, his home country. While working as a university administrator there, Santos published two novels, *The Volcano* and *Villa Magdalena*, both in 1965; his more celebrated book, *The Praying Man*, was published almost two decades later.

The post-civil rights 1970s witnessed the ongoing production of novels by Asian American writers. The Indian-born Stephen Gill arrived in Canada in 1965 and was instrumental in the formation of the Cornwall Writer's Guild in 1973; the organization became defunct within several years. Gill then founded Vesta Publications, to publish his own works as well as to help novice writers. Gill's three novels, *Immigrant*, *Why*, and *The Loyalist City*, came out within three years, and all are concerned with identity and acceptance issues of young characters living in large Canadian cities such as Montreal. Perhaps the most notable fiction writers of the 1970s were Maxine Hong Kingston and Bharati Mukherjee, both born in 1940; both continued to write novels in the 1980s and 1990s. While Kingston's *The Woman Warrior* is not a novel per se, it contains elements of fiction and fantasy, most notably the chapter titled "White Tiger." Mukherjee, on the other hand, published *The Tiger's Daughter* in 1971 and *Wife* in 1975; both are novels about immigrants living in an uncomfortable and painful in-between world.

Kingston continued to play a prominent role on the literary front in the 1980s, along with Mukherjee, Amy Tan, and the Japanese Canadian writer Joy Kogawa, among others. Kingston's *China Men* won the National Book Award in 1981; in 1989 she published a pure fiction work titled *Tripmaster Monkey*, the first chapter of which, "Trippers and Askers," was anthologized in volume 2 of the fifth edition of *The Norton Anthology of American Literature*. The numerous literary awards that Kingston has garnered for her books over a period of fifteen years indicate that she has not only become a mainstream literary figure in contemporary America but also helped enhance the visibility of Asian American literature as a whole. Mukherjee's *Jasmine*, also published in 1989, shows the possibilities that the West has to offer to the new immigrant, and celebrates the acquisition and evolution of new identities for a South Asian immigrant woman. Winner of a National Book Critics Circle Award, Mukherjee authored five novels that have gained attention from both Asian American and mainstream scholars.

Tan's *The Joy Luck Club* appeared in 1989 as well, and was soon afterward made into a movie with almost all Asian American actors. The publication of the novel and the production of the movie helped further establish Asian American literature in the university curriculum as well as in the popular culture. Kogawa's *Obasan*, on the other hand, makes a powerful statement about the Japanese Canadian internment by the Canadian government in World War II. The novel won several awards, including the prestigious Books in Canada First Novel Award in 1981. Kingston, Mukherjee, Tan, and Kogawa formed an unorchestrated, resonant chorus that rang across the two English-speaking countries of North America ever more clearly and distinctly.

Tan published two more novels in the 1990s, *The Kitchen God's Wife* and *The Hundred Secret Senses*, both of which attracted some critical notice but not as much fanfare as her first novel. Her *Bonesetter's Daughter* came out in 2002. Novels of the 1990s show a greater variety of writers, styles, and themes. The Hawai'i-based Lois-Ann Yamanaka uses Hawaiian pidgin in novels like *Wild Meat and Bully Burgers*, *Blu's Hanging*, and *Heads by Harry*. Immigrant issues are not very conspicuous in her work, but sexual and ethnic identities and interracial relationships hold a great deal of thematic significance. Nora Okja Keller, the Korean-born German/Korean American author of *Comfort Woman*, is also based in Hawai'i. Her novel deals with the horrendous and humiliating experiences of some Korean women forced to serve Japanese soldiers during World War II. Keller's second novel, *Fox Girl*, narrates the story of young Korean teenagers abandoned by American GIs after the Korean War. Both works probe issues that have not been seriously examined before and are therefore welcome additions to the ever-expanding Asian American literary canon.

Novelists of this time period also include Chang-rae Lee, who wrote *Native Speaker* (1995) and *A Gesture Life* (1999); both works probe identity issues concerning Asian Americans. From 1992 to 1999, Marie Lee published six novels for young adult readers, including the better-known *Finding My Voice*, *If It Hadn't Been for Yoon Jun*, and *Necessary Roughness*. Also noteworthy is SKY (Sharon) Lee, the Chinese Canadian author of *Disappearing Moon Café* (1991), a novel that focuses on the lives of four generations of the Wong family in Vancouver, Canada. Kyoko Mori's *Shizuko's Daughter* (1993) was written for young adult readers, just like her *One Bird* (1995); both recount the same story about the loss of the protagonist's mother, but from different perspectives. *Bone* by Fae Myenne Ng also appeared in 1993, to wide audience and critical acclaim. The story of a Chinese immigrant family, *Bone* portrays the experience of immigration and intergenerational relations. Sri Lankan-born Shyam Selvadurai published *Funny Boy* in 1994 and won the Lambda Literary Foundation's Award for Best Gay Male Novel from the United States. One of the youngest Asian American novelists, Holly Uyemoto, published her first novel, *Rebel Without a Clue* (1989), at the age of nineteen, and her second, *Go* (1995), at age twenty-five. Both works understandably, if not predictably, tell coming-of-age stories. Susan Choi's *The Foreign Student* (1998) depicts a relationship between a Korean student and a young American woman from the South.

Some writers who started their careers in the 1970s have continued to exercise their creative talents for decades since. The novelists mentioned above were mostly born in the post-civil rights 1960s, and whether they are Canadians or Americans by virtue of citizenship and/or residence, they have demonstrated a great thematic variety and stylistic distinctions. But whatever they write and however they deal with their subjects, their novels continue to gain importance due to the increasing force, volume, and significance of their literary output.

Poetry

Asian American poetry, seemingly less discussed than the prose forms of fiction, has nonetheless developed steadily over at least a century. Sadakichi Hartmann wrote poems under Whitman's influence in the late 1880s. However, eight decades then elapsed without a genuinely noticeable flourishing of poetry by Asian Americans. According to George Uba in "Coordinates of Asian American Poetry," "Asian American poetry is writing appearing in English by a person wholly or partially of Asian ancestry who self-defines the product as poetry or verse and who has inhabited the United States or Canada" (309). This broad definition allows a great deal of flexibility in classifying Asian American poets, as in the case of Hartmann. But when the labels "American" and "Canadian" imply citizenship, not just residential status, the definition seems more restrictive. But citizenship aside, there had been poets of Asian descent writing in the United States and Canada before 1970, a demarcation line that Uba draws between poetry written by Asians in North America and Asian American poetry, the latter being written after the Third World student strikes of 1968–69. "The 1970s were significant both for the acceleration of literary production and for the efforts to define an Asian American literature," claims Uba. "The development of a Pan-Asian, Third World consciousness was the ground from which an Asian American literature was to emerge" (312). He seems to suggest that that literature became a politically more conscious and purposively more coherent branch of American literature after the formation of an Asian American consciousness around 1970. Uba recognizes a number of poets between Hartmann and that year: the Japanese American Yone Noguchi, the Filipino Americans José Garcia Villa and Carlos Bulosan, the Japanese Canadian Joy Kogawa, and the Chinese Canadian Fred Wah, among others.

Villa sustained a long and outstanding career of at least forty years, from 1939, when he published *Many Voices* in Manila, to 1979, when his *Appassionata* came out in New York. In fact, his last poetry collection, *The Parlement of Giraffes,* was published posthumously in 1999. Curiously enough, hardly any other Asian American poets before the 1970s matched either the quality or the quantity of Villa's work. Even in the two decades following the end of World War II, very few Asian American poets appeared, while a considerable number of novelists and autobiographers emerged. Other than the fact that Asian American literature as a whole, let alone poetry, was quite a way from being recognized, critics have cited the loss of generic preeminence in the twentieth century as a contributing factor to poetry's lack of popularity with writers and readers. Sunn Shelley Wong discusses this as well as the difficulty of reading poetry in "Sizing up Asian American Poetry." Asian Americans who were writing poems in the 1950s, such as Diana Chang, are rare. In the mid-1970s, when there was a surge of interest in anthologizing Asian American writings, Chang had a few poems printed in anthologies like Wand's *Asian-American Heritage* and magazines like *New York Quarterly* and *Bridge*. However, she did not reach a creative peak until the early 1980s, with two collections, *The Horizon Is Definitely Speaking* and *What Matisse Is After.*

While early poets such as Hartmann, Noguchi, and Villa were all foreign-born and did not concern themselves with ethnicity and race-related themes as much as the American-born poets since World War II, they blazed a path for subsequent writers, though they have not been as deeply discussed as those who rose in the 1970s and later. Victoria Chang, herself a poet and editor, divides Asian American poets into two generations: Ai, Cathy Song, John Yau, Li-Young Lee, Marilyn Chin, and Garrett Hongo "were the first generation of Asian American poets to receive wide-spread recognition in the American literary community" (xv); the second (new) generation that has come of age are included in her collection, *Asian American Poets* (2004). Chang is careful to point out that by "first generation" she does not mean that "no other Asian American poets existed before them"; she suggests instead that these writers have achieved "widespread literary recognition" (xxix*m*), although whether some have indeed been well recognized beyond the borders of Asian American literature remains in question. Some important poets of that generation are missing from Chang's list, such as Lawson Fusao Inada, Arthur Sze, and Janice Mirikitani.

Considering that occasional poems were written and published from the end of World War II to 1970 and most of them attracted little or no critical and popular notice, the decade of the 1970s was truly remarkable in terms of the volume of production. From 1968 to 1978, G. S. Sharat Chandra was publishing poems in India, England, and the United States, his earliest collection, *Bharata Natyam Dancer and Other Poems*, coming out in 1968, followed by *April in Nanjangud* in 1971, *Once or Twice* in 1974, and *The Ghost of Meaning* in 1978. Yukihide Maeshima Hartman put out two volumes, *A One of Me* in 1970 and *Hot Footsteps* in 1976. Lawson Fusao Inada, among the earliest writers to explore the Japanese American internment, published 3 *Northwest Poets* with Albert Drake and Douglas Lawder in 1970, and a collection of his own, *Before the War*, in 1971. Mei-Mei Berssenbrugge produced her first collection, *Fish Souls*, in 1971 and went on to publish *Summits Move with the Tide* in 1974 and *Random Possession* in 1979. Agha Shahid Ali published *Bone-Sculpture* in 1972 and *In Memory of Begum Akhtar and Other Poems* in 1979. Albert Saijo, a stylistically innovative poet often associated with Jack Kerouac and Lew Welch, coauthored *Trip Trap: Haiku Along the Road from San Francisco to New York* with those two writers in 1973.

Arthur Sze wrote his own poems while translating Chinese poetry; his publications include *The Willow Wind* in 1972 and *Two Ravens* in 1976. Ai published *Cruelty* in 1973. Rienzi Crusz put out *Flesh and Thorn* in 1974. Meena Alexander was able to complete four volumes within three years: *The Bird's Bright Wing* in 1976, *I Root My Name* and *In the Middle Earth* in 1977, and *Without Place* in 1978. Jessica Hagedorn was likewise productive in this time period; with Alice Karle, Barbara Szerlip, and Carol Tinker, she published *Four Young Women* in 1973, followed by a poetry and prose collection titled *Dangerous Music* in 1975. Hagedorn remained active as an editor and writer throughout the following two decades. Deeply affected by the wartime internment, Mitsuye Yamada wrote about her ordeals in *Camp Notes and Other Poems* (1976). Nellie Wong has written poetry for two decades, publishing her first collection, *Dreams in Harrison Park*, in 1977. Garrett Hongo, Alan Chong Lau, and Lawson Fusao Inada brought out a noteworthy collection called *The Buddha Bandits Down Highway 99* in 1978. Another activist poet, Janice Mirikitani, put forth *Awake in the River* in 1978. John Yau, who has been writing and publishing poetry and works in other genres for nearly three decades, started his prolific career with *Crossing Canal Street* in 1976, followed by *The Reading of an Ever-changing Tale* in 1977 and *Sometimes* in 1979.

This cursory listing of selected poetry collections underlines some important 1970s literary and political movements that involved Asian Americans. George Uba writes, "The 1970s were significant both for the acceleration of literary production and for the efforts to define an Asian American literature," and thus, "Fueled by the social upheavals of the late 1960s and early 1970s, including the black power and antiwar movements, nascent efforts were undertaken not merely to identify Asian American literary works but also to name an actual literary tradition" (312). Anthologies like Chin et al.'s *Aiiieeeee!* and Hsu and Palubinskas's *Asian-American Authors*, among others, represent efforts to identify and recover works by writers of Asian descent. Poetry volumes like those mentioned above reflect politically conscious efforts to create a tradition for Asian American literature, which were very successful in retrospect, as many of the poems written in the 1970s activist era continue to be read and critiqued today. These poets, along with some prose writers of the era, formed a considerable literary, and indirectly political, force that not only made their voices heard through their writings but also established an identity for what they had produced—Asian American literature, though the umbrella term was to remain vague and open for decades to come. The rise of this literature occurred in the wake of three highly significant events in twentieth-century American history: the Vietnam War and the antiwar protests; the civil rights movement, spearheaded by African American activists, that was instrumental in the birth of Asian American studies on university campuses; and the Third World student protest at San Francisco State and other California universities. These events provided catalysts and material for Asian American writers, with poets in the vanguard, many dealing with the material in various forms and styles in their works.

In comparison, the 1980s poetry is postactivist and thematically more diversified. Most of the poets of the 1970s continued to write and publish; in fact, many of them further established themselves in the continuously changing canon of Asian American poetry. This is certainly true of Ai, Alexander, Ali, Berssenbrugge, Crusz, Hartman, Hongo, Mirikitani, Sze, Yamada, and Yau, who all produced at least one, and in many cases multiple volumes in the 1980s. Shirley Geok-lin Lim, one of Asian America's most prolific and versatile writers, completed several: *Crossing the Peninsula and Other Poems*, *No Man's Grove and Other Poems*, and *Modern Secrets*. Pat Matsueda published *X* in 1983 and *The Fish Catcher* in 1985. Himani Bannerji put forth *A Separate Sky* in 1982 and *Doing Times* in 1986. One of the most-discussed Hawaiian poets, Cathy Song made her literary debut with *Picture Bride* in 1983, followed by *Frameless Windows, Squares of Light* in 1988 and *School Figures* in 1994. Merle Woo's *Yellow Woman Speaks*, speaking out on the oppression and marginalization of women, was published in 1986.

In Hawai'i too, Wing Tek Lum brought out *Expanding the Doubtful Points* in 1987. Marilyn Mei Ling Chin published the collection *Dwarf Bamboo* the same year, and continued with *The Phoenix Gone, the Terrace Empty* in 1994. Kimiko Hahn started to write poems in the late 1980s, publishing *We Stand Our Ground*, in collaboration with Gale Jackson and Susan Sherman, in 1989, and her own volume, *Air Pocket*, the following year. Lonny Kaneko's *Coming Home from Camp*, from 1986, deals with the wartime internment of Japanese Americans. That year also saw the appearance of a unique book, *Shallow Graves: Two Women and Vietnam*, written collaboratively by the Vietnamese Tran Thi Nga and the American Wendy Larsen. Few poetry collections by Asian Americans in the 1980s were more critically acclaimed than Li-Young Lee's *Rose*, though Lee's second volume, *The City in Which I Love You* (1990), went on to become very noteworthy as well. Juliet Sanae Kono's *Hilo Rains*, poems about Hawai'i, was published in 1988. David Mura's *After We Lost Our Way* followed the next year. Thus, Asian American poetry continued to flourish, with a greater range of themes and subject matters and a greater range of poets.

Poets active in the 1970s and/or 1980s who continued to be so in the 1990s include Ai, Alexander, Ali, Berssenbrugge, Chandra, Chin, Crusz, Hagedorn, Hahn, Hartman, Inada, Lee, Lim, Mirikitani, Mura, Sze, and Yau, to mention the most obvious. In fact, these writers dominated the field of Asian American poetic production, though the 1990s, like all other decades, had its own representatives. The Hawaiian poet Eric Chock wrote *Last Days Here*, published in 1990 by Bamboo Ridge Press, which he was involved in establishing. While Divakaruni launched her poetry career with the 1987 collection *Dark Like the River*, all her other volumes published to date were written in the 1990s: *The Reason for Nasturtiums*, *Black Candle*, and *Leaving Yuba City*. Myung Mi Kim's first four poetry collections were all produced in the 1990s: *Under Flag*, *The Bounty*, *Dura*, and *Spelt*.

The Singaporean Canadian Lydia Kwa published a few scattered poems in the late 1980s, but most of her other pieces came out in 1994, in a collection titled *The Colours of Heroines.* Another Canadian Asian poet, Evelyn Lau, published *You Are Not Who You Claim* in 1990, *Oedipal Dreams* in 1992, and *In the House of Slaves* in 1994. Filipino American poet Fatima Lim-Wilson had two volumes, *Wandering Roots/From the Hothouse* in 1991 and *Crossing the Snow Bridge* in 1995. Of the three books by Indian Canadian poet Uma Parameswaran, *Trishanku* was published in 1988, *The Door I Shut Behind Me* in 1990, and *Trishanku and Other Writings* in 1998. Rita Wong, a Chinese Canadian, contributed many individual poems to the contemporary literary scene and published a single volume, *monkeypuzzle,* in 1998.

A very distinct characteristic of Asian American poetry of the 1990s is the expansion of the field, most notably the emergence of numerous Canadian writers and poets adding to the growing corpus of Asian American literature, defined broadly and loosely. Another characteristic is the obvious departure from the more familiar themes of the 1970s and '80s, such as generational clashes, cultural differences, nostalgia for the homeland, racism, and sexism; poets in the 1990s instead turned to contemporary themes more in tune with those addressed by mainstream writers: social and economic issues, globalism, and gay and lesbian concerns, among others. In the beginning years of the twenty-first century, there have appeared a few volumes by both veteran and novice poets. These include Alan Chong Lau's *Blues and Greens* in 2000, Ali's *Rooms Are Never Finished* in 2001, Alexander's *Illiterate Heart* in 2002, Myung Mi Kim's *Commons* in 2002, and Victoria Chang's *Circle* in 2005; many other poets published scattered pieces in magazines and anthologies. Multiple-author collections by novice poets in the twenty-first century are still emerging, but we already have a fair sample of their thematic scope and stylistic innovations. For example, Victoria Chang's *Asian American Poetry* presents twenty-eight poets from an emerging generation of writers, almost all of whom are unfamiliar names and newcomers to the contemporary literary scene. Contemporary Asian American writers now compete with mainstream writers for space in classroom anthologies, and a number of them have been successful, but the question remains how much longer the label "Asian American" will remain viable and distinct when its writers stand shoulder to shoulder with their mainstream colleagues and their thematic concerns are more American than just Asian American issues.

Short Fiction

The earliest Asian American short stories are believed to have been written by the Eaton sisters in the late nineteenth century, and the first collection, *Mrs. Spring Fragrance* by Edith Eaton/Sui Sin Far, was published in 1912. Surprisingly, as Amy Ling observes, "After the early work of Sui Sin Far at the beginning of the twentieth century, the next notable Chinese American short story collections did not appear until the latter two decades of the century with Frank Chin's *The Chinaman Pacific & Frisco R.R. Co.* (1988) and David Wong Louie's *Pangs of Love* (1991)" (37). The key word in Ling's observation is "notable," but it is true that between World War I and World War II, while there were stories written and published by Asian Americans, few collections existed. In 1949, however, an important collection appeared, *Yokohama, California,* by the critically acclaimed Toshio Mori. A couple of well-known pieces originated from it: "Slant-Eyed Americans" and "The Woman Who Makes Swell Doughnuts." Though Mori went on to publish *The Chauvinist and Other Stories* in 1979 and, posthumously, *Unfinished Message* in 2000, these later collections had less impact than his first. Bienvenido Santos had been writing short stories in the 1930s and '40s but did not publish a collection, *You Lovely People*, until 1955. Another collection that is more in tune with Asian American themes and settings is Monfoon Leong's *Number One Son*, published by East/West in 1975. Leong was born in San Diego's Chinatown and wrote about his experience living there as well as about cross-cultural issues.

The 1970s was a relatively quiet period for short fiction writing. Diana Chang was publishing stories in various venues but has not collected them. Patsy Sumie Saiki published a volume called *Sachie, A Daughter of Hawaii*, in Honolulu in 1977. Another collection that came out late in that decade is Bienvenido Santos's *Scent of Apples*. While Santos continued to produce fiction and poetry throughout the 1980s and 1990s, *Scent of Apples* remains important partly because it is his only book published in the United States, partly because it won an American Book Award, and partly because he vividly portrays Filipino old-timers in America. In comparison, the 1980s was a more active decade for short story writing. Saiki brought out two more volumes, *Ganbare! An Example of Japanese Spirit* (1981) and *Japanese Women in Hawaii* (1985). Like her first book, *Sachie*, the new collections focus on Japanese in Hawaiʻi. Another Hawaiian writer, Susan Nunes, produced *A Small Obligation and Other Stories of Hilo* in 1982, stories often about mixed-race people (particularly Japanese and Portuguese, like Nunes herself) living in a complicated world of competing cultures and ethnicities. The same year saw the appearance of Shirley Geok-lin Lim's first story collection, *Another Country and Other Stories*, which, like some of her other works, was published in Singapore. Ty Pak's 1983 collection, titled *Guilt Payment*, focuses on male Koreans living in Hawaiʻi.

The 1980s was a noteworthy era also because of the publications of several well-known collections. Darrell H.Y. Lum, writing in the controversial Hawaii Pidgin English, brought out a collection of stories and drama titled *Sun*. One of the most acclaimed collections, *Seventeen Syllables: 5 Stories of Japanese American Life*, by Hisaye Yamamoto, was published in Tokyo in 1985, and the following year the author received the American Book Award for Lifetime Achievement. Two other similar collections, *Seventeen Syllables and Other Stories* and *Seventeen Syllables*, came out in 1988 and 1994, respectively, though most of these stories were written in the 1940s. Several masterpieces of Yamamoto's—classics among Asian American short stories—are widely taught and discussed, including the title story "Seventeen Syllables," "Yoneko's Earthquake," and "The Legend of Miss Sasagawara." These pieces represent what the *Aiiieeeee!* editors have described as "the most highly developed" Asian American writing in terms of technique and style (266). The Philippine-born Cecilia Manguerra Brainard also depicts historical and cultural issues in *Women with Horns and Other Stories*, published in 1987. Bharati Mukherjee published two volumes in this period as well: *Darkness* in 1985 and *The Middleman and Other Stories* in 1988. Also important is Frank Chin's *The Chinaman Pacific & Frisco R.R. Co.*, published in 1988, in which the author "dazzles readers with his verbal pyrotechnics and saddens readers with his intense love/hate reaction to the Chinese American identity" (Ling, "The Asian American Short Story," 37).

Asian American short fiction did not fully flower until the 1990s. This decade was characterized by not only a great number of writers working in this genre but also a variety of themes and styles never seen before. Indeed, the number of collections produced in this decade seems staggering in comparison with each of the previous decades. Darrell Lum produced a new volume, *Pass on, No Pass Back* in 1990. David Wong Louie's *Pangs of Love*, "marked by sophistication and humor" (Ling, "The Asian American Short Story," 37), appeared in 1991. In 1992, Bamboo Ridge Press released Gary Pak's *The Watcher of Waipuna and Other Stories*, which explores themes and issues unique to the Hawaiian community with which the author is so familiar. The same year saw the publication of a collection by another Hawaiian writer of Japanese ancestry, Sylvia A. Watanabe: *Talking to the Dead*. This short story cycle set in Maui depicts the life of a Japanese American community. Evelyn Lau's volume titled *Fresh Girls and Other Stories*, published in 1993, reflects her life experience as a teenage prostitute. Another Canadian woman writer of Indian descent, Shani Mootoo, also published a collection that year, *Out on Main Street and Other Stories*, which, like Lau's work, deals with the experience of women, though the latter focuses more on Indian diasporic characters.

In 1995, Cecilia Manguerra Brainard brought out a second collection, *Acapulco at Sunset and Other Stories*, in the Philippines. Chitra Banerjee Divakaruni published *Arranged Marriage* that year. Divakaruni's stories explore Indian women's lives from multiple perspectives as she examines the custom of arranged marriage in India. Also in 1995, Shirley Lim put forth a second book of stories, *Life's Mysteries*. Kathleen Tyau's *A Little Too Much Is Enough* (1995) was chosen as the Best Book of the Year by the Pacific Northwest Booksellers Association in 1996. The Massachusetts-born John Yau wrote a collection titled *Hawaiian Cowboys* that explores multiethnic issues. In 1997 Peter Bacho, primarily a novelist, contributed *Dark Blue Suit and Other Stories*, which deals with first-generation Filipino immigrants in the United States. Shirley Lim's third collection, *Two Dreams*, also came out that year. A number of collections were published in 1998, including G. S. Sharat Chandra's *Sari of the Gods*, which probes self-identity lived between cultures. John Yau followed his *Hawaiian Cowboys* with a new collection, *My Symptoms*, that explores themes of sexual liberation, among other things. The year 1999 saw the publication of several notable collections: Gish Jen's *Who's Irish*, Jhumpa Lahiri's *Interpreter of Maladies*, Evelyn Lau's *Choose Me*, Ty Pak's *Moonbay*, and Kathleen Tyau's *Makai*. Lahiri won the prestigious Pulitzer Prize in fiction in 2000.

Finally, the beginning years of the twenty-first century have witnessed a strong start in the production field of short stories. Russell Leong's *Phoenix Eyes and Other Stories* (2000) casts a spotlight on Asian American males. Divakaruni's new volume *The Unknown Errors of Our Lives*, which came out in 2001, contains stories concerned with the social and familial conditions of immigrant women in America. Alex Kuo's *Lipstick and Other Stories*, published in Hong Kong in 2001, includes stories about his life in China and the United States. Don Lee wrote a book of stories titled *Yellow* that also came out in 2001; set in a fictional town in California, *Yellow* probes issues relevant to Korean Americans on the West Coast. The same year saw the appearance of Karen Tei Yamashita's *Circle K Cycles*, an unusual book that chronicles the author's six-month stay in Seto, Japan, and includes journal entries, photos, and short stories, among other elements.

The list of short story writers herein is limited to authors of collections published in the beginning years of the twenty-first century and is by no means exhaustive. As Amy Ling predicted in 2001, "the short story as a genre—a form that can be completed without a lengthy investment of time; that permits a narrow focus on one theme, character, or mood; and that is flexible and accessible in magazines as well as books—is thriving among Asian Pacific Americans" ("The Asian American Short Story" 40). If the field of Asian American short stories remained largely open before the 1980s, that landscape started to change in the middle of that decade; it certainly took on a new look in the 1990s, as the enumeration of the titles—only the notable ones—from that period clearly indicates. The rise of the Asian American short story has been underlined by the rise to prominence of small presses like

Bamboo Ridge Press in Hawai'i, and by the willing attention that major mainstream commercial presses—Norton, Penguin, Houghton Mifflin, HarperCollins, Doubleday, Hyperion, and Farrar, Straus & Giroux, to mention only a few—have paid to the creative efforts of Asian Americans. It seems clear that the days of continued marginalization of Asian American writing are fading into history; the time of Asian American writers sharing the spotlight in the American literary scene has dawned.

Works Cited

Baym, Nina. Preface. *The Norton Anthology of American Literature*, 4th ed. (New York: Norton, 1994), 2:xxix–xxxii.

——. Preface. *The Norton Anthology of American Literature*, 5th ed. (New York: Norton, 1998), 2:xxix–xxxii.

Chang, Victoria. Introduction. In Victoria Chang, ed., *Asian American Poetry: The Next Generation* (Urbana: University of Illinois Press, 2004), xv–xxx.

Cheung, Floyd. "Yung Wing." In Guiyou Huang, ed., *Asian American Autobiographers: A Bio-Bibliographical Critical Sourcebook* (Westport, CT: Greenwood Press, 2001), 413–17.

Cheung, King-Kok. *Articulate Silences: Hisaye Yamamoto, Maxine Hong Kingston, Joy Kogawa.* Ithaca, NY: Cornell University Press, 1993.

Cheung, King-Kok, ed. *An Interethnic Companion to Asian American Literature.* New York: Cambridge University Press, 1997.

Chin, Frank. *The Chickencoop Chinaman* and *The Year of the Dragon.* Seattle: University of Washington Press, 1981.

Chin, Frank, Jeffery Paul Chan, Lawson Fusao Inada, and Shawn Wong. Preface. *Aiiieeeee!: An Anthology of Asian American Writers* (New York: Mentor, 1991), xi–xxii.

Foner, Philip, and Daniel Rosenberg, eds. *Racism, Dissent, and Asian Americans from 1850 to the Present.* Westport, CT: Greenwood Press, 1993.

Huang, Guiyou. "Be/coming American." In Guiyou Huang, ed., *Asian American Autobiographers: A Bio-Bibliographical Critical Sourcebook* (Westport, CT: Greenwood Press, 2001), 1–16.

——. "The Makers of the Asian American Poetic Landscape." In Guiyou Huang, ed., *Asian American Poets: A Bio-Bibliographical Critical Sourcebook* (Westport, CT: Greenwood Press, 2002), 1–14.

——. "The Asian American Short Story: The Cases of Sui Sin Far, Yamamoto, and Peñaranda." In Guiyou Huang, ed., *Asian American Short Story Writers: An A-to-Z Guide* (Westport, CT: Greenwood Press, 2003), xiii–xxxii.

Katrak, Ketu H. "South Asian American Literature." In King-Kok Cheung, ed., *An Interethnic Companion to Asian American Literature* (New York: Cambridge University Press, 1997), 192–218.

Kim, Elaine. *Asian American Literature: An Introduction to the Writings and Their Social Context.* Philadelphia: Temple University Press, 1982.

Kim, Esther. "David Henry Hwang." In Miles Xian Liu, ed., *Asian American Playwrights: A Bio-Bibliographical Critical Sourcebook* (Westport, CT: Greenwood Press, 2002), 126–44.

Kingston, Maxine Hong. "Cultural Mis-readings by American Reviewers." In Guy Amirthanayagam, ed., *Asian and Western Writers in Dialogue: New Cultural Identities* (London: Macmillan, 1982), 55–65.

———. *China Men*. New York: Vintage International, 1980.

Lee Yan Phou. *When I Was a Boy in China*. Boston: Lothrop, 1887.

Li, David Leiwei. *Imagining the Nation: Asian American Literature and Cultural Consent.* Stanford: Stanford University Press, 1998.

Lim, Shirley Geok-lin. Introduction. In Shirley Geok-lin Lim, ed., *Asian-American Literature* (Lincolnwood, IL: NTC Publishing Group, 2000), xix–xxii.

———. "Twelve Asian American Writers: In Search of Self-Definition." In A. LaVonne Brown Ruoff and Jerry W. Ward Jr., eds., *Redefining American Literary History* (New York: MLA, 1990), 237–50.

Ling, Amy. *Between Worlds: Women Writers of Chinese Ancestry*. New York: Pergamon, 1990.

———. "The Asian American Short Story." In Blanche H. Gelfant and Lawrence Graver, eds., *The Columbia Companion to the Twentieth-Century American Short Story* (New York: Columbia University Press, 2001), 34–41.

Ling, Jinqi. *Narrating Nationalism: Ideology and Form in Asian American Literature.* New York: Oxford University Press, 1998.

Lowe, Lisa. "Heterogeneity, Hybridity, Multiplicity: Making Asian American Differences." *Diaspora* 1, no. 1 (1991): 24–44.

———. *Immigrant Acts: On Asian American Cultural Politics*. Durham: Duke University Press, 1996.

Moser, Linda Trinh. "Sadakichi Hartmann." In Guiyou Huang, ed., *Asian American Poets: A Bio-Bibliographical Critical Sourcebook* (Westport, CT: Greenwood Press, 2002), 125–32.

Roh-Spaulding, Carol. "Diana Chang." In Emmanuel Nelson, ed., *Asian American Novelists: A Bio-Bibliographical Critical Sourcebook* (Westport, CT: Greenwood Press, 2000), 38–43.

Sumida, Stephen H. "Asian/Pacific American Literature in the Classroom." Forum: What Do We Need to Teach? *American Literature* 65, no. 2 (June 1993): 348–53.

Tapping, Craig. "South Asia Writes North America: Prose Fictions and Autobiographies from the Indian Diaspora." In Shirley Geok-lin Lim and Amy Ling, eds., *Reading the Literatures of Asian America* (Philadelphia: Temple University Press, 1992), 285–301.

Thomas, Brook. "*China Men*, *United States v. Wong Kim Ark*, and the Question of Citizenship." *American Quarterly* 50, no. 4 (December 1998): 689–717.

Uba, George. "Coordinates of Asian American Poetry: A Survey of the History and a Guide to Teaching." In Sau-ling Cynthia Wong and Stephen H. Sumida, eds., *A Resource Guide to Asian American Literature* (New York: MLA, 2001), 309–31.

Uno, Roberta. "*Tea*, by Velina Hasu Houston." In Sau-ling Cynthia Wong and Stephen H. Sumida, eds., *A Resource Guide to Asian American Literature* (New York: MLA, 2001), 193–99.

Wong, Sau-ling Cynthia. *Reading Asian American Literature: From Necessity to Extravagance.* Princeton: Princeton University Press, 1993.

———. "Navigating Asian American Panethnic Literary Anthologies." In Sau-ling Cynthia Wong and Stephen H. Sumida, eds., *A Resource Guide to Asian American Literature* (New York: MLA, 2001), 235–51.

Wong, Sunn Shelley. "Sizing up Asian American Poetry." In Sau-ling Cynthia Wong and Stephen H. Sumida, eds., *A Resource Guide to Asian American Literature* (New York: MLA, 2001), 285–309.

Yung Wing. *My Life in China and America*. New York: Holt, 1909.

Part II
A–Z Entries

1. Anthologies

Asian-American Authors. Ed. Kai-yu Hsu and Helen Palubinskas. Boston: Houghton Mifflin, 1972. 184 pp.

This earliest anthology of writings by Asian Americans was truly a pioneering effort. In fact, the collection was so ahead of its time that there had been no real discussion or definition of what was "Asian American," not to mention "Asian American literature." The editors start by acknowledging this absence: "Authors may define the term Asian-American in different ways. In this anthology every effort was made to represent the works of writers of Asian origin who have had extensive living experience in America. Those born and reared in America were considered first; then those who came to this country when very young and remained here" (1). Hsu and Palubinskas cite space limitations as a primary reason for including writers of only three ethnicities: Chinese, Japanese, and Filipino. While the editors make no explicit statement about the book's purpose and goal, they seem to structure the selections around one vital issue: Asian American identity in cultural, ethnic, social, and political terms. The anthology represents Asian Americans' perpetual search for self in a time and place characterized by identity crisis. The writers included want to represent themselves rather than having white writers do it for them: they not only are eager to express their identity and articulate their experience, they also want "to torpedo the stereotype" (5).

Hsu and Palubinskas break the anthology into three sections: "Chinese American Literature," "Japanese American Literature," and "Filipino American Literature." Each is prefaced by a general introduction surveying the writers represented, followed by a brief chronology of the group in question. Each selection is preceded by an introduction about the author that provides biographical information or includes their remarks. The Chinese American section includes eight writers: an excerpt from Pardee Lowe's autobiography *Father and Glorious Descendant*, a chapter from Jade Snow Wong's autobiography *Fifth Chinese Daughter*, an excerpt from Virginia Lee's semiautobiographical novel *The House That Tai Ming Built*, Frank Chin's short story "Food for All His Dead," an excerpt from Diana Chang's novel *The Frontiers of Love*, Jeffery Paul Chan's short story "Auntie Tsia Lay Dying," Shawn H. Wong's poem "Letter to Kay Boyle," and a short poem by Russell C. Leong titled "Threads." The Japanese American section consists of five items: Toshio Mori's short story "The Eggs of the World," an excerpt titled "One Sunday in December" from Daniel Inouye's autobiography *Journey to Washington*, six poems from Lawson Fusao Inada's *West Side Songs*, Hisaye Yamamoto's short story "The Brown House," and two poems by Iwao Kawakami, "The Room" and "San Bruno." Despite the editors' claim that the characteristics of an "emerging Filipino-American literature" are vague due to the quantity of Filipino emigration, the Filipino American section contains more writers than either of the other two sections. A group of nine authors includes Joaquin Legaspi's two poems, "Sphinx" and "Query," two poems (numbers 57 and 60) from José Garcia Villa's collection *Have*

Come, Am Here, Alfred A. Robles's poem "It Was a Warm Summer Day," two poems by Bayani L. Mariano, "What We Know" and "A Letter to Nancy," N. V. M. Gonzalez's short story "The Morning Star," Samuel Tagatac's poem for Mrs. Potash titled "A Funeral," J. C. Dionisio's short story "A Summer in an Alaskan Salmon Cannery," Bienvenido N. Santos's short story "Scent of Apples," and Oscar F. Peñaranda's short story "The Price."

Useful features of *Asian-American Authors* include the general introduction to the anthology, the short introductions to each of the three sections, and the biographical information on all the writers anthologized, accompanied by a black-and-white photo of each author. While this is a slim volume, totaling only 184 pages, it is an important editorial achievement for being the first Asian American anthology.

* * *

Asian-American Heritage: An Anthology of Prose and Poetry. Ed. David Hsin-Fu Wand. New York: Washington Square Press, 1974. 308 pp.

Published in the same year as Frank Chin et al.'s *Aiiieeeee!*, Wand's *Asian-American Heritage* is another early anthology of Asian American writing; however, it presents broader coverage of both genres and ethnic groups. Chin et al.'s book and Hsu and Palubinskas's anthology both focus on three ethnicities—Chinese, Japanese, and Filipino—while Wand's includes Chinese, Japanese, Korean, Filipino, and Pacific Islander. The idea to anthologize writings by Pacific Islanders, in this case Hawaiian and Samoan writers, was no doubt rare in 1974, when Asian American literature in general had not acquired an identity of its own and when its borders were wide open.

Acknowledging the uniqueness of Asians' experience in America, the editor intends to provide an opportunity for the American public to examine their writings and to get to know the people who produce it. Wand hopes that his anthology "will be the beginning of a series dealing with Third World writers working in the United States," arguing that a systematic and balanced study of American literature is not possible "without a thorough examination of the infusion and interplay of these diverse literary heritages in the American tradition" (xi). Wand's preface and introduction show a keen awareness of the history and breadth of Asian American literary production and express regret about his inability to include other writers due to limitations of space and other factors. In the introduction, Wand attempts to answer the emerging, difficult question of "What is an Asian-American?" (2). It seems that *nisei*, *sansei*, and *yonsei* are unquestionably Asian American because they are born and raised in the United States and write in English; but *issei* like Yone Noguchi and the first generation like Stephen S.N. Liu and David Rafael Wang (pseudonym of editor David Hsin-Fu Wand himself), who immigrated to the United States at an early age, raise questions about the sensibility of birth. Wand, unlike Frank Chin and his editorial group, who selected only writers born and raised in America, includes foreign-born writers, such as Younghill Kang and Richard E. Kim from Korea and Carlos Bulosan from the Philippines, all of whom came to the United States at a relatively young age and wrote about their American experience.

Wand's anthology classifies Asian American writers on the basis of ancestry and the geographical locations of their forebears (5). Thus the rationale for including Filipino American writers is that Filipinos originated from the Philippine Islands, located in Southeast Asia; Filipino Americans are "ipso facto" Asian Americans. A justification is also made for placing Polynesian oral literature in *Asian-American Heritage*, albeit with some effort. Wand's definition of "Polynesians" includes Hawaiians, Samoans, and Tahitians, whose spoken languages are considered dialects of the same tongue and are closely related. Even though Polynesians are culturally and racially different from East Asians, geographically, argues Wand, Polynesia, like the Philippine Islands, belongs to Southeast Asia. Polynesian American literature "belongs to Asian-American literature because Hawaiians and Samoans are native Americans of the fiftieth state, which is geographically a part of Southeast Asia" (13). Since the editor is not aware of writers who think and write in Hawaiian, he presents "English versions of Hawaiian and Samoan oral poetry," rendered into English by poets like Armand Schwerner and David Rafael Wang.

The five represented genres are conveniently placed in five sections in the anthology: stories, poetry, essays, novel excerpts, and oral poetry, each preceded by a concise commentary (from two to nine pages long) that introduces the themes of the selections. The book includes roughly two dozen authors of five different ethnic backgrounds (if one considers Hawaiian, Samoan, and Tahitian as of Polynesian ethnicity). Well-known writers who are still widely read and taught in colleges and universities, such as Richard Kim, Toshio Mori, Hisaye Yamamoto, Diana Chang, Wing Tek Lum, Janice Mirikitani, José Garcia Villa, Younghill Kang, John Okada, and Carlos Bulosan, are included; works of lesser-known writers, such as Ling Chung, Suzi Mee, and Irwin Paik, are also available.

Three other valuable aspects of this early anthology are photographs, biographical sketches of writers, and a glossary of foreign terms. The photos are significant because they provide a strong visual sense of historical events, such as the presidential Executive Order 9066 and its impact on Japanese American life on the farm and in internment camps. The biographical sketches, along with author photos, introduce these Asian Americans. The glossary, meant for the mainstream audience who may be unfamiliar with Asian American languages and cultures, explains ethnic and native terms such as *haole, pake, issei, karate,* and so on. Three decades after its publication, *Asian-American Heritage* remains useful to students and teachers for its fair and balanced coverage of genres and ethnic groups, and for the editorial apparatus with which the editor makes the book accessible.

* * *

Aiiieeeee!: An Anthology of Asian American Writers. **Ed. Frank Chin, Jeffery Paul Chan, Lawson Fusao Inada, and Shawn Wong. Washington, DC: Howard University Press, 1974; New York: Mentor Books, 1991. 294 pp.** One of the earliest Asian American literary anthologies, first published by Howard University Press in 1974, *Aiiieeeee!* is certainly one of the most used, most quoted, and most controversial anthologizing efforts in the relatively short history of Asian American studies and literary production. Edited by four young, dynamic writers, all of whom went on to become well-known figures in their own right—critic, playwright, poet, novelist—within and beyond the Asian American literary community, the book consists of writings by fourteen authors of three ethnicities: Chinese, Japanese, and Filipino. Though it is called an "Asian American" anthology, its editors obviously define the term narrowly. While the collection presents multigenre texts—short stories, novel excerpts, and acts from plays—its preface, and a new preface titled "*Aiiieeeee!* Revisited: Preface to the Mentor Edition," written in October 1991, express strong views on the status of Asian American writing. There is also an introduction to Chinese and Japanese American literature, coauthored by the editors, as well as a separate introduction to Filipino American literature written by S. E. Solberg.

The editorial group headed by Chin draws some hard lines in defining and expressing the Asian American identity, arguing that Asian Americans have "evolved cultures and sensibilities distinctly not Chinese or Japanese and distinctly not white American," and that their anthology is "exclusively Asian American," which means written by "Filipino, Chinese, Japanese Americans, American born and raised" (xi). These Americans of Asian descent, the editors argue, possess an "Asian American sensibility," the birth of which is used "as the measure of being an Asian American" (xiii). Thus, Americanized writers such as Lin Yutang (author of *A Chinatown Family*, among others) and C. Y. Lee (author of *Flower Drum Song*) are excluded because of their presumed foreign sensibility, but "the birth of the sensibility," not "the actual birth" (xiii), enables the inclusion of Louis Chu, who came to the United States at age nine. One accomplishment that the editors intend is to show off the voices of seven generations of Chinese Americans and four generations of Japanese Americans. "America's dishonesty—its racist white supremacy passed off as love and acceptance—has kept seven generations of Asian American voices off the air, off the streets, and praised us for being Asiatically no-show. A lot is lost forever. From the few decades of writing we have recovered from seven generations, it is clear that we have a lot of elegant, angry, and bitter life to show. We know how to show it. We are showing off. If the reader is shocked, it is due to his own ignorance of Asian America. We are not new here. Aiiieeeee!!" (xxii).

Because of the paucity of Asian American literary writings, and because of racist suppression, Chin and his colleagues were convinced that those generations had been effectively muzzled and Asian Americans had been left "in a state of self-contempt, self-rejection, and disintegration" (xii). Therefore, gathering and publishing available Asian American writings became for them an important and necessary step to right the wrongs that had been done. Even more important, showcasing their own work forms a powerful resistance to the white man's representations of Asians, especially Asian males, in American literature, as represented by Earl Derr Biggers's series of Charlie Chan novels. Ultimately, *Aiiieeeee!* indicates to the reading public that Asian Americans can, and do, represent themselves.

The 1991 preface to the Mentor edition not only reinforces the political and literary messages of the earlier preface but also expresses the editors' defiant and disappointed feeling because they were convinced that their anthologizing effort was ignored by yellow and white critics. By 1991, the sequel to *Aiiieeeee!*, *The Big Aiiieeeee!*, edited by the same group, had been published, after what they believe to be seventeen years of silence on the part of literary critics and "culture vultures" (xxiv). While the tone in the new preface continues to be bitter and belligerent, the editors emphasize the Asian American sensibility less and stress their Asian roots more (Chinese and Japanese classics, Genghis Khan, the pope's biased understanding and handling of Oriental cultures), material that appeared again in Frank Chin's oft-quoted "This Is Not an Autobiography," published in *Genre*, and in his "Come All Ye Asian American Writers of the Real and the Fake" in *The Big Aiiieeeee!*. The introductions to Chinese and Japanese American literature provide a useful survey of major writers from the two groups, analyzing some works, such as John Okada's novel *No-No Boy* and Lawson Fusao Inada's poetry, among many other things. Solberg's introduction to Filipino American literature offers a survey of writers from the colonial period to the postcolonial years, including Carlos Bulosan, Benny F. Feria, Bienvenido Santos, and N. V. M. Gonzalez.

Of the fourteen selected writers, four are women (Diana Chang, Momoko Iko, Hisaye Yamamoto, and Wakako Yamauchi), and Jeffery Paul Chan, Diana Chang, Frank Chin, Louis Chu, Wallace Lin (pseudonym of Russell Leong), and Shawn Hsu Wong are Chinese American; Momoko Iko, Toshio Mori, John Okada, Hisaye Yamamoto, and Wakako Yamauchi are Japanese American; Carlos Bulosan, Oscar Peñaranda, and Sam Tagatac are Filipino American. The bounds and boundaries of "Asian American" have been quite fluid since the inception of Asian American studies in the late 1960s. Chin et al.'s anthology represents the earliest attempt at defining Asian American literary parameters, including only three ethnic groups. Nonetheless, the publication of *Aiiieeeee!* and its sequel *The Big Aiiieeeee!* helped map the initial boundaries of Asian American literary studies and define important Asian American issues, including racism, manhood, and history; despite its challenging and often angry tone, the collection has drawn the attention of many critics—mainstream and Asian American—to an emerging literature. Even with its narrow ethnic scope and its controversial advocacy of the Asian American sensibility, *Aiiieeeee!* raises urgent issues regarding the identity of Asian Americans and the parameters of Asian American literature.

* * *

Breaking Silence: An Anthology of Contemporary Asian American Poets. **Ed. Joseph Bruchac. Greenfield Center, NY: Greenfield Review Press, 1983. 295 pp.**
Almost all Asian American literary anthologies are edited by Asian American writers and/or scholars. *Breaking Silence* is an exception, which constitutes evidence of

the meaningfulness of Asian American work to what Bruchac calls "a non-Asian American such as myself"; thus, "In a way, this is an outsider's view of contemporary Asian American poetry" (xiv). Nonetheless, the editor solicited work from 200 individual poets and selected 50 American poets of Asian ancestry who were writing before and at the time the anthology was being prepared. Indeed, the collection represents a variety of poets with widely different ethnic and cultural backgrounds from the United States, Canada, and the Pacific Islands. The title is taken from "a powerful poem" by Janice Mirikitani, for "It exemplifies what I feel is happening with Asian American writers in the United States and Canada.... They are adding to the literature and life of their nations and the world, breaking both silence and stereotypes with the affirmation of new songs" (xiv–xv). This is among the earliest single-genre anthologies of Asian American works. According to Bruchac, the birth of this book can be traced back to a special issue of *The Greenfield Review*, published in the spring of 1977, that focused on Asian American writers.

Bruchac acknowledges previous works and efforts that prepared the way for his collection, naming influential Asian American publications such as *Bridge*, *Yardbird Reader*, *Aiiieeeee!*, *AMERICAN BORN AND FOREIGN*, and the Canadian anthology *PAPER DOORS*, among others. These are a healthy indication of the rise of and attention paid to Asian American creative writing after its long oblivion. Due to the efforts of people like "the *Aiiieeeee* Boys," *Amerasia*, *The Greenfield Review*, and *Bridge*, "there opened up a body of listeners and readers who had space on their blank pages for Asian American work" (xiv). While the anthology focuses on writers of Chinese, Japanese, Filipino, and Korean ethnic origins, it projects the vision of a broadening field of literary production by

Asian Americans: "In a few years, the new generation of immigrants from southeast Asia—Thai, Hmong, Vietnamese—may be producing their Jessica Hagedorns, Frank Chins, Lawson Inadas, Laureen Mars" (xiv).

Accompanying each poet's selections is a photo or picture, followed by a brief biographical sketch. In some cases the poet gives a statement on their method. For example, the Filipino American poet Virginia Cerenio comments: "Writing is a fusion of art & politics; a tool for capturing those emotions that can only be imagined between the lines in history books. Anger cannot make poems, it is the beauty of the expression of anger that makes poems. In crafting a writing style, I seek to contain the tension and balance between art & politics" (10).

Some poets chose not to include a photo: Diane Hai-Jew, Garrett Kaoru Hongo, George Leong, and Wing Tek Lum, to name four. Lum states, "It is my strong preference not to have a photo, statement, etc. Let the poems speak for themselves" (171). Still others, such as Alan Chong Lau and Kitty Tsui, present their images via other media—Lau with a potato block print made himself and Tsui with a drawing by Karen Sjöholm. Such self-presentation and self-identification shows the diversity of Asian American poetic voices in terms of gender, politics, writing style, and other characteristics. Many other familiar names can be found in the volume: Diana Chang, Marilyn Chin, Eric Chock, Lawson Fusao Inada, Joy Kogawa, Janice Mirikitani, David Mura, Cathy Song, Arthur Sze, and Merle Woo, as well as some new names: Jaime Jacinto, Geraldine Kudaka, Diane Mei Lin Mark, and Dwight Okita, to mention just a few. The anthology as a whole presents a broad range of themes and techniques, as diverse as the poets themselves and as varied as the ethnicities and cultures they come from, if not representing them. Because of the quality and quantity of works, as well as

the wide spectrum of writers this anthology represents, it remains a viable textbook for courses in Asian American poetry or literature in general.

* * *

***The Hawk's Well: A Collection of Japanese American Art and Literature,* vol. 1. Ed. Jerrold Asao Hiura. San Jose, CA: Asian American Art Projects, 1986. 200 pp.**
A single-ethnicity, interdisciplinary collection, *The Hawk's Well* gathers six genres of art and literature in one modest volume: prints (Tom Kamifuji), pen and inks (Sharyn Nagako Yoshida), serigraphs/poetry (Richard Hamasaki and Mark Hamasaki), calligraphy (Shioh Kato), short story (Yoshiko Uchida), and poetry (Janice Mirikitani, James Masao Mitsui, Jerrold Asao Hiura, and Zukin Hirasu). The anthology, the first in a series of collections of creative works by Pacific Basin people, is part of *Tides Anthology,* published by Asian American Art Projects. Even though *The Hawk's Well* took shape exactly a dozen years after the publication of Frank Chin et al.'s *Aiiieeeee,* the editor seems to follow the groundwork laid by that pioneering anthology and even echoes its resounding theme of "Asian American sensibility." James Mitsui, for example, is described as having "developed a sensibility that is neither distinctly Asian nor white American but an elegant and purposeful jab into the middle of it all" (12). And like its predecessor, this volume intends to educate the reading public about Japanese America and to counter mainstream ignorance of the creative systems of Asian Americans.

While the volume as a whole is interdisciplinary, the introduction focuses on literary writers ranging from early Japanese American authors to *sansei* authors like Lawson Fusao Inada, Lane Nishikawa, Lonny Kaneko, Philip Gotanda, Ronald Tanaka, Amy Sanbo, and Janice Mirikitani. The editor identifies the primary aim as "to introduce Japanese American artists and writers through a significant body of their work and to bring the art of Japanese America into a common theme with its evolving literature" (23). To achieve this, Hiura divides the collection into four parts, respectively titled with the four major elements of the universe, "Fire," "Water," "Earth," and "Air." In Part I, "Fire," besides poems by Hiura, there are pen and inks, photos of Los Angeles's Little Tokyo circa 1937, photos of the Hiura family in 1920, and photos of a cemetery monument in Manzanar, a concentration camp for Japanese internees during World War II. Part II, "Water," opens with a famous quotation from Lao Tzu, the author of the foundation work of Taoism, *Tao Te Ching*: "Under heaven / nothing is more soft and yielding / than water. / Yet, for attacking the solid and the strong, / nothing is better" (62). Photos of Japanese dancers and of evacuees at Terminal Island, California (1942) are presented along with prose and poetry by Mirikitani, including her now familiar "Awake in the River." Part III, "Earth," includes a short story by Yoshiko Uchida, "Something to Be Remembered By," as well as poems by James Mitsui, among which is a sarcastic piece called "Fishing in Eagle Harbor with Garrett Hongo." Part IV, "Air," consists of serigraphs, calligraphy, and photographs of railroad workers circa 1909, and photographs of Filipino emigrants in 1934. Poetry by Zukin Hirasu is thematically more varied than in the earlier parts. There are poems about places—Japan, China, Europe, Italy, I Hotel, Rapallo—and poems about historical figures—Lin Piao (Chairman Mao's designated successor who died in a plane crash), Gaudier Brzeska (the French artist and writer), Ezra Pound (the American expatriate and imagist poet), and Ernest Fenollosa (the American Orientalist).

The Hawk's Well showcases a variety of genres of literature and art, and it therefore serves audiences of different artistic penchants. But the poetry stands above all other genres in the collection because of its quality and quantity.

* * *

Songs of Gold Mountain: Cantonese Rhymes from San Francisco Chinatown. Ed. and trans. Marlon K. Hom. Berkeley and Los Angeles: University of California Press, 1987. 322 pp.

Songs of Gold Mountain is a rare collection of poems written by early Chinese immigrants to the United States, specifically in San Francisco, California. The main title of the collection uses a well-known metaphor, Gold Mountain, invented by early nineteenth-century Chinese immigrants and still used by contemporary Chinese and Chinese Americans; the subtitle refers to a specific Chinese subgroup, the Cantonese—Chinese people originally from Guangdong (formerly Canton), a southern province that shares the Pearl River Delta and that borders Hong Kong, a region known in modern Chinese history for its export or outflow of labor to the West as well as to South Pacific islands. These same adventurous people participated in the construction of America's transcontinental railroad and established all the major Chinatowns in North America, the best known being the Chinatown of San Francisco, which was nicknamed Gold Mountain and which in turn became a metonymy for the United States that represented American plenty when gold was discovered in the Sierra Nevada mountains.

The "Cantonese Rhymes" were for the most part written by Chinese immigrants from Canton province, all 220 pieces were initially composed in Chinese and translated into English by the editor, Marlon Hom. These poems were selected from 1,640 original entries collected in two anthologies called *Jinshan ge ji* (literally, Collected Songs of Gold Mountain) (808 pieces) and *Jinshan ge erji* (Collected Songs of Gold

Mountain II) (832 pieces), published in Chinese in 1911 and 1915, respectively, in San Francisco's Chinatown. Hom's collection presents his translation as well as the original Chinese poem for each piece, with two sets of notes, one for the English version and one for the Chinese original. This textual arrangement gives readers of both Chinese and English a great deal of convenience. And because the poems reflect a broad range of issues concerning Chinese immigrants in the late nineteenth and early twentieth centuries, the collection conveys a sense of history as lived by the writers of these songs (poems, ballads, lyrics).

Marlon Hom's seventy-page introduction, "An Introduction to Cantonese Vernacular Rhymes from San Francisco Chinatown," offers one of the most thorough and comprehensive discussions of the literary history of Chinese America, looking into major societal, political, and cultural issues of important time periods in the Chinese American experience from the earliest days in 1849, when news of the discovery of gold in California traveled to China. Hom also debunks stereotypes of "unassimilable" Chinese immigrants; he argues, for example, that the formation of Chinatown was not a result of the immigrants' unwillingness to assimilate; rather, it was an alternate way of responding to racism. "Chinatown was created as a means of survival during a time of rampant racial intolerance, when the Chinese were forced to retreat from an integrated existence to an alienated one" (15). In the section "Cantonese Rhymes from San Francisco Chinatown," Hom traces the development of early Chinatown literature, discussing in detail the publication by Tai Quong Company (a noted Chinatown bookseller and publisher) of the two collections of *Songs of Gold Mountain* that form the basis of this anthology.

The songs or rhymes are divided into eleven categories, each revolving around one major theme: "Immigration Blues," "Lamentations of Stranded Sojourners," "Lamentations of Estranged Wives," "Nostalgic Blues," "Rhapsodies on Gold," "Songs of Western Influence and the American-borns," "Nuptial Rhapsodies," "Ballads of the Libertines," "Songs of the Young at Heart," "Songs of Prodigals and Addicts," and "Songs of the Hundred Men's Wives." Each section opens with a short introduction to its themes and draws a brief historical, and sometimes literary, context in which to productively read the selected pieces. Unfortunately, none of the original songs had or was given a title. Nevertheless, this is an ideal book for bilingual readers of English and Chinese. Anyone interested in the development of early Chinese American literary writings will find it a valuable source as well as a good classroom text in immigration history and ethnic studies.

* * *

***The Forbidden Stitch: An Asian American Women's Anthology.* Ed. Shirley Geok-lin Lim, Mayumi Tsutakawa, and Margarita Donnelly. Corvallis, OR: Calyx Books, 1988. 290 pp.**

Published by Calyx, a women's collective, and called the first Asian American women's anthology, *The Forbidden Stitch* presents a broad spectrum of writers, genres, themes, and styles; and because it includes visual artworks, this collection is truly interdisciplinary. Each of the three editors writes an introduction that explains the need for an Asian American women's anthology and lays out the scope of the work. In "A Dazzling Quilt," Shirley Geok-lin Lim argues that "Asian American woman" is a "homogenizing labeling of an exotica" because such women exhibit "a bewildering display of differences. We do not share a common history, a common original culture or language, not even a common physique or color. We are descended from Hindus of Uttar Pradesh, Chinese from Hong Kong, Japanese from Honshu, Ilocanos from the Philippines, Vietnamese from Saigon (now Ho Chi Minh City), Koreans, Malaysians, Pakistanis" (10). This volume attests to the plurality of Asian American voices, a plurality that casts doubt on any thematic unity. Therefore, Lim points out, one of the editors' aims is "to awaken the reader to the vitality of cultural difference itself, its visible markers in the lives (and spelling!) of these women. If the stitch is multi-colored and complexly knotted, still it holds together a dazzling quilt" (11).

Mayumi Tsutakawa, in "Escape from Anonymity," identifies "discovering new voices and planning their escape from the fate of anonymity" as her dual goal in editing the anthology. This goal is clearly realized, as the book represents a wide diversity of Asian women who claim their native soil in both or either of the two continents of Asia and North America, though there is no single definition of Asian/Pacific American literature or uniformly homogenizing theme that connects all these writers. The anthology is therefore an effort to showcase "contemporary ideas and new works by individual artists" (13). It adds new voices of women born in South and Southeast Asian countries. Margarita Donnelly, as managing editor, explains in "Difficult Birthing" why and how it took so long, from 1985 to 1989, for the book to be born, a difficult and painful process associated with being the first Asian American women's anthology, which she believes is "an important indicator of the level of invisibility Asian American women experience in this society" (15). The collection was truly a labor of love for its three editors.

The Forbidden Stitch is divided into four sections—poetry, prose, art, and reviews— followed by contributor notes and index, and a fairly comprehensive bibliography.

Marilyn Chin's well-known piece, "We Are Americans Now, We Live in the Tundra," opens the poetry section that consists of twenty-eight women poets whose work is scattered in five different parts of the book. Most of the poets are represented by one poem; however, Diana Chang, Tina Koyama, Merle Woo, Myrna Peña Reyes, Mei-Mei Berssenbrugge, Sharon Hashimoto, and Shirley Geok-lin Lim each have two pieces included. Conspicuously absent from the volume is Cathy Song, who by 1988 had had her award-winning *Picture Bride* published. The prose section consists of fifteen short narratives, from some well-established writers such as Yoshiko Uchida, Shirley Geok-lin Lim, Fae Myenne Ng, and Diana Chang, as well as a few new voices, such as Talat Abbasi, Siu Wai Anderson, and Anjana Appachana. The art section offers works by fourteen artists in various media, including photos, portraits, drawings, mixed media, works of porcelain, clay, acrylics, sand, wood, ceramics, collage, terra cotta and earth, print, weaving, sculpture, canvas, and more. The last section, reviews, features twelve scholars' reviews and review essays of poetry collections, novels, anthologies, and short stories, including reviews of well-known works such as Cathy Song's *Picture Bride*, Elaine Kim's *Asian American Literature* and *With Silk Wings*, Joy Kogawa's *Obasan*, Jessica Hagedorn's *Dangerous Music*, Diana Chang's *What Matisse Is After*, Fay Chiang's *In the City of Contradictions*, Ruthanne Lum McCunn's *Thousand Pieces of Gold*, Linda Ty-Casper's *Wings of Stone*, Jeanne Wakatsuki Houston's *Beyond Manzanar*, Cherríe Moraga and Gloria Anzaldúa's anthology *This Bridge Called My Back*, Marilyn Chin's *Dwarf Bamboo*, Helen Chetin's *Angel Island Prisoner 1922*, three collections by Shirley Lim, two collections by Mei-Mei Berssenbrugge, and three volumes by Ai.

Following these interesting and insightful reviews are notes on the sixty contributors and three editors. Even more valuable is the bibliography of works by Asian American women, under twelve subheadings (anthologies, fiction, interviews, and so on). Because the four sections of the anthology are spatially intertwined and do not follow a sequential order, the organization makes access difficult, though the title *Forbidden Stitch* and the Chinese embroidered purse, stitched, are reminders of the layers as well as the diverse patterns of the quilt image; it thus makes sense to have the genres spread throughout the book rather than limiting each to a designated space in the anthology.

* * *

***Making Waves: An Anthology of Writings by and About Asian American Women.* Ed. Asian Women United of California. Boston: Beacon, 1989. 481 pp.**
Like Joseph Bruchac's anthology that takes its title, *Breaking Silence,* from a poem by the Japanese American poet Janice Mirikitani, the volume *Making Waves,* collectively edited by Asian Women United of California, a nonprofit organization founded in 1976 to promote the social, economic, and general welfare of Asian American women, uses the water image in the title and throughout the seven parts of the book at the suggestion of Mirikitani. Elaine Kim, who wrote the landmark book *Asian American Literature* (1982), generated the idea for this anthology. It is a multigenre collection of essays, poems, short stories, and memoirs by women writers of Asian descent, primarily unpublished works since the early 1970s; hence a collection of original works produced within the time frame of a decade and a half. The anthology not only represents writers of large and culturally well-established ethnic groups such as Chinese, Japanese, Koreans, and Filipinos, it also uses many avenues to reach other Asian ethnic communities in its concerted

effort to demonstrate heterogeneity. Thus new, emerging literary voices from South and Southeast Asia are included. "By South Asian," the editors write, "we mean those whose roots extend to India, Pakistan, Bangladesh, and the other countries in that area" (viiii); "Southeast Asian" refers to women from the Indochinese Peninsula—Vietnam, Cambodia, and Laos—as well as women from Burma and Thailand (x). This editorial approach to a broader representation of Asian American literary production evinces an increasing awareness of the expansion of the field resulting from the increased volume of Asian immigration into the United States from other geographical locations than the Far East, as well as Asian American women's desire to express their own American experience.

A general introduction titled "A Woman-Centered Perspective on Asian American History" by Sucheta Mazumbdar provides an overview that "explores the lines along which women have shaped, and been shaped by, the history of Asian America" (1). This history starts in 1848, when gold was discovered in the California Sierra Nevada foothills and attracted Chinese men from across the Pacific Ocean, followed by a small number of Chinese women, picture brides from Japan and Korea who would not meet their husbands until they gained the shores of Gold Mountain, and sewing women in the garment industry in New York City, and winds up with Asian American political activism in the 1970s. The twenty-two-page survey of Asian American women's lives provides a historical context in which to read and understand the literature presented in the anthology, which is divided into seven parts, each focusing on a major theme. "These themes . . . help organize the diversity of subjects which range from memories of Asian American women in their homelands to current issues in the United States, from personal relationships to those in the workplace, from introspection to war" (x).

Part 1, "From Shore to Shore: Immigration," presents poems (Meena Alexander, Sakae S. Roberson, Chunmi Kim, Myrna Peña Reyes, and Cathy Song) and prose (Connie Young Yu, Dorothy Cordova, Sun Bin Yim, and Van Luu). Part 2, "Crashing Waves: War," examines war-related issues that affect Asian American women with poems by Janice Mirikitani and Brenda Paik Sunoo, and essays by Elaine Kim and Valerie Matsumoto, a memoir by K. Kam, and stories told in diary form by Evelyn Lee and Gloria Oberst. Part 3, "Moving Currents: Work," includes poems by Kathy Wong and Kitty Tsui, and essays that investigate the working conditions of Asian women—such as *issei* women in Hawai'i (Gail M. Nomura), Punjabi cannery workers in California (Marcelle Williams), women in the garment industry (Diane Yen-Mei Wong with Dennis Hayashi), and women in Silicon Valley (Rebecca Villones), women in broadcasting (Felicia Lowe)—and Asian American women's struggle for recognition (Deborah Woo).

Part 4, "Where Rivers Merge: Generations," contains a poem by Beheroze F. Shroff and stories by R. A. Sasaki, Kartar Dhillon, Cecilia Manguerra Brainard, and Virginia Cerenio, all of which deal with generational and cultural conflicts in Asian American communities. Part 5, "Clearing the Mist: Identity," centers around the complex and often perplexing question of the identity of the ethnic self. The introduction states, "Identity is a simple word yet it raises many complex issues and causes much introspection. We grapple not only with our individual understanding of ourselves, men, and other women, but also with broader influences of history, society, cultural heritage, and traditional structures" (239). Thus, poems by Angela Lobo-Cobb and Johnny Sullivan Price and articles by Kesaya E. Noda, Wakako Yamauchi, Nellie Wong, Sucheng Chan, Barbara M. Posadas, and Pamela H. all concern Asian American women's issues—their stereotype as passive and submissive, gender relationships, interracial marriage, disability, and gay and lesbian issues. Part 6, "Thunderstorms: Injustice," confronts issues such as violence, racism, and sexism. A poem by Chea Villanueva, stories by Meena Alexander and Valerie Matsumoto, and essays by Renee E. Tajima, Venny Villapando, Nilda Rimonte, and Rashmi Luthra examine these topics with actual events and historical experiences. Part 7, "Making Waves: Activism," includes works by poets Janice Mirikitani and Valorie Bejarano, activist Juanita Tamayo Lott, feminist scholar Esther Ngan-Ling Chow, Nancy Dio (interview with Mrs. Chang Jok Lee), Yoichi Shimatsu and Patricia Lee, Jyotsna Vaid, and Judy Chu.

The editorial collective introduces each of the seven parts by summarizing the themes and subjects of the pieces that follow. This provides the reader with a historicized as well as contextualized perspective. To further help the user of the anthology, "A Chronology of Asian American History," compiled by Judy Yung, is appended, and to give a sense of the heterogeneous cultural, ethnic, and educational backgrounds, notes on all fifty-three contributors are provided, followed by useful notes on works as well as subjects. All the textual apparatus facilitate use of an anthology conceived and created entirely by American women of Asian descent. *Making Waves* will remain a useful textbook for courses in Asian American literature, history, ethnic studies, and women's studies.

* * *

Between Worlds: Contemporary Asian-American Plays. Ed. Misha Berson. New York: Theatre Communications Group, 1990. 196 pp.

At the end of her introduction to the anthology, editor Misha Berson states, "This book, the first anthology of plays by Asian-American writers, was conceived in the spirit of that emergent culture, that ever-evolving mosaic of the American Dream" (xiv). Berson's qualifier "emergent" was certainly true of the genre of Asian American drama, which, by 1990 when her anthology came out, had only a few prominent voices. And like anthologies such as Hsu and Palubinskas's *Asian-American Authors* and Chin et al.'s *Aiiieeeee!* published in the early 1970s, *Between Worlds* includes six playwrights with ancestral roots in only three Asian countries: China, Japan, and the Philippines. But the writers are of three generations and diverse religious and linguistic backgrounds. Berson's introduction offers a brief history of the theatrical development of Asian American drama writing and staging, and explains how racism and ethnic stereotyping curbed interest in writing by and about Asian Americans. Plays by white writers before the 1950s generally created and reinforced stereotypical images of Asians in America, and "such caricatures had little to do with actual human behavior, and nothing at all to do with Asian self-definition" (x). So the time had come "for Asian Americans to begin telling their own stories in their own authentic voices" (xii). Since the 1960s a group of Asian American playwrights emerged to do just that. Berson chose Ping Chong, Philip Kan Gotanda, Jessica Hagedorn, David Henry Hwang, Wakako Yamauchi, and Laurence Yep for inclusion in her anthology, in part because their plays reflect "the tremendous diversity of Asian Americans as artists and individuals—a diversity long denied by the 'majority' culture" (xiii).

The six playwrights are represented by seven plays: *Nuit Blanche: A Select View of Earthlings* by Ping Chong, *The Wash* by Philip Kan Gotanda, *Tenement Lover:* *no palm trees/in new york city* by Jessica Hagedorn, *As the Crow Flies* and *The Sound of a Voice* by David Henry Hwang, *And the Soul Shall Dance* by Wakako Yamauchi, and finally, *Pay the Chinaman* by Laurence Yep. It is almost redundant to say that some of these pieces have now become well-established—performed, read, and studied—dramas in the Asian American literary canon today, *And the Soul Shall Dance* and *The Wash* being just two examples. Each is preceded by a specially written narrative that provides some biographical details about the author in their own words and that sheds light on the work(s) chosen for the anthology and on the author's other works. All six writers discuss themes, issues, influences, and styles in their statements. Besides this narrative sketch and a photo of each playwright, the editor provides two other items to aid the reader, "Biographical Information" and "About the Play." These amenities contextualize the selected plays and illuminate all the works collected in the volume, as the writers share similarities in their viewpoints on identity, history, racial biases, otherness, and more. As the first anthology of Asian American plays, Berson's *Between Worlds* does an excellent job of presenting some of the most impressive works that emerged between the mid-1970s and 1990.

* * *

Home to Stay: Asian American Women's Fiction. **Ed. Sylvia Watanabe and Carol Bruchac. Greenfield Center, NY: Greenfield Review Press, 1990. 321 pp.**
Home to Stay is a single-genre, single-gender, and multiethnic collection of fiction (short stories and novel excerpts) mostly by Asian American women, though several authors represented are not Asian American but rather women who, by historical circumstances or chance, find themselves involved in Asian American experiences.

Marnie Mueller, for example, is a Caucasian woman born in Tule Lake, one of ten Japanese American relocation camps where her father was serving as a guard. Mueller writes in the introduction to her piece "Changes": "Sitting at the long table in the library's main room, I began to weep—perhaps for the tragedy of the camps and the suffering people had experienced. I give myself that much. But closer to the truth, I suspect, is that I wept for relief that my own history had been confirmed at last" (35). Another non-Asian woman, Deborah Fass, a descendant of Eastern European Jewish immigrants, went to Japan to study Japanese literature and teach English as a second language, and married a Japanese musician. Three other writers included are not "typical" Asian Americans either: Sussy Chako is Chinese/Indonesian American; Shirley Geok-lin Lim, Chinese/Malaysian American; and Diana Davenport, half Native Hawaiian.

The volume's range of ethnicities is also apparent in its inclusion of writers such as Arun Mukherjee, an Indian Canadian. Of the twenty-nine contributors, a good number are well-known names on the Asian American literary scene: Maxine Hong Kingston, Meena Alexander, Gish Jen, Fae Myenne Ng, Amy Tan, Chitra Divakaruni, Wakako Yamauchi, Jessica Hagedorn, Hisaye Yamamoto, Shirley Geok-lin Lim, Bharati Mukherjee, and Sylvia Watanabe. Most are represented by only one piece; however, Yamauchi, Yamamoto, and Brainard each have two. A couple of the selections are taken from high-profile prose narratives, such as Kingston's *China Men* and Tan's *The Joy Luck Club*; several are widely read pieces, like Yamauchi's "And the Soul Shall Dance," Mukherjee's "The Management of Grief," and Watanabe's "Talking to the Dead."

Carol Bruchac conceived of this anthology, which she and Sylvia Watanabe coedited, each contributing a brief intro-duction. Watanabe points to the breadth of representation: women of Chinese, Filipino, Indian, Japanese, Korean, Malaysian, Pakistani, and Vietnamese descent, as well as non-Asians, are included; this helps to illustrate the diversity of ethnic voices under the all-encompassing rubric "Asian American," a term that has never really stabilized since its inception back in the 1960s. Despite this diversity, contends Watanabe, "the stories in this book have arisen smack-dab out of the mainstream of American tradition," and "these stories tell and re-tell the old American story of coming home to stay" (xi). Watanabe's introduction suggests that Asian American writing has its roots deep in the soil of American culture and experience, and in it the mainstream tradition is obvious, so if one wants to push the argument a step further, Asian American literature is an organic branch of American literature, albeit with an ethnic slant. Bruchac's introduction, on the other hand, not only provides a historical backdrop to the conception and compilation of the anthology but also discusses the major themes that run through many of its pieces. "It takes the reader from stories with an historical perspective...to the voices of girls and young women, through family and relationship stories, stories of madness, aging and racism, ending with stories of death and celebration" (xiv).

Another valuable, and visual, aspect of the anthology is the authors' photos, accompanied by biographical sketches and statements on the art of writing. These statements, some sketchy and others more elaborate, help the reader understand the authors' works and why they write as women and as Asian Americans.

* * *

The Big Aiiieeeee!: An Anthology of Chinese American and Japanese American Litera-

ture. Ed. **Jeffery Paul Chan, Frank Chin, Lawson Fusao Inada, and Shawn Wong. New York: Meridian, 1991. 619 pp.**

Edited by the same group of editors as *Aiiieeeee!* (1974), except that the new volume has Jeffery Paul Chan as the primary editor instead of Frank Chin, *The Big Aiiieeeee!* is a sequel to the earlier book, produced seventeen years later. Even though the sequel is a bulkier volume of literature than its predecessor, its focus is narrower as a result of a decision to include only two Asian subgroups, Chinese and Japanese, as opposed to three in *Aiiieeeee!*, which also included Filipinos. In their introduction, the editors describe the contents of their anthology and explain, in broad terms, their principles of inclusion:

> Here, we offer a literary history of Chinese American and Japanese American writing concerning the real and the fake, we describe the real, from its sources in the Asian fairy tale and the Confucian heroic tradition, to make the work of these Asian American writers understandable in its own terms. We describe the fake—from its sources in Christian dogma and in Western philosophy, history, and literature—to make it clear why the more popularly known writers such as Jade Snow Wong, Maxine Hong Kingston, David Henry Hwang, Amy Tan, and Lin Yutang are not represented here. Their work is not hard to find. (xv)

While the above-named authors, among others, are considered fake by the editors, four works are regarded as real: Diana Chang's *Frontiers of Love*, Louis Chu's *Eat a Bowl of Tea*, Shawn Wong's *Homebase*, and Frank Chin's short story collection, *The Chinaman Pacific & Frisco R.R. Co.*

The goal of celebrating the real and exposing the fake in Asian American writing is further explicated in a ninety-two-page essay by Frank Chin, provocatively titled "Come All Ye Asian American Writers of the Real and the Fake," that, while attacking what Chin calls "Asian American writers in the Christian autobiographical tradition," traces the cultural and literary roots of the heroic tradition in Asian American writing to Chinese and Japanese classics, such as *Water Margin*, *Romance of the Three Kingdoms*, *Journey to the West* (all Chinese), and *Chushingura* (Japanese). Chin also presents the original Chinese "Ballad of Mulan" along with his own translation of it as proof of Maxine Hong Kinston's "fake" use of Chinese myths and fairy tales. Chin also finds "fake" Asian Americans in the history of the Japanese experience in the United States, such as the Japanese American Citizens League (JACL) represented by Mike Masaoka during the Japanese internment in World War II.

Unlike its precursor *Aiiieeeee!*, however, *The Big Aiiieeeee!* includes more women writers: Sui Sin Far, Wakako Yamauchi, Violet Kazue Matsuda de Cristoforo, Michi Weglyn, and Joy Kogawa. Genre coverage also broadens: besides the familiar—short stories, poems, novel excerpts, acts of plays, memoirs, etc., there are a phrase book (Wong Sam and Assistants), history research (Peter T. Suzuki), debate (Minoru Yasui), and an autobiographical picture book (Taro Yashima). Both Wong Sam and Assistants' *An English-Chinese Phrase Book* and Violet Kazue Matsuda de Cristoforo's *Poetic Reflections of the Tule Lake Internment Camp 1944* (English–Japanese) are bilingual, as are the poems from *Songs of Gold Mountain*, translated by Marlon K. Hom, that record the experience of early Chinese immigrants at the Angel Island Wooden Barracks in San Francisco Bay. Taro Yashima's autobiographical picture book *Horizon Is Calling* tells of the birth of the artist/author's third child and includes pictures by the boy, with English and Japanese captions at the bottom of each picture. A similar textual strategy is used in Frank Chin's long essay containing a section on "Lin Chong's Revenge," with six illustrations based on the Chinese novel *Romance of the Three Kingdoms*.

Some writing from Hawai'i is also present: an excerpt from Kazuo Miyamoto's novel *Hawaii: End of the Rainbow*, an excerpt from Milton Murayama's novel *All I Asking for Is My Body*, and poems by the Hawaiian-born and mainland-educated Wing Tek Lum. Also noteworthy is the inclusion of an excerpt from the Japanese Canadian Joy Kogawa's novel *Obasan*. The introductory note explains, "it is presented here because of its rare sense of history and its description of the quality of the relationship between Issei and Nisei" (470). The anthology also includes a piece from each of its four editors: the short story "Cheap Labor" by Jeffery Paul Chan, the short story "The Only Real Day" by Frank Chin, an excerpt from Shawn Wong's novel *Homebase*, and five poems by Lawson Fusao Inada, the last of which, "On Being Asian American," appropriately concludes the anthology. Despite its narrow ethnic focus, *The Big Aiiieeeee!*'s coverage of genres and its introduction to Chinese and Japanese American literature make it an interesting anthology for study and classroom use.

* * *

Island: Poetry and History of Chinese Immigrants on Angel Island, 1910–1940. Ed. **Him Mark Lai, Genny Lim, and Judy Yung. Seattle: University of Washington Press, 1991. 174 pp.**

Island is a unique anthology in the history of Asian American literature. As its title rightly indicates, this is a collection of poetry and history; in fact, poetry is presented as history. Unlike most other anthologies of a literary nature, this collection focuses on one ethnicity: the Chinese, specifically the Cantonese of China; one time period:

1910–1940; one locale: Angel Island in the San Francisco Bay; and one genre: translations of Chinese poetry carved on the walls of the wooden barracks at the Angel Island Immigration Station, better known to the Chinese immigrants/detainees as "Muk Wu" (Wooden Barracks); also known to many as the Ellis Island of the West Coast. The three editors, Lai, Lim, and Yung, took on a project more than professional and historical—it is very personal: all three are offspring of Angel Island inmates, and translated these poems as a "personal hobby" (8). The collection contains two other valuable kinds of historical records: photographs of Angel Island Immigration Station buildings and of Chinese detainees, and oral histories recorded and preserved from interviews with thirty-nine people (thirty-one men and eight women), thirty-two of whom were detainees on the island. As the editors put it, "Overall, the oral history of the detainees gives a fairly consistent and accurate picture of the immigrants' daily life on Angel Island" (9).

To understand the translated poetry, readers will do well to have some knowledge of the history of Chinese immigration from 1910 to 1940, which is concisely recounted in the thirty-page introduction by the editors: the opening and closing of the immigration station on the island; why the Cantonese fled their homeland to the United States; how and why the U.S. government created racist legislation such as the Chinese Exclusion Act of 1882; how Chinese male and female immigrants/detainees were treated during their imprisonment while awaiting their turn for interrogation; and ultimately, how the detainees "vented their frustration by writing or carving Chinese poems on the detention center's walls as they waited for the results of appeals or orders for their deportation" (23). These poets were largely Cantonese villagers from the Pearl River Delta region in Guangdong province

(Canton). More than 135 poems written on the walls of the barracks have been recorded, many of which are still visible today (23). Of these, the editors of *Island* selected sixty-nine on the basis of content and artistry. However, the remaining sixty-six pieces are presented in the appendix. All the poems, according to the editors, occupy a unique place in the literary culture of Asian America because they "unconsciously introduced a new sensibility, a Chinese American sensibility using China as the source and America as a bridge to spawn a new cultural perspective" (28).

The five main sections of the anthology constitute the bulk of the book, each with its own theme and title, followed by poems fitting in that category, which in turn are followed by oral histories: "The Voyage, Poems 1–11," "The Detainment, Poems 12–33," "The Weak Shall Conquer, Poems 34–46," "About Westerners, Poems 47–56," "Deportees, Transients, Poems 57–69." An outstanding selection is a considerably longer poem (two and a half pages in English translation and four in the original Chinese), titled "Imprisonment in the Wooden Building," first published in San Francisco's Chinese-language newspaper, *Chinese World*, on March 16, 1910. Almost all the pieces were written anonymously; only occasionally would an author leave his family name, and no woman detainee was known to have written a poem during their imprisonment. Most of the poems were in regulated Chinese form, i.e., with a fixed number of lines and a fixed number of words in each line, often with rhymes. With some exceptions, most of the poems were in four lines, each with seven words (also seven syllables), and could easily fall into the category of classical Chinese *ci*. Indeed, as they are presented in both English and Chinese, the poems can be much better appreciated if the reader has knowledge of both languages, though the notes in English will certainly help those who do not know Chinese.

The oral histories are valuable because they were obtained from people who lived through the horrendous experience on Angel Island. The interviewees—mostly men and a few women, ranging from age six to thirty-three when they were detained—recount their personal ordeals. For example, a Mr. Gin, six years old in 1915, became dirty and full of lice because nobody took care of him during his three months of detention before he was allowed to land; the interpreter told him that he was lucky "because the sight of lice crawling all over me caused the inspector to cut short questioning" (115).

Other textual apparatus include footnotes for appendix poems, sources of poems, sources of photographs, an English bibliography, and a Chinese references list. This collection of poems, photographs, and oral histories provides insights into a dark era of exclusion in the history of immigration in the United States. Even though it stands as a record of one ethnic Asian group, it reflects the pattern of U.S. immigration policy toward all Asian subgroups. It is beyond any doubt an invaluable source for the study of immigration history. As the editors state, "The poems are a vivid fragment of Chinese American history and a mirror capturing an image of that past" (28).

* * *

Charlie Chan Is Dead: An Anthology of Contemporary Asian American Fiction. Ed. Jessica Hagedorn. New York: Penguin, 1993. 569 pp.

In her introduction, editor Jessica Hagedorn states, "As the first anthology of Asian American fiction by a commercial publisher in this country, *Charlie Chan Is Dead* proudly presents forty-eight writers. Almost half are being published in a major collection for the first time" (xxviii). That this anthology was produced by a major publisher indicates a wider recognition of

Asian American literary writing in the early 1990s, as well as a genuine need for Asian American anthologies in the classroom. Elaine Kim wrote the preface, where she ruminates, "For the most part, I read Asian American literature as a literature of protest and exile, a literature about place and displacement, a literature concerned with psychic and physical 'home'—searching for and claiming a 'home' or longing for a final 'homecoming'" (ix). Indeed, Kim's preface itself protests mainstream America's "grotesque representations of Asian Americans, for she feels 'an urgent need to insist that these were not 'our realities.' Our strategy was to assert a self-determined Asian American identity in direct opposition to these dehumanizing characterizations" (ix). Undoubtedly Hagedorn's anthology reflects efforts at such self-determination. And for Kim, "this anthology celebrates many ways of being Asian American today, when the question need no longer be 'either/or.' This anthology gives us *both* Asian American literature *and* world literature: Asian American literary work may be about Asian American experiences, but this is never *all* it is about" (xiii).

Hagedorn offers generous praise of the "absolute breakthrough" anthology *Aiiieeeee!* edited by Frank Chin et al. (though Chin declined to be included in her own collection), for sparking energy and interest among Asian American writers and scholars in the 1970s. Nonetheless, Hagedorn admits, *Charlie Chan Is Dead* is an anthology created for "selfish reasons," a book she wanted to read that had never before been available (xxx), which is another comment of protest against the absence of mainstream publications of Asian American literary efforts in the preceding decades. A single-genre collection of contemporary Asian American fiction, the book anthologizes mostly short stories, and some excerpts from longer narratives.

Many names and titles are familiar to readers—Meena Alexander ("Manhattan Music"), Jeffery Paul Chan ("The Chinese in Haifa"), Diana Chang ("Falling Tree"), Hisaye Yamamoto DeSoto ("Eucalyptus"), Hagedorn ("Film Noir"), Gish Jen ("The Water-Faucet Vision"), Darrell Lum ("Fourscore and Seven Years Ago"), Toshio Mori ("The Chauvinist"), Bharati Mukherjee ("A Father"), Bienvenido Santos ("Immigration Blues"), Amy Tan ("Alien Relative"), José Garcia Villa ("Untitled Story"), and Lois-Ann Yamanaka ("Empty Heart"), among others. Excerpts from Cynthia Kadohata's *The Floating World*, Maxine Hong Kingston's *Tripmaster Monkey: His Fake Book*, Joy Kogawa's *Itsuka*, Ruthanne Lum McCunn's *Thousand Pieces of Gold*, Han Ong's *The Stranded in the World*, and Shawn Wong's *American Knees* are also included. New, younger writers are R. Zamora Linmark ("They Like You Because You Eat Dog, So What Are You Gonna Do About It?" [8 vignettes]), and John J. Song ("Faith"). As Hagedorn points out, there is an array of cultural backgrounds, ages, ranges, and literary styles represented in the anthology. However, a large number of the writers had been well established by the time the anthology was published in 1993, and though the editor "was definitely interested in 'riskier' work" (xxviii) and did include a few new voices, her collection is more safe than experimental. But its focus on one genre and the contemporary era, its biographical notes on authors, and a selected reading list at the end make this one of the most useful collections of Asian American fiction.

In February 2004, a revised and updated edition, *Charlie Chan Is Dead 2: At Home in the World: An Anthology of Contemporary Asian American Fiction*, was published by Penguin, with a preface by Elaine Kim and an introduction by Hagedorn.

* * *

The Politics of Life: Four Plays by Asian American Women. Ed. and with an introduction and commentaries by Velina Hasu Houston. Philadelphia: Temple University Press, 1993. 274 pp.

The Politics of Life is a single-genre anthology of dramatic literature by three Asian American playwrights, edited by one of them, Velina Hasu Houston. The collection consists of a substantial introduction by the editor, two plays by the Japanese American Wakako Yamauchi, *12–1–A* and *The Chairman's Wife*; one piece by the Chinese American author Genny Lim, *Bitter Cane*; and finally, one play by Houston herself, *Asa Ga Kimashita* (*Morning Has Broken*).

Houston's introduction opens with a quotation from the Japanese American poet Kazuko Shiraishi that uses the metaphor of "the pistol of confession" to explain the rationale for her own anthology of Asian American dramatic literature: "We must challenge America's understanding of our history and her perceptions about our present and future.... *Confession* means we have developed a rich voice and we must be heard. It means we challenge all manifestations of oppression. The playwrights in this volume wield their own unique pistols, firing in different directions, but never missing their marks" (2). This book is another effort to protest the marginalization of not just Asian American writing but specifically dramatic literature produced by Asian American women; it is also a renewed attempt to dismantle stereotypes of those women, created especially by the "European American patriarch." The collection therefore carries the dual missions of meeting professional needs and of exercising feminism and antiracism. Houston defines feminism as not just a political ideology but also "self-empowerment, self-definition, and self-determination for women as they try to bring the scales of economic, professional, domestic, and educational justice into balance" (12).

The plays included reflect "an artistic consciousness of the significance of the essential elements of drama," and they were chosen because the authors are pioneers, whose work in the American theater "has opened avenues of opportunities for other Asian American women playwrights to have their work presented" (3). Houston calls Yamauchi's *And the Soul Shall Dance*, Lim's *Paper Angels*, and her own *Tea* "groundbreakers" that exemplify self-empowerment and self-determination. Dramatic literature by Asian Americans, argues Houston, "cannot be published unless a European American chooses to analyze, edit, and present us. In effect, we must have a chaperone or it is difficult to come to the party.... I simply am pointing to the need for self-determination" (16). Editing and producing their own anthologies is both a professional statement of Asian American dramatic coming-of-age and a political act toward literary independence and self-determination: "We have grown up now" (20).

Even though only three playwrights and four plays are included, the editor separates them into two generations: Yamauchi represents the first wave of Asian American women playwrights and Lim and Houston the early part of a second wave; all three examine the lives of Asians and Asian Americans who deal with the daily struggles "to balance the presence of the political in their lives with their personal humanity" (25). Yamauchi's *12–1–A* (block 12, barrack 1, unit A in the concentration camp) delves into the Japanese American incarceration in Poston, Arizona, where Yamauchi herself was interned during World War II. Her second selection in the volume, *The Chairman's Wife*, dramatizes the eventful life of Madame Mao (Chiang Ching), the wife of Chairman Mao Tse-tung. Lim's *Bitter Cane* deals with the political and socioeconomic exploitation of Chinese laborers recruited to work on the sugarcane plantations of

Hawai'i. Finally, Houston's partly autobiographical *Asa Ga Kimashita* looks into the economic and political consequences of the U.S. occupation's land reclamation regulations enforced in Japan after World War II.

To facilitate reading and understanding of the plays, Houston provides detailed biographical commentaries on each of the three playwrights, as well as lists of their works and their production history. While the introduction and the commentaries serve a generally useful but sometimes jingoistic purpose, the reader will benefit more from a direct reading of the dramas themselves.

* * *

Unbroken Thread: An Anthology of Plays by Asian American Women. **Ed. Roberta Uno. Amherst: University of Massachusetts Press, 1993. 328 pp.**

Unbroken Thread is a single-genre, single-gender anthology of six plays by Asian American women playwrights from three generations. The pioneering writers—the first generation—are Wakako Yamauchi and Momoko Iko; the second generation is represented by Genny Lim and Velina Hasu Houston; and the younger playwrights are Jeannie Barroga and Elizabeth Wong. "All six playwrights are American-born daughters of Asian immigrants, and their voices span the genres of naturalism, impressionism, ritual drama, postmodern collage, and media-influenced episodic drama," writes Roberta Uno in her introduction (1). While the writers are all of Asian descent, they belong with different ethnic groups: Genny Lim and Elizabeth Wong are Chinese American; Wakako Yamauchi and Momoko Iko, Japanese American; Houston, Amerasian (Japanese/African/Native American); Jeannie Barroga, Filipino American.

The six plays are Lim's *Paper Angels*, Yamauchi's *The Music Lessons*, Iko's *Gold Watch*, Houston's *Tea*, Barroga's *Walls*, and

Wong's *Letters to a Student Revolutionary.* "Each is a groundbreaking work and addresses in its own way the experiences of Asians in America" (1), and they all focus on themes of isolation and captivity, offering "special insights into the lives, roles, and relationships of Asian American women" (2). The sharing of themes suggests what ties the works together in one volume: "The common thread that runs through these plays is their authors' sensitivity to the lives of Asian Americans, particularly women, in a changing world" (2). But there is also an important political end implied in collecting these dramas: it allows the women playwrights to express their presence in a traditionally women-silencing culture and provides them with an outlet for their views on issues about which they have had little say in the past. Uno's introduction discusses the silence and marginalization of Asian Americans on stage and in writing, while offering a brief survey of the history of Asian American theatrical writing from 1924, when Gladys Li published the play *The Submission of Rose Moy*, to the early 1990s, when dramatic performances were taking place in more recently arrived communities of Southeast Asians and South Asians.

Between 1983 and 1991 and before the publication of *Unbroken Thread* in 1993, Uno had interviewed four of the represented playwrights (all but Barroga and Houston) and the Asian American actor Mako, so she was able to include their comments and biographical details in the introductions preceding the six dramas, which offer historical and literary background to the plays. The appendix is a nineteen-page list of plays by sixty-nine Asian American women for readers who wish to further research the field. This anthology is an ideal textbook for a semester-long course in Asian American drama by women or in Women's Studies.

* * *

Quiet Fire: A Historical Anthology of Asian American Poetry, 1892–1970. Ed. **Juliana Chang. New York: Asian American Writers' Workshop, 1996. 164 pp.**

Thirteen years elapsed between the publications of two major Asian American poetry anthologies, Joseph Bruchac's *Breaking Silence* in 1983 and Juliana Chang's *Quiet Fire* in 1996. While the former features contemporary American poets of Asian descent in the early 1980s, the latter focuses on the evolution of the development of Asian American poetry, specifically from 1892, when the quintessential American poet Walt Whitman died and his half-German, half-Japanese disciple Sadakichi Hartmann started to establish himself as a playwright and poet, and when Sui Sin Far, a pioneer Eurasian fiction writer, was publishing her short stories. While Bruchac's *Breaking Silence* takes its title from a Janice Mirikitani poem, *Quiet Fire*'s title has its origin in Patricia Y. Ikeda's "Recovery." "Fire is the powerful force that destroys traces of history, leading to the subject's sense of both loss and desire. But fire also represents potential…illumination, a powerful radiation" (xviii), writes Juliana Chang. The anthology is a recovery act "against amnesia," intended to "serve as an archival counter-memory, illuminating the gaps in what has been presented as "American poetry" and "American culture" (xv). But the collection is not limited to written and published works; it "considers nontraditional oral and written forms as poetic discourse," including Japanese folk song-derived plantation work songs, Cantonese rhymes from Chinatown, and translations of Chinese poems carved on the walls of the Angel Island detaining station (xvii). Besides mainland American and Hawaiian poets, Canadian Asian poets, such as Fred Wah and Joy Kogawa, are also represented. As the image of fire connotes both destruction and illumination, writes Chang, "This collection provides some traces and remnants that…will prove illuminating of an Asian American poetic history" (xix). Her purpose is to unearth obscured poetry "that deserves wider recognition" (xx).

The pages of this historical anthology do convey a sense of the evolution of the Asian American poem, revealing not only a longer history than many care to know but also a wide range of ethnicities and cultures—Chinese, Filipino, Indian, and Japanese—as well as a broad spectrum of styles and bilingualism. While most of the poems collected were written in English, one anonymous piece, "Hole-Hole Bushi," is presented in both English transliteration and translation; six pieces selected from *Songs of Gold Mountain* (ed. and trans. Marlon K. Hom) are followed by the original Chinese poems, basically in free verse. Three other similar poems from *Island* (ed. and trans. Him Mark Lai, Genny Lim, and Judy Yung) are included, that in the original are all four-line poems, with seven words (also seven syllables) in each line. There are seven pieces from *Sounds from the Unknown: A Collection of Japanese-American Tanka*, each presented in transliteration and translation. The rest of the poems, the majority in the anthology, are the works of twenty-six poets, including familiar names like Jun Fujita, Toyo Suyemoto, Hisaye Yamamoto, José Garcia Villa, Diana Chang, Carlos Bulosan, Joy Kogawa, Jessica Hagedorn, G. S. Sharat Chandra, and Lawson Inada, and some less familiar names, such as Masao Handa, H. T. Tsiang, Bunichi Kagawa, and Charles Yu. The Asian American status of a few of these poets has been debated; for example, Sadakichi Hartmann and Yone Noguchi both were born in Japan, wrote in Japanese and English, and spent more years of their lives in the East than in the West; and Wen I-To wrote predominantly in Chinese and was well established as a New Culture poet in China, and is not likely to be considered by many contemporary Asian American scholars as a Chinese American poet.

Three other characteristics make Chang's anthology valuable. First are biographical notes, which, though sketchy in most cases, are nonetheless useful to the reader who wants to find out about an individual poet. Second are "Reminiscences: Asian North American Poetry Scenes (ca. 1970 to mid-1980s)," compiled by Walter K. Lew, written by several authors—Fay Chiang (New York, 1986) on "Looking Back: Basement Workshop, 1971–86"; Alan Chong Lau (Seattle, 1984) on "Up, Down, and Beyond the West Coast"; Eric Chock (Honolulu, 1994) on "The Beginnings of Asian American Poetry in Hawaii: A Local Viewpoint"; Kimiko Hahn (New York, 1994) on "Word"; and Gerry Shikatani (Montreal, 1994) on "Here, Not There." Each short but concise essay focuses on a major locale where Asian American poetry has developed and put down roots, celebrating the poetry from different ethnic and geographical perspectives that further supplement the reading and teaching of the works selected. Finally, the bibliography at the end provides a seven-page list of single-author volumes and a list of forty-seven anthologies of Asian American poetry. *Quiet Fire* is not a thorough or comprehensive anthology, nor was it meant to be, but it is selective and to some degree representative. It highlights nearly a century of Asian American poetry in the making, and it is an ideal textbook for specialized courses in Asian American poetry.

* * *

***Asian American Drama: 9 Plays from the Multiethnic Landscape.* Ed. Brian Nelson. New York: Applause, 1997. 422 pp.**
Nelson's is one of the largest single-genre anthologies of drama by Asian Americans. It consists of nine plays by ten playwrights, as well as a foreword by David Henry Hwang

and an introduction by Dorinne Kondo. Titled "The Myth of Immutable Cultural Identity," Hwang's foreword considers the issue of cultural authenticity and its bearings on cultural identity, arguing that the latter is not immutable; "Yet the premise that an immutable cultural identity actually exists has gone largely unchallenged" (vii). To his gratification, the nine plays gathered in Nelson's volume "challenge notions of cultural purity and racial isolationism; indeed, they explode the very myth of an immutable cultural identity" (vii–viii). Hwang insists that voices of different races and ethnicities blend into each other: "In these plays, a Japanese American male can become the literary voice of angry white men, or a man and woman can mutate together from one ethnic identity to another, in search of common connection and higher love" (viii). These views are echoed in Kondo's introduction: "the publication of *Asian American Drama: Nine Plays from the Multiethnic Landscape* occurs within a shifting racial matrix in which conventional definitions of race are being challenged, proliferated, and transformed, even as race continues to have powerful, often oppressive, effects in the world. Perhaps most crucially, the connection begins to take account of the significant continuities and changes in the very articulation of what it means to be 'Asian American'" (ix).

The plays included are Philip Kan Gotanda's *Day Standing on Its Head*, Amy Hill's *Tokyo Bound*, Velina Hasu Houston's *As Sometimes in a Dead Man's Face*, David Henry Hwang's *Bondage*, Lane Nishikawa and Victor Talmadge's *The Gate of Heaven*, Dwight Okita's *The Rainy Season*, Garret H. Omata's *S.A.M. I Am*, Rob Shin's *The Art of Waiting*, and Denise Uyehara's *Hiro*. A few of these playwrights are familiar, even famous figures in both the Asian American and mainstream American theatrical circles—Gotanda, Hwang, and Houston, whose plays have been staged in mainstream (nonminority, non-Asian American) theaters. However, all their selected works chart the continuities and transformations of Asian American identities and challenge stereotypical views of Americans of Asian descent while creating new forms of ethnic and racial identities that are "complex, contradictory and multiple" (Kondo xiv).

Preceding each of the nine dramas are ancillary materials providing information about the production history of the play and comments by the editor, and, for potential directors who intend to stage the play, contact information for performance rights. In the unique case of Gotanda, the playwright offers some notes on producing his work. Editor Nelson contributes two pages of "Editor's Notes" that offer evaluative remarks on the themes and styles of each of the nine plays, as well as the rationale for including specific works. For example, Nelson explains why he picked Denise Uyehara's *Hiro* over her *Hobbies*: "Perhaps *Hobbies* would have been the more natural selection for a volume about multiethnic issues. But I have included *Hiro* in this volume instead, because it's a type of multicultural play that seems remarkably rare: a play about people of color, in which their color is not a plot point" (387). Such a judicious approach underlies all the selections in the volume.

* * *

But Still, Like Air, I'll Rise. Ed. Velina Hasu Houston. Philadelphia: Temple University Press, 1997. 520 pp.

The title of Houston's anthology is taken from a poem by the poet laureate Maya Angelou, "Still I Rise," which exudes an ebullient feeling of positivism and hope. One of the largest, if not the largest of Asian American drama anthologies, this volume was published in the same year as Brian Nelson's *Asian American Drama: 9 Plays from the Multiethnic Landscape.* That book includes nine plays and Houston's contains eleven. Roberta Uno, herself a playwright and editor of the 1993 anthology of Asian American plays titled *Unbroken Thread,* wrote the foreword. Discussing the meaningfulness of phone conversations with her editor/playwright friend Houston and an upsetting phone call from an unnamed Asian American woman journalist wanting to learn about "major figures" in Asian American theater, Uno stresses the importance of providing a context for Asian American writing while acknowledging the diversity and breadth of theatrical works by ethnic Americans. Houston's collection, says Uno, "defies the narrow and reductionist categorization that is frequently imposed on our dramatic work by those seeking a convenient way to place it as literature or market it to an audience"; "It is clearly a source for theater production as much as it is an academic resource, challenging and redefining the dramatic literary canon and the frameworks used for its analysis and interpretation" (xi). The goal is then both political and practical: "It takes its place among a small but growing number of texts that enable theater artists to expand their vision and repertoire and allow scholars to consider theater from a place of immersion and practice" (xi).

Editor Houston likewise expresses a good deal of enthusiasm, optimism, and ambition in her introduction: "The dramatic voices contained in this volume are too eclectic, intense, powerful, and rich not to leave a permanent mark on the American psyche, and perhaps beyond the boundaries of this continent" (xvi). To counter marginalization of Asian Americans and critique protectionism of mainstream American theater, Houston offers a wide spectrum of dramatic voices from Asian America, "as pan-Asian as I could make it" (xxi). The result is a showcase of eleven plays: Jeannie Barroga's *Talk-Story,* Philip Kan Gotanda's *Day Standing on Its Head*, Houston's own *Kokoro* (True Heart), Huynh Quang Nhuong's *Dance of the Wandering Souls*, David Henry Hwang's *Bondage*, Victoria Nalani Kneubuhl's *The Conversion of Ka'ahumanu*, Sung Rno's *Cleveland Raining*, Dmae Roberts's *Breaking Glass*, Lucy Wang's *Junk Bonds*, Elizabeth Wong's *Kimchee and Chitlins*, and Chay Yee's *A Language of Their Own*. These writers and works represent a considerable array of Asian/Pacific ethnicities—Chinese, Filipino, Japanese, Samoan Hawaiian, Singaporean, and Vietnamese—and offer a broad sampling of dramas by playwrights from hitherto marginal segments of American theater. While a number of the included plays are familiar to many readers/viewers, most notably Gotanda's *Day Standing on Its Head*, Hwang's *Bondage*, and Wong's *Kimchee and Chitlins*, the rest are newer pieces that add power to an ever-growing canon of Asian American drama, of which Houston's anthology provides a commendable example.

* * *

Watermark: Vietnamese American Poetry & Prose. Ed. Barbara Tran, Monique T.D. Truong, and Luu Truong Khoi. New York: Asian American Writers' Workshop, 1998. 227 pp.

Like *Making Waves*, edited by Asian Women United of California, which uses water images throughout, *Watermark* embodies a passionate love of water that comes to represent a culture and a people—Vietnamese and Vietnamese Americans. This book, edited by three Vietnamese American scholars and writers, consists of forty pieces of literature in two genres by twenty-four writers, both established and emergent. An excerpt from Huynh Sanh Thong's "Live by water, die for water" serves as a brief introduction that explains the lexical and emotional significance of the Vietnamese word

nuóc: "The word for 'water' and the word for 'a homeland, a country, a nation' are spelled the same way in the romanized script and are pronounced the same way" (vi). And "Those who have not discerned that dual acception of the one word *nuóc* have missed the origin of Vietnamese culture and what merges all its disparate elements into a coherent system" (vi). This modest-sized anthology is meant to facilitate understanding of one subgroup, Vietnamese Americans, who had been very much on the fringes of the Asian American literary landscape dominated by the larger ethnic groups such as Chinese, Japanese, Koreans, and Filipinos.

The water image is further delineated in the editors' note that unconventionally appears toward the very end of the book, where they explain, "We were asked to build a structure with only one constraint: it must hold water. We agreed on this one term, but agreed also that we should stick close to the landscape. The structure must hold water, yes, but we would make no attempts to redirect the flow or dictate its uses" (224). The result of this approach is a well-structured anthology that represents some well-known Vietnamese American writers, and many younger, emerging literary voices, in both poetry and prose. Fifteen each have one piece printed, while eight others have more than one: Linh Dinh, five; Christian Langworthy and Truong Tran, four; Mông Lan, three; Dao Strom, lê thi diem thúy, Andrew Lam, and Bao-Long Chu, two each. A number of the writers are widely recognized for their literary, legal, and social activities, including Monique T.D. Truong, lê thi diem thúy, Andrew Lam, Trinh T. Minh-ha, and Lan Cao. Some of the contributors were born in Vietnam: Lan Cao, Linh Dinh, Maura Donohue, Andrew Lam, Bich Minh Nguyen, Dao Strom, Trac Vu (all in Saigon), and Quang Bao, lê thi diem thúy, Nguyen Ba Trac, Thuong Vuong-Riddick (in other parts of the country).

Themes of the poems, short stories, and excerpts (three, besides Thong's quoted earlier—from Barbara Tran's *Rosary*, Maura Donohue's *When You're Old Enough*, and Lan Cao's *Monkey Bridge*) range from self to memories of war, the history of Vietnam, family deaths, and hardships of immigration. Following the texts proper are two other useful items: notes on the cultural, ethnic, geographical, and educational backgrounds of the contributors as well as the three editors, and "A Note to the Reader" that urges readers to use the anthology to look at their own hands "in a new way" (224). As one of very few Vietnamese American anthologies, and despite its relatively modest size, *Watermark* increases the visibility of Vietnamese American literature as a viable branch of Asian American writing that is gaining more and more critical acclaim.

* * *

Asian-American Literature: An Anthology. **Ed. Shirley Geok-lin Lim. Lincolnwood, IL: NTC Publishing Group, 2000. 563 pp.**

Lim's is one of the more recent multigenre anthologies of Asian American writing. According to the editor, its major goal is "to offer teachers, students, and the general public an inclusive introduction to Asian-American writing ... a broad sampler of works whose critical reception has already marked them as belonging to an Asian-American canon or which represent emergent voices, communities, and concerns" (xv). Lim's collection is divided into eight chapters, each of which centers around a major thematic core: "The Immigrant Experience," "Asian Affiliations," "Struggles and Recognitions," "The Individual Inside/ Against the Ethnic Community," "Gender Identities, Gender Relations," "Parents and Families," "American Place and Displacement," and "Language and Vision."

Each chapter is prefaced by a concise headnote that provides a social and literary context for reading the material to follow, and each selection is preceded by a short introduction to the author and the text. Both well-known and newer writings are included, selected on the basis of "literary quality" and "historical and thematic significance" (xv), though the editor acknowledges the contested criterion of "quality." Eighty-three writers are included under eight separate headings, some in more than one chapter; they range from pioneering fiction writers such as Sui Sin Far, Carlos Bulosan, and John Okada, to high-profile authors of the 1970s and 1980s such as Frank Chin, Maxine Hong Kingston, Bharati Mukherjee, and Amy Tan, to younger contemporary writers such as novelist Cynthia Kadohata and playwright Philip K. Gotanda.

Compared with earlier Asian American anthologies that tend to collect writings by authors with national origins in the Far Eastern countries of China, Japan, and Korea, Lim's effort features a broad array of national origins: Burmese, Chinese, Filipino, Hawaiian-Asian, Indian, Indonesian, Japanese, Korean, Malaysian, Pakistani, and other groups. In terms of genre representation, while most of the anthology is composed of short stories, novel excerpts, and poems, it also selects some drama, nonfiction memoirs, and oral narratives.

Lim states that her anthology does not attempt to demonstrate that "Asian-American works come from or contribute to a cohesive and united tradition" (xvi). The various thematic concerns, literary strategies, narrative techniques, and other elements showcase a rich, colorful spectrum of writings in differing styles and genres. It clearly is a multiple-author and multigenre book that enriches the literature curriculum for the university (and high school) classroom. If not directly challenging the Euro-Americentric approaches taken by more traditional works such as *The Norton Anthology of American Literature*, Lim's certainly competes for attention in textbook selections.

Different from Asian American anthologies of the 1970s and early 1980s that focus more on male authors, especially Frank Chin et al.'s *Aiiieeeee!* and its sequel *The Big Aiiieeeee!*, Lim's book devotes a great amount of space to women writers of Asian descent, which reflects not only the expansion of the production field of Asian American literature as a result of the civil rights movement of the 1960s but also the rise of women writers as a result of the feminist movements in the 1960s and 1970s. Lim observes that "single-genre anthologies have been a useful means of exploring the cultural diversity of Asian-American writing" (xxi). The diversity in national origins, gender, and genres in this anthology is manifest in its heterogeneous representations that "help to overturn stereotypes of inscrutable Asian-Americans" (xix).

* * *

Asian American Poetry: The Next Generation. Ed. Victoria Chang. Urbana: University of Illinois Press, 2004. 194 pp.

In *Asian American Poetry*, "Noguchi" is not Yone Noguchi of the late nineteenth century, but Rick Noguchi of the early twenty-first; "Cathy" is not Cathy Song, winner of the 1982 Yale Younger Poets Series, but Cathy Park Hong; "Chang" is not Diana Chang, author of many novels and poems, but Jennifer Chang and Tina Chang; "Santos" is not the fiction writer Bienvenido Santos but Marisa de los Santos. These names are just some indications that this volume is a combined effort of new and younger Asian American poets writing at the turn of the twenty-first century. While the editor subtitles her collection "The Next Generation," she frequently refers to the poets as "the

new generation" in her introduction, thus separating them from the first generation of Asian American poets, of whom she mentions Garrett Hongo, Cathy Song, John Yau, Ai, and Li-Young Lee, who have received widespread recognition in the American literary community. While Chang cites Asian American poets from roughly a century ago—Sadakichi Hartmann, Yone Noguchi, and H. T. Tsiang—and from half a century ago—Toyo Suyemoto, José Garcia Villa, and Carlos Bulosan—she considers those who wrote from the 1970s to the 1990s as the first generation. Those who were born between 1961 and 1981—poets forty years of age and younger—are the new generation.

But the newness is not merely represented by youth. The writing styles, subject matters, experiments with language, and ethnic and demographic shifts the poets represent all contribute to the new voices from contemporary Asian America. Chang's goal is not to simply compile the broadest and widest collection of Asian American poetry, but to make the difficult choices that will help readers gain exposure to the highest quality work. Chang decided to gather such a volume for three reasons: an increasing interest in Asian American writing; a desire for editorial expertise—there has been a mushrooming of poetry anthologies across the country; and a new generation of Asian American poets that has emerged and is helping expand the Asian American literary canon.

To make her case for a new poetry anthology, Chang relies on the U.S. Census Bureau's 2000 statistics that recorded a considerable increase in the population that is responsible for the new ethnic makeup of Asian Americans—indeed, the "newness" is partly defined by the demographic change: as a result of interracial marriages between Asians and Caucasians and between Asians and other races, one can no longer unproblematically identify a writer's ethnicity by his or her name. For examples, who can tell for sure, from the surnames only, of what race(s) are poets such as Brenda Shaugnessy, Pimone Triplett, Lee Ann Roripaugh, Jon Pineda, Brian Komei Dempster, Paisley Rekdal, and C. Dale Young? And when they do not write about "typical" Asian American issues (immigration, internment, the transcontinental railroad, picture brides, generational gaps and cultural clashes between parents and children), it is next to impossible to pinpoint ethnicity, either by name or by subject matter. In terms of subjects, though, the work included is as much Asian American as it is American, for it represents considerable departures from Asian American themes and reflects contemporary issues often written about by mainstream authors.

Unlike some writers before the 1970s who were born outside the United States, the new generation of poets in Chang's volume are mostly native-born, and there seems to be a de-emphasis, if not depoliticization, of Asian American themes and an increased attention to mainstream topics. In other words, their themes are more mainstream American, dealing with current issues such as gay and lesbian lifestyles, voyeurism, and rape that transcend racial, gender, and cultural boundaries. In the protest period of Asian American writing, up to the 1980s, many wrote to protest their inferior treatment by the mainstream society, seeking a voice to define their own identity in a racist milieu. Chang's collection seems to suggest that protest literature by Asian Americans is showing signs of an end, and that new, distinct voices are no longer mere tributaries to

the mainstream literature; rather, they show a strong tendency to compete for spaces in it. This of course does not mean that the collection has no Asian American markers other than ethnicities, names of the poets, and names of Asian places such as Japan, New Delhi, and Benigno Aquino Airport. Some still write about parent-child relationships, rebellion, ethnic food, memories of the past and home countries, cultural misunderstanding, and Japanese internment camps.

The poets included are new also because they experiment with language, the line and space, the stanza, rhyme, and form. There are a number of prose poems, some in a diary format; there are unconventional titles like Amy Quan Barry's and Paisley Rekdal's that use mathematical formulas. Other formal experiments include Jennifer Chang's and Mong-Lan's innovative uses of line, space, and stanza; Warren Liu's double line (for lack of a better expression); and Adrienne Su's single line (with fragments/phrases/images) for stanzas. In short, readers of this collection will find a variety of styles, a range of topics, a diversity of voices, and a kaleidoscope of forms. Chang's introduction ties together poems by twenty-eight writers. Marilyn Chin calls her two-page foreword "a means to pass the torch as a symbolic gesture" (xiii) and the anthology "a scintillating canvas with varying hues and emotions" (xiv). Both Chin's foreword and Chang's introduction provide a historicizing and contemporary context for the selected poems in the anthology. Teachers and students will find valuable things experienced and now expressed in this collection.

2. Autobiographies/Memoirs

Meena Alexander. See Alexander in "Poetry."

Carlos Bulosan (1911–1956). A pioneer Filipino American autobiographer, novelist, poet, and labor activist, Bulosan was born in Binalonan, Pangasinan, the Philippines. He received only three years of schooling in his home country, but he was an avid reader, wrote for the school newspaper, and was involved in the publication of the school literary magazine. At the age of nineteen, Bulosan immigrated to the United States, landing in Seattle, Washington, and started to work menial jobs throughout the depression years in California, Washington, Oregon, and in the fish canneries in Alaska. He became a union activist in a labor organization called UCAPAWA—United Cannery, Agricultural, Packing and Allied Workers of America, and he served as its yearbook editor in 1952. Bulosan's health had often been plagued by lung diseases, for which he was hospitalized for two years in the late 1930s; in 1956 he died of pneumonia, complicated by poverty and alcoholism.

In a short life of forty-five years, Bulosan produced a considerable number of works in different genres: short stories, novels, poetry, and autobiography. Before World War II, he published two volumes of poetry: *Letter from America* (Prairie City, IL: The Press of J. A. Decker, 1942) and *The Voice of Bataan* (New York: Woward-McCann, 1943); two short story collections: *The Laughter of My Father* (New York: Harcourt, Brace and Company, 1944), and *The Philippines Is in the Heart* (Quezon City, Philippines: New Day, 1978). *The Power of the People*, a novel, was posthumously published in 1977 (Ontario, Canada: Tabloid Books) and republished in 1995 as *The Cry and the Dedication* (Philadelphia: Temple University Press). Bulosan is primarily known for *America Is in the Heart: A Personal History* (New York: Harcourt, Brace and Company, 1946), an autobiographical novel that stands tall in the twentieth-century canon of Asian American literary writings.

America Is in the Heart can be considered a lightly veiled recounting of Bulosan's own life story, or the personal history of the book's narrator, variably called Carlos, Carl, or Allos throughout the book. Like Bulosan himself, the narrator left his home country to realize his dreams in America. His father, concerned about his son's survival in the new country, stated that he could always come back home to Binalonan, where the author was born and lived for nineteen years. And like Bulosan, the narrator was a migrant worker in the fields of California and a cannery worker in Alaska and Seattle. Like many other Filipinos of the time period, he and his fellow workers were subject to economic exploitation and racial oppression, which often culminated in filthy working conditions and racial violence perpetrated on them. *The Laughter of My Father*, consisting of twenty-four short stories, is also autobiographical of the Bulosan family and their community in the village of Binalonan. *The Philippines Is in the Heart*, written to balance the America-centered *America Is in the Heart* and published posthumously in 1978 (edited by E. San Juan Jr.), portrays a variety of characters ranging from Americans to affluent Filipinos to peasants and tribal people.

For more information, see:

Alquizola, Marilyn. "The Fictive Narrator of *America Is in the Heart*." In Gail Nomura, Stephen H. Sumida, Russell Endo, and Russell Leong, eds., *Frontiers of Asian American Studies* (Pullman: Washington State University Press, 1989), 211–17.

——. "Subversion or Affirmation: The Text and Subtext of *America Is in the Heart*." In Shirley Hune, Hyung-Chan Kim, Stephen S. Fugita, and Amy Ling, eds., *Asian Americans: Comparative and Global Perspectives* (Pullman: Washington State University Press, 1991), 191–209.

Campomanes, Oscar, and Todd Gernes. "Two Letters from America: Carlos Bulosan and the Act of Writing." *MELUS* 15, no. 3 (Fall 1988): 15–46.

Daroy, Petronilo. "Carlos Bulosan: The Politics of Literature." *Saint Louis Quarterly* 6, no. 2 (June 1968): 193–206.

Evangelista, Susan. *Carlos Bulosan and His Poetry: A Biography and an Anthology.* Quezon City, the Philippines: Ateneo de Manila University Press, 1985.

Han, John Jae-Nam. "Carlos Bulosan." In Guiyou Huang, ed., *Asian American Autobiographers: A Bio-Bibliographical Critical Sourcebook* (Westport, CT: Greenwood Press, 2001), 27–35.

Morantte, P. C. *Remembering Carlos Bulosan: His Heart Affair with America.* Quezon City, the Philippines: New Day, 1984.

Mostern, Kenneth. "Why Is America in the Heart?" *Critical Mass: A Journal of Asian American Cultural Criticism* 2, no. 2 (Spring 1995): 35–65.

San Juan Jr., E. "Carlos Bulosan." In Mari Jo Bulhe, Paul Buhle, and Harvey Kaye, eds., *The American Radical* (New York: Routledge, 1994), 253–60.

——. *Carlos Bulosan and the Imagination of the Class Struggle.* New York: Oriole Editions, 1972.

——. "Carlos Bulosan: The Poetics and Necessity of Revolution." *The Researcher* 2 (1969): 113–23.

Slotkin, Joel. "Igorots and Indians: Racial Hierarchies and Conceptions of the Savage in Carlos Bulosan's Fiction of the Philippines." *American Literature* 72, no. 4 (December 2000): 843–66.

Stuart Santiago, Maria Katrina. "Carlos Bulosan in the History of the Philippine Short Story in English." *Diliman-Review* 47, no. 3–4 (1999): 54–63.

Zhang, Aiping. "Carlos Bulosan." In Guiyou Huang, ed., *Asian American Short Story Writers: An A-to-Z Guide* (Westport, CT: Greenwood Press, 2003), 23–30.

Cynthia Chou (1926–). Born and educated in China, Chou lived and worked in several major Chinese cities—Beijing, Tianjin, Nanjing, and Shanghai. She and her husband also lived in Taiwan for nearly three years before deciding to move to Colombo, Ceylon, where they resided for another three years. In 1955 they relocated again, this time to New York, where her husband took a job with an engineering consulting company. In 1957 she completed a master's degree in education at Teachers College of Columbia University. During her time at Columbia and then at Michigan Tech University, where her husband was teaching, Chou was invited to speak about her life experiences. These speeches laid the groundwork for her autobiography, *My Life in the United States*, published in 1970 (North Quincy, MA: Christopher Publishing House), the only book she has produced so far.

My Life in the United States consists of twenty-eight chapters that delineate the author's American experience as an immigrant. While the work's thematic emphasis rests on the United States, it does recount stories and events that happened in China and Ceylon, the other two major locales where Chou and her husband lived before immigrating to North America. A conventional autobiography, *My Life in the United States* starts with the narrator's arrival in New York City in 1955 and closes with her plan to write an autobiography in the mid-1960s, so the book chronicles approximately ten years of her life. Like other autobiographies written by first-generation immigrants, Chou's depicts firsthand encounters with a new culture in New York and fresh experiences with immigrant issues such as clashing cultural values, generational conflicts, and Americanization. The last ten chapters shift focus to Chou's life in Michigan and mainly deal with her experience as a speaker and informant on Asian cultures. She delves into her itinerant life in different parts of Asia and South Asia; these chapters also illuminate the process of writing *My Life in the United States*.

Cynthia Chou is known to a relatively small Asian and Asian American audience and there have been virtually no studies of her work, except for Shuchen S. Huang, "Cynthia L. Chou," in Guiyou Huang, ed., *Asian American Autobiographers: A Bio-Bibliographical Critical Sourcebook* (Westport, CT: Greenwood Press, 2001), 57–59.

Benny Feria (1911–1978). First-generation Filipino American autobiographer and poet Feria was born in the San Narciso of Zambale, the Philippines. He developed an interest in writing at a very early age and started to keep diaries at age ten. Feria was brought up in poverty and believed that his life would improve if he moved to the United States, which he did in July 1926. After a brief stay in San Francisco, he did farm work in Fresno, California for a while, then settled down in Chicago, where he washed dishes to make money for college at DePaul University and then the University of Chicago. In 1940 Feria started a newspaper called the *Commonwealth Press*, later renamed *The United Filipino Press*. In 1947 he published a collection of poems titled *Never Tomorrow* (New York: Exposition Press), but his better-known work would be his autobiography, *Filipino Son*, published in 1954 (Boston: Meador Press).

Feria's poetry has received hardly any critical notice. *Never Tomorrow* explores the life experiences of Filipino immigrants in the new land of America and their struggles to put down roots and establish identity in an adopted culture. *Filipino Son* deals with similar themes. In nineteen chapters, the autobiographer spends the absolute majority of the narrative space discussing his life in the United States, specifically from his arrival in San Francisco to the publication of his poetry collection, *Never Tomorrow*, a time span of approximately two decades. Though a Filipino, the protagonist in the autobiography loves America as the land of plenty and opportunity, so he made an early decision, at age fifteen, to improve his life by going there to achieve economic success through hard work in a system governed by principles of freedom and democracy. In his eagerness to present America as the ideal land of happiness, Feria characterizes the Philippines as the opposite. Like some autobiographies by Asian immigrants in the early half of the twentieth century, and keenly aware of the white audience it was going to address, *Filipino Son* is cautious in its selection of topics and themes and hardly touches upon harsh, political issues such as the racism and economic exploitation that many Filipinos were subject to in the historical period that the book covers.

For more information, see:

Fuse, Montye P. "Benny F. Feria." In Guiyou Huang, ed., *Asian American Autobiographers: A Bio-Bibliographical Critical Sourcebook* (Westport, CT: Greenwood Press, 2001), 83–87.

Gonzalez, N. V. M. and Oscar V. Campomanes. "Filipino American Literature." In King-Kok Cheung, ed., *An Interethnic Companion to Asian American Literature* (New York: Cambridge University Press, 1997), 62–124.

Phung Thi Le Ly Hayslip (1949–). Born and raised in the small village of Ky La in Vietnam, Le Ly Hayslip experienced a childhood and young adulthood of war, patriotism, and violence. In her early teens, Le Ly joined the Viet Cong and became a celebrated revolutionary hero. But after she was captured and then released by the Army of the Republic of Vietnam, she suffered torture and rape at the hands of both the Republican forces and Viet Cong soldiers. After her revolutionary career was thus effectively halted, Le Ly escaped to Saigon, where she worked different legitimate and illegitimate jobs. At age nineteen she married a man thirty-four years her senior who promised they would go to the United States, which she did in 1973. Her husband died several years later, and Le Ly married Ed Hayslip, who eventually died of carbon monoxide poisoning. Le Ly then devoted all her energy to running restaurants and managing rental properties and with all the money she saved, she established a humanitarian organization, the East Meets West Foundation, in 1986 to not only help her home country but also create a material link between Vietnam and the United States, two former foes. In 1989, with the assistance of Jay Wurts, Le Ly published her first autobiography, *When Heaven and Earth Changed Places: A Vietnamese Woman's Journey from War to Peace* (New York: Doubleday); four years later, her second autobiography, *Child of War, Woman of Peace*, written with James Hayslip, came out (New York: Doubleday, 1993).

In *When Heaven and Earth Changed Places*, Le Ly reminisces about events that occurred between her early years in her home village of Ky La and Saigon and her return to Vietnam in 1986, after she had achieved financial success in the United States. The book narrates the hardships and challenges of war and poverty that she faced while growing up in Vietnam. It also provides details about how she became a hero for the National Liberation Front (Viet Cong) and how she was arrested by the Republican forces; because of this, she was suspected of treason by the Viet Cong. The book narrates her efforts to establish a humanitarian foundation and her return to Vietnam, when the United States had not reestablished diplomatic ties with the former war enemy. Le Ly's second book, *Child of War, Woman of Peace*, is a sequel that focuses on her life in the United States, though it depicts her numerous trips back to Vietnam after her first return in 1986. While she spends considerable time and space describing her philanthropic efforts, she also interjects episodes of her romantic affairs with different men. The second book also illuminates Le Ly's first as she discusses its writing process, among other things.

For more information, see:

Bow, Leslie. "Le Ly Hayslip's Bad (Girl) Karma: Sexuality, National Allegory, and the Politics of Neutrality." *Prose Studies* 1, no. 17 (April 1994): 141–60.

Ho, Khanh. "Le Ly Hayslip." In King-Kok Cheung, ed., *Words Matter: Conversations with Asian American Writers* (Honolulu: University of Hawai'i Press, 2000), 105–22.

Janette, Michele. "Phung Thi Le Ly Hayslip." In Guiyou Huang, ed., *Asian American Autobiographers: A Bio-Bibliographical Critical Sourcebook* (Westport, CT: Greenwood Press, 2001), 111–14.

Nguyen, Viet Thanh. "Representing Reconciliation: Le Ly Hayslip and the Victimized Body." *Positions: East Asian Cultures Critique* 5 (1997): 605–42.

——. "*When Heaven and Earth Changed Places* and *Child of War, Woman of Peace*, by Le Ly Hayslip." In Sau-ling Cynthia Wong and Stephen H. Sumida, eds., *A Resource Guide to Asian American Literature* (New York: MLA, 2001), 66–77.

Shipler, David K. "A Child's Tour of Duty." Rev. of *When Heaven and Earth Changed Places*, by Le Ly Hayslip, *New York Times Book Review*, June 25, 1990, 1+.

* * *

Garrett Hongo. See Hongo in "Poetry."

* * *

Bill Hosokawa (1915–). A Japanese American autobiographer, Hosokawa was born and raised in Seattle, Washington. He graduated from the University of Washington in 1937 with a journalism degree and started a promising career as a journalist that was disrupted by World War II. Hosokawa and his family were forced to relocate to Heart Mountain, Wyoming, where they were interned until 1943. During that time, Hosokawa founded and edited a newspaper titled the *Heart Mountain Sentinel*. Hosokawa has lived in Denver since 1946. He worked at *The Denver Post* until 1983, and in 1985 he joined the staff of *Rocky Mountain News*, where he worked until retirement in 1992. He is the author of a dozen books, mostly nonfiction, including *Nisei: The Quiet Americans* (New York: William Morrow, 1969), *Thunder in the Rockies: The Incredible Denver Post* (New York: William Morrow, 1976), *JACL in Quest of Justice* (New York: William Morrow, 1982), and *Old Man Thunder, Father of the Bullet Train* (Denver: Sogo Way, 1997). In Asian American literary circles, Hosokawa is known for his two autobiographical works: *Thirty-five Years in the Frying Pan* (New York: McGraw Morrow-Hill, 1978) and *Out of the Frying*

Pan: Reflections of a Japanese American (Niwot: University Press of Colorado, 1989). In addition, he has collaborated with other writers on a number of works, including Jim Yoshida's autobiography, *The Two Worlds of Jim Yoshida* (New York: William Morrow, 1972).

Hosokawa's work as a newspaperman and his efforts to promote U.S.–Japanese relations have been recognized as well. In 1974 he was appointed honorary consul general of Japan in Colorado and was decorated with the Order of the Rising Sun by the Japanese government, and in 1987 he received a Gold Rays with Neck Ribbon. He was awarded an honorary Doctor of Humane Letters by the University of Denver in 1990.

Hosokawa's personal experience of internment during World War II, his encounters with racial discrimination, and the Asian American experience in general are the principal concerns of many of his newspaper columns, which he eventually collected into *Thirty-five Years in the Frying Pan* and *Out of the Frying Pan*, published eleven years apart. Hosokawa digs to the bottom of the Japanese American internment that he, his wife Alice, and their son Michael endured at Heart Mountain by tracing both the political and the racial motivations of the government's decision to incarcerate Japanese Americans on the West Coast. Hosokawa investigates the causes of such mistreatment by scrutinizing the links between race and political status in the United States and the reasons the Bill of Rights applies to certain citizens and not others, like his family and his ethnic group, under extreme circumstances such as a war.

For more information, see:

Emi, Frank Seishi. "Draft Resistance at the Heart Mountain Concentration Camp and the Fair Play Committee." In Gail M. Nomura, Russell Endo, Stephen H. Sumida, and Russell Leong, eds., *Frontiers of Asian American Studies* (Pullman: Washington State University Press, 1989), 41–49.

O'Brien, Amy C. "Bill Hosokawa." In Guiyou Huang, ed., *Asian American Autobiographers: A Bio-Bibliographical Critical Sourcebook* (Westport, CT: Greenwood Press, 2001), 121–25.

Walker, Tom. "Dignity Unscarred by Internment-Camp Stay." *Denver Post*, December 13, 1998, G-06.

* * *

Jeanne Wakatsuki Houston (1935–) and **James D. Houston** (1934–). Jeanne Wakatsuki was born to a Japanese American family in Inglewood, California, and grew up in Ocean Park, where they made a living by fishing. At the age of seven, her entire family was relocated to Manzanar, in eastern California, by the authority of President Roosevelt's executive order to evacuate Japanese Americans on the West Coast. Her tough childhood was further complicated by family problems such as her father's inability to support his family because he was inhibited from returning to the fishing industry after the war, but Jeanne excelled in primary and high schools. She attended San Jose State College, studying sociology and journalism, and there she met her future husband James D. Houston, whom she married in 1957. James Houston was born in San Francisco and is the author of several novels. In the late 1960s Jeanne and James started to collaborate on writing about Jeanne's personal experience of internment at Manzanar, and in 1973, they published an autobiography under the title *Farewell to Manzanar: A True Story of Japanese American Experience During and After the World War II Internment* (Boston: Houghton Mifflin).

As the subtitle indicates, *Farewell to Manzanar* presents firsthand accounts of the experience of Japanese American internment at one particular concentration camp during World War II. While the book is largely autobiographical and focuses on the Wakatsuki family, the Houstons reconstruct the internment experience from a larger historical perspective. Like other, similar accounts of the Japanese American wartime incarceration, *Farewell to Manzanar* does not merely recount or denounce the internment, it explores and confronts the role of racism in the U.S. government's implementation of the executive order. The Houstons contrast the different lifestyles that the Wakatsukis had before, during, and after the internment and the war. They detail the less than perfect, but happy life of Jeanne and her family as fishermen before her father Ko's arrest and his ensuing imprisonment in Bismarck, North Dakota. Ko's problems affected the family's stability, which contributed to Jeanne's distancing from both him and her family. She chronicles her struggles with her racial and cultural identity as well as her efforts to assimilate into the mainstream culture, both characterized by her desire for acceptance in a racially divided society. The end of *Farewell to Manzanar* stages Jeanne's return to the concentration camp with her husband and their three children, thereby providing both physical and psychological closure to what she believes to be a shameful experience.

Most notices of *Farewell to Manzanar* are reviews. See:

Bryant, Dorothy. Rev. of *Farewell to Manzanar*. *The Nation* (November 9, 1974): 469.

Chappell, Virginia. "But Isn't This the Land of the Free?: Resistance and Discovery in Student Responses to *Farewell to Manzanar*." In Carol Severino, Johnella E. Butler, and Juan C. Guerra, eds., *Writing in Multicultural Settings* (New York: MLA, 1997).

LaViolette, Forrest E. Rev. of *Farewell to Manzanar*. *Pacific Affairs* 47 (1974): 405–6.

Moser, Linda Trinh. "Jeanne Wakatsuki Houston and James D. Houston." In Guiyou Huang, ed., *Asian American Autobiographers: A Bio-Bibliographical Critical Sourcebook* (Westport, CT: Greenwood Press, 2001), 127–33.

Okamura, Raymond Y. "*Farewell to Manzanar*: A Case of Subliminal Racism." *Amerasia Journal* 3, no. 2 (1976): 143–47.

Ruttle, Lee. Rev. of *Farewell to Manzanar*. *Pacific Citizen* (January 5, 1975): 5.

Rabinowitz, Dorothy. Rev. of *Farewell to Manzanar*. *Saturday Review World* (November 6, 1973): 34.

Sakurai, Patricia A. "The Politics of Possession: The Negotiation of Identity in *American in Disguise, Homebase,* and *Farewell to Manzanar*." In Sakurai, *Privileging Positions: The Sites of Asian American Studies* (Pullman: Washington State University Press, 1995), 157–70.

Wilson, Robert A. Rev. of *Farewell to Manzanar*. *Pacific Historical Review* 43 (1974): 621–22.

* * *

Peter Hyun (1906–1993). Korean Hawaiian autobiographer Hyun was born in Lihue, Hawai'i. He lived in three cultures—the United States, China, and Korea—and knew five languages—Chinese, English, Japanese, Korean, and Tagalog. He was also widely traveled: when he was nine months old, his parents took him to their home country of Korea, but as living there under Japanese colonial rule became increasingly difficult and dangerous, the Hyuns moved to

Shanghai, China; when Hyun was eighteen, the family returned to Hawai'i, where his father took the pastorship of a Korean Methodist church in Honolulu. Hyun himself moved again when he went to study religion at DePauw University in Indiana, but he did not become a minister; instead, he became involved in the theater in several different places, including New York City and Cambridge, Massachusetts. Hyun also pursued acting and directing, in both of which he achieved considerable success. He quit the theater and movie industry in the late 1930s, having encountered enough racial slurring and discrimination. In 1944 he joined the U.S. Army and worked as an interpreter for the American military government in Korea, before he was arrested and expelled for his connections with North Korean leaders. Returning to the mainland, Hyun worked different jobs, including a stint teaching English as a second language in Mexico.

In 1986, Hyun published his first autobiography, *Man Sei! The Making of a Korean American* (Honolulu: University of Hawai'i Press); his second autobiography, *In the New World: The Making of a Korean American* (Honolulu: University of Hawai'i Press), came out in 1995, two years after his death. These works truly reflect his rich, multicultural, polyglot, and interethnic experiences throughout East Asia and North America. His frequent relocations required acquisition of new languages and acquaintance with new cultures and peoples, and Hyun engages these topics in both books that share one subtitle, though *Man Sei!* focuses on his life experience in China and *In the New World* concentrates more appropriately on the American years of his colorful career. The former depicts his personal life against the important historical backdrop of Korea's struggle for independence from Japan and the Hyuns' exile experience in China. In Japanese-occupied Korea, Hyun and his fellow Koreans were forced to study the language and history of the colonizer; in China, he and his family, made homeless by the Japanese occupation, endured insults. Thus, national and international politics, racial and ethnic differences, war and nationalism are all important subjects in *Man Sei!*. The new world in Hyun's *In the New World* is the United States. Even though America is Hyun's birthplace and country of citizenship, he still had to endure linguistic and racial discrimination when he struggled with English, when he lived in pidgin-speaking Hawai'i, and when he was pursuing an acting/directing career.

For more information, see:

Barzman, Norma. "The Best Years; Seniors; Inside a Mobile; Peter and Luisa Hyun Find the Peaceful Seaside Supports the Books They're Both Writing." *Los Angeles Times,* June 14, 1990, Ventura County ed., J12.

Huot, Nikolas. "Peter Hyun." In Guiyou Huang, ed., *Asian American Autobiographers: A Bio-Bibliographical Critical Sourcebook* (Westport, CT: Greenwood Press, 2001), 135–39.

"Hyun, Peter," in Susan M. Trosky, ed., *Contemporary Authors*, vol. 136 (Detroit: Gale, 1992), 198–99.

Jacobson, M. F. Rev. of *In the New World: The Making of a Korean American. Choice* 33, no. 5 (January 1996): 857.

McCune, Evelyn. Rev. of *Man Sei! The Making of a Korean American. Korean Studies* 11 (1987): 85–87.

Nahm, Andrew C. Rev. of *Man Sei! The Making of a Korean American*, by Peter Hyun, and *Korea Under Colonialism: The March First Movement and Anglo-Japanese Relations*, by Dae-Yeol Ku. *Journal of Asian Studies* 47, no. 2 (May 1988): 385–87.

Yang, Eun-Sik. "When Korea Fought Japan." Rev. of *Man Sei! The Making of a Korean American. Los Angeles Times,* September 13, 1987, final ed., Book Review, 18.

Daniel Inouye (1924–) and **Lawrence Elliott**. The son of Japanese immigrants, Inouye is known for his distinguished record as a legislative leader and as a World War II combat veteran who earned the nation's highest award for military valor, the Medal of Honor. Born and raised in Honolulu, Hawai'i, Inouye grew up in a bicultural and bilingual family in a poor neighborhood. When the Japanese attacked Pearl Harbor in December 1941, young Dan Inouye rushed into service as the head of a first-aid litter team. In 1942, while a premed freshman at the University of Hawai'i, Inouye joined 4,000 *nisei* volunteers as a combat member of the 442nd Infantry Regiment that was to be stationed in Naples, Italy, to fight the Germans and Italians. Inouye was injured in the right arm by an enemy bullet on April 21, 1945; the arm was soon thereafter amputated in an army hospital in Battle Creek, Michigan. On May 27, 1947, Inouye was honorably discharged and returned home with a Distinguished Service Cross, along with a Bronze Star and a Purple Heart with cluster, among other medals and citations. His Distinguished Service Cross was upgraded to the Medal of Honor on June 21, 2000.

With financial assistance from the G.I. Bill, Inouye graduated from the University of Hawai'i in 1950 and from the George Washington University Law School with a J.D. in 1952. Returning to Hawai'i, he entered politics in 1954 and was elected to the Hawai'i Territorial House of Representatives. In 1958, he was elected to the Territorial Senate. When Hawai'i gained statehood in 1959, he was elected its first congressman and was re-elected to a full term in 1960. Inouye was first elected to the U.S. Senate in 1962 and is now serving his seventh consecutive term as the third most senior member of the Senate. In 1967, before his reelection, he wrote an autobiography with the assistance of Lawrence Elliott, published as *Journey to Washington* (Englewood Cliffs, NJ: Prentice-Hall).

Journey to Washington chronicles the growth of a young Japanese American boy into a war hero and eventually a prominent legislator. It is the success story of an ethnic American. The book narrates Inouye's childhood experience up to the point of his entry into national politics. A dominant theme of the book is patriotism, or rather, the narrator's loyalty to his country, though it also enumerates his acts of heroism. Inouye expresses an unequivocal American identity even as a student in the classroom, or when Pearl Harbor called on Americans—the mainstream population and Japanese Americans—to join the fight against fascism, be it German, Italian, or Japanese. A strong sense of determination, resilience, and optimism is clearly conveyed throughout the book. Whether faced with racial problems in school, racial hatred following Pearl Harbor, or life-threatening situations in World War II, Inouye remains determined to succeed in his American dream through a hard-work ethic and a belief in American ideals and values. He devotes space to his war experience on both the French and Italian fronts. There are eyewitness accounts of casualties as well as atrocities of war that would be counterbalanced by the eventual triumph of the Allied forces.

For more information, see:

Goodsell, Jane. *Daniel Inouye.* New York: Thomas Y. Crowell, 1977.
Han, John Jae-Nam. "Daniel K. Inouye." In Guiyou Huang, ed., *Asian American*

Autobiographers: A Bio-Bibliographical Critical Sourcebook (Westport, CT: Greenwood Press, 2001), 141–47.

Henderson, Robert. Rev. of *Journey to Washington. Library Journal* (May 1, 1967): 1826.

Humphrey, Hubert H. Foreword to *Journey to Washington*, by Daniel Inouye and Lawrence Elliott (Englewood Cliffs, NJ: Prentice-Hall, 1967), vii–ix.

Johnson, Lyndon Baines. Foreword to *Journey to Washington*, by Daniel Inouye and Lawrence Elliott (Englewood Cliffs, NJ: Prentice-Hall, 1967), v–vi.

Mansfield, Mike. Foreword to *Journey to Washington*, by Daniel Inouye and Lawrence Elliott (Englewood Cliffs, NJ: Prentice-Hall, 1967), xi–xv.

Rev. of *Journey to Washington. Choice* (November 1968): 1222.

Richard E. Kim. See Kim in "Fiction."

* * *

Maxine Hong Kingston. See Kingston in "Fiction."

Li-Young Lee. See Lee in "Poetry."

* * *

Mary Paik Lee (1900–1995). Lee is one of the few Korean American writers, or Koreans in America for that matter, born in present-day North Korea. Born Paik Kuang Sun in Pyongyang, Lee left Japanese-occupied Korea for Hawai'i at the tender age of five and a year later moved on to California; she lived in various places in that state for the rest of her life—Riverside, Los Angeles, and San Francisco, among others. She married in 1919 and became Mary Paik Lee upon being granted U.S. citizenship in 1960. Lee worked various jobs, including rice farming with her husband. She authored one book, her autobiography, *Quiet Odyssey: A Pioneer Korean Woman in America* (Seattle: University of Washington Press, 1990), published five years before her death in 1995. Although the book bears Lee's name, it was edited and somewhat manipulated by the Asian American historian Sucheng Chan, who not only influenced the titling of the book but also provided a preface, an introduction, and appendixes that would affect readings of and responses to it.

Lee's initial title for her memoir was *One Korean Family in America*. Indeed, as Anita Mannur writes, "Lee's memoirs focus entirely on describing the story of one family and its experiences. To a certain extent, it functions as an autoethnography that broadly speaks to (and of) the experiences of Korean immigrants at that period in time" (200). And like many immigrant narratives, *Quiet Odyssey* delineates the physical hardships and racist assaults that her family endured, especially in their early years living in California; in San Francisco and Riverside, racial stereotyping and verbal abuse accompanied them in the streets and in school. Lee's family encountered racism during World War II not particularly because they were Koreans but because they looked no different than the Japanese, with whom America was at war. The Koreans, like the Chinese, suffered unjustly for being look-alikes. Lee's book, however, does not present a totally racist picture of American values and life; it advocates a strong work ethic and urges faith in the American dream of success.

For more information, see:

Chiu, Monica. "Constructing 'Home' in Mary Paik Lee's *Quiet Odyssey: A Pioneer Korean Woman in America.*" In Susan L. Roberson, ed., *Women, America, and Movement: Narratives of Relocation* (Columbia: University of Missouri Press, 1998), 121–36.

Leonard, Karen. Rev. of *Quiet Odyssey: A Pioneer Korean Woman in America. Journal of American Ethnic History* 12, no. 2 (1993): 78–80.

Lin, Patricia. Rev. of *Quiet Odyssey: A Pioneer Korean Woman in America. MELUS* 17, no. 1 (1991): 114–17.

Louie, Miriam Ching. Rev. of *Quiet Odyssey: A Pioneer Korean Woman in America. Amerasia Journal* 16, no. 2 (1990): 168–72.

Mannur, Anita. "Mary Paik Lee." In Guiyou Huang, ed., *Asian American Autobiographers: A Bio-Bibliographical Critical Sourcebook* (Westport, CT: Greenwood Press, 2001), 199–202.

* * *

Ling-ai Li (ca. 1910–). Also known as Gladys, Li was born in Hawai'i to immigrant parents who came from Canton, southern China, in 1896, but unlike many other Chinese immigrants of the time who went to Hawai'i as sugarcane plantation workers, her parents were medical doctors. Li attended the University of Hawai'i and earned a B.A. in 1930. In college she wrote a number of poems and three plays, *The Submission of Rose Moy* (published in *The Hawaii Quill Magazine* 1 [June 1928]: 7–19), *The Law of Wu Wei* (*The Hawaii Quill Magazine* 2 [January 1929]: 20–26), and *The White Serpent* (*The Hawaii Quill Magazine* 5 [May 1932]: 24–31). From 1933 she spent several years in China studying music and Chinese theater. During her time there and later in New York, Li directed documentary films as well as plays. While engaged in theater work and other responsibilities Li kept writing, and in 1944 she published a novel for young adults, *Children of the Sun in Hawaii* (Boston: D. C. Heath, 1944). Li's most acclaimed work is *Life Is for a Long Time: A Chinese Hawaiian Memoir* (New York: Hastings House, 1972). In 1975 Li was awarded the Bicentennial Woman of the Year award by the National Association of Women Artists of America.

Li's plays explore racial and cultural issues. *The Submission of Rose Moy* dramatizes intergenerational conflicts between a father and his daughter in a Chinese Hawaiian family. *The Law of Wu Wei* examines the impact of cultural traditions on gender relations. *The White Snake* is Li's adaptation of an age-old Chinese folktale called *The Story of the White Snake. Children of the Sun in Hawaii,* her only novel, depicts the life of a native Hawaiian boy called Kimo living in the diverse community of multiple races and ethnicities in Hawai'i. While Li calls *Life Is for a Long Time* a memoir, it is biographical, for it mainly deals with the immigrant life of her parents in Hawai'i. Khai-Fai Li and his wife Tai-Heong Kong were trained to become medical doctors in China. They moved to the United States to pursue a life of happiness, but their medical diplomas were not recognized, so they became menial laborers instead. The memoir presents stories of hardships but, more important, stories of triumphs: Li's parents overcame the nonrecognition of their Chinese medical degrees by taking and passing the medical exam and became not only qualified doctors but also benefactors of their community through building hospitals, establishing a Chinese school, and founding a newspaper. Ultimately, *Life Is for a Long Time* portrays the pains and gains of immigrant life as well as the prevailing desire for survival.

For more information, see:

Huang, Shuchen S. "Ling-ai (Gladys) Li." In Guiyou Huang, ed., *Asian American Autobiographers: A Bio-Bibliographical Critical Sourcebook* (Westport, CT: Greenwood Press, 2001), 203–7.

Rev. of *Life Is for a Long Time: A Chinese Hawaiian Memoir. Publishers Weekly* 4 (September 1972): 44.

* * *

Shirley Geok-lin Lim. See Lim in "Poetry."

* * *

Alice P. Lin (1942–). A Chinese American autobiographer, Lin was born into a military family in Chengdu, Sichuan province, China. Right before the Communists took over in 1949, the Lins escaped to Taiwan, leaving her grandmother and other relatives on the mainland. In Taiwan, Lin attended Donghai University; then she was accepted into the Graduate School at the University of Michigan, from which she received a master's degree in social work. A few years later she earned a doctoral degree in social policy and planning from Columbia University. Since then Lin has worked in various government and academic positions. While publishing in academic journals, she wrote an autobiography called *Grandmother Had No Name* (San Francisco: China Books and Periodicals, 1988). The book has not been widely noted, but the New York Library Association cited it as the Book of the Year in 1991.

The title of *Grandmother Had No Name* suggests that Lin's book is more biographical than autobiographical. Ruru Li considers the book a blend of autobiography and social history (393). Indeed, the author presents a gallery of images of women, especially her maternal grandmother and one of her aunts, whom she did not get to know in the first thirty years of her life because of the long severance of ties between Taiwan and mainland China, where Lin's relatives were left behind. The book almost exclusively focuses on female characters, delving into the lives of important women members of her family in China. Lin's grandmother's anonymity—Grandmother has no name—is not the result of a choice but rather of oppressive patriarchal traditions that not only erase women's identities as individual human beings but also impose on them roles and responsibilities that they fulfill without being recognized and appreciated. Lin's First Aunt—Grandmother Li's first daughter—is another significant figure in the book. A self-sacrificing woman like her mother, First Aunt shoulders family responsibilities while being trapped in an unhappy marriage. The most autobiographical moments of the book occur in chapters where Lin reflects on her relocations and adjustments, first to Taiwan and then to the United States. While the book's spotlight remains on women members of her family, Lin does take time to discuss contemporary women's issues gleaned from her visits to China, including women's roles in society, working conditions, increasing numbers of women in leadership positions in China, and so on.

For more information, see:

Huot, Nikolas. "Alice P. Lin." In Guiyou Huang, ed., *Asian American Autobiographers: A Bio-Bibliographical Critical Sourcebook* (Westport, CT: Greenwood Press, 2001), 221–25.

Li, Ruru. Rev. of *Grandmother Had No Name. China Quarterly* 126 (June 1991): 393–94.

* * *

Aimee E. Liu. See Liu in "Fiction."

M

Adeline Yen Mah (1937–). Chinese American autobiographer and physician Mah was born in Tianjin, China, to an affluent family of businesspeople, but her mother's death two weeks after her birth and her father's remarriage to a young French Chinese girl meant a lonely, physically and emotionally abusive childhood. Mah lived in Hong Kong before she went to study medicine in London, and eventually she immigrated to the United States. All her years in China, Mah struggled to gain acceptance and love from her wealthy father and her cruel stepmother, but to no avail. Her horrific life as an unwanted daughter inspired her to write an autobiography entitled *Falling Leaves: The True Story of an Unwanted Chinese Daughter*; it was first published in England in 1997 and made its American debut in 1998 (New York: Wiley). The book was also published in Chinese in Taiwan, under the Chinese title *Falling Leaves Return to Their Roots,* in 1999, the same year Mah reworked her memoir for younger readers and published it as *Chinese Cinderella* (New York: Delacorte).

Falling Leaves is an appeal to the moral conscience of societies worldwide on behalf of unwanted children, as well as a genuine quest for justice for the neglected and forgotten. The narrative focuses on the relationship of Adeline and her stepmother Niang (a northern Chinese term for mother), and to a lesser extent, on the relationship of Adeline, her father, and her aunt. Adeline presents vivid accounts of her stepmother's mood swings and her verbal and physical violence toward her own child, Susan, as well as toward her stepdaughter.

Merciless and unforgiving, Niang squarely keeps her promises, especially her vengeful vows. Whatever she is, she is not the traditional subservient, meek housewife of early to mid-twentieth-century China. While Adeline cannot appreciate her stepmother's strong-willed unconventionality, she sees strength and power in the unconventional life and career of another woman of her family, her Westernized grandaunt, who was never married, worked to support herself, and founded a women's bank in Shanghai. Still another strong woman, in a different way, is Adeline's Aunt Baba, her father's spinster sister, who endured hardships in her own life but never wavered in her duty and love to Adeline. Adeline, the protagonist of the autobiography, ultimately triumphs not in China but in the United States. Oddly, *Falling Leaves* turns out to be a book about a family of strong women, though the strongest apparent also happens to be the cruelest and most unforgiving.

For more information, see:

Dean, Kitty Chen. Rev. of *Falling Leaves. Library Journal 123,* no. 2 (February 1, 1998): 96.

McLellan, Dennis. "A Daughter Returns Again to Her Roots." *Los Angeles Times,* December 19, 1999, 10.

Seaman, Donna. "Falling Leaves Return to Their Roots." *Booklist* (February 1, 1998): 884.

Simpson, John M. Rev. of *Falling Leaves. USA Today,* March 26, 1998, 10D.

Stuttaford, Genevieve. Rev. of *Falling Leaves. Publishers Weekly* (January 5, 1998): 48.

Yardley, Jonathan. "Growing Up Unwanted: A Tale of Survival." *Washington Post,* March 11, 1998, D2.

Yen, Xiaoping. "Adeline Yen Mah." In Guiyou Huang, ed., *Asian American Autobiographers: A Bio-Bibliographical Critical Sourcebook* (Westport, CT: Greenwood Press, 2001), 239–42.

* * *

Anchee Min. See Min in "Fiction."

* * *

David Alan Mura. See Mura in "Poetry."

Haing S. Ngor (ca. 1941–1996). Cambodian American actor and autobiographer Ngor was born in a small village near the capital city, Phnom Penh, Cambodia, and received a medical education in obstetrics and gynecology. He worked as a doctor for the government's military hospital until the Khmer Rouge arrived, and in 1980 he escaped to the United States by way of Thailand. Ngor's work in the new country was helping other Cambodian refugees while developing his skills in film acting. In Roland Joffé's film *The Killing Fields* (Warner Bros., 1984), he played Dith Pran, a Cambodian photographer who befriended Sydney Schanberg, a *New York Times* correspondent stationed in Cambodia from 1972 to 1975, during the Vietnam War, and for that role Ngor won an Academy Award for Best Supporting Actor in 1985. In 1987 Ngor's autobiography, *A Cambodian Odyssey*, written with Roger Warner, was published (New York: Macmillan). In 1993 he appeared in Oliver Stone's film *Heaven and Earth* (Warner Bros.), which combined the Vietnamese American writer Le Ly Hayslip's two autobiographical works, *When Heaven and Earth Changed Places* (1989) and *Child of War, Woman of Peace* (1993). In February 1996, Ngor's life was cut short when he was gunned down in Los Angeles's Chinatown by three Asian American gangsters.

A Cambodian Odyssey records vividly and passionately Ngor's experiences under the genocidal regime of Pol Pot of the Khmer Rouge, which tortured and maimed him. Ngor's accounts of actual events appear rather detached but often are graphic. One of the most touching episodes concerns his own wife, Chang My Huoy. In loving detail, Ngor describes his admiration and affection for his wife, who died giving birth to their child. His father, another major figure depicted in the autobiography, represents familial and cultural traditions of Cambodia. Ngor's book of course also examines his own life and work in the United States. Even though he was a medical doctor usefully employed in a hospital in Phnom Penh until 1975, when Pol Pot's guerrilla forces invaded, Ngor could no longer practice medicine, so he turned to helping refugees from his home country. Ultimately, his work dramatizes humans' capability for cruelty as well as their ability for survival, though ironically, Ngor himself survived the horrors of war and the cruelty of torture only to be murdered by violence in the streets of Los Angeles in a time of peace.

For more information, see: Amy C. O'Brien, "Haing S. Ngor," in Guiyou Huang, ed., *Asian American Autobiographers: A Bio-Bibliographical Critical Sourcebook* (Westport, CT: Greenwood Press, 2001), 287–90.

Induk Pahk (1896–1980). A Korean American autobiographer, educator, and translator, Pahk was born into a very religious family in a small village outside Pyongyang, the capital city of present-day North Korea.

As formal education was off limits to young girls in those days, Pahk's mother sent her to school disguised as a boy. Pahk completed her elementary education in a Methodist missionary school in Pyongyang; then she attended Ewha Girls High School in Seoul and went on to Ewha Women's College, graduating in 1916. In 1926 she was invited to study at Wesleyan College in Georgia, but she graduated with a master's degree from Columbia University in New York. She traveled back to Korea and became involved with the Political Education Committee of the Patriotic Women's Society, and before the outbreak of the Korean War she returned to the United States to give speeches to the American public on a range of topics concerning Korea. She went back to Korea again with the mission to build a school and in 1964, she established the Induk Vocational School for Boys, now evolved into the thriving Induk Technical High School and the Induk College.

Between 1933 and 1977, Pahk published numerous books in Korean and English, as well as translations of two religious texts published in Seoul. More important, she authored three autobiographies, *September Monkey* (New York: Harper & Brothers, 1954), *The Hour of the Tiger* (New York: Harper & Row, 1965), and *The Cock Still Crows* (New York: Vantage Press, 1977). Pahk's time was divided between the United States and South Korea until she died in Seoul in 1980. Her autobiographies have quite different thematic orientations from most other similar works written by Korean Americans because her works concentrate heavily on Korean culture and her travels in the United States. While crisscrossing the two countries and giving speeches in the United States, Pahk kept highly minute details of her itineraries and activities in her journals, which lent great ease to writing the autobiographies and authenticity to the material presented. *September Monkey* recounts the major events between her birth and the beginning of her U.S. lecture tours. In 642 speeches, she provided information about Korean history, culture, and contemporary economic and political situations during and after the Korean War. While the earlier part of *The Hour of the Tiger* recaps the contents of Pahk's first book, the second half focuses on an important phase of her career—the time and effort she devoted to fund raising in the United States to build a school for boys in Korea and the opening of the school in Seoul. Pahk's third book is partly autobiographical and partly nonfiction: *The Cock Still Crows* repeats some of the same stories and events narrated in the first two volumes; it also catalogues various details related to the fund raisers she organized, names of donors to her school, as well as her school's mission statement and curriculum, among many other things. Read together, the three autobiographies limn the narrator as a Korean hero as well as a bridge effectively connecting the East and the West.

For more information, see:

Oh, Seiwoong. "Induk Pahk." In Guiyou Huang, ed., *Asian American Autobiographers: A Bio-Bibliographical Critical Sourcebook* (Westport, CT: Greenwood Press, 2001), 299–303.

Oka, Takashi. "Land of the Morning Calm." Rev. of *September Monkey*. *Christian Science Monitor*, October 28, 1954, 11.

Rev. of *The Hour of the Tiger*. *Booklist* 62 (February 1, 1966): 506+.

Rev. of *The Hour of the Tiger*. *Christian Century* 82 (December 8, 1965): 1515.

Rev. of *The Hour of the Tiger*. *Kirkus Reviews* 33 (October 15, 1965): 1088.

Rev. of *The Hour of the Tiger*. *Library Journal* 91 (January 15, 1966): 245.

Rev. of *September Monkey*. *Booklist* 51 (November 15, 1954): 130.

Rev. of *September Monkey*. *Kirkus Reviews* 22 (October 15, 1954): 721.

Rev. of *September Monkey*. *New York Herald Tribune Book Review*, November 21, 1954, 14.

Smith, Robert Aura. "Ambassador from Korea." Rev. of *September Monkey*. *New York Times Book Review*, November 7, 1954, 34.

S

Monica Sone (1919–). Born Kazuko Monica Itoi in Seattle, Washington, to first-generation parents of Japanese ancestry, Sone grew up on the waterfront of Seattle and attended a public American school during the day and a Japanese-language school in the after hours, studying Japanese language, culture, literature, and deportment. When Kazuko was seven, her parents took the family to Japan to visit her grandfather. When the Pacific War broke out, her family was first relocated to a temporary concentration camp in Puyallup State Fairgrounds and then interned at Camp Minidoka, Idaho, where Kazuko spent almost a year before she left to attend Wendell College in Indiana; she ended up completing a degree in clinical psychology at Western Reserve University. She took the name Monica Sone after she married a fellow *nisei*, Gary Sone. She published her autobiography, *Nisei Daughter*, in 1953 (Boston: Little, Brown).

Appearing eight years after Jade Snow Wong's third-person autobiography *Fifth Chinese Daughter* (1945), Sone's *Nisei Daughter* was inspired by that second-generation Chinese American's autobiography that narrates a young girl's coming-of-age and independence in prewar and wartime San Francisco. Sone's autobiography deals with essentially the same time periods, though its geographi-

cal locale is mostly Seattle, another major West Coast city where Japanese Americans fell victim to President Roosevelt's Executive Order No. 9600 that started the Japanese internment. Sone recounts almost idyllic memories of her childhood on the waterfront, where her parents owned a small hotel, but contrasting with this near-perfect prewar life are the hardships and humiliating ordeals she and her family suffered at the concentration camps. Sone returned to Minidoka to visit her parents a year after her departure for college; the reunion and her personal experience finally help confirm her identity as a Japanese American. She wrote this book partly to educate her readers about her family and their community, partly to denounce the government's racist mistreatment of a people, and partly to describe the realization of her bicultural heritage and explore the development of her own cultural and racial identity. Also scrutinized are the psychological aftereffects of camp life on *nisei* Japanese Americans and how they internalized the racialized victimization.

For more information, see:

Holte, James Craig. "Monica Sone." In *The Ethnic I: A Sourcebook for Ethnic-American Autobiography* (Westport, CT: Greenwood Press, 1988), 161–66.

Kapai, Leela. "Monica Sone." In Guiyou Huang, ed., *Asian American Autobiographers: A Bio-Bibliographical Critical Sourcebook* (Westport, CT: Greenwood Press, 2001), 321–27.

Lim, Shirley Geok-lin. "Japanese American Women's Life Stories: Maternality in Monica Sone's *Nisei Daughter* and Joy Kogawa's *Obasan*." *Feminist Studies* 16, no. 2 (Summer 1990): 289–312.

Rayson, Ann. "Beneath the Mask: Autobiographies of Japanese-American

Women." *MELUS* 14, no. 1 (Spring 1987): 43–57.

Sumida, Stephen H. "Protest and Accommodation, Self-Satire and Self-Effacement, and Monica Sone's *Nisei Daughter.*" In James Robert Payne, ed., *Multicultural Autobiography: American Lives* (Knoxville: University of Tennessee Press, 1992), 207–43.

Yamada, Mitsuye. Rev. of *Nisei Daughter. MELUS* 7, no. 3 (Fall 1980): 91–92.

Yamamoto, Traise. "*Nisei Daughter*, by Monica Sone." In Sau-ling Cynthia Wong and Stephen H. Sumida, eds., *A Resource Guide to Asian American Literature* (New York: MLA, 2001), 151–58.

* * *

Sara Suleri (1953–). Pakistani American writer and academic Suleri was born in Karachi, Pakistan. Her father was a Pakistani journalist and political activist and her mother, an English professor from Wales. Suleri attended Kinnaird College, a Christian women's institution in Lahore, Pakistan; after graduating in 1974, she went on to obtain a master's degree from Punjab University in Lahore in 1976. She immigrated to the United States to attend Indiana University, where she completed a doctoral degree in English in 1983. Since then she has been teaching English at Yale, where she was a founding editor of *The Yale Journal of Criticism* and currently serves on the editorial boards of *YJC*, *The Yale Review*, and *Transition*. In 1989 Suleri published an autobiography, *Meatless Days* (Chicago: University of Chicago Press), which won the 1989 Pushcart Prize. Her scholarly book, *The Rhetoric of English India* (Chicago: University of Chicago Press, 1992), has also been critically acclaimed.

Meatless Days is a rich book that deals with important topics—colonialism and postcolonialism, the personal/private versus the political/public, Indian diaspora, the partition of India and the independence of Pakistan, the family and the nation, and women's experience of these political turmoils and historical events. In general terms, the autobiography narrates Suleri's life experience in three major geographical locales: her childhood in Pakistan, her immigrant life in England, and her experience in the United States. The subjects range from politics to religion to family relations, gender issues, and more. On the personal level, Suleri presents accounts of her relationships with her parents and siblings, though she devotes much more narrative space to the portrayal of her father, Pip, a real patriot and author of two books, *The Road to Peace in Pakistan* (1944), a political treatise, and *My Leader* (1945), a biography of Muhammad Ali Jinnah, known as Quaid-e-Azam or "Great Leader," the founding father and first governor general of Pakistan. Pip is depicted as a very complex man of politics but not of family, as he ignores his wife, Mair Jones, and his children, due to his profound involvement in politics. This seems to have contributed to Sara Suleri's decision to leave Pakistan for the United States, against his wishes.

While her father takes the role of the patriarch in Suleri's family and in the autobiography, her mother—her father's second wife—is movingly portrayed as a hardworking, patient mother and wife committed to her family and her responsibilities. While seemingly detached from the religious and political causes her husband pursues, she stands strong when he is imprisoned and tenaciously runs his newspaper in his absence. Other family members represented include Suleri's paternal grandmother and her sister, who was killed in a suspicious car accident. The uniting voice is of course Suleri's; toward the end of her narrative, she looks at her own academic life and writing career in the United States.

For more information, see:

Bizzini, Silvia C. "Sara Suleri's *Meatless Days* and Maxine Hong Kingston's *The Woman Warrior*: Writing, History and the Self After Foucault." *Women: A Cultural Review* (Spring 1996):55–65.

Dayal, Samir. "Style Is (Not) the Woman: Sara Suleri's *Meatless Days*." In Deepika Bahri and Mary Vasudeva, eds., *Between the Lines: South Asians and Postcoloniality* (Philadelphia: Temple University Press, 1996), 250–69.

Grewal, Inderpal. "Autobiographic Subjects and Diasporic Locations: *Meatless Days* and *Borderlands*." In Inderpal Grewal and Caren Kaplan, eds., *Scattered Hegemonies: Postmodernity and Transnational Feminist Practices* (Minneapolis: University of Minnesota Press, 1994), 231–54.

Koshy, Susan. "Mother-Country and Fatherland: Re-membering the Nation in Sara Suleri's *Meatless Days*." In Brinda Rose, Bishnupriya Ghosh, and Chandra T. Mohanty, eds., *Interventions: Feminist Dialogues on Third World Women's Literature and Film* (New York: Garland, 1997), 45–61.

Kruckels, Brigit. "'Men Live in Homes, Women Live in Bodies': Body and Gender in Sara Suleri's *Meatless Days*." In Monika Fludernik, ed., *Hybridity and Postcolonialism: Twentieth-Century Indian Literature* (Tübingen, Germany: Stauffenburg, 1998), 167–86.

Lovesey, Oliver. "'Postcolonial Self-Fashioning' in Sara Suleri's *Meatless Days*." *Journal of Commonwealth Literature* 32, no. 2 (1997): 35–50.

Oed, Anja. "Aspects of (Self)Representation in Sara Suleri's *Meatless Days*; or, What Does It Mean to Write a Book Beyond What It Is About." In Monika Fludernik, ed., *Hybridity and Postcolonialism: Twentieth-Century Indian Literature* (Tübingen, Germany: Stauffenburg, 1998), 187–97.

Ramraj, Ruby S. "Sara Suleri." In Guiyou Huang, ed., *Asian American Autobiographers: A Bio-Bibliographical Critical Sourcebook* (Westport, CT: Greenwood Press, 2001), 335–43.

Ray, Sangeeta. "Memory, Identity, Patriarchy: Projecting a Past in the Memories of Sara Suleri and Michael Ondaatje." *Modern Fiction Studies* 39, no. 1 (Spring 1993): 37–58.

Warley, Linda. "Assembling Ingredients: Subjectivity in *Meatless Days*." *Autobiography Studies* 7, no. 1 (1992): 107–23.

Nguyèn Thi Thu-Lâm (1940–). Born into a well-to-do and politically active family, Thu-Lâm spent the first three decades of her life in various locales of Vietnam, including Hanoi and Saigon, and was intermittently educated. Thu-Lâm married twice, the first time as a means of escape from her family, especially her mother, and the second time to an American lawyer; that ended in divorce. She started to work with Americans in Vietnam in 1963 but experienced constant sexual harassment; she then started her own business in laundry and other services, including a business in Hawai'i in the 1970s, and became financially successful, though by the time she divorced her second husband, her possessions were reduced considerably. After moving to Oakland, California, she started a new life and in 1989 published her autobiography, *Fallen*

Leaves (New Haven, CT: Yale Council on Southeast Asia Studies).

Like Le Ly Hayslip's *When Heaven and Earth Changed Places* and *Child of War, Woman of Peace*, Thu-Lâm's *Fallen Leaves* is among the rare few autobiographies by Vietnamese Americans that offer narratives of the Vietnam War from Vietnamese perspectives. And like Hayslip's two memoirs, Thu-Lâm's account includes her own life stories along with Vietnamese history that contextualizes her own events and the Vietnam War. The autobiographical segments of the book focus on her childhood under French colonial rule as well as the Japanese occupation. Vietnam's struggle to free itself from these foreign powers informs and influences Thu-Lâm's personal life, as is evident in her narration of scenes of violence perpetrated against Vietnamese civilians. The other struggle portrayed in the book is personal and financial, as Thu-Lâm attempts to free herself from abusive marriages and to gain economic independence and financial success. Another major foreign presence in both Vietnam and her autobiography is the United States and its multifaceted influence on Vietnam's lifestyles and culture. Thu-Lâm welcomes the American-style capitalism and became an American entrepreneur in the 1970s and '80s.

Renny Christopher's book, *The Vietnam War/The American War: Images and Representations in Euro-American and Vietnamese Exile Narratives* (Amherst: University of Massachusetts Press, 1995), contains insightful discussions of *Fallen Leaves*. See also:

Janette, Michele. "Nguyèn Thi Thu-Lâm." In Guiyou Huang, ed., *Asian American Autobiographers: A Bio-Bibliographical Critical Sourcebook* (Westport, CT: Greenwood Press, 2001), 371–74.

Phan, Don T. "The Vietnamese on Vietnam and America." Rev. of

Fallen Leaves. Los Angeles Times April 1, 1990, Book Review, 2.

Yoshiko Uchida (1921–1992). *Nisei* Japanese American autobiographer and writer of children's books Uchida was born in Alameda and grew up in Berkeley, California. When she was twelve, her parents took her and her sister to Japan for family visits. Uchida completed high school at sixteen and went on to attend the University of California at Berkeley. Her studies were interrupted in her senior year by the forced relocation of her family after the Pacific War broke out in December 1941. The Uchidas were interned at Camp Topaz, Utah, in September 1942, and Yoshiko was released in May 1943. The following year she completed a master's degree in education at Smith College. In her writing career of approximately four decades she wrote thirty books, twenty-seven of which are for children. Of these, the first published is *Dancing Kettle and Other Japanese Folk Tales* (San Diego: Harcourt Brace, 1949); other books in this category include *The Journey to Topaz* (New York: Charles Scribner, 1971), *Samurai of Gold Hill* (New York: Charles Scribner, 1971), *Journey Home* (New York: Atheneum, 1978), and *A Jar of Dreams* (New York: Atheneum, 1981). In 1987, she published *Picture Bride: A Novel* (Flagstaff, AZ: Northland Press). In 1982 she published her first autobiography, *Desert Exile: The Uprooting of a Japanese-American Family* (Seattle: University of Washington Press), and in 1991 another, *The Invisible Thread: An Autobiography* (New York: Simon and Schuster).

Although Uchida is perhaps better known as a writer of children's books (some of which won awards), a couple of her works are autobiographical—*Journey to Topaz* and *Journey Home*; her more strictly autobiographical works, however, remain *Desert Exile* and *The Invisible Thread*, both of which are noteworthy for their accounts of the Japanese American internment experience. *Desert Exile*, like some other autobiographical works that focus on the experience of internment, delves into issues of identity, racial and cultural heritage, and the psychological effects of the racially motivated exile of Japanese Americans. Uchida not only narrates her blissful childhood lived among different ethnic groups and then her racially more aware years during college, she also examines her ambivalence about being American in Japan and being Japanese in America. In her account of camp life she devotes a considerable amount of space to her *issei* parents as well as her own experience of the internment. *The Invisible Thread*, published almost a decade after *Desert Exile*, recaptures the essence of Uchida's first autobiography except that it is aimed at a younger audience and offers new perspectives informed by Japanese Americans' redress movement. Uchida expresses positive views of Japan and reiterates affirmatively her Japanese American identity.

For more information, see:

Culley, John J. Rev. of *Desert Exile*. *Western Historical Quarterly* 14, no. 4 (October 1983): 485–86.

Daniels, Roger. Rev. of *Desert Exile*. *Pacific Historical Review* 52, no. 2 (May 1983): 234–35.

Ghymn, Esther Mikyung. "Yoshiko Uchida's Positive Vision." In Ghymn, *The Shapes and Styles of American Asian Prose Fiction* (New York: Peter Lang, 1992), 67–89.

Kapai, Leela. "Yoshiko Uchida." In Guiyou Huang, ed., *Asian American Autobiographers: A Bio-Bibliographical Critical Sourcebook* (Westport, CT: Greenwood Press, 2001), 375–81.

Lebra, Atkie Sugiyama. Rev. of *Desert Exile*. *Pacific Affairs* 56, no. 2 (Summer 1983): 386–87.

Katherine Wei (1930–). A Chinese American autobiographer and a respected bridge player, Wei was born into an intellectual family in Beijing, China. In 1937, when Japan invaded, Wei and her family moved from Beijing to Hunan, then to Chongqing (the wartime capital of China), and finally to Shanghai. In 1949 she immigrated to New York, where she studied at Columbia University's School of Nursing. Wei is the family name of her second husband, a shipowner in Houston whom she married after she divorced her first husband in 1968. Wei wrote her autobiography *Second Daughter: Growing up in China, 1930–1949* (Boston: Little, Brown, 1984), with the assistance of the novelist and playwright Terry Quinn. Wei's talent for bridge has garnered her numerous titles and awards, including Grand Master, the World Bridge Federation's highest rank, and induction into the Bridge Hall of Fame in 1999. In addition, she has published books and articles on the game of bridge, including *Precision's One Club* (Louisville, KY: Baron/Barclay Bridge Supplies, 1981), coauthored with Judi Radin.

The title of Wei's autobiography, *Second Daughter*, refers to her own positioning among her female siblings—Wei is the second of four daughters and, as the subtitle reveals, the book focuses on her childhood and young womanhood in China until 1949, the year the Communists took over and Wei left to study in the United States. But the book does not solely narrate the author's life experiences; her mother and grandfather also figure prominently. The mother embodies the contradictions of a traditional Chinese woman/mother and a Westernized individual who seeks liberation and equality of the sexes. Being a zealous admirer of American cultural values and life-styles, Katherine's mother went to great lengths to arrange opportunities for meetings between her daughter and a would-be America-bound Chinese student, whom Katherine did marry in New York in 1950. Katherine's grandfather, on the other hand, is portrayed as a stereo-typical patriarch in old China who kept con-cubines, smoked opium, and wrote poetry, among other pastimes. *Second Daughter* devotes space to Katherine's delayed visit to her mother in 1981, when American citizens were allowed to travel to China, but it was an anticlimactic meeting due to the emotional chasm that had grown between them during the thirty-two years of separation and lack of communication in any form.

For more information, see:

Davin, Delia. Rev. of *Second Daughter*. *Times Literary Supplement*, April 5, 1985, 375.

Stuttaford, Genevieve. Rev. of *Second Daughter*. *Publishers Weekly* (June 15, 1984): 68.

Teo, Elizabeth. Rev. of *Second Daughter*. *Library Journal* 109 (August 1984): 1442.

Yen, Xiaoping. "Katherine Wei." In Guiyou Huang, ed., *Asian American Autobiographers: A Bio-Bibliographical Critical Sourcebook* (Westport, CT: Greenwood Press, 2001), 383–87.

* * *

Jade Snow Wong (1922–). A pioneering figure in Asian American literary history and one of the most noted Asian American autobiographers, Wong was born and raised in San Francisco, California. She grew up in San Francisco's Chinatown under significant influences of traditional Chinese cultural val-

ues; she learned classical Chinese literature from her father, who was a Protestant minister and a garment manufacturer, at once tradition-conscious and open-minded. Wong completed an A.A. at San Francisco Junior College in 1940, then went on to study at Mills College, earning a B.A. in 1942. After graduation she worked as a researcher at a shipyard and then as a ceramic artist. In 1945, she published her autobiography, *Fifth Chinese Daughter* (New York: Harper); three decades later, she produced another book, *No Chinese Stranger* (New York: Harper & Row, 1975), which was marketed as a piece of travel writing though it is also autobiographical. Wong's first book garnered her a great deal of fame and attention: on the strength of her words, the U.S. Department of State invited her to go on a four-month tour of Asia to spread the message of American democracy and to personalize the success story of a U.S. minority group. Wong also received an honorary doctorate of humane letters from her alma mater, Mills College, as well as a Silver Medal from the Commonwealth Club of San Francisco.

Fifth Chinese Daughter was a unique book in the mid-1940s because it was written as an autobiography and yet narrated from the third-person point of view; it was widely noted also because of its firsthand account of the success story of a young minority woman from a tradition-bound Chinese family. The autobiography's favorable historical reception may have partly contributed to its revival in the 1980s, when Asian American literature was attracting a great surge of interest from both Asian American and mainstream American readers, writers, and scholars. Wong's book traces the experiences of a young Chinatown girl who learns about her American world through her first-generation Chinese immigrant parents and their colleagues and relatives, and who struggles between the traditional values of Chinese culture upheld by her parents and new American values represented by the world outside Chinatown, most notably

Mills College. The desire to be independent, loyalty to her parents, and the determination to receive a college education all come alive through detailed descriptions of Jade Snow's upbringing as the fifth daughter of a Chinese family that valued the birth of a boy more than that of a girl. Her parents' industry and intelligence, the garment workers' daily chores and pastimes, Chinatown life before World War II, and Chinese cuisine and customs are all given flesh-and-blood depictions. As an autobiography, though, Jade Snow Wong's book portrays her own ups and downs through college, and her growth into a successful ceramic artist who won the admiration and support of many, including her parents and the Mills College faculty. *No Chinese Stranger*, Wong's second book, has received considerably less critical and popular notice than her first. It chronicles her experience traveling to China as well as her life since the publication of *Fifth Chinese Daughter*.

For more information, see:

Cobb, Nora. "Food as an Expression of Cultural Identity in Jade Snow Wong and *Songs for Jadina*." *Hawaii Review* 12 (1988): 12–16.

Chen, Fu-jen. "Jade Snow Wong." In Guiyou Huang, ed., *Asian American Autobiographers: A Bio-Bibliographical Critical Sourcebook* (Westport, CT: Greenwood Press, 2001), 389–96.

Evans, Ernestine. "A Chinese-American Girl's Two Worlds." *The New York Herald Tribune Book Review* 27 (1950): 4.

Lim, Shirley Geok-lin. "The Tradition of Chinese American Women's Life Stories: Thematics of Race and Gender in Jade Snow Wong's *Fifth Chinese Daughter* and Maxine Hong Kingston's *The Woman Warrior*." In Margo Culley, ed., *American Women's Autobiography:*

Fea(s)ts of Memory (Madison: University of Wisconsin Press, 1992), 252–67.

Sue, Karen. "Jade Snow Wong's Badge of Distinction in the 1990s." *Hitting Critical Mass: A Journal of Asian American Cultural Criticism* 2 (1994): 3–52.

Wyatt, E. V. R. "Books: 'Fifth Chinese Daughter.'" *Commonweal* LIII (1950): 182.

Yin, Kathleen Loh Swee and Kristopher F. Paulson. "The Divided Voice of Chinese-American Narration: Jade Snow Wong's *Fifth Chinese Daughter*." *MELUS* 9 (1982): 53–59.

Jim Yoshida (1921–). *Nisei* Japanese American autobiographer Yoshida was born in Seattle, Washington. After high school he was admitted to Willamette University in Oregon, but he could not attend because on his trip to Japan in the summer of 1940 he was detained in that country; then he was drafted into the Japanese army and wore its military uniform for ten years. To regain his American citizenship Yoshida was forced to resort to legal means, suing the U.S. government, and he eventually returned to the United States in 1953. He collaborated with Bill Hosokawa, the author of the autobiographies *Thirty-five Years in the Frying Pan* (1978) and *Out of the Frying Pan* (1989), in writing *The Two Worlds of Jim Yoshida*, published in 1972 (New York: William Morrow), six years before Hosokawa wrote his own first autobiography.

The Two Worlds of Jim Yoshida is very different from all other autobiographies written about Japanese American experiences right before, during, and immediately after World War II, for the majority of them focus on the evacuation and internment of Japanese on the West Coast. Yoshida's work deals with a unique experience of an American of Japanese origin detained in his ancestral country, with which the United States was at war and for which he was forced to serve. It is the story of a man without a country. When World War II broke out, Jim took his father's ashes to Japan, where he was trapped and drafted to fight in the Japanese Imperial Army in China. The two worlds Yoshida refers to are the United States and Japan, between which he was torn emotionally while physically he was stuck in Japan. The autobiography delineates two major issues: Yoshida's conscription and service in the Japanese army, and his legal battle with the U.S. government to reclaim his American citizenship. In between, to atone for what he did during his Japanese years, Yoshida volunteered his service to his birth country of America by willingly joining U.S. troops in Korea to fight another war in the early 1950s. Even though *The Two Worlds of Jim Yoshida* chronicles the eventful and painful years of his life between the ages of eighteen and thirty-three, the work seems to be an expression of resignation about the events that occurred in war times.

Elaine H. Kim's *Asian American Literature: An Introduction to the Writings and Their Social Context* (Philadelphia: Temple University Press, 1982) includes a brief discussion of Yoshida's book as an early Asian American autobiography. A bio-critical essay, "Jim Yoshida," by Amy O'Brien, appears in Guiyou Huang, ed., *Asian American Autobiographers: A Bio-Bibliographical Critical Sourcebook* (Westport, CT: Greenwood Press, 2001), 409–11.

3. Drama

Brenda Wong Aoki (1953–). Aoki is a child of four different ethnic heritages: Chinese, Japanese, Scottish, and Spanish. Born in Salt Lake City, Utah, and raised in Los Angeles, California, Aoki earned a B.A. from the University of California at Santa Cruz in 1976. Keenly interested in performing arts and music, Aoki was involved in the establishment of the Asian American Dance Collective and the Asian American Theater Company; she even studied Noh and Japanese classical theater in Japan. The major venue of her artistic expression has been solo performance.

The plays Aoki has published include *The Queen's Garden*, in Kathy A. Perkins and Roberta Uno, eds., *Contemporary Plays by Women of Color* (New York: Routledge, 1996), 14–31; an excerpt of *Mermaid Meat: A Piece for Symphony*, in Jo Bonney, ed., *Extreme Exposure: An Anthology of Solo Performance Texts from the Twentieth Century* (New York: Theatre Communications Group, 2000), 271–75; an excerpt of *Random Acts of Kindness*, in Jo Bonney, ed., *Extreme Exposure: An Anthology of Solo Performance Texts from the Twentieth Century* (New York: Theatre Communications Group, 2000), 267–70. The plays that have been produced but remain unpublished are *Obake! Some Japanese Ghosts* (or *Obake! Tales of Spirits*

Past and Present) (1988); *Random Acts of Kindness* (1992); and *Uncle Gunjiro's Girlfriend* (1998). Of these, *The Queen's Garden* won four Dramalogue awards and a San Diego Critics Circle Award; *Mermaid Meat* garnered an American Society of Composers, Authors, and Publishers special award.

Obake!, The Queen's Garden, Random Acts of Kindness, Mermaid, and *Uncle Gunjiro's Girlfriend* have all been produced as solo performances. Aoki incorporates Japanese folktales and her own life experiences into her work to explore varied themes such as love and passion, secrets and betrayal, and family-related issues. *Obake!* presents five vignettes that retell stories as far apart as the Japanese American writer Hisaye Yamamoto's celebrated short story "The Legend of Miss Sasagawara," the notorious Monkey King of China, and recollections of Aoki's grandfather. *Random Acts of Kindness*, also autobiographical, relates the story of a solo performer and her worries about aging and ethnic heritage. *Mermaid Meat* is about the love shared by an old fisherman and a mermaid he reels in from the sea, and the fisherman's daughter eating the mermaid's flesh and the mermaid forgiving her. Also autobiographical, *Uncle Gunjiro's Girlfriend* probes Aoki's family secrets: her grand-uncle's interracial marriage with the daughter of the archdeacon of San Francisco's Grace Cathedral, who, after her Japanese husband's death, attempts to escape incarceration with her children during World War II.

For more information, see:

Cheng, Scarlet. "Speaking of the Spoken: Brenda Wong Aoki Bases Her *Uncle Gunjiro's Girlfriend* on a Long-held Family Secret." *Los Angeles Times,* April 30, 2000, Calendar: 48+.

Churnin, Nancy. "Memories of the Gang Trap." Rev. of *The Queen's Garden. Los Angeles Times,* November 6, 1992, F1.

de Jesús, Melinda L. "Brenda Wong Aoki." In Miles Xian Liu, ed., *Asian American Playwrights: A Bio-Bibliographical Critical Sourcebook* (Westport, CT: Greenwood Press, 2002), 1–5.

Helig, Jack. Rev. of *Random Acts of Kindness. Readers: Chicago's Free Weekly* 27, no. 2 (April 17, 1998): 2.

Hurwitt, Robert. "Brenda Wong Aoki." In Jo Bonney, ed., *Extreme Exposure: An Anthology of Solo Performance Texts from the Twentieth Century* (New York: Theatre Communications Group, 2000), 265–66.

——. "A Tale of Love and Racism." Rev. of *Uncle Gunjiro's Girlfriend. San Francisco Chronicle,* October 12, 1998, D1.

North, Cheryl. "It's a Scream at Berkeley Symphony." Rev. of *Mermaid Meat. Oakland Tribune,* May 17, 1997, Cue: 1, 5.

Winn, Steven. "Aoki's Garden Needs Weeding." Rev. of *The Queen's Garden. San Francisco Chronicle,* October 10, 1992, C6.

——. "Aoki Tells Adult Tales with Flair." Rev. of *Obake! Some Japanese Ghosts. San Francisco Chronicle,* September 14, 1990: E7.

Jeannie Barroga (1949–). Filipina American playwright Barroga was born and raised in Milwaukee, Wisconsin, where she also attended the University of Wisconsin, graduating with a B.A. in fine arts in 1972. Barroga moved to the San Francisco Bay area after graduation and started to write plays in 1979. Since then she has had a productive career as playwright, producer, director, literary manager, and teacher, though she is best known for writing more than fifty plays, most of which remain unpublished. Her published works that have also been staged include *Two Plays: Kenney Was a Shortstop and The Revered Miss Newton* (San Francisco: Philippines Resource Cen-ter, 1993); *Walls,* in Roberta Uno, ed., *Unbroken Thread: An Anthology of Plays by Asian American Women* (Amherst: University of Massachusetts Press, 1993), 201–60; excerpts of *Talk-Story,* in Velina Hasu Houston, ed., *But Still, Like Air, I'll Rise: New Asian American Plays* (Philadelphia: Temple University Press, 1997), 1–47. A number of her many unpublished manuscripts have been produced: *Lorenzo, Love* (1985), *When Stars Fall* (1985), *Eye of the Coconut* (1986), *Sistersoul* (1986), *Family* (1988), *My Friend Morty* (1989), *Kin* (1990), *Sabi-Sabi* (1994), *Rita's Resources* (1995), *A Good Face* (1996), and *Tracking Kilroy* (2000). Barroga's theatrical achievements won her the Joey Award and the Tino Award, both from TeleTheatre, and the Maverick Award from the Los Angeles Women's Festival, among other honors.

Barroga's plays explore ethnic issues, particularly the Filipino experience in mainstream America. *Eye of the Coconut,* for example, looks at the life of a Filipino American family in Milwaukee through intergenerational clashes over issues such as assimilation and ethnic identity. The theme of family and the setting of Milwaukee appear again in *Rita's Resources*, a play that deals with the meaning of the American dream to a Filipina seamstress living in the Wisconsin city. A Filipina is the protagonist in another Barroga work, *Talk-Story*, about a copy girl who wants to become a newspaper columnist so that she can express herself and tell her father's stories. *Kenny Was a Shortstop* continues the use of a female protagonist; Cora, a reporter, discovers and writes about the gang-related killing of a young Filipino called Kenny. In *Walls*, Barroga's most produced play, a Chinese American reporter, Vi, investigates issues surrounding the Vietnam War and its traumatic effects on race relations and ethnic identities. The walls in the play, used in the same sense as used by Robert Frost in his famous poem "Mending Wall," function symbolically as vehicles of division and separation.

For more information, see:

Hurwitt, Robert. "Coconut Falls from Sitcom Tree: Asian Theater Play Finds the Laughs Are Hard to Come By." *San Francisco Examiner*, January 31, 1991, C1.

Johnson, Wayne. "*Eye of the Coconut* Takes a Warm Look at a Filipino-American Family in Transition." *Seattle Times*, October 15, 1987, E9.

Lee, Josephine. "Walls." In Lee, *Performing Asian America: Race and Ethnicity on the Contemporary Stage* (Philadelphia: Temple University Press, 1997), 208–15.

Peterson, Jane T. and Suzanne Bennett, eds. *Women Playwrights of Diversity: A Bio-Bibliographical Sourcebook*. Westport, CT: Greenwood Press, 1997.

Tian, Jie. "Jeannie Barroga." In Miles Xian Liu, ed., *Asian American Playwrights: A Bio-Bibliographical Critical Sourcebook* (Westport, CT: Greenwood Press, 2002), 6–13.

Weiner, Bernard. "A Dramatic Reflection of the Wall." *San Francisco Chronicle*, April 28, 1989, E8.

Frank Chin (1940–). The son of an immigrant Chinese father and a mother who was a fourth-generation resident of Chinatown in Oakland, California, Chin is difficult to pigeonhole. Even though he is discussed here under drama, he is almost equally known as a novelist, playwright, short story writer, critic, and editor. He is beyond any doubt among the most controversial of contemporary Asian American writers. Chin started his literary career with *The Chickencoop Chinaman*, the first play written by an Asian American to be staged in New York (1972); in 1974 he wrote *The Year of the Dragon*, which also was produced in New York (both plays were collected and published by the University of Washington Press in 1981). However, the work that made him famous and influential during these early years was an editorial project called *Aiiieeeee!: An Anthology of Asian American Writers* (Washington, DC: Howard University Press, 1974), coedited with Jeffery Paul Chan, Lawson Fusao Inada, and Shawn Wong, one of the first major literary anthologies by and for Asian Americans that articulated an "Asian American sensibility." The same group of four collaborated again in 1991 to produce a larger anthology called *The Big Aiiieeeee!: An Anthology of Chinese American and Japanese American Literature* (New York: Meridian). In 1988, Chin published a collection of short stories titled *The Chinaman Pacific & Frisco R.R. Co.* (Minneapolis: Coffee House Press). In the early 1990s he turned his creative energy to novel writing; the results are *Donald Duk* (Minneapolis: Coffee House Press, 1991) and *Gunga Din Highway* (Minneapolis: Coffee House Press, 1994). In 1998, the University of Hawaiʻi released his collection *Bulletproof Buddhists, and Other Essays.*

Evidence of Chin's controversial standing in the literary community can be seen in a number of his widely quoted essays, including the famous and harshly worded "This Is Not an Autobiography" in *Genre* 18 (Summer 1985): 109–30, and the lengthy introduction to *The Big Aiiieeeee!* titled "Come All Ye Asian American Writers of the Real and the Fake" (1–92). These pieces present Chin as a cultural nationalist who appears both combative and argumentative in his articulation of the so-called "Asian American sensibility" and the definition of the "real" and the "fake" among Asian American writers. Chin has also led a group of male writers who protest the emasculation of the Asian male and the deprivation of their manhood. Indeed, many of Chin's works—novels, stories, plays, and essays—explore these racially loaded topics related to gender, identity, and cultural authenticity. The last issue in particular has thrown him into what have been described as "acrimonious" verbal fights with some women writers, most notably Maxine Hong Kingston: it is difficult not to see something of Kingston in the fictional character Pandora Toy in Chin's *Gunga Din Highway*, and something of Chin in Kingston's male protagonist Wittman Ah Sing in *Tripmaster Monkey: His Fake Book.*

While *Gunga Din Highway* satirizes the sellout of the real Asian American culture, *Donald Duk* celebrates Asian American pride and history as represented by the Chinese laborers who built America's transcontinental railroad. Chin's plays, both written and first produced in the early 1970s, focus more on identity issues. *The Chickencoop Chinaman*, for example, deals with the futile search for a father figure. *The Year of the Dragon* offers a gloomy look into the life of a Chinatown family on the brink of disintegration due to identity crisis. *The Chinaman Pacific & Frisco R.R. Co.*, Chin's only short story collection to date, consists of eight stories written between 1970 and 1978; most of them are autobiographical and focus on the Chinese American experience.

In *The Year of the Dragon*, Pa Eng and China Mama embody traditional values to which Pa Eng wants to hold his sons, especially his elder son Fred, by imposing his own wishes. Even though Fred resists and then rebels against his father's will, he seems to want to impose the same things on his younger brother Johnny, who rebels against both his father and his brother. Chinatown in Chin's play functions as an ambiguous symbol of both tradition and change. While the locale allows tradition-bound people like Pa Eng to survive and even prosper (he is Chinatown's mayor), it also is a meeting place for old and new cultural values. For example, Fred works as a tour guide who shows white tourists around Chinatown, a job he does not exactly appreciate but stays with because this way he can continue his father's business as a tour and travel agency. In the meantime, Fred perceives the enclave he knows inside and out as a trap that limits his potential and self-worth, which explains why he urges his brother to go east to college, so that Johnny will not be like him, anchored down without any mobility and therefore no prospect for success beyond the confines of Chinatown.

Studies of Chin's works abound. See:

Cheung, King-Kok. "The Woman Warrior Versus the Chinaman Pacific: Must a Chinese American Critic

Choose Between Feminism and Heroism?" In Marianne Hirsche and Evelyn Fox Keller, eds., *Conflicts in Feminism* (New York: Routledge, 1990), 234–51.

Chiu, Jeannie. "Uncanny Doubles: Nationalism and Repression in Frank Chin's 'Railroad Standard Time.'" *Hitting Critical Mass: A Journal of Asian American Cultural Criticism* 1, no. 1 (Fall 1993): 93–107.

Chua, Cheng Lok. "*The Year of the Dragon,* by Frank Chin." In Sauling Cynthia Wong and Stephen H. Sumida, eds., *A Resource Guide to Asian American Literature* (New York: MLA, 2001), 175–84.

Davis, Robert Murray. "Frank Chin: An Interview with Robert Murray Davis." *Amerasia* 14, no. 2 (1988): 81–95.

——. "West Meets East: A Conversation with Frank Chin." *Amerasia Journal* 24, no. 1 (1998): 87–103.

Huang, Guiyou. "Frank Chin." In Emmanuel Nelson, ed., *Asian American Novelists* (Westport, CT: Greenwood Press, 2000): 48–55.

——. "Frank Chin." in Miles X. Liu, ed., *Asian American Playwrights* (Westport, CT: Greenwood Press, 2002), 24–32.

Kim, Elaine H. "'Such Opposite Creatures': Men and Women in Asian American Literature." *Michigan Quarterly Review* 29, no. 1 (Winter 1990): 68–93.

Kurahashi, Yuko. "Gender, Culturalism, and Between Worlds: *The Year of the Dragon* and *And the Soul Shall Dance.*" In Kurahashi, *Asian American Culture on Stage: The History of the East West Players* (New York: Garland Publishing, 1999), 69–89.

Lau, Joseph S.M. "The Albatross Exorcised: The Rime of Frank Chin." *Tamkang Review* 12, no. 1 (1981): 93–105.

Li, David Leiwei. "The Formation of Frank Chin and Formations of Chinese American Literature." In Shirley Hune, et al., eds., *Asian Americans: Comparative and Global Perspectives* (Pullman: Washington State University Press, 1991): 211–23.

MacDonald, Erik. "'The Fractured I ≠ the Dissolved Self': Ethnic Identity in Frank Chin and Cherrie Moraga." In *Theater at the Margins: Text and Post-Structured Stage* (Ann Arbor: University of Michigan Press, 1993), 137–72.

McDonald, Dorothy Ritsuko. Introduction to *Chickencoop Chinaman* and *The Year of the Dragon* (Seattle: University of Washington Press, 1981), ix–xxix.

Moran, Edward. "Frank Chin." *Current Biography* 60, no. 3 (March 1999): 17–20.

Nguyen, Viet Thanh. "The Remasculization of Chinese America: Race, Violence, and the Novel." *American Literary History* 12, no. 1 (2000): 130–57.

Zhang, Aiping. "Frank Chin." In Guiyou Huang, ed., *Asian American Short Story Writers: An A-to-Z Guide* (Westport, CT: Greenwood Press, 2003), 51–60.

* * *

Ping Chong (1946–). Chinese American playwright, performing artist, and theater director Chong was born in Toronto, Canada, and was raised in New York's Chinatown. He attended New York University to study film, but live performance seemed more appealing. He studied filmmaking and graphic design at the School of Visual Arts and Pratt Institute before he launched his theatrical career. From 1964 to 1966 he joined the choreographer/

composer Meredith Monk's House Foundation and worked with Monk on several drama projects. In 1971, Chong embarked on a career as a performance artist, directing and performing his first play, *Lazarus,* in 1973 (Lee Nagrin Studio, New York City). In 1975 he founded The Fiji Theatre Company, later renamed Ping Chong and Company, that staged his plays. His works have been presented in major U.S. cities and throughout North America, Europe, and Asia, in venues such as the Brooklyn Academy of Music's Next Wave Festival and the Spoleto Festival USA. Chong has published only three of his numerous theatrical works: *Kind Ness, Plays in Progress* 8, no. 9 (1986): 1–43; *Snow, Plays in Progress* 10, no. 9 (1988): 1–62; and *Nuit Blanche,* in Misha Berson, ed., *Between Worlds: Contemporary Asian-American Plays* (New York: Theatre Communications Group, 1990), 7–28. He has dozens of unpublished drama manuscripts, screenplays, and multimedia works; of these, *Undesirable Elements* has been widely produced.

Chong has received numerous awards and honors, including an Outstanding Achievement in Music Theatre Award (shared with Meredith Monk) in 1986, the Village Award in 1988, a USA Playwrights' Award in 1988, the Bessie Award in 1990 and 1998, and the Obie Award from the *Village Voice* in 1977 and 2000.

Chong's first major dramatic production, *Nuit Blanche: A Select View of Earthlings,* premiered in New York in 1981. This is a story about human conditions across time and around the world, ranging from South America and other Third World locations, where the disastrous effects of colonialism and imperialism on indigenous cultures are examined and criticized, to the United States, specifically the Carolinas, where the focus is on the effects of slavery. *Kind Ness* premiered in 1986 and has been staged in many northeastern cities and occasionally abroad. Set in 1960s–'70s American suburbia,

the play dramatizes the story of five children and one gorilla named Buzz and satirizes human exploitation of intelligent animals such as the precocious primate. *Snow,* first produced in 1988 in Minneapolis, crosses the international space of history and geography, involving Germany, Japan, France, and America in different historical periods covering World War I, post-World War II, the Meiji era in Japan, and the seventeenth and nineteenth centuries. The common thread that connects histories, cultures, and peoples is the natural element of snow; amid cultural and natural dissimilarities are similarities that characterize humans. Chong's unpublished but frequently staged work is *Undesirable Elements,* for which he created different versions for performance in Chicago, Cleveland, Minneapolis, Seattle, Rotterdam, and Tokyo. The play is a series of performance pieces tailored to specific locations, and it examines the effects of culture, history, and race on the lives of people with diverse backgrounds.

For more information, see:

Berson, Misha. "Collage of Culture— *Undesirable Elements* Explores Seattle Faces." *Seattle Times,* February 3, 1995, H26.

Carroll, Noël. "A Select View of Earthlings: Ping Chong." *Drama Review* 27, no. 1 (1983): 72–81.

Chong, Ping. "Notes for 'Mumblings and Digressions: Some Thoughts on Being an Artist, Being an American, Being a Witness....'" *MELUS* 16, no. 3 (1989–90): 62–67.

Gussow, Mel. "*Nuit Blanche.*" *The New York Times,* January 23, 1981, C8.

Hering, D. "Ping Chong and Company." *Dance Magazine* 65, no. 2 (1991): 115–16.

Howard, Beth. "Ping Chong: Creating a Visual and Aural Feast." *Theatre Crafts* 24, no. 3 (1990): 27–31, 59–60.

Moynihan, D. S. "Ping Chong's *Nuit Blanche*." *Drama Review* 25, no. 1 (1981): 101–5.

Neely, Kent. "Ping Chong's Theatre of Simultaneous Consciousness." *Journal of Dramatic Theory and Criticism* 6, no. 2 (1992): 121–35.

——. "Theatre Review—*Snow*," *Theatre Journal* 41, no. 2 (1989): 234.

Sandla, Robert. "Practical Visionary: Ping Chong." *Theatre Week* 2, no. 20 (1989): 26–33.

Sugano, Douglas. "Ping Chong." In Miles Xian Liu, ed., *Asian American Playwrights: A Bio-Bibliographical Critical Sourcebook* (Westport, CT: Greenwood Press, 2002), 33–40.

Westfall, Suzanne. "Ping Chong's *Terra In/Cognita*: Monsters on Stage." In Shirley Geok-lin Lim and Amy Ling, eds., *Reading the Literatures of Asian America* (Philadelphia: Temple University Press, 1992), 359–73.

G

Philip Kan Gotanda (1951–). A *sansei* Japanese American playwright and screenwriter, Gotanda was born in Stockton, California, where his father settled after his release from internment at Rohwer Camp, Arkansas, during World War II. After a year studying at the University of California at Santa Cruz, Gotanda left the United States to hone his ceramic techniques in Japan for a year, then returned to complete his degree in Japanese arts at the University of California at Santa Barbara in 1973. Even though Gotanda was alternately interested in arts, music, and playwriting, he earned a degree from Hastings School of Law in 1978. While he continued his musical creations,

he sustained his interest in playwriting. He established professional and personal ties with Frank Chin's Asian American Theater Company in San Francisco; he also played guitar with another celebrated Asian American playwright, David Henry Hwang, in the 1970s.

Gotanda's first theatrical attempt was *The Avocado Kid, or Zen and the Art of Guacamole*, produced at East West Players in 1979 and at the Asian American Theater Company in 1981. The following years witnessed a salvo of successful productions and publications: *The Dream of Kitzmura*, in Robert Hurwitt, ed., *West Coast Plays* 15/16 (Los Angeles: California Theater Council, 1983), 191–223; *The Wash*, in Robert Hurwitt, ed., *West Coast Plays* 21/22 (Los Angeles: California Theater Council, 1987), 119–65; *Fish Head Soup*, in *Fish Head Soup and Other Plays*, intro. Michael Omi (Seattle: University of Washington Press, 1995), 1–67; *A Song for a Nisei Fisherman*, In *Fish Head Soup and Other Plays* (Seattle: University of Washington Press, 1995), 199–258; *Yankee Dawg You Die* (New York: Dramatists Play Service, 1991); *Day Standing on Its Head* (New York: Dramatists Play Service, 1994); *Ballad of Yachiyo, American Theatre Magazine* (February 1996):27–42; and *in the dominion of night*, coauthored with Dan Kuramoto, Danny Yamamoto, and Taiji Miyagawa (privately published, 1996). Gotanda's unpublished manuscripts include *The Avocado Kid, or Zen and the Art of Guacamole* (1979), *Bullet Headed Birds* (1981), *Sisters Matsumoto* (1997), *Yohen* (1997), and *Floating Weeds* (2000). In addition, Gotanda has written screenplays: *The Wash* (1988); *The Kiss* (1992); *Drinking Tea* (1996); and *Life Tastes Good* (1999). Of these, the most produced and reviewed are *Yankee Dawg You Die*, *The Wash*, and *The Dream of Kitamura*. *A Song for a Nisei Fisherman*, *Ballad of Yachiyo*, *Day Standing on Its Head*, and *Sisters Matsumoto* have also received considerable popular notice.

Gotanda has been recognized with Guggenheim, McKnight, National Endowment for the Arts, and Rockefeller fellowships, as well as the National Artist Award from the PEW Charitable Trust and Theatre Communications group and a Lila Wallace-Reader's Digest Writer's Award.

Much of Gotanda's dramatic writing concerns the Japanese American experience, particularly the Japanese American internment and its aftermath, and American racism on both the institutional and the individual levels. *The Ballad of Yachiyo*, based on the story of his paternal aunt's suicide, was produced and published in the mid-1990s; it grew out of Gotanda's experience studying with the ceramic artist Hiroshi Seto in Japan around 1970. *The Dream of Kitamura* stages the story of a third-generation Japanese American law professor's midlife experience. *A Song for a Nisei Fisherman* is a biographical play based on the life of Gotanda's father. The protagonist, Itsuta "Ichan" Matsumoto, like Gotanda's father, had an impoverished childhood in Hawai'i and suffered during the Japanese American internment in World War II; the play also delineates his roles as a father and husband. The dissolution of a *nisei* marriage provides the plot for *The Wash*, which, though set in the 1980s, examines the psychological effects of the Japanese American camp experience, as reflected in the experiences of the wife, Masi Matsumoto, who decides to free herself from an abusive marriage. In *Sisters Matsumoto*, set in 1945 in Gotanda's own birthplace, the audience again sees the devastating impact of the internment on Japanese American families and how it becomes internalized in characters like the Matsumoto sisters and in other families, like Henry's.

While racism is not directly approached in the above-mentioned plays, it is the central target of exploration in *Yankee Dawg You Die*, probably Gotanda's most produced and studied drama. This play does not solely focus on Japanese American characters, as is often the case in other Gotanda works; it instead presents an Asian American cast and considers their experiences of racism and racial stereotyping. The play crosses ethnicities—the two major characters, Vincent Chang and Bradley Yamashita, are respectively Chinese and Japanese American; spans generations—Chang and Yamashita are of different generations; explores gay issues in the Asian American community; and just as important, critiques racism. All these intertwining factors are played out in the entertainment industry, in which Asian American actors perform or struggle with their racial and sexual identities while battling the mainstream media's representations of them onstage and stereotyping offstage.

Reviews of productions of Gotanda's plays are abundant. The following is a select listing of more substantial studies of his works:

Berson, Misha. "Gotanda's Plays Explore Lives of Asian-Americans." *American Theatre* (September 1988): 54–55.

Cho, Nancy. "*Yankee Dawg You Die*, by Philip Kan Gotanda." In Sau-ling Cynthia Wong and Stephen H. Sumida, eds., *A Resource Guide to Asian American Literature* (New York: MLA, 2001), 185–92.

Hurwitt, Robert. "Song of a Sansei Playwright: An Interview with Philip Kan Gotanda and Richard Seyd." In Hurwitt, *West Coast Plays* 21/22 (Los Angeles: California Theater Council, 1987), 166–74.

Hwang, David Henry. "Philip Kan Gotanda." *Bomb* (Winter 1998): 20–26.

Kaplan, Randy Barbara. "Philip Kan Gotanda." In Miles Xian Liu, ed., *Asian American Playwrights: A Bio-Bibliographical Critical Sourcebook* (Westport, CT: Greenwood Press, 2002), 69–88.

Kurahashi, Yuko. "*The Avocado Kid.*" In Kurahashi, *Asian American Culture on Stage: The History of the East West Players* (New York: Garland, 1999), 114–17.

———. "Philip Kan Gotanda's Personal Saga, *A Song for a Nisei Fisherman.*" In Kurahashi, *Asian American Culture on Stage: The History of the East West Players* (New York: Garland, 1999), 162–66.

Lee, Josephine. Rev. of *Fish Head Soup and Other Plays. Amerasia Journal* 23, no. 1 (1997): 181–83.

Moy, James. "David Henry Hwang's *M. Butterfly* and Philip Kan Gotanda's *Yankee Dawg You Die*: Repositioning Chinese American Marginality on the American Stage." *Theatre Journal* 42 (March 1990): 48–56.

Omi, Michael. Introduction to *Fish Head Soup and Other Plays*, by Philip Kan Gotanda (Seattle: University of Washington Press, 1995), xi–xxvi.

Siegel, Nina. "*Ballad of Yachiyo.*" Interview with Philip Kan Gotanda. *American Theatre* (February 1996): 25–26.

Swanson, Meg and Robin Murray. "Yankee Dawg You Die." In Swanson and Murray, *Playwrights of Color* (Yarmouth, ME: Intercultural Press, 1999), 107–28.

Velina Hasu Houston (1957–). One of the most prolific playwrights of Japanese, African American, and Native American descent, Houston was born in Tokyo to a Japanese mother and an African/Native American father, who was a U.S. occupation soldier after World War II. Houston moved to the United States with her parents in 1959, first living in New York and then settling down in Junction City, Kansas, where, after her father's death in 1969, she lived with her mother until she went to college. Houston earned a B.A. in journalism, mass communications, and theater from Kansas State University in 1979, before she went on to study theater arts and screenwriting and obtained an M.F.A. from UCLA in 1981. Her master's thesis, "Asa Ga Kimashita" (Morning Has Broken), workshop produced at UCLA in 1981, later became one of her most produced plays and was published in *The Politics of Life: Four Plays by Asian American Women*, edited by Houston herself (Philadelphia: Temple University Press, 1993), 205–74.

Tea, undoubtedly Houston's most famous and most staged work, was published in Roberta Uno, ed., *Unbroken Thread: An Anthology of Plays by Asian American Women* (Amherst: University of Massachusetts Press, 1993), 155–200. Other plays followed: *The Matsuyama Mirror*, in Craig Slaight and Jack Sharrar, eds., *Short Plays for Young Actors* (North Stratford, NH: Smith and Kraus, 1996), 77–106; *As Sometimes in a Dead Man's Face*, in Brian Nelson, ed., *Asian American Drama: 9 Plays from the Multiethnic Landscape* (New York: Applause, 1997), 71–125; *Kokoro* (True Heart), in Houston, ed., *But Still, Like Air, I'll Rise: New Asian American Plays* (Philadelphia: Temple University Press, 1997), 89–129; and *Hula Heart*, in Coleman A. Jennings, ed., *Eight Plays for Children: The New Generation Project* (Austin: University of Texas Press, 1999), 77–104. Houston has also written dozens of unpublished manuscripts, of which the following have been produced at least once: *Switchboard* (1976), *Nobody Like Us* (1979), *Thirst* (1981), *American Dreams* (1983), *Amerasian Girls* (1983), *Albatross* (1988), *Christmas Cake* (1990), *Cultivated*

Lives (1994), *Ikebana* (1999), and *Waiting for Tadashi* (1999), among other pieces. Houston has written numerous screenplays as well, mostly for PBS. She has edited two drama anthologies, already mentioned: *The Politics of Life* (1993) and *But Still, Like Air, I'll Rise* (1997).

Houston's theatrical accomplishments have won her a number of prestigious awards, including the Lorraine Hansberry Playwriting Award in 1982, the first prize David Library Playwriting Award in 1982, the *LA Weekly* Drama Critics Award for *Asa Ga Kimashita* in 1984, *DramaLogue* Outstanding Achievement in Theater Award for the Old Globe production of *Tea* in 1988, the Critics Choice Awards from the *Los Angeles Times* and *DramaLogue*, both in 1991, and the Po'Okela Award in 1996, among other prizes and fellowships.

Though not exactly autobiographical, Houston's plays often reflect her family's history and her own interracial background, as well as several constant themes: women, race relations, gender issues, and national boundaries. Her earliest drama, *Asa Ga Kimashita*, is essentially a Japanese play, as it deals with Japan's transition from the prewar traditional patriarchal family structure to the postwar, more democratic practice in family relations, and the effects this shift has on gender roles in the Shimada family. The play is also transnational and interracial, for it involves Japan and the United States as well as an African American soldier in the American occupying forces. Setsuko, the daughter of Kiheida and Fusae Shimada in *Asa Ga Kimashita*, is the protagonist of Houston's next play, *American Dreams*. Setsuko faces another set of problems and issues as she struggles with a new life in America with her African/Native American husband Creed Banks: the racism and sexism she encounters come not only from the mainstream society but also from the African American community, historically victims

of racism and classism. Setsuko's American dreams are therefore wrought with frustration and humiliation coupled with uncertainties about her cultural identity.

The Matsuyama Mirror, another Japanese play set in the Edo feudal period, examines the maturation process of a young Japanese girl, Aiko, from innocent girlhood to womanhood. This growth does not occur without losses—it takes her mother's sudden death, her father's remarriage, and her own first menstruation to initiate Aiko into adulthood. *Kokoro* shifts the scene to America and examines the causes and implications of a traditional Japanese practice, parent-child suicide, carried out in the new world. Yasako, the wife of Hiro Yamashita, finding it impossible to deal with both the irreconcilable differences of opinion with her husband and his extramarital affairs, decides to drown herself and her daughter in the sea. The socially accepted practice of suicide in one culture (Japan) is placed under the legal microscope of another (America) to demonstrate cultural differences and clashes as experienced by immigrants in contemporary American life.

Houston's most staged and best-known drama is undoubtedly *Tea*. First premiered at New York City's Manhattan Theatre Club in 1987, the play has been staged twice in Japan and in many mainland U.S. cities as well as in Hawai'i. Somewhat biographical of Houston's own mother, *Tea* focuses on five Japanese war brides who try to make sense of their lives in a Kansas town. In much the way the Chinese mothers gather to share stories and strategize about the future around a mahjong table in Amy Tan's *The Joy Luck Club*, the Japanese women meet at the tea ceremony in the house of a friend who recently committed suicide, to reflect on their lives as wives, mothers, and immigrants. The tea event, while retaining its social meaning, also creates a forum for sharing experience and articulating hopes.

Reviews and notices of Houston's play productions can be easily found in popular publication venues. What follows is a list of mostly article-length studies:

Hoang, Hahn. "Amazing Grace: Velina Hasu Houston Draws Strength and Inspiration from the .Hard Adventure of Growing up Black and Japanese." *Transpacific* (July–August 1991): 37–45.

Hongo, Florence M. "Velina Hasu Houston: Truly Japanese and American." In Hongo, *Strength and Diversity: Japanese American Women*, 1885 to 1990 (San Francisco: National Japanese American Historical Society, 1990), 29–30.

Lee, Josephine. *Performing Asian America: Race and Ethnicity on the Contemporary Stage.* Philadelphia: Temple University Press, 1997.

Ling, Amy. "Velina Hasu Houston, Playwright and Poet," in Ling, ed., *Yellow Light: The Flowering of Asian American Arts* (Philadelphia: Temple University Press, 1999), 236–40.

Shimakawa, Karen. "Swallowing the Tempest: Asian American Women on Stage." *Theatre Journal* 47, no. 3 (October 1995): 367–81.

Uno, Roberta. "*Tea*, by Velina Hasu Houston." In Sau-ling Cynthia Wong and Stephen H. Sumida, eds., *A Resource Guide to Asian American Literature* (New York: MLA, 2001), 193–99.

Usui, Masami. "Velina Hasu Houston." In Miles Xian Liu, ed., *Asian American Playwrights: A Bio-Bibliographical Critical Sourcebook* (Westport, CT: Greenwood Press, 2002), 103–20.

——. "Creating a Feminist Transnational Drama: *Oyako Shinju* (Parent–Child Suicide) in Velina Hasu Houston's *Kokoro* (True Heart)." *Japanese Journal of American Studies* 11 (2000): 173–98.

——. "Dreams and Nightmares, Nightmares and Dreams in Velina Hasu Houston's *American Dreams.*" *Kansai American Journal* 35 (1998): 32–53.

——. "Japan's Post-war Democratization—Agrarian Reform and Women's Liberation in Velina Hasu Houston's *Asa Ga Kimashita* (Morning Has Broken)." *AALA Journal* 5 (1998): 11–25.

——. "Voices from the 'Netherworld': Japanese International Brides in Velina Hasu Houston's *Tea.*" *Chu-Shikoku Studies in American Literature* 34 (June 1998): 45–64.

"Velina Hasu Houston." In Jane T. Peterson and Suzanne Bennet, eds., *Women Playwrights of Diversity* (Westport, CT: Greenwood Press, 1997), 166–70.

* * *

David Henry Hwang (1957–). Chinese American playwright Hwang was born in Los Angeles to a Chinese-born father and a Philippines-born mother, both of Chinese descent, and was raised in a comfortable middle-class neighborhood in San Gabriel, in Southern California. Against his father's hope that he would major in business, Hwang studied English at Stanford and developed a keen interest in drama writing, which he started to do without any training, for no playwriting program existed at Stanford then. Hwang sought help from other sources, such as fiction writers at the university and playwrights at the Padua Hills Playwrights' Festival in the summer of 1978, when he developed ideas for his first play, *FOB*. Hwang graduated from Stanford in 1979, the same year he submitted *FOB* to the Playwrights Conference of the O'Neill

Theatre Center, which accepted it for stage reading. In June 1980 the play premiered successfully at New York City's Public Theater and won Hwang an Obie Award. Hwang then went on to obtain an education in playwriting at the Yale University School of Drama, which he attended from fall 1980 to spring 1981. In the next two years he wrote three more plays: *The Dance and the Railroad*, *The House of Sleeping Beauties*, and *The Sound of a Voice*. After a hiatus of two years brought on by mixed criticism of his earlier works, Hwang wrote *Rich Relations*, and in 1986 he started on his most famous work, *M. Butterfly*, which premiered at the National Theatre in Washington, DC in 1988, and won the Outer Critics Circle Award and the Tony Award for best play of 1988. Other plays soon followed: *Face Value*, *Bondage*, *Trying to Find Chinatown*, and *Golden Child*. All found their way into anthologies: *Broken Promises: Four Plays* (New York: Avon Books, 1983); *FOB: and, The House of Sleeping Beauties: Two Plays* (New York: Dramatists Play Service, 1983); *FOB and Other Plays* (New York: New American Library, 1990); *Trying to Find Chinatown: and Bondage* (New York: Dramatists Play Service, 1996); *Trying to Find Chinatown: The Selected Plays* (New York: Theatre Communications Group, 2000). In addition, Hwang has created librettos as well as screenplays: *Korea: Homes Apart*, *M. Butterfly*, *Golden Gate*, and *Seven Years in Tibet*.

Of Hwang's numerous plays, *FOB* and *M. Butterfly* are perhaps the most familiar to American and Asian American audiences, though his other dramas have attracted considerable critical and popular attention as well. *FOB*, written when Hwang was in college in his early twenties, shows a keen awareness of issues of ethnicity, immigration, and East–West relations enacted by two opposing characters, an FOB (fresh off the boat) Chinese and an ABC (American-born Chinese). Though of the same ethnicity, the FOB Steven and the ABC Dale act and speak differently due to their separate cultural values and national origins. These values are reflected through Steve's relationships with Dale and his cousin Grace. The play dramatizes cultural differences and identity politics as the three characters debate and argue about their perceptions of reality and myth in Chinese and American cultures. *The Dance and the Railroad*, featuring two railroad construction workers, Lone and Ma, and appropriating both Western and Asian theater forms, is set on a transcontinental railroad construction site in 1867 California, a historical and geographical background against which Chinese Americans experience both assimilation and exclusion as well as the temptation and trepidations of their American dream. In *Bondage* and *Trying to Find Chinatown*, Hwang focuses on the racial and sexual identities and how they are constructed and perceived. Hwang's most personal and autobiographical plays are *Family Devotions*, *Rich Relations*, and *Golden Child*. *Family Devotions* explores the negative influence of Christian fundamentalism on a Chinese American Christian family; *Rich Relations* is about a dysfunctional Christian family and the absurdities the protagonist, Hinson, and his family commit; *Golden Child*, written after the birth of the author's son, deals with the history of the main character, Andre Kwang, and his family when faced with the onslaught of Christian influence and modernization, as seen through the eyes of Eng Ahn.

Hwang's most celebrated and studied play is undoubtedly *M. Butterfly*. As Esther Kim writes, "Using the form of theatre (both Western and Chinese) and the mode of metatheatrical performance, Hwang explores in *M. Butterfly* the discrepancies of gender, sexuality, and Orientalism as they show on the surface as opposed to their truthfulness. This dynamic interplay of perception and deception makes *M. Butterfly* one of the most important American dramas in the twentieth century" (132). The play weaves vital contemporary issues of sexism, racism, colonialism, imperialism, homosexuality, East–West relations, war, and revolution into the single relationship of a Western man and a perceived Chinese woman; it creates a powerful drama of human passion and capacity for understanding and misunderstanding across cultures, nations, and genders. Although Hwang had not read Edward Said's *Orientalism* prior to writing the play and therefore received no direct influence from that influential book, the play forcefully and heart-wrenchingly captures the essence of racial, sexual, and political tensions in East–West historical relations, almost exactly the way that Said views them.

There is an abundance of studies of Hwang's work. The following is a select listing:

Cooperman, Robert. "Across the Boundaries of Cultural Identity: An Interview with David Henry Hwang." In Marc Maufort, ed., *Staging Difference: Cultural Pluralism in American Theatre and Drama* (New York: Peter Lang, 1995), 365–73.

——. "New Theatrical Statements: Asian Western Mergers in the Plays of David Henry Hwang." In Marc Maufort, ed., *Staging Difference: Cultural Pluralism in American Theatre and Drama* (New York: Peter Lang, 1995), 201–13.

Deeney, John. "Of Monkeys and Butterflies: Transformations in M. H. Kingston's *Tripmaster Monkey* and D. H. Hwang's *M. Butterfly.*" *MELUS* 18, no. 4 (Winter 1993–1994): 21–39.

DiGaetani, John L. "An Interview with David Henry Hwang." In DiGaetani, *A Search for a Postmodern Theater: Interviews with Contemporary Playwrights* (Westport, CT: Greenwood Press, 1991), 161–74.

Eng, David L. "In the Shadow of a Diva: Committing Homosexuality in David Henry Hwang's *M. Butterfly.*" *Amerasia Journal* 20, no. 1 (1994): 93–116.

Frockt, Deborah. "David Henry Hwang." In Jackson R. Bryer, ed., *The Playwright's Art: Conversations with Contemporary American Dramatists* (New Brunswick, NJ: Rutgers University Press, 1995), 123–46.

Kim, Esther S. "David Henry Hwang." In Miles Xian Liu, ed., *Asian American Playwrights: A Bio-Bibliographical Critical Sourcebook* (Westport, CT: Greenwood Press, 2002), 126–44.

Kondo, Dorinne. "*M. Butterfly*: Orientalism, Gender, and a Critique of Essentialist Identity." *Cultural Critique* 16 (Fall 1990): 5–29.

Love, Colleen. "*M. Butterfly* and the Rhetoric of Antiessentialism: Minority Discourse in an International Frame." In David Palumbo-Liu, ed., *The Ethnic Canon: Histories, Institutions, and Interventions* (Minneapolis: University of Minnesota Press, 1995), 260–89.

Moy, James S. "David Henry Hwang's *M. Butterfly* and Philip Kan Gotanda's *Yankee Dawg You Die*: Repositioning Chinese American Marginality on the American Stage." *Theatre Journal* 42, no. 1 (1990): 48–56.

Pao, Angela. "The Critic and the Butterfly: Sociocultural Contexts and the Reception of David Henry Hwang's *M. Butterfly.*" *Amerasia Journal* 18, no. 3 (1992): 1–16.

——. "*M. Butterfly*, by David Henry Hwang." In Sau-ling Cynthia Wong and Stephen H. Sumida, eds., *A Resource Guide to Asian American Literature* (New York: MLA, 2001), 200–8.

Remen, Kathryn. "The Theatre of Punishment: David Henry Hwang's *M. Butterfly* and Michel Foucault's *Discipline and Punish*." *Modern Drama* 37, no. 3 (Fall 1994): 391–400.

Shimakawa, Karen. "'Who's to Say?' or, Making Space for Gender and Ethnicity in *M. Butterfly*." *Theatre Journal* 45, no. 3 (1993): 349–61.

Shin, Andrew. "Projected Bodies in David Henry Hwang's *M. Butterfly* and *Golden Gate*." *MELUS* 27, no. 1 (Spring 2002): 177–97.

Skloot, Robert. "Breaking the Butterfly: The Politics of David Henry Hwang." *Modern Drama* 33, no. 1 (March 1990): 59–66.

Street, Douglas. *David Henry Hwang*. Boise, ID: Boise State University, 1989.

Trudeau, Lawrence J. "David Henry Hwang." In Trudeau, ed., *Asian American Literature: Reviews and Criticism of Works by American Writers of Asian Descent* (Detroit: Gale Research, 1999), 151–68.

I

Momoko Iko (1940–). Iko was born to Japanese parents in Wapato, Washington, just two years prior to her family's forced relocation to the Heart Mountain concentration camp in Wyoming during World War II. Though she was too young to remember what happened to her family of eight during those years, that event would later haunt her work. Iko started her college education at Northern Illinois University and completed a B.A. in English at the University of Illinois at Urbana-Champaign in 1961. She also studied at Mexico's Instituto Allende and the University of Iowa's creative writing program. She started to write while at Northern Illinois and out of an unpublished novel she formed a two-act play, *Gold Watch*, in 1970. Act 1 was anthologized in Frank Chin et al.'s *Aiiieeeee!* (Washington, DC: Howard University Press, 1974), 88–114, and the whole play was published in Roberta Uno, ed., *Unbroken Thread: An Anthology of Plays by Asian American Women* (Amherst: University of Massachusetts Press, 1993), 111–53. Iko's unpublished manuscripts include *When We Were Young* (1973), *Flowers and Household Gods* (1975), *Second City Flat* (1976), *Hollywood Mirrors* (1978), and *Boutique Living and Disposable Icons* (1987). Iko has won awards from the East West Players, as well as fellowships from the Rockefeller Foundation, the Zellerbach Foundation, and the National Endowment for the Arts.

Gold Watch, Iko's signature play, has enjoyed the most productions, followed by *Flowers and Household Gods*. First produced at Los Angeles's Inner City Cultural Center in 1972, *Gold Watch* was believed to be the first play written by an Asian American woman produced in the continental United States (Parascandola 148). Set in the farming community of Wapato in the Yakima Valley, Washington, the story begins on Labor Day weekend of 1941 and spans the Japanese bombing of Pearl Harbor and the U.S. government's evacuation of Japanese Americans in spring 1942. The protagonist, Masu Murakami, leads the community's resistance against relocation. A subplot is Masu's relationship with his son Tadao, who becomes the owner of his father's gold watch when Masu is killed while fighting the nightriders. The play celebrates the human courage to survive as well as the family's struggle for dignity. *Flowers and Household Gods*, although also about the Japanese American family, is set in the modern metropolis of Chicago in 1968. Delving into the lives of three generations of the Kagawa family—now faced with the death of the matriarch and the alcoholism of the patriarch, and haunted by the memories of internment during the war—the play dramatizes the struggle between cultures and generations exacerbated by clashing social and cultural values.

Three article-length studies of Iko's drama are available:

Parascandola, Louis J. "Momoko Iko." In Miles Xian Liu, ed., *Asian American Playwrights: A Bio-Bibliographical Critical Sourcebook* (Westport, CT: Greenwood Press, 2002), 145–50.

Sumida, Stephen H. "*Gold Watch*, by Momoko Iko." In Sau-ling Cynthia Wong and Stephen H. Sumida, eds., *A Resource Guide to Asian American Literature* (New York: MLA, 2001), 209–20.

Uno, Roberta. "Momoko Iko." In Uno, ed., *Unbroken Thread: An Anth-ology of Plays by Asian American Women* (Amherst: University of Massachusetts Press, 1993), 103–9.

Most other notices are reviews:

Backalenick, Irene. "Not Without Flaws, but Well Worth Seeing." Rev. of *Boutique Living and Disposable Icons*, *Westport News*, July 1, 1988, 45.

Francia, Luis H. Rev. of *Flowers and Household Gods*. *Village Voice* 26, no. 18 (1981): 88.

Gussow, Mel. "Ethnic Identity Confusion for Japanese-Americans." Rev. of *Boutique Living and Disposable Icons*. *The New York Times*, June 30, 1988, C20.

——. "Stage: Nisei Internment." Rev. of *Flowers and Household Gods*. *The New York Times*, April 21, 1981, C7.

Henninger, Daniel. "Visions: Public TV Takes a Chance." Rev. of *Gold Watch*. *National Observer*, November 13, 1976, 22.

Hornby, Richard. "Rich Pacifics." Rev. of *Boutique Living and Disposable Icons*, *New York Press*, July 1, 1988, 3–4.

Margulies, Lee. "Fight for Dignity in *Gold Watch*." *Los Angeles Times*, November 11, 1976, section 4, 28.

O'Connor, John. Rev. of *Gold Watch*. *The New York Times*, November 11, 1976, 81.

Susan Kim (1958–). A Korean American playwright, Kim was born in New York City and spent some childhood years in the New England states of Massachusetts and New Hampshire. She graduated from Wesleyan University with a B.A. and worked a few years in public television in New York before she took writing classes. Kim wrote her first play, *Open Spaces*, in 1988; it won a Drama League Award. Her published dramas include *Scientist Meets Fish*, in Kerry Muir, ed., *Childplay: A Collection of Plays and Monologues for Children* (New York: Proscenium Publishers, 1995), 161–68; *To Bee or Not to Bee*, in Kerry Muir, ed., *Childplay: A Collection of Plays and Monologues for Children* (New York: Proscenium Publishers, 1995), 195–200; and *Dreamtime for Alice*, in Curt Dempster, ed., *Ensemble Studio Theatre Marathon '99: The One-Act Plays* (New York: Faber and Faber, 2000), 99–118. Besides *Open Spaces*, Kim's unpublished dramas include *Death and the Maiden* (1990), *Rapid Eye Movement* (1991), *Swimming Out to Sea*

(1992), *The Arrangement* (1993), *The Joy Luck Club* (1993), *Seventh Word, Four Syllables* (1993), *The Door* (1999), and *Where It Came From* (2000).

Kim's work generally focuses on women's plight. *The Joy Luck Club* was adapted from Amy Tan's celebrated novel of the same title and has been staged in China and the United States; of all Kim's dramaturgical efforts, it has received the most reviews. *Dreamtime for Alice* has also garnered a few notices in the popular press. *Rapid Eye Movement* dramatizes the terror that a woman called Lorraine feels living a middle-class life. *Seventh Word, Four Syllables* depicts Gabby's efforts to free herself from her controlling husband. And *Where It Came From* examines the impact of childhood on the adult behavior of a woman named Sara. In all these plays, female characters occupy center stage; their plight in connection with gender, race, and class is put on the spot and scrutinized.

For more information, see:

Brandi, Nick. "Keeping Up the Pace." Rev. of *Dreamtime for Alice*. *Show Business* 2–8 (June 1999): 11–12.

Ewald, Laura. Rev. of *Ensemble Studio Theatre Marathon '99: The One-Act Plays*. *Library Journal* 125 (2000): 93.

Gussow, Mel. "A First Lady's Fantasy of Travel Back in Time." Rev. of *Seventh Word, Four Syllables*. *The New York Times*, June 10, 1993, C18.

———. "Women Taking Their Places, Rightful or Not." Rev. of *Rapid Eye Movement*. *The New York Times*, September 25, 1992, C3.

Marks, Peter. "In 4 One-Acts, The Soul Is Crushed at Every Age." Rev. of *Dreamtime for Alice*. *The New York Times*, May 25, 1999, B1.

Ruta, Suzanne. "The Jab of the One-Act." Rev. of *Death and the Maiden*.

The New York Times, May 20, 1990, section 2, 12.

Smith, Andrew L. "Susan Kim." In Miles Xian Liu, ed., *Asian American Playwrights: A Bio-Bibliographical Critical Sourcebook* (Westport, CT: Greenwood Press, 2002), 151–55.

L

lê thi diem thúy (1972–). First-generation Vietnamese American lê was born in Phan Thiet, a fishing community not far from Ho Chi Minh City. lê and her father left Vietnam in 1979 and settled in Southern California. She completed a B.A. in cultural studies at Hampshire College in Amherst, Massachusetts. For a class assignment in college she wrote her first play, *Mua He Do Lua/Red Fiery Summer*, which she solo performed in the mid-1990s. The play was published in Rajini Srikanth and Esther Yae Iwanaga, eds., *Bold Worlds: A Century of Asian American Writing* (New Brunswick, NJ: Rutgers University Press, 2001), 387–97. lê's more recent play, *the bodies between us*, was published in Roberta Uno and Lucy Mae San Pablo Burns, eds., *The Color of Theatre: Race, Culture, and Contemporary Performance* (New York: Continuum, 2002). In addition, lê has published a number of poems in Asian American anthologies.

Both of lê's plays take the form of solo performance and both are concerned with familial and personal issues played out against larger national and international topics. *Red Fiery Summer* has been produced in the United States, Canada, and Ireland. It is a play that performs two kinds of life: in war-torn Vietnam and in peaceful Southern California; lê's parents' love story, dramatized against the backdrop of the Vietnam War, makes the play a powerful statement on the war and on the media's representation of it in the West. *the bodies between us*, divided into four sections titled "orange," "earth," "water," and "sky," engages with the relationship between lê and her father and relates the hardships and ordeals suffered by refugees leaving Vietnam in search of a safe land.

For more information, see:

Bao, Quang. "lê thi diem thúy: A Life of Her Own." *VietMagnet* (March 1997): 1–2.

Garvey, Hugh. "Writers on the Verge: lê thi diem thúy." *Voice Literary Supplement* 22 (June 2, 1998): 78–80.

de Jesús, Melinda L. "lê thi diem thúy." In Guiyou Huang, ed., *Asian American Poets: A Bio-Bibliographical Critical Sourcebook* (Westport, CT: Greenwood Press, 2002), 201–4.

Trotter, Mary. "Performance Review: The Fourth International Women Playwrights Conference." Rev. of *Red Fiery Summer*. *Theatre Journal* 49, no. 4 (December 1997): 532.

Uno, Roberta. "lê thi diem thúy." In Miles Xian Liu, ed., *Asian American Playwrights: A Bio-Bibliographical Critical Sourcebook* (Westport, CT: Greenwood Press, 2002), 170–74.

* * *

Ling-ai Li. See Li in "Autobiographies/Memoirs."

* * *

Genny Lim (1946–). A Chinese American playwright, poet, and editor, Lim was born in San Francisco to immigrant parents from Guangzhou (Canton), southern China. She attended Columbia University and received a certificate in broadcast journalism in 1973. After working different jobs for several years, Lim returned to school and earned a B.A. in theater arts in 1978 and then an M.A. in creative writing in 1988, both at San Francisco State University. Her studies led her to editing one of the most important anthologies in Chinese American history and literary history: *Island: Poetry and History of Chinese Immigrants on Angel Island, 1910–1940*, trans. Him Mark Lai and Judy Yung (San Francisco: San Francisco Study Center, 1980). Two other edited anthologies followed: *The Chinese American Experience: Papers from the Second National Conference on Chinese American Studies (1980)* (San Francisco: Chinese Historical Society of America, 1984), and *Unsilenced Voices: An Anthology of Poems* (San Francisco: Fine Arts Museum of San Francisco, 1991). A collection of her poetry came out in 1989, titled *Winter Place: Poems* (San Francisco: Kearny Street Workshop). Lim has also written and produced plays: *Paper Angels*, written in 1978 and premiered in 1980, was published in 1991, along with another piece, *Bitter Cane*, in *Paper Angels and Bitter Cane* (Honolulu: Kalamaku Press); *The Only Language*, an excerpt from the screenplay *The Only Language She Knows*, appeared in *Bamboo Ridge* 30 (1986): 34–41; *Pigeons*, in *Bamboo Ridge* 30 (1986): 57–79; and excerpts from *La China Poblana* in Amy Ling, ed., *Yellow Light: The Flowering of Asian American Arts* (Philadelphia: Temple University Press, 1999), 216–21. In addition, Lim has written about a dozen unpublished manuscripts.

Lim's list of awards includes the American Book Award for *Island: Poetry and History of Chinese Immigrants on Angel Island, 1910–1940;* the Downtown Village Award for *Paper Angels;* and the Distinguished Award for Culture from the San Francisco Chinese Culture Center Foundation, among other awards and recognitions for her performance and community work.

While Lim's *Pigeons, Winter Place, La China Poblana,* and *The Only Language She Knows* have received limited reviews of their productions, *Paper Angels* and *Bitter Cane* have been critically acclaimed. As its title suggests, *Paper Angels* is set in 1905 on Angel Island, the notorious detention center for Chinese immigrants for decades. The play examines the physical and psychic effects of detention, and more broadly, of the 1882 Exclusion Act designed to bar Chinese immigrants from entering the United States, on four male and three female Chinese immigrants who crossed the vast ocean with dreams of success, only to be detained and humiliated. *Bitter Cane* takes place in the sugarcane plantations of Hawai'i and explores the sojourner experience of Chinese laborers dealing with issues of family history, love, and honor as well as struggles and hardships of all kinds in an alien culture.

A good number of reviews of Lim's work are of her edited anthology *Island* and of her play *Paper Angels*; only a couple are of *Bitter Cane*. More substantial studies include:

Houston, Velina Hasu. "Genny Lim." In Houston, ed., *The Politics of Life: Four Plays by Asian American Women* (Philadelphia: Temple University Press, 1993), 151–62.
Lee, Josephine. *Performing Asian America: Race and Ethnicity on the Contemporary Stage.* Philadelphia: Temple University Press, 1997.
Liu, Miles Xian. "Genny Lim." In Liu, ed., *Asian American Playwrights: A Bio-Bibliographical Critical Sourcebook* (Westport, CT: Greenwood Press, 2002), 189–200.

* * *

Paul Stephen Lim (1944–). Born to Chinese parents in Manila, the Philippines, Lim emigrated to the United States when he was twenty-four years of age. He attended the University of Kansas for his B.A. (1970) and M.A. (1974), both in English. Lim wrote his first play, *Conpersonas*, in 1976, while he was working on a doctoral degree he did not finish, for he wanted to devote all his energy

to playwriting. He has written a dozen plays, of which eight have been published: *Conpersonas: A Recreation in Two Acts* (New York: Samuel French, 1977); excerpts of *Points of Departure: A Play in One Act*, *Bridge: An Asian American Perspective* 5, no. 2 (1977): 27–29; *Flesh, Flash and Frank Harris: A Recreation in Two Acts* (Louisville, KY: Aran Press, 1985); *Hatchet Club*, *Plays* 1, no. 1 (1985): 17–62; *Homerica: A Trilology on Sexual Liberation* (Louisville, KY: Aran Press, 1985); *Woeman: A New Play* (Louisville, KY: Aran Press, 1985); *Figures in Clay: A Threnody in Six Scenes and a Coda* (Louisville, KY: Aran Press, 1992); and *Mother Tongue: A Play* (Louisville, KY: Aran Press, 1992). His unpublished manuscripts include *Chambers: A Recreation in Four Parts* (1977), *Lee and the Boys in the Backroom: A Play in Two Acts* (1987, based on William Burroughs's novel *Queer*), and *Report to the River* (1997). Lim also coauthored *Zooks* with Steve Rice (1980). Lim is the recipient of a good number of awards and fellowships for his plays and short stories, including the highly prestigious Palanca Memorial Award for Literature from the Philippines in 1975, and a gold medallion from the Kennedy Center for his contribution to the theater in Region V of the ACTF (American College Theatre Festival) in 1996.

Lim is a Chinese Filipino American gay playwright and his work, with autobiographical elements, reflects his concerns with sexual relationships and with gender and racial politics. *Conpersonas* dramatizes these issues through suicide victim Miles Zeigler's relationships with three other characters: his male lover, his fiancée, and his twin brother. The play shows that a person's identity is defined by the relationships—sexual and/or social—that the individual cultivates and maintains. Homosexual relationships are the thematic focus of *Figures in Clay*. Set in Lawrence, Kansas, the play presents three gay men from three different generations and two races involved in a triangular relationship, with David Lee, a Chinese Filipino American, occupying the center. *Mother Tongue* utilizes the same setting and principal characters from *Figures in Clay*, as the two plays were written in the same time period. *Mother Tongue* examines the intersections of the dynamics of race, gender, sexual orientations, and profession, issues that affect the lifestyle of the Chinese Filipino American David Lee. A thematic shift occurs in *Report to the River*, a work that looks hard into crime and punishment that stir up a small midwestern town. Set by the Kaw River, which divides Lawrence, Kansas, the drama centers on the death of a young man, Mikey, at the hands of a homeless man, Jake. The conviction of the perpetrator, while bringing the case to a close, shows how a community can be divided in their perceptions of a crime, a division that is symbolized by the river, the crime scene to which all the police officers report.

For more information, see:

Biles, Jan. "Original Scripts Stun Audience." Rev. of *Report to the River*. *Lawrence Daily Journal-World*, October 10, 1997, 76.

Frank, Glenda. Rev. of *Flesh, Flash and Frank Harris*. *N.Y. Theatre Voice* (March 1984): 12.

Jones, John Bush. "Theater in Mid-America." Rev. of *Conpersonas*. *Kansas City Times*, October 30, 1975, n.p.

Komai, Chris. "Lim's Mother Tongue in Many Voices." *RAFU* (March 2, 1988): 1–2.

Liu, Miles Xian. "Paul Stephen Lim." In Liu, ed., *Asian American Playwrights: A Bio-Bibliographical Critical Sourcebook* (Westport, CT: Greenwood Press, 2002), 201–11.

Moore, Jim. "Points Is Sharp." Rev. of *Points of Departure*. *Los Angeles Herald Examiner*, November 3, 1977, B3.

Dwight Okita (1958–). *Sansei* Japanese American playwright and poet Okita was born in Chicago and attended the University of Illinois at Chicago, from which he earned a B.A. in creative writing in 1983. Okita's published plays include *The Rainy Season*, in Brian Nelson, ed., *Asian American Drama: 9 Plays from the Multiethnic Landscape* (New York: Applause, 1997), 209–62; with Anne V. McGravie, Nicholas A. Patricca, and David Zak, *The Radiance of a Thousand Suns: The Hiroshima Project: A Drama with Music* (Woodstock, IL: Dramatic Publishing Company, 1998); *Richard Speck*, in Amy Ling, ed., *Yellow Light: The Flowering of Asian American Arts* (Philadelphia: Temple University Press, 1999), 256–57; and *Asian Men on Asian Men: The Attraction*, in Amy Ling, ed., *Yellow Light: The Flowering of Asian American Arts* (Philadelphia: Temple University Press, 1999), 258–59. Among the unpublished manuscripts are *Dream/Fast* (1987), *Letters I Never Wrote* (1991), *The Salad Bowl Dance* (1993), *The Spirit Guide* (1994), and *My Last Week on Earth* (1998). Okita has also published a collection of poetry, *Crossing with the Light* (Chicago: Tia Chucha, 1992). His awards include an Illinois Arts Council fellowship for poetry.

Okita's work explores the experience of three types of Asian Americans: Japanese, gays, and women. *Richard Speck* features an Asian American woman who dreams of Richard Speck, the nurse killer who murdered three Asian American nurses.

The internment and return of a Japanese American woman to her Chicago home form the central plot of *The Salad Bowl Dance.* Gay love between a Japanese American man and a Brazilian man constitutes the main story line of *The Rainy Season. The Radiance of a Thousand Suns,* a collaborative work with three other authors, considers the effects of the nuclear age. Okita's poetry collection, *Crossing with the Light,* contains sixty poems that describe relationships of different kinds, among other subjects.

For more information, see:

Bommer, Lawrence. "'Rainy Season' Dries Up After First Act." *Chicago Tribune,* February 25, 1993, 13.

Chiu, Christina. "Dwight Okita." In *Lives of Notable Asian Americans: Literature and Education* (New York: Chelsea House, 1996), 107–13.

Han, John Jae-Nam. "Dwight Okita." In Miles Xian Liu, ed., *Asian American Playwrights: A Bio-Bibliographical Critical Sourcebook* (Westport, CT: Greenwood Press, 2002), 263–70.

Hayford, Justin. Rev. of *The Rainy Season. Reader* (February 26, 1993): 32.

Mauro, Lucia. Rev. of *The Radiance of a Thousand Suns: The Hiroshima Project: A Drama with Music. New City,* July 27, 1995, 31.

Smith, Sid. "'Monsters' Adds Up When Pieces Join Together." Rev. of *Richard Speck. Chicago Tribune,* November 20, 1991, 26.

Warburton, Richard. Rev. of *Dream/Fast. Windy City Times,* June 18, 1987, n.p.

Uma Parameswaran. See Parameswaran in "Poetry."

Dmae Roberts (1957–). Born in Taiwan to a Chinese mother and an American father, Roberts moved to the United States at age eight and grew up in Junction City, Oregon. She graduated from the University of Oregon with a B.A. in journalism in 1984. Roberts has written a great many radio productions, including *Legacies: Tales from America,* which was widely broadcast. Three of her plays have been produced and published: *Picasso in the Back Seat* (Seattle: Rain City Projects, 1995); *Breaking Glass,* in Velina Hasu Houston, ed., *But Still, Like Air, I'll Rise: New Asian American Plays* (Philadelphia: Temple University Press, 1997), 271–330; and *Tell Me, Janie Bigo,* with Brenna Sage (Portland: MediaRites, 1998). Her unpublished works—all but one have been staged—include *Mei Mei, a Daughter's Song* (1990), *Lady Buddha* (1997), and *Volcano Embrace* (1999). Roberts has received a number of awards, including the George Foster Peabody Award for the radio docuplay, *Mei Mei, a Daughter's Song;* the Portland Drama Critics Circle Award for Best Original Play and the Oregon Book Award for Best Play, both for *Picasso;* the United Nations Silver Award; and the Robert F. Kennedy Journalism Award, among other awards and fellowships.

Picasso in the Back Seat explores the relationship between arts and the consumer. Two thieves steal a Picasso painting called *Tete,* and the search for and recovery of the work have transformative effects on all the characters involved—the thieves, the curator, and a homeless woman. The play's moral dimensions dramatize the ability of art to transform and morally improve the human spirit. *Breaking Glass* is a more personal work that deals with domestic problems facing a mixed-race family: a Chinese mother, a Caucasian father, and two interracial children. The family not only struggles with domestic relationships but also has to deal with racism in the Oregon town of Junction City. While this play looks more into the father–son (Buddy and Jimmy) relationship, *Mei Mei, a Daughter's Song* focuses on the mother–daughter relationship (Mei Jen and Cyndy). *Lady Buddha*, whose title suggests mercy, demonstrates the need for compassion from all humans.

For more information, see:

Fitzgibbon, Joe. "Dmae Roberts Seeks Peace and Justice Through Drama." *Portland Oregonian*, October 1, 1998, 3.

Kantor, Jill. "Comedic Janie Bigo Can't Quite Hit Its Mark." *Portland Oregonian*, September 29, 1998, E4.

Storhoff, Gary. "Dmae Roberts." In Miles Xian Liu, ed., *Asian American Playwrights: A Bio-Bibliographical Critical Sourcebook* (Westport, CT: Greenwood Press, 2002), 298–302.

Watternberg, Richard. "Volcano Embrace Taps Tectonic Terrors." *Portland Oregonian*, November 12, 1999, E6.

S

Edward Sakamoto (1940–). Japanese Hawaiian playwright Sakamoto was born and raised in Honolulu. He graduated from the University of Hawai'i in 1962. Sakamoto wrote his first play, *In the Alley*, during his junior year in college; since then he has written fifteen more plays—all of which have been produced and seven of which have been published: *In the Alley*, in Dennis Carroll, ed., *Kumu Kahua Plays* (Honolulu: University of Hawai'i Press, 1983), 123–42; *The Life of the Land*, in Sakamoto, *Hawai'i No Ka Oi: The Kamiya Family Trilogy* (Honolulu: University of Hawai'i Press, 1995), 91–138; *Manoa Valley*, in *Hawai'i No Ka Oi: The Kamiya Family Trilogy* (Honolulu: University of Hawai'i Press, 1995), 49–90; *The Taste of Kona Coffee*, in *Hawai'i No Ka Oi: The Kamiya Family Trilogy* (Honolulu: University of Hawai'i Press, 1995), 1–46; *A'ala Park*, in Sakamoto, *Aloha Las Vegas and Other Plays* (Honolulu: University of Hawai'i Press, 2000), 25–70; *Aloha Las Vegas*, in *Aloha Las Vegas and Other Plays* (Honolulu: University of Hawai'i Press, 2000), 131–90; *Stew Rice*, in *Aloha Las Vegas and Other Plays* (Honolulu: University of Hawai'i Press, 2000), 71–130. Unpublished manuscripts are *Yellow Is My Favorite Color* (1972), *That's the Way the Fortune Cookie Crumbles* (1976), *Voices in the Shadows* (1978), *Pilgrimage* (1980), *Chikamatsu's Forest* (1986), *Our Hearts Were Touched with Fire* (1993), *Lava* (1997), and *Dead of the Night* (1999). For *Chikamatsu's Forest* and *Stew Rice*, Sakamoto was awarded two Hollywood Dramalogue Critic's awards, and for *Aloha Las Vegas* he received the Po'okela Award for Excellence in Original Script; in 1997 he received the Hawai'i Award for Literature.

Most of Sakamoto's plays are set in Hawai'i and about Hawai'i—including the collection named *Aloha Las Vegas*—and are often closely connected to the notion of home. *In the Alley* delves into the dynamics of racial conflict in Hawai'i. Departure from and return to the island and the accompanying physical and sentimental emotions about Hawai'i and the mainland inform the settings and characterizations of plays like *Stew Rice* and *The Life of the Land*. The characters' attempt to fit in on the mainland and the awkwardness of being treated as different in Hawai'i when they return create the dramatic tensions in these plays.

The majority of scholarly work on Sakamoto is reviews of productions:

Carroll, Dennis. "Sakamoto in the Theatre: Displaced Protagonists, Challenged Spectators." Introduction to *Aloha Las Vegas and Other Plays* (Honolulu: University of Hawai'i Press, 2000), 1–23.

Drake, Sylvie. "*Stew Rice*: Nostalgia and Reality." *Los Angeles Times,* January 11, 1988, Calendar, 6.

Novick, Julius. "Paradise Island." Rev. of *The Life of the Land. Village Voice* 32, no. 25 (1987): 98.

Odo, Franklin S. "Can You Go Home Again? Edward Sakamoto's Plays and Japanese Americans in Hawai'i." Foreword to *Hawai'i No Ka Oi: The Kamiya Family Trilogy* (Honolulu: University of Hawai'i Press, 1995), ix–xxv.

Huot, Nikolas. "Edward Sakamoto." In Miles Xian Liu, ed., *Asian American Playwrights: A Bio-Bibliographical Critical Sourcebook* (Westport, CT: Greenwood Press, 2002), 303–9.

Rozmiarek, Joseph T. "The Local Appeal of Las Vegas." Rev. of *Aloha Las Vegas. Honolulu Advertiser,* September 22, 1992, B3.

* * *

R. A. Shiomi (1947–). Born in Toronto, Canada, to parents of Japanese ancestry, Shiomi majored in history and received a B.A. from the University of Toronto in 1970; two years later, he completed a teaching certificate at Simon Fraser University. In 1992 he moved to Minneapolis, Minnesota, where he cofounded Theater Mu, which specializes in Asian American dramatic productions. Shiomi is best known for his play *Yellow Fever*, which premiered at San Francisco's Asian American Theater Company in 1982 and was published in Canada (Toronto: Playwrights Union of Canada, 1984), as well as in the United States, in Meg Swanson and Robin Murray, eds., *Playwrights of Color* (Yarmouth, ME: Intercultural Press, 1999), 657–86. Shiomi has also written and coauthored a dozen unpublished manuscripts; those that he wrote alone include *Prime Time* (1984), *Rosie's Café* (1985), *Play Ball* (1989), *Uncle Tadao* (1990), *Land of a Million Elephants* (1994), *The Raven in the Starfruit Tree* (1999), *The Tale of the Dancing Crane* (1999), and *The Song of the Pipa* (2000).

Some of Shiomi's work deals with Japanese Canadian themes. *Rosie's Café* depicts postinternment Japanese Canadian life of resistance and assimilation, *Play Ball* explores racism against Japanese Canadians, and *Uncle Tadao* dramatizes a Japanese American man's efforts to come to grips with the internment and his brother's suicide. *Land of a Million Elephants, River of Life,* and *The Raven in the Starfruit Tree* focus on Southeast Asian tales or characters, while *The Song of the Pipa,* incorporating the famous narrative poem of the same title by the Tang dynasty Chinese poet Bai Jüyi, portrays the life of a *pipa* player during the Cultural Revolution. *Yellow Fever,* Shiomi's most popular work, is a detective play set in Powell Street in Vancouver. The drama follows the Japanese Canadian Sam Shikaze's investigation of the kidnapping of the Cherry Blossom Queen. The investigative process exposes the ubiquitous presence of racism as well as the fears and tribulations Japanese Canadians are still going through, trying to recuperate from the internment trauma.

For more information, see:

Kaplan, Jon. "New York: Sam Shikaze, Private Eye." Interview with R. A. Shiomi. *Canadian Theatre Review* 46 (Spring 1986): 98–100.

Lee, Josephine D. "R. A. Shiomi." In Miles Xian Liu, ed., *Asian American*

Playwrights: A Bio-Bibliographical Critical Sourcebook (Westport, CT: Greenwood Press, 2002), 315–20.

——. "Between Immigration and Hyphenation: The Problems of Theorizing Asian American Theater." *Journal of Dramatic Theory and Criticism* 13, no. 1 (1998): 45–69.

——. "'Speaking a Language That We Both Understand': Reconciling Feminism and Cultural Nationalism in Asian American Theater." In Jeffrey D. Mason and J. Ellen Gainor, eds., *Performing America: Cultural Nationalism in American Theater* (Ann Arbor: University of Michigan Press, 1999), 139–59.

Oliver, Edith. Rev. of *Rosie's Café. The New Yorker* (October 26, 1987): 130.

——. Rev. of *Yellow Fever. Contractor* 30 (1983): 86.

Swanson, Meg and Robin Murray. "Introduction to *Yellow Fever*." In Swanson and Murray, eds., *Playwrights of Color* (Yarmouth, ME: Intercultural Press, 1999), 641–56.

* * *

Diana Son (1965–). Korean American playwright Son was born in Philadelphia and raised in Dover, Delaware. She went to New York University to study dramatic literature; in June 1987, the year she graduated, La Mama Experimental Theatre Club, where she was interning, staged her play *Wrecked on Brecht*, which launched her career as a playwright. Son's published plays include *R.A.W* (*'Cause I'm a Woman*), in Kathy A. Perkins and Roberta Uno, eds., *Contemporary Plays by Women of Color: An Anthology* (New York: Routledge, 1996), 290–96; excerpts of *BOY*, in Stephen Vincent Brennan, ed., *New Voices of the American Theater* (New York: Henry Holt, 1997), 110–15; *Happy Birthday Jack*, in Michael Bigelow Dixon and Amy Wegener, eds., *Humana Festival '99: The Complete Plays* (Lyme, NH: Smith and Krause, 1999), 355–58; and *Stop Kiss* (Woodstock, NY: Overlook Press, 1999). Son has also written five unpublished manuscripts: *Wrecked on Brecht* (1987), *Stealing Fire* (1992), *The Joyless Bad Luck Club* (1993), *2000 Miles* (1993), and *Fishes* (1995). The awards she has received include the GLAAD (Gay and Lesbian Alliance Against Defamation) Media Award for Outstanding New York Theatre Production on Broadway or Off-Broadway, and the Berilla Kerr Award for Playwriting.

Son's most frequently staged works are her three full-length plays, *R.A.W.* (*'Cause I'm a Woman*), *BOY*, and *Stop Kiss*, and like some of her other works, these pieces address women's, especially ethnic women's, issues. *R.A.W.* exposes the falsity of demeaning stereotypes of Asian American women. The stereotypical images of Asian women as geishas, exotic virgins, china dolls, and suicidal Miss Saigons are turned inside out and subverted to vivify the women's individual humanity as well as to show the diversity of their experiences and backgrounds. Also subversive is *BOY*, a dramatic satire of blatant sexism and socially constructed gender identity. Mama and Papa Uber Alles, having had three daughters, wish to have a son but get a fourth daughter instead. Naming the girl "Boy" and pretending she is male sets up the stage for confused gender identity and its social consequences. The complexity of gender identity is examined again in *Stop Kiss*, another play that centers on women characters, from the perspective of two female lovers, Callie and Sara. Their kiss, being witnessed by a man, feeds questions about gender identity as well as identity in general.

For more information, see:

Ascheim, Skip. "Playwright Diana Son in Search of Identity." *Boston Globe*, March 5, 2000, N9.

Berson, Misha. "The 'Kiss' of Success: Diana Son Embraces Her Good Fortune Writing for Stage and Television." *Seattle Times,* January 20, 2000, G26.

Janich, Kathy. "A Conversation with *Stop Kiss* Playwright Diana Son." *Atlantic Journal and Constitution,* April 21, 2000, 6Q.

Kim, Esther S. "Diana Son." In Miles Xian Liu, ed., *Asian American Playwrights: A Bio-Bibliographical Critical Sourcebook* (Westport, CT: Greenwood Press, 2002), 321–27.

Steele, Mike. "*BOY* Explores Cultural Construction of Gender." *Star Tribune* (Minneapolis), April 30, 1999, 5E.

Winer, Laurie. "'BOY's Search Leads Down a Funny but Rocky Path." *Los Angeles Times,* June 19, 1996, F1.

Elizabeth Wong (1958–). Chinese American playwright Wong was born in South Gate, California, and grew up in Los Angeles Chinatown. She graduated from the University of Southern California with a degree in journalism in 1980. Having worked for eight years as a news reporter for television and then for newspapers, she took playwriting classes at the Yale School of Drama before she was accepted into the Tisch School of the Arts at New York University, from which she earned an M.F.A. in playwriting in 1991. The key that opened the door to NYU was a drama script that she was required to write, titled *The Aftermath of a Chinese Banquet.* Two other plays, her best known to date, were also written during her time at Tisch: *Letters to a Student Revolutionary,* written in 1989 and published in 1993, in Roberta Uno, ed., *Unbroken Thread: An Anthology of Plays by Asian American Women* (Amherst: University of Massachusetts Press, 1993), 261–308; and *Kimchee and Chitlins,* written in 1990 and published in 1996 (Woodstock, IL: Dramatic Publishing Company).

Wong's other published plays include *Assume the Position, Script Magazine* (1990):42–84; excerpts of *China Doll,* in Kathy Perkins and Roberta Uno, eds., *Contemporary Plays by Women of Color: An Anthology* (New York: Routledge, 1996), 310–16; *Let the Big Dog Eat,* in Michael Bigelow Dixon and Amy Wegener, eds., *Humana Festival '98: The Complete Plays* (Lyme, NH: Smith and Krause, 1998), 357–67; *Inside a Red Envelop,* in Michael Wright, ed., *Playwriting Master Class: The Personality of Processes and the Art of Rewriting* (Portsmouth, NH: Heinemann, 2000), 15–27; and *Punk Girls: On Divine Omnipotence and the Longstanding Nature of Evil,* in Kent Brown, ed., *Scenes and Monologues for Young Actors* (Woodstock, IL: Dramatic Publishing Company, 2000), 229–31. For a short while Wong was a staff writer for the television program *All-American Girl,* which starred the Korean American comedian Margaret Cho. In addition, about a dozen of Wong's drama manuscripts remain unpublished. Wong has received numerous awards and prizes, including the Playwright Forum Award from Theatre Works in Colorado Springs in 1990 and the Association for Theatre in Higher Education's Jane Chambers Award in 1995.

The themes of Wong's work range wide. *Punk Girls,* for example, probes the minds of postadolescents about their understanding of the existence of evil. *Let the Big Dog Eat* pokes fun at Ted Turner's generous contribution to the United Nations. *China Doll* is about the Chinese American actress Anna May Wong pursuing the Hollywood dream, interwoven with a critique of racism and sexism. But the more popular piece that delves deep into race issues is *Kimchee and Chitlins*. Set in Brooklyn, New York, the play investigates the racial tensions between Korean Americans and African Americans. Even though the protagonist, Suzie Seeto, is Chinese American, the conflict hinges on Brooklyn's black community's boycott of Korean grocers, behind which is a web of racial, cultural, and economic entanglements. Wong's most acclaimed play, however, remains *Letters to a Student Revolutionary*, a work based on her own personal experience corresponding with a woman in China and on one of the most heart-wrenching events in contemporary Chinese political history, the 1989 Tiananmen Square massacre. The first dramatic work in America to respond to the bloody events in Beijing, the play chronicles the decade-long correspondence between Bibi, a Chinese American woman news reporter, and Karen, a young Chinese woman, which suddenly ceases after the massacre. The course of their correspondence dramatizes how American and Chinese understanding or misunderstanding of values such as freedom and democracy—things that the students in Tiananmen demanded, and for which some died—are exposed, questioned, and reevaluated.

For more information, see:

Bommer, Lawrence. "Culture Clash." Rev. of *Kimchee and Chitlins*. *Chicago Tribune*, May 6, 1993, 511C.

Collins, Scott. "'Kimchee, Chitlins' Leaves a Mixed Taste." Rev. of *Kimchee and Chitlins*. *Los Angeles Times*, July 29, 1994, F25.

Feingold, Michael. "Savage Tongue." Rev. of *Letters to a Student Revolutionary*. *Village Voice* 36, no. 22 (1991): 99.

Foley, Kathleen F. "Striking *Letters to a Student Revolutionary*." Rev. of *Letters to a Student Revolutionary*. *Los Angeles Times*, May 13, 1994, F16.

Gussow, Mel. "Letters Across a Cultural Divide." Rev. of *Letters to a Student Revolutionary*. *The New York Times*, May 16, 1991, current events ed., C18.

Kaplan, Randy Barbara. "Elizabeth Wong." In Miles Xian Liu, ed., *Asian American Playwrights: A Bio-Bibliographical Critical Sourcebook* (Westport, CT: Greenwood Press, 2002), 347–60.

Lee, Josephine. "Asian American Doubles and the Soul Under Capitalism." In Lee, *Performing Asian America: Race and Ethnicity on the Contemporary Stage* (Philadelphia: Temple University Press, 1997), 163–88.

Torres, Vicki. "Prophetic Drama Evokes Some Jitters." Rev. of *Kimchee and Chitlins*. *Los Angeles Times*, May 26, 1992, B3.

Uno, Roberta. "Introduction to *Letters to a Student Revolutionary*." In Uno, ed., *Unbroken Thread: An Anthology of Plays by Asian American Women* (Amherst: University of Massachusetts Press, 1993), 261–63.

* * *

Merle Woo (1941–). A Chinese/Korean American playwright and poet, Woo was born in San Francisco to a Chinese-born father and an American-born Korean mother. Woo attended Catholic schools and San Francisco State University, from which she earned a B.A. in English in 1965. While pursuing graduate studies, Woo witnessed the Third World Student Strikes. In 1969 she completed her M.A. in English. Woo has taught at San Francisco State and the University of California at Berkeley, where she has been active in gay/lesbian issues and with the Freedom Socialist Party. Woo's involvement in drama started with a performing role in Lonny Kaneko's play *Lady Is*

Dying in 1977. Around this time Woo, Nellie Wong, and Kitty Tsui formed a performance group called Unbound Feet Three; they split in 1981. In 1979 Woo published a play, *Home Movies: A Dramatic Monologue*, in Karen Brodine, ed., 3 *Asian American Writers Speak Out on Feminism*, by Nellie Wong, Merle Woo, and Mitsuye Yamada (San Francisco: SF Radical Women, 1979); act 1, scene 1 of *Balancing* was published in Asian American Studies, ed., *Hanai: An Anthology of Asian American Writings* (Berkeley: Asian American Studies, UC-Berkeley Department of Ethnic Studies, 1980). In 1986 Woo published a collection of poetry titled *Yellow Woman Speaks: Selected Poems* (Seattle: Radical Women Publications).

Home Movies, an outcry against both sexism and racism, takes the form of a monologue spoken by an elderly woman who is watching a black-and-white film in a convalescent hospital; as she watches a white man sexually assault a young Asian woman, she reminisces about her own experience of abuse by her former employer. Woo's other play, *Balancing*, deals with the struggles for love and acceptance between a mother and her teenage daughter. Woo's poetry collection, *Yellow Woman Speaks*, explores similar issues and topics: women's experience, feminism, immigration blues, identity politics, and lesbianism. Some pieces—"The Subversive: For Nellie Wong," for example—are about fellow poets and friends who share Woo's feminist cause, and some focus on family figures, such as "For Dick Woo (Woo Nay)," for her father, and "Korea," for her aunt. The title poem likens the yellow woman to a powerful beast that vows to fight the abuse and exploitation of Asian women.

For more information, see:

Clarke, Janet Hyunju. "Merle Woo." In Miles Xian Liu, ed., *Asian American Playwrights: A Bio-Bibliographical Critical Sourcebook* (Westport, CT: Greenwood Press, 2002), 361–66.

Hayes, Loie B. "Merle Woo." In Christa Brelin and Michael J. Tyrkus, eds., *Outstanding Lives: Profiles of Lesbians and Gay Men* (Detroit: Visible Ink Press, 1997), 389–92.

——. "Merle Woo." In Michael J. Tyrkus, ed., *Gay and Lesbian Biography* (Detroit: St. James Press, 1997), 464–65.

Huang, Su-ching. "Merle Woo." In Guiyou Huang, ed., *Asian American Poets: A Bio-Bibliographical Critical Sourcebook* (Westport, CT: Greenwood Press, 2002), 323–29.

"Merle Woo." In Frank V. Castronova, ed., *Almanac of Famous People*, 6th ed., vol. 1 (Detroit: Gale, 1998), 1808.

Wakako Yamauchi (1924–). *Nisei* Japanese American playwright Yamauchi was born and raised in Westmoreland, in the Imperial Valley of Southern California. Like her lifelong friend, short story writer Hisaye Yamamoto, during World War II, she and her family were interned at Poston, Arizona; her father died there. Yamauchi received some high school education but no formal training in creative writing, though she studied screenwriting briefly with the Writers Guild of America's Open Door Project. She had always enjoyed the stories her mother told her about her Japanese heritage, as well as the many stories and poems she read in her youth. She found playwriting a useful form of creative expression because plays performed on stage offer the opportunity to engage the audience and connect with them.

Yamauchi's first play, *And the Soul Shall Dance*, initially written as a short story published in 1966, was adapted into a play and first produced at Los Angeles's East West Players in 1977. Excerpts were published in 1978, and the full version appeared in Rick Foster, ed., *West Coast Plays* 11–12 (Berkeley: California Theatre Council, 1982), 117–64. Other plays followed in the 1990s: *The Music Lesson*, premiered at the New York Public Theater in 1980, was published in 1993, in Roberta Uno, ed., *Unbroken Thread: An Anthology of Plays by Asian American Women* (Amherst: University of Massachusetts Press, 1993), 53–104. *12–1–A*, first produced in 1982, and *The Chairman's Wife*, premiered in 1990, were both published in Velina Hasu Houston, ed., *Politics of Life: Four Plays by Asian American Women* (Philadelphia: Temple University Press, 1993), 45–100, 101–49. Yamauchi's unpublished manuscripts include *Shirley Temple Hotcha* (1977), *Not a Through Street* (1981), *The Trip* (1982), *A Good Time* (1983), *The Memento* (1983), *Songs That Made the Hit Parade* (1988), and *Stereoscope I: Taj Mahal* (1988). In addition, she has published *Songs My Mother Taught Me: Stories, Plays, and Memoir*, edited by Garrett Hongo (New York: Feminist Press, 1994).

Almost all of Yamauchi's writings are concerned with Japanese American history, immigration, and rural farming; World War II imprisonment; and postwar readjustment. *And the Soul Shall Dance* tells the story of two farming families—the Muratas and the Okas—that face the challenges of survival during the Great Depression years in Southern California. The families struggle not only to cope with intergenerational tensions (*issei* and *nisei*) domestically but also to balance their life in America with their nostalgic views of Japanese traditions. Based on her short story "In Heaven and Earth" and set in a farming community, *The Music Lesson* continues the theme of survival, but it also probes the mother-daughter relationship complicated by the added pressure of sexual awakening in Aki, the adolescent daughter of Chizuko Sakata, a widow mother, as the two negotiate their own relationship and their feelings for Kawaguchi, a migrant worker. *12–1–A*, set in Poston, Arizona, in 1942, the year Yamauchi and her family were interned in the same locale, deals with the Japanese American experience at internment camps. The play traces the experiences of three families—the Tanakas, the Yoshidas, and the Ichiokas—all of whom live in barrack 12–1–A, and all of whom are forced to endure filthy conditions on a daily basis while struggling with confused notions of citizenship and cultural identity. The irony they face is the fact that while *nisei* males such as Ken Ichioka enlist to defend their country, their *issei* parents remain incarcerated in the camps; thus the characters live amid alternations of hope and despair until the play's curtain falls. While Yamauchi's other works delve into the Japanese American experience during and after the war, *The Chairman's Wife* shifts to late-twentieth-century China and chronicles the life of Chiang Ching, the widow of Chairman Mao Tse-tung. Set against the backdrop of Chinese students' prodemocracy demonstrations in Tiananmen Square, the play moves back and forth in time to examine the different periods in Chiang Ching's career and trace her rise to power and subsequent fall. Along the way, it explores the effects she has had on present-day Chinese politics and culture.

For more information, see:

Arnold, Stephanie. "Producing *And the Soul Shall Dance*." In Arnold, ed., *The Creative Spirit* (Mountain View, CA: Mayfield, 1998), 151–64.

Berson, Misha. "Wakako Yamauchi." In Berson, ed., *Between Worlds: Contemporary Asian American*

Plays (New York: Theatre Communications Group, 1990), 128–31.

Holden, Stephen. "Trying to Adapt to Inhospitable Terrain." Rev. of *And the Soul Shall Dance. The New York Times,* March 25, 1990, late edition, 63.

Houston, Velina Hasu. "Wakako Yamauchi." In Houston, ed., *The Politics of Life: Four Plays by Asian American Women* (Philadelphia: Temple University Press, 1993), 33–43.

McDonald, Dorothy Ritsuko and Katherine Newman. "Relocation and Dislocation: The Writings of Hisaye Yamamoto and Wakako Yamauchi." *MELUS* 7, no. 3 (1980): 21–38.

Osborn, William P. and Sylvia Watanabe. "A *MELUS* Interview: Wakako Yamauchi." *MELUS* 23, no. 2 (1998): 101–10.

Partnow, Elaine T. and Lesley Anne Hyatt. "Wakako Yamauchi." In Partnow and Hyatt, *The Female Dramatist: Profiles of Women Playwrights from the Middle Ages to Contemporary Times* (New York: Facts on File, 1998), 223–24.

Pollard, Lauren Ray. "12–1–A: Revisiting the Internment Tragedy." *Seattle Times,* October 17, 1995, final edition, F4.

Sugano, Douglas I. "Wakako Yamauchi." In Miles Xian Liu, ed., *Asian American Playwrights: A Bio-Bibliographical Critical Sourcebook* (Westport, CT: Greenwood Press, 2002), 367–76.

Sumida, Stephen H. "*And the Soul Shall Dance,* by Wakako Yamauchi." In Sau-ling Cynthia Wong and Stephen H. Sumida, eds., *A Resource Guide to Asian American Literature* (New York: MLA, 2001), 221–32.

Uno, Roberta. "Wakako Yamauchi." In Uno, ed., *Unbroken Thread: An Anthology of Plays by Asian American Women* (Amherst: University of Massachusetts Press, 1993), 53–58.

Wood, Joe. "Cameos: *And the Soul Shall Dance.*" *Village Voice* 35, no. 14 (1990): 110.

Yogi, Stan. "Rebels and Heroines: Subversive Narratives in the Stories of Wakako Yamauchi and Hisaye Yamamoto." In Shirley Geok-lin Lim and Amy Ling, eds., *Reading the Literatures of Asian America* (Philadelphia: Temple University Press, 1992), 131–50.

* * *

Laurence Michael Yep (1948–). A third-generation Chinese American playwright, novelist, and writer of children's books, Yep was born in San Francisco and raised in a predominantly poor black neighborhood. In 1966 Yep enrolled at Marquette University, Wisconsin, to study journalism but left to attend the University of California at Santa Cruz, from which he received a B.A. in 1970. He went on to pursue graduate studies at the State University of New York at Buffalo and earned a Ph.D. in 1975, the same year that he published his well-received chidlren's book, *Dragonwings* (New York: Harper, 1973), one of more than thirty-three children's books he produced between 1973 and 1997, when he published *The Khan's Daughter* (New York: Scholastic). While Yep seems more recognizable as a children's book writer, he has written three novels: *Seademons* (New York: Harper, 1977), *Shadow Lord* (New York: Pocket, 1985), and *Monster Makers, Inc.* (New York: Arbor House, 1986). Yep's prose work also includes a few short stories. As a playwright, Yep has produced work of considerable quality. *Pay the Chinaman* premiered in 1987 in San Francisco and was published in Misha Berson, ed., *Between Worlds: Contemporary Asian-American Plays* (New York: Theatre

Communications Group, 1990), 180–96. *Dragonwings* was first staged in Berkeley, California, and published in *American Theatre* 9, no. 5 (1992): 1–13. *Fairy Bones* premiered at Zephyr Theater in San Francisco and has not been published.

Pay the Chinaman is a play about survival and deals with two Chinamen who both cheat, one named Con Man and the other, Young Man. Set in the last two decades of the nineteenth century, when anti-Chinese sentiment ran high and violence was rampant, the play shows Chinese men's suffering poverty caused by lack of employment and racial discrimination. Both Chinamen in the play cheat to get each other's money while coping with their past and struggling with the present. The play *Dragonwings* was adapted from one of Yep's eight children's books that deal with dragons in some form (the titles of these books all include the word "dragon"). As in the earlier play, Yep does not use realistic names for the characters in *Dragonwings*: in the early decades of the twentieth century, Moon Shadow, an adult now, talks about his life with his mother in China two decades earlier, and tells the audience about his father, Windrider, who makes a living working in his uncle Bright Star's laundry in San Francisco in the United States. After Moon Shadow joins his father, the two start to make Windrider's dream of building and flying a plane come true, though the plane's crash and Windrider's injury thwart their success in the land of opportunities. The play also explores the topic of racial harmony as the principal characters build friendships outside of their own ethnic enclave and find employment with whites that enables them to settle down in their adopted land.

For more information, see:

Erstein, Hap. "Dragonwings Lift Youngsters to Joys of Books." *Washington Times,* October 20, 1992, final edition, E4.

Johnson-Feelings, Dianne. *Presenting Laurence Yep.* New York: Twayne, 1995.

"Laurence (Michael) Yep." In Jean C. Stein, Daniel G. Marowski, and Sharon R. Gunton, eds., *Contemporary Literary Criticism,* vol. 35 (Detroit: Gale, 1985), 468–74.

Liu, Fiona Feng-Hsin. "Images of Chinese-Americans and Images of Child-Readers in Three of Laurence Yep's Fictions." Ph.D. diss., Pennsylvania State University, 1998.

Mehan, Uppinder. "Laurence Michael Yep." In Miles Xian Liu, ed., *Asian American Playwrights: A Bio-Bibliographical Critical Sourcebook* (Westport, CT: Greenwood Press, 2002), 377–83.

Sarver, Linda. "Between Worlds: *The Sound of a Voice* and *Pay the Chinaman.*" *Theatre Journal* 47, no. 1 (1995): 145–48.

4. Fiction

Meena Alexander. See Alexander in "Poetry."

Peter Bacho. See Bacho in "Short Fiction."

* * *

Himani Bannerji (1942–). Born in Gangatia, the Mymensingh district of present-day Bangladesh, Bannerji went to school first in Dhaka and then in Calcutta. She earned a B.A. from Visva Bharati in Santiniketan and an M.A. in English from Jadavpur University in Calcutta. In 1969 Bannerji immigrated to Canada; in 1970 she completed a second M.A. in English at the University of Toronto, where she started a Ph.D. program in sociology in 1980 and completed it in 1988, with a dissertation titled "The Politics of Representation: A Study of Class and Class Struggle in the Theatre of West Bengal," which turned into a book titled *Mirror of Class: Essays on Political Theatre* (Calcutta: University of Calcutta Press, 1998).

While she continues to publish in the field of her doctoral specialization, Bannerji has devoted a great deal of creative energy to writing fiction and poetry. Her first novel, *The Two Sisters*, was published in 1978 (Toronto: Kids Can Press); a collection of poems, *A Separate Sky*, in 1982 (Toronto: Domestic Bliss); and a second collection, *Doing Time*, in 1986 (Toronto: Sister Vision Press). Her sec-ond novel, *Coloured Pictures*, did not come out until 1991 (Toronto: Sister Vision Press). In addition to novels and poetry, Bannerji has written short stories and essays. Though she has not produced a short story collection, she has published several volumes of essays, including *The Writing on the Wall: Essays on Culture and Politics* (Toronto: TSAR, 1993), *Thinking Through: Essays on Feminism, Marxism, and Anti-Racism* (Toronto: Women's Press, 1995), *The Dark Side of the Nation: Essays on Multiculturalism, Nationalism, and Gender* (Toronto: Canadian Scholars' Press, 2000), *Jibanananda, Sudhindranath* (Essays on Modern Bengali Poetry) (Calcutta: Dey's Publishing, 2000), and *Inventing Subjects: Studies in Hegemony, Patriarchy and Colonialism* (New Delhi: Tulika, 2001). She also coauthored (with Linda Carty, Kari Dehli, Susan Heald, and Kate McKenna) *Unsettling Relations: The University as a Site of Feminist Struggle* (Toronto: Women's Press, 1992). Besides, Bannerji has edited *Returning the Gaze: Essays on Racism, Feminism and Politics* (Toronto: Sister Vision Press, 1993), and coedited (with S. Mojab and J. Whitehead) *Of Property and Propriety: The Role of Gender and Class in Imperialism and National-*

ism (Toronto: University of Toronto Press, 2001).

Bannerji is difficult to categorize, as she seems equally known for her novels, poetry, essays, and short stories. Literary critics have, however, focused their studies on her novels and poetry. Her first novel, *The Two Sisters*, containing folktales in Bengali and English, has now gone out of print. Her second, *Coloured Pictures*, has received a little more critical attention. Written for younger audiences, the novel narrates the story of a thirteen-year-old South Asian girl named Sujata and her social studies teacher, Stephen Stephenson, as they struggle against cultural stereotyping and racially motivated violence. Bannerji's poetry echoes many themes she explores in her novels and critical essays. *A Separate Sky*, a collection of twenty-five of her own poems and eight translations from Bengali, examines aspects of Canada's multiculturalism. The poems in *Doing Time* broaden and deepen issues raised in the earlier volume by looking into immigration, genders, ethnicities, patriarchy, and imperialism.

Bannerji's multigenre versatility and high productivity have not garnered a commensurate level of critical acclaim. While some reviews of her books exist, the majority of *Unsettling Relations: The University as a Site of Feminist Struggles*, reviews of her novels and poetry are limited. A few article-length studies are valuable sources:

Chakraborty, Chandrima. "Himani Bannerji." In Guiyou Huang, ed., *Asian American Poets: A Bio-Bibliographical Critical Sourcebook* (Westport, CT: Greenwood Press, 2002), 37–44.

——. "Himani Bannerji." In Guiyou Huang, ed., *Asian American Short Story Writers: An A-To-Z Guide* (Westport, CT: Greenwood Press, 2003), 5–10.

Jacob, Susan. "Breaking the Circle: Recreating the Immigrant Self in Selected Works of Himani Bannerji." In Coomi S. Vevaina and Barbara Godard, eds., *Intersexions: Issues of Race and Gender in Canadian Women's Writing* (New Delhi: Creative, 1996), 189–96.

Kain, Geoffrey. "Himani Bannerji." In Emmanuel Nelson, ed., *Asian American Novelists: A Bio-Bibliographical Critical Sourcebook* (Westport, CT: Greenwood Press, 2000), 8–12.

Kumar, Alka. "Voicing the Other: Himani Bannerji's Poetics of Protest." *Central Institute of English and Foreign Languages Bulletin* 9, no. 1 (June 1997): 99–112.

Shahani, Roshan G. "'Some Kind of Weapon': Himani Bannerji and the Praxis of Resistance." In Coomi S. Vevaina and Barbara Godard, eds., *Intersexions: Issues of Race and Gender in Canadian Women's Writing* (New Delhi: Creative, 1996), 179–88.

* * *

Cecilia Manguerra Brainard (1947–). The youngest of four children born and raised on the island of Cebu in the central Philippines, Brainard enjoyed a happy, affluent childhood, but her idyllic life was disrupted by the death of her engineer father, a loss that she coped with by writing a diary. Brainard went to Maryknoll College in Quezon City in 1964 and received a B.A. in communication arts in 1968; the following year she immigrated to the United States, partly to escape the oppressive dictatorship of the Ferdinand Marcos regime, and started graduate school at UCLA to study film. She worked different jobs, including public relations and fund raising, before she started to write columns for the *Philippine American News*, which she did from 1981 until 1988. She also wrote essays that were collected and published in *Philip-*

pine Woman in America (Quezon City: New Day, 1991), as well as pieces in various periodicals. *Song of Yvonne*, her first novel, was published in 1991 (Quezon City: New Day); in the United States, it was published as *When the Rainbow Goddess Wept* in 1994 by Dutton, and then reprinted in 1995 by Plume in New York. Besides essays and novels, Brainard has written and edited collections of short fiction. Her own stories were collected in *Woman with Horns and Other Stories* (Quezon City: New Day, 1987), and in *Acapulco on Sunset and Other Stories* (Manila: Anvil, 1995). Her edited works include *Seven Stories from Seven Sisters: A Collection of Philippine Folktales* (Los Angeles: Philippine American Women Writers and Artists, 1992), *Fiction by Filipinos in America* (Quezon City: New Day, 1993), *The Beginning and Other Asian Folktales* (Los Angeles: Philippine American Women Writers and Artists, 1995), *Contemporary Fiction by Filipinos in America* (Manila: Anvil, 1997), and *Growing up Filipino: Stories for Young Adults* (Santa Monica, CA: PALH, 2003). Brainard coed-ited, with Edmundo F. Litton, *Journey of 100 Years: Reflections on the Centennial of Philippine Independence* (Santa Monica: Philippine American Women Writers and Artists, 1999).

Brainard is a recipient of a number of awards, including the 1985 Fortner Prize for her stories, a California Arts Council Artists' Fellowship in Fiction in 1989, and the Outstanding Individual Award from the City of Cebu in 1997.

Song of Yvonne has its historical setting in World War II, when the Philippines was occupied by the Japanese and was experiencing all kinds of atrocities. The story is presented through the eyes of a young girl who goes through the ordeal along with her people and her country. Brainard's short story collection, *Acapulco at Sunset and Other Stories*, narrates the life story of a Filipina living in Mexico. Even though Brainard is one of the most prolific contemporary Filipina American writers, scholarship on her novels and short stories is yet to develop. A few reviews of her works, interviews, and a biographical essay are available. See:

Aubry, Erin. "A Child's Vision of Life During Wartime." *Los Angeles Times,* November 15, 1994, E-8.

Beltran, Marie G. "Woman with Stories and Other Concerns." *Filipinas* (May 1995): 29, 56.

Casper, Leonard. Rev. of *Song of Yvonne. Philippine Studies* 41 (2nd Quarter 1993): 251–53.

Cruz, Isagani R. "The Pleasures of Ubec, Otherwise Known as Cebu." *Starweek: The Sunday Magazine of the Philippine Star,* October 29, 1995, 20.

Huebler, Dana. "An Interview with Cecilia Manguerra Brainard." *Poets and Writers Magazine* (March–April 1997): 96–105.

Otano, Alicia Otano. "Cecilia Manguerra Brainard." In Guiyou Huang, ed., *Asian American Short Story Writers: An A-to-Z Guide* (Westport, CT: Greenwood Press, 2003), 17–21.

Ty, Eleanor. "Cecilia Manguerra Brainard." In Emmanuel Nelson, ed., *Asian American Novelists: A Bio-Bibliographical Critical Sourcebook* (Westport, CT: Greenwood Press, 2000), 29–33.

* * *

Carlos Bulosan. See Bulosan in "Autobiographies/Memoirs."

Theresa Hak Kyung Cha (1951–1982). Born in Pusan, Korea, and killed by an unknown assailant in New York, Cha lived a very short but productive life as a writer and performer. The Cha family moved to Hawaiʻi in 1962, then relocated in 1964 to San Francisco, where Theresa attended the Catholic School Convent of the Sacred Heart. For college she first went to the University of San Francisco and then the University of California at Berkeley, where she studied ceramics and performance but received a B.A. in comparative literature in 1973 and a second B.A. in art in 1975. Her interest in film and art took her to Paris to study film theory in 1976. Cha returned to Berkeley to complete an M.A. in 1977 and an M.F.A. in art in 1978. She became a naturalized U.S. citizen in 1977 and moved to New York in 1980 to work as an editor and writer for Tanam Press. In 1981 she received a National Endowment for the Arts Fellowship for a film project that took her to Korea. In 1980, Tanam published a collection of articles on film theory edited by Cha, titled *Apparatus: Cinematographic Apparatus: Selected Writings;* the same press published her autobiographical novel, *Dictee,* in 1982, the year that she married her husband and was tragically killed at age thirty-one.

Cha's only full-length book, *Dictee* has been studied as both a novel and an autobiography, but the work does not fit squarely into either category. It is not a linear narrative with a sustained plot, nor is it a conventional autobiography that deals with the life of one subject, for it contains French and English dictation (hence the title), letters, maps, history, and photographs, and it is written in three languages: English, French, and Chinese. The experiment with both the language and the form has led critics to use terms like "postmodern" and "postcolonial" to describe its style and content. The power and limits of language, the function of memory in self-representation, histories and diasporas of the Korean people, and the fluidity or fragmented nature of national and personal identities all converge in this slim volume, making *Dictee* a rich, multilayered work rarely found in the canons of mainstream American or Asian American literature.

Though *Dictee* is the only book Cha wrote during her short life, it went from oblivion following the years of its publication in 1982 (out of print until 1994) to a resurrection of critical interest in the early 1990s to being one of the most studied works in Asian American literature. For more information, see:

Chang, Juliana. "Transforming This Nothingness: Theresa Hak Kyung Cha's *Dictee.*" *Critical Mass* 1, no. 1 (1993): 75–82.

Kang, Laura Hyun Yi. "The 'Liberatory Voice' of Theresa Hak Kyung Cha's *Dictee.*" In Elaine H. Kim and Norma Alarcon, eds., *Writing Self/Writing Nation: Essays on Theresa Hak Kyung Cha's* Dictee (Berkeley, CA: Third Woman Press, 1994), 73–99.

——. "*Dictee*, by Theresa Hak Kyung Cha," in Sau-ling Cynthia Wong and Stephen H. Sumida, eds., *A Resource Guide to Asian American Literature* (New York: MLA, 2001), 32–44.

Kim, Elaine H. "Poised on the In-between: A Korean American's Reflections on Theresa Hak Kyung Cha's *Dictee.*" In Elaine H. Kim and Norma Alarcon, eds., *Writing Self/Writing Nation: Essays on Theresa Hak Kyung Cha's* Dictee (Berkeley, CA: Third Woman Press, 1994), 3–30.

Lin, Yi-Chun Tricia. "Theresa Hak Kyung Cha." In Emmanuel S. Nelson, ed., *Asian American Novelists: A Bio-Bibliographical Critical Sourcebook* (Westport, CT: Greenwood Press, 2000), 34–37.

Lowe, Lisa. "Unfaithful to the Original: The Subject of *Dictee.*" In Elaine H. Kim and Norma Alarcon, eds., *Writing Self/Writing Nation: Essays on Theresa Hak Kyung Cha's* Dictee

(Berkeley, CA: Third Woman Press, 1994), 35–69.

Martin, Stephen-Paul. "Theresa Cha: Creating a Feminine Voice." In *Open Form and the Feminine Imagination: The Politics of Reading in Twentieth-Century Innovative Writing* (Washington, DC: Maisonneuve Press, 1988), 187–205.

Min, Eun Kyung. "Reading the Figure of Dictation in Theresa Hak Kyung Cha's *Dictee.*" In Sandra Kumamoto Stanley, ed., *Other Sisterhoods: Literary Theory and U.S. Women of Color* (Urbana: University of Illinois Press, 1998), 309–24.

Moira, Roth. "Theresa Hak Kyung Cha, 1951–1982: A Narrative Chronology." In Elaine H. Kim and Norma Alarcon, eds., *Writing Self/Writing Nation: Essays on Theresa Hak Kyung Cha's* Dictee (Berkeley, CA: Third Woman Press, 1994), 151–60.

Nishime, Leilani. "Theresa Hak Kyung Cha." In Guiyou Huang, ed., *Asian American Autobiographers: A Bio-Bibliographical Critical Sourcebook* (Westport, CT: Greenwood Press, 2001), 37–41.

Sakai, Naoki. "Distinguishing Literature and the Work of Translation: Theresa Hak Kyung Cha's *Dictee* and Repetition Without Return." In *Translation and Subjectivity: On "Japan" and Cultural Nationalism* (Minneapolis: University of Minnesota Press, 1997), 18–39.

Shih, Shu-mei. "Nationalism and Korean American Women's Writing: Theresa Hak Kyung Cha's *Dictee.*" In Jeanne Campbell Reesman, ed., *Speaking the Other Self: American Women Writers* (Athens: University of Georgia Press, 1998), 144–62.

Spahr, Juliana. "Postmodern Readers and Theresa Hak Kyung Cha's *Dictee.*" *College Literature* 23, no. 3 (1996): 23–43.

Stephens, Michael. "Korea: Theresa Hak Kyung Cha." In *The Dramaturgy of Style: Voice in Short Fiction* (Carbondale: Southern Illinois University Press, 1986), 184–210.

Viray, Ma. "Diagrams and Declensions—A Reading of *Dictee* (a Novel by Hak Kyung Cha, Theresa)." *Amerasia* 14, no. 1 (1988): 143–47.

Wilson, Rob. "Falling Into the Korean Uncanny: On Reading Theresa Hak Kyung Cha's *Dictee.*" *Korean Culture* 12 (Fall 1991): 33–37.

Wolf, Susan. "Theresa Cha: Recalling Telling Retelling." *Afterimage* 14, no. 1 (Summer 1986): 11–13.

Wong, Shelley Sunn. "Unnaming the Same: Theresa Hak Kyung Cha's *DICTEE.*" In Lynn Keller and Cristanne Miller, eds., *Feminist Measure: Soundings in Poetry and Theory* (Ann Arbor: University of Michigan Press, 1994), 43–68.

* * *

Diana Chang (1934–). Born in New York City to a Chinese father and a Eurasian mother, Chang was raised and educated in English-language schools in China. She lived in three major Chinese cities, Beijing, Nanjing, and Shanghai, before returning to the United States after World War II to attend high school; she completed her education at Barnard College in 1949. Chang is a prolific and versatile writer who works in four genres: novels, poetry, short stories, and essays. Although she is better known as a novelist, she is also an accomplished painter who has exhibited her work jointly with other artists and singly. Between 1956 and 1978, Chang published six novels:

The Frontiers of Love (New York: Random House, 1956), *A Woman of Thirty* (New York: Random House, 1959), *A Passion for Life* (New York: Random House, 1961), *The Only Game in Town* (New York: Signet, 1963), *Eye to Eye* (New York: Harper and Row, 1974), and *A Perfect Love* (New York: Grove, 1978). In the 1980s and 1990s, she turned her creative energy to writing poetry, producing four volumes: *The Horizon Is Definitely Speaking* (Port Jefferson, NY: Backstreet Editions, 1982), *What Matisse Is After* (New York: Contact II Publications, 1984), *Earth, Water, Light: Landscape Poems Celebrating the East End of Long Island* (Northport, NY: Birnham Wood Graphics, 1991), and *The Mind's Amazement: Poems Inspired by Paintings, Poetry, Music, Dance* (Islip, NY: Live Poets Society, 1998). Even though no collections of her own short fiction have been published, more than thirty of her short stories appeared in magazines, collections, and anthologies between 1975 and 1997. Chang is a recipient of several major literary awards, including a Fulbright Fellowship and a John Hay Whitney Fellowship. Among her other literary achievements is her service as editorship for *The American PEN* for several years.

Chang has been credited as the first American-born Chinese to write and publish a novel in the United States. *Frontiers of Love*, set in wartime Shanghai, explores identity issues concerning three Eurasians living in the southeast Chinese metropolis: Mimi Lambert, Feng Huang, and Sylvia Chen. Each of the characters responds to their biracial and bicultural identity differently, which results in downfalls (Mimi Lambert and Feng Huang), or in ambivalence about the self-identity (Sylvia Chen). *A Woman of Thirty* delineates the affair of a young woman, Emily Merrick, with a married man and explores how her infatuation prompts her to examine the conflict of moral and religious values and her desire to achieve her human potential.

The Only Game in Town once again focuses on Caucasian characters who are forced to deal with issues of identity and maturation. Chang's later novels, *A Passion for Life* and *Eye to Eye*, magnify "the scope and intensity of this crisis of identity" (Roh-Spaulding 39), as *A Woman of Thirty* did earlier.

Chang's short stories, like her novels and poetry, "deal with a wide range of subject matter: mortality, love, sexuality, alienation, and identity" (Clarke 46). As de Almeida observes, "The status of agency vis-à-vis reified or easily consumed representations and 'authenticity,' the reservoir of ethnic markers par excellence, is a central concern for Chang in not only her first novel, but her early poetry as well" (66). Some poems in *The Horizon Is Definitely Speaking* address existential concerns; a few pieces in *What Matisse Is After* look into Asian American identities; and *The Mind's Amazement* deals with the subjects mentioned in the subtitle: painting, poetry, music, and dance.

A considerable number of reviews of *The Frontiers of Love* are available in various venues. Of particular use is Leo Hamalian's informative "A MELUS Interview: Diana Chang," *MELUS* 20, no. 4 (1995): 29–43, which offers details about her personal and creative life. Shirley Geok-lin Lim's introduction to the University of Washington edition provides a contemporary context for reading the novel (Seattle: University of Washington Press, 1994), v–xxiii. Other useful studies include:

de Almeida, Eduardo. "Diana Chang." In Guiyou Huang, ed., *Asian American Poets: A Bio-Bibliographical Critical Sourcebook* (Westport, CT: Greenwood Press, 2002), 65–69.

Clarke, Janet Hyunju. "Diana Chang." In Guiyou Huang, ed., *Asian American Short Story Writers: An A-to-Z*

Guide (Westport, CT: Greenwood Press, 2003), 45–50.

Fink, Thomas. "Chang's 'Plunging Into View'." *Explicator* 55, no. 3 (1997): 175–77.

Grow, L. M. "On Diana Chang's 'Four Views in Praise of Reality'." *Amerasia* 16, no. 1 (1990): 211–15.

Ling, Amy. "Writer in the Hyphenated Condition: Diana Chang." *MELUS* 7, no. 4 (1980): 69–83.

Medwick, Lucille. "The Chinese Poet in New York." *New York Quarterly* 4 (1970): 94–115.

Roh-Spaulding, Carol. "Diana Chang." In Emmanuel Nelson, ed., *Asian American Novelists: A Bio-Bibliographical Critical Sourcebook* (Westport, CT: Greenwood Press, 2000), 38–43.

Spaulding, Carol Vivian. "Blue-Eyed Asians: Eurasians in the Work of Edith Eaton/Sui Sin Far, Winnifred Eaton/Onoto Watanna, and Diana Chang." Ph.D. diss., University of Iowa, 1997.

Wu, Kitty Wei-hsiung. "Cultural Ideology and Aesthetic Choices: A Study of Three Works by Chinese American Women: Diana Chang, Bette Bao Lord, and Maxine Hong Kingston." Ph.D. diss., University of Maryland, 1989.

* * *

Frank Chin. See Chin in "Drama."

* * *

Louis Hing Chu (1915–1970). Born in Toishan (Taishan), Guangdong (Canton) province, China, Chu immigrated with his parents to Newark, New Jersey, at the age of nine. He attended Upsala College and graduated with a bachelor's degree in English with a minor in sociology; in 1940 he obtained an M.A. in sociology from New York University, with a thesis titled "The Chinese Restaurants in New York City." From 1943 to 1945 he served in a unit of the U.S. Army Signal Corps stationed in Kunming, Yunnan province, China. After his tour of duty there, Chu put what he had learned in college to use in the service of the Chinese community in New York: he worked as an executive secretary for the Soo Yuen Benevolent Association and then as director of a center for the elderly, the Golden Age Club, until he died in February 1970. But no matter what he did for a livelihood, Chu never gave up his dream of becoming a writer: in 1961 he published *Eat a Bowl of Tea* (New York: L. Stuart), known to be his only novel, though during his lifetime he had not been recognized as a novelist or as any kind of writer, for that matter. Besides his master's thesis and the novel, Chu also wrote a short story, "Bewildered."

Eat a Bowl of Tea portrays the life of New York's Chinatown from an insider's perspective. Racial, patriarchal, and familial tensions all converge in the relationship of Wang Wah Guy and his son Ben Loy. Wang was made a Chinatown bachelor by the 1924 National Origins Law that prohibited the entry of Chinese wives into the United States, including his own. This personal experience drove him to deal with his son through control. The picture that Chu presents is "distinctly different from the stereotypes that had already existed and been accepted as the standard images of Chinese and Chinese community"; instead, Chinatown is depicted as "nonexotic, realistic with its weaknesses and strengths ... invested with feelings and emotions reflective of a full consciousness of self"; thus Chu views problems there "not as Chinese problems but as Chinese American problems" (Wang 70).

When *Eat a Bowl of Tea* was first published in 1961, only a few reviews appeared;

since its republication in 1979, the novel has experienced a revival that has yielded a substantial amount of criticism. Jeffery Paul Chan, "Introduction" to *Eat a Bowl of Tea* (Seattle: University of Washington Press, 1970, 1–5) is a useful early notice of the novel. Elaine Kim's *Asian American Literature: An Introduction to the Writings and Their Social Context* (Philadelphia: Temple University Press, 1982) contains discussions of Chu's work (109–21). See also:

Chua, Cheng Lok. "Golden Mountain: Chinese Versions of the American Dream in Lin Yutang, Louis Chu, and Maxine Hong Kingston." *Ethnic Groups* 4 (May 1982): 33–59.

Hsiao, Ruth Y. "Facing the Incurable: Patriarchy in *Eat a Bowl of Tea*." In Shirley Geok-lin Lim and Amy Ling, eds., *Reading the Literatures of Asian America* (Philadelphia: Temple University Press, 1992), 151–62.

Ling, Jinqi. "Reading for Historical Specificities: Gender Negotiations in Louis Chu's *Eat a Bowl of Tea*." *MELUS* 20, no. 1 (Spring 1995): 35–52.

Li Shu-yan. "Otherness and Transformation in *Eat a Bowl of Tea* and *Crossings*." *MELUS* 18, no. 4 (Winter 1993–1994): 99–111.

Shih, David. "*Eat a Bowl of Tea*, by Louis Chu." In Sau-ling Cynthia Wong and Stephen H. Sumida, eds., *A Resource Guide to Asian American Literature* (New York: MLA, 2001), 45–53.

Wang, Shunzhu. "Louis Hing Chu." In Emmanuel S. Nelson, ed., *Asian American Novelists: A Bio-Bibliographical Critical Sourcebook* (Westport, CT: Greenwood Press, 2000), 68–75.

D

Chitra Banerjee Divakaruni (1956–). Indian American novelist, poet, short story writer, and community activist Divakaruni was born and raised in Calcutta in a traditional middle-class Indian family; in Calcutta she completed her school and college educations. Her father's interest in the United States prompted the family to move there. Divakaruni obtained an M.A. in English from Wright State University in Dayton, Ohio, in 1977, then enrolled at the University of California at Berkeley, earning a doctorate in English in 1984. Even though she wrote a dissertation on the Renaissance playwright Christopher Marlowe's drama, her creative efforts focus on topics closer to her life experiences, such as immigration and women's issues.

Divakaruni's writing career took off with poetry: her first collection, *Dark Like the River* (Calcutta: Writers Workshop) was published in 1987; a second volume, *The Reason for Nasturtiums* (Berkeley: Berkeley Poets Workshop and Press) in 1990; *Black Candle: Poems About Women from India, Pakistan, and Bangladesh* (Corvallis, OR: Calyx Books) in 1991; and *Leaving Yuba City: New and Selected Poems* (New York: Doubleday) in 1997. Her short stories are collected in two volumes: *Arranged Marriage* (New York: Doubleday, 1995), which won the 1996 Before Columbus Foundation American Book Award and the PEN Oakland Josephine Miles Prize, and *The Unknown Errors of Our Lives* (New York: Doubleday, 2001). But Divakaruni is more widely known for her novels: *The Mistress of Spices* (New York: Doubleday, 1996) was chosen by the *Los Angeles Times* as one of the best books of 1997; *Sister of My Heart* (New York: Doubleday) came out in 1999, and *The*

Vine of Desire (New York: Doubleday) in 2002. As a community activist, Divakaruni is known for helping found MAITRI, a telephone helpline for South Asian women in the San Francisco Bay area.

Divakaruni's poetry anticipates many themes that she explores in both her short· and long fiction. Her primary concern is South Asian women immigrants in situations of violence, marriage and family, and history, as well as racial problems and legal restrictions on nonwhite immigrants like Punjabi farmers who came to Yuba City, California. Her short stories, while continuing these themes, probe more deeply into related issues of women's survival, relationships (including mother-daughter relationships), role in the family and in society, and the consequences of immigration and Americanization. *Arranged Marriage*, a critically acclaimed collection, "is thematically unified and explores, questions, rearticulates, and redefines the South Asian cultural construction of the feminine" (Moka-Dias 88). Divakaruni's novels are women-centered as well, featuring mostly female protagonists. *The Mistress of Spices*, for example, examines the immigrant life of Tilo, the Spice-Mistress, the healer who embodies love and survival as well as power. *The Sister of My Heart*, as the title suggests, centers on the relationship of Anju and Sudha, two cousins who grow up as sisters under unfortunate circumstances.

Studies of Divakuruni's work are still emerging. Other than many reviews, some articles are valuable to an understanding of her multigenre corpus:

Davis, Rocío G. "Everyone's Story: Narrative *You* in Chitra Divakaruni's 'The Word Love.'" In Rocío G. Davis and Sämi Ludwig, eds., *Asian American Literature in the International Context: Readings on Fiction, Poetry, and Performance* (Hamburg: LIT Verlag, 2002), 173–83.

——. "Chitra Banerjee Divakaruni." In Guiyou Huang, ed., *Asian American Short Story Writers: An A-To-Z Guide* (Westport, CT: Greenwood Press, 2003), 65–71.

"Chitra Banerjee Divakaruni: Poet and Fiction Writer." In Amy Ling, ed., *Yellow Light: The Flowering of Asian American Arts* (Philadelphia: Temple University Press, 1999), 136–48.

"Chitra Divakaruni." In Roshni Rustomji-Kerns, ed., *Living in America: Poetry and Fiction by South Asian American Writers* (Boulder, CO: Westview Press, 1995), 47–49, 95–99.

Moka-Dias, Brunda. "Chitra Banerjee Divakaruni." In Emmanuel Nelson, ed., *Asian American Novelists: A Bio-Bibliographical Critical Sourcebook* (Westport, CT: Greenwood Press, 2000), 87–92.

Rasian, Dharini. "Chitra Banerjee Divakaruni." In King-Kok Cheung, ed., *Words Matter: Conversations with Asian American Writers* (Honolulu: University of Hawai'i Press), 140–53.

Shah, Purvi. "Chitra Banerjee Divakaruni." In Guiyou Huang, ed., *Asian American Poets: A Bio-Bibliographical Critical Sourcebook* (Westport, CT: Greenwood Press, 2002), 93–99.

Srikanth, Rajini. "Chitra Banerjee Divakaruni: Exploring Human Nature Under Fire." *Asian Pacific American Journal* 5, no. 2 (1996): 94–101.

Streuber, Sonja H. "Chitra Banerjee Divakaruni." In Guiyou Huang, ed., *Asian American Autobiographers: A Bio-Bibliographical Criti-*

cal Sourcebook (Westport, CT: Greenwood Press, 2001), 67–75.

Indira Ganesan (1960–). Indian American novelist Ganesan was born in Srirangam, southern India, and spent a few years of her childhood in Uttar Pradesh, northern India. At age five she followed her father to the United States, where he had been pursuing graduate education. Although she studied at a Catholic women's college in Madras, India, for a year, she was primarily educated in the United States, earning a degree in English from Vassar College in New York in 1982, and an M.F.A. from the Writers' Workshop at the University of Iowa in 1984. Ganesan won fellowships to attend the MacDowell Colony and the Fine Arts Work Center in Massachusetts, which prepared her to write fiction. Her first novel, *The Journey*, appeared in 1990 (New York: Knopf); a second, *The Inheritance*, came out in 1998 (New York: Knopf). In addition to writing novels and short stories, Ganesan has taught at various colleges and universities throughout the United States.

The Journey narrates the story of a young Indian American woman, Renu Krishnan, as she returns from America to a fictionalized place in India (Pi, an island in the Bay of Bengal) on the occasion of her cousin's untimely death in a train accident. The novel probes issues of cultural and social differences that are responsible for prejudices and stereotypes. Ganesan anatomizes the familiar Indian practice of arranged marriages. *The Inheritance*, a bildungsroman that seems to have garnered more critical attention than *The Journey*, also set on the fiction island of Pi in India, is about a fifteen-year-old girl, Sonil, who embarks on a journey of recovery from a chronic illness as well as of discovery of herself and of her parents.

As Ganesan has published only two novels to date, both relatively recent, there have been more reviews than full-length studies of her work. But a few items are noteworthy:

Chander, Harish. "Indira Ganesan." In Emmanuel Nelson, ed., *Asian American Novelists: A Bio-Bibliographical Critical Sourcebook* (Westport, CT: Greenwood Press, 2000), 99–104.

Nair, Hema. "Interview with Indira Ganesan by Hema Nair." *Little India* (June 1998): 8.

Wright, Marilou Briggs. "Indira Ganesan." In Emmanuel Nelson, ed., *Writers of the Indian Diaspora* (Westport, CT: Greenwood Press, 1993), 115–21.

Chuang Hua (?). Little is known of the personal life of the author of *Crossings*, except that she was born in China, which she left with her family in 1937, the year the Sino-Japanese War broke out, probably to escape that conflict. The family first lived in England and then settled in the United States, where Chuang Hua received some schooling; she also spent some time in Paris and then returned to New York.

Chuang Hua is known to have authored only one book, *Crossings*, first published by Dial Press in 1968 and republished by Northeastern University Press in 1986. The book was marketed as a novel. Amy Ling, however, reads it as an autobiography, while Veronica Wang calls it an "autobiographical novel." *Crossings* is narrated by a third-person narrator, Fourth Jane. As its title suggests, the work is a study of various kinds of crossings—geographical, racial, cultural, and metaphorical—that Jane makes of oceans and continents in quest of the self.

A few studies are available:

Brickner, Richard. "Crossings." *The New York Times,* March 9, 1969, 38.

Douglass, Lesley Chin. "Finding the Way: Chuang Hua's *Crossings* and Chinese Literary Tradition." *MELUS* 20, no. 1 (Spring 1995): 53–65.

Li Shu-yan. "Otherness and Transformation in *Eat a Bowl of Tea* and *Crossings.*" *MELUS* 18, no. 4 (Winter 1993–1994): 99–110.

Ling, Amy. Foreword, *Crossings* (Boston: Northeastern University Press, 1986).

——. "A Rumble in Silence: *Crossings* by Chuang Hua." *MELUS* 9, no. 3 (Winter 1982): 29–37.

Wang, Veronica. "In Search of Self: The Dislocated Female Émigré Wanderer in Chuang Hua's *Crossings.*" In Barbara Frey Waxman, ed., *Multicultural Literatures Through Feminist/Poststructuralist Lenses* (Knoxville: University of Tennessee Press, 1993), 22–36.

Xiao, Hailing. "Chuang Hua." In Emmanuel Nelson, ed., *Asian American Novelists: A Bio-Bibliographical Critical Sourcebook* (Westport, CT: Greenwood Press, 2000), 117–19.

Xu, Wenying. "Chuang Hua." In Guiyou Huang, ed., *Asian American Autobiographers: A Bio-Bibliographical Critical Sourcebook* (Westport, CT: Greenwood Press, 2001), 61–66.

* * *

Jessica Tarahata Hagedorn (1949–). A versatile Filipina American literary figure—novelist, poet, performance artist, and songwriter—Hagedorn was born in Manila and immigrated to San Francisco with her mother at the age of fourteen. In the Philippines Hagedorn attended the Catholic Assumption Convent, where she developed interests in theater, music, movies, and literature. In San Francisco she completed her high school education at the nationally known Lowell High School, where she became more interested in rock 'n' roll and black culture. Even though she received no formal college education, she studied theater arts at the American Conservatory Theater in San Francisco; she also participated in the Kearny Street Writers' Workshop, which introduced her to contemporary political and cultural issues concerning Asian America. In 1975 she published her first collection of poetry and prose, *Dangerous Music* (San Francisco: Momo's Press); two other volumes, *Pet Food and Tropical Apparitions* (San Francisco: Momo's Press) and *Danger and Beauty* (New York: Penguin), came out in 1981 and 1993, respectively. Her first novel, *Dogeaters* (New York: Pantheon) was published in 1990, and a second, *The Gangster of Love* (Boston: Houghton Mifflin), in 1996. Hagedorn's literary talents are also evident in the plays and teleplays that she wrote, including *Chiquita Banana* (1972), *Where the Mississippi Meets the Amazon* (1977), *Tenement Lover* (1981), *Teenytown* (with Laurie Carlos and Robbie Champagne) (1990), and other pieces. Hagedorn's editorial work includes the anthology *Charlie Chan Is Dead: An Anthology of Contemporary Asian American Fiction* (New York: Penguin, 1993).

Hagedorn's contributions to literature have been recognized with numerous awards: the American Book Award from the Before Columbus Foundation, the Lila Wallace–Reader's Digest Fund Writer's Award, and a

National Endowment for the Arts Creative Writing Fellowship.

Though Hagedorn's literary talents are multifarious, her major accomplishments have been in fiction and poetry. In her two novels, writes Ruby S. Ramraj, "Hagedorn focuses on themes that are recognizably postmodern and postcolonial in her exploration of the lives of characters in multicultural and multiracial worlds" (111). *Dogeaters,* set in Manila during the 1950s and 1980s, is narrated by a female character, Rio Gonzaga, who represents the life of the upper class, and a male character, Joey, who embodies the lower class. Like *Dogeaters, The Gangster of Love* also utilizes two narrators, the primary voice of Raquel (Rocky) Rivera, alternating with that of her fellow musician, Elvis Chang, in a few sections of the novel. New York is the backdrop against which the themes of the novel—identity politics, relationships, and social and cultural alienation—are played out.

Hagedorn's poetry has also been critically acclaimed. Early pieces appearing in *Four Young Women: Poems by Jessica Tarahata Hagedorn, Alice Karle, Barbara Szerlip, and Carol Tinker,* edited by the San Francisco-based poet Kenneth Rexroth (New York: McGraw-Hill, 1973), include "Autobiography Part One: Manila to San Francisco" and "The Death of Anna May Wong," and "focus on the fragmentation, dislocation, alienation, and insurgency of the Asian Pacific immigrant" (Uba 103). The 1975 collection, *Dangerous Music,* a result of the poet's temporary return to her birth country, deals with her feelings about the Philippines, among other themes. *Pet Food and Tropical Apparitions* is more feminist in its political orientation and explores issues of sexuality, particularly in relation to racial identity.

Hagedorn's multigenre work has been widely discussed. In addition to a number of reviews, there are many articles and essays on her work. See:

Aguilar-San Juan, Karin. "The Exile Within/The Question of Identity: Jessica Hagedorn." Interview in Aguilar-San Juan, ed., *The State of Asian America: Activism and Resistance in the 1990s* (Boston: South End Press, 1994), 173–82.

Balce, Nerissa S. "*Dogeaters,* by Jessica Hagedorn." In Sau-ling Cynthia Wong and Stephen H. Sumida, eds., *A Resource Guide to Asian American Literature* (New York: MLA, 2001), 54–65.

Bonetti, Kay. "Jessica Hagedorn." In Kay Bonetti, Greg Michalson, Speer Morgan, Jo Sapp, and Sam Stowers, eds., *Conversations with American Novelists: The Best Interviews from The Missouri Review and the American Audio Prose Library* (Columbia: University of Missouri Press, 1997), 217–33.

Casper, Leonard. "Bungungot and the Philippine Dream in Hagedorn." *Solidarity* 127 (July–September 1990): 152–57.

Covi, Giovanna. "Jessica Hagedorn's Decolonization of Subjectivity: Historical Agency Beyond Gender and Nation." In Yiorgos Kalogera and Domna Pastourmatzi, eds., *Nationalism and Sexuality: Crisis of Identity* (Thessalonici, Greece: Aristotle University, 1996), 63–80.

De Manuel, Maria Teresa. "Jessica Hagedorn's *Dogeaters*: A Feminist Reading." *Likha* 12, no. 2 (1990–1991): 10–32.

Evangelista, Susan. "Jessica Hagedorn: A Pinay Poet." *Philippine Studies* 35, no. 4 (1987): 475–87.

———. "Jessica Hagedorn and Manila Magic." *MELUS* 18, no. 4 (Winter 1993–1994): 41–52.

Gillian, Jennifer. "Border Perceptions: Reading U.S. Intervention in Roosevelt and Hagedorn." In Will Wright et al., eds., *The Image of the Frontier in Literature, Media, and Society* (Pueblo: University of Southern Colorado, 1997), 121–25.

Gima, Charlene Setsue. "Writing the Pacific: Imagining Communities of Difference in the Fiction of Jessica Hagedorn, Keri Hulme, Rodney Morales, and Gary Pak." Ph.D. diss., Cornell University, 1997.

Lee, Rachel C. "The Americas of Asian-American Literature: Nationalism, Gender and Sexuality in Bulosan's *America Is in the Heart*, Jen's *Typical American*, and Hagedorn's *Dogeaters*." Ph.D. diss., University of California at Los Angeles, 1995.

Lee, A. Robert. "*Eat a Bowl of Tea*: Asian Americans in the Novels of Gish Jen, Cynthia Kadohata, Kim Ronyoung, Jessica Hagedorn, and Tran Van Dinh." *Ethnicity and Representations in American Literature*, special issue of *Yearbook of English Studies* 24 (1994): 263–80.

Ramraj, Ruby S. "Jessica Hagedorn." In Emmanuel Nelson, ed., *Asian American Novelists: A Bio-Bibliographical Critical Sourcebook* (Westport, CT: Greenwood Press, 2000), 110–16.

Uba, George. "Jessica Hagedorn." In Guiyou Huang, ed., *Asian American Poets: A Bio-Bibliographical Critical Sourcebook* (Westport, CT: Greenwood Press, 2002), 101–11.

Zhang, Aiping. "Jessica Hagedorn." In Guiyou Huang, ed., *Asian American Short Story Writers: An A-to-Z Guide* (Westport, CT: Greenwood Press, 2003), 93–100.

Gish Jen (1956–). The second of five children in a Chinese family, Jen was born in Yonkers and raised in Scarsdale, New York. She attended Harvard and graduated in 1977; she completed the M.F.A program at the University of Iowa in 1983. Jen had always wanted to be a writer, and obtaining the M.F.A. paved the way for a writing career. Even though her short story collection, *Who's Irish?*, was published after her two novels, *Typical American* (Boston: Houghton Mifflin, 1991) and *Mona in the Promised Land* (New York: Vintage, 1996), Jen started her writing career with short stories, many of which appeared in journals and magazines as well as anthologies, both ethnic and mainstream. Some pieces have been anthologized in *The Best American Short Stories: 1988*, *The Best American Short Stories: 1995*, and *The Best American Short Stories of the Century* (1999). The publications of critically acclaimed fiction have secured Jen a place in both contemporary Asian American and mainstream American literary canons. She has received numerous prestigious awards, including a National Endowment for the Arts Award (1988) and a Lannan Literary Award for fiction (1999).

Typical American, Jen's first novel, explores an immigrant theme: the pursuit of the American dream by a Chinese American family. *Mona in the Promised Land* continues this theme but focally narrates the title character Mona's attempt to convert to Judaism. In Jen's collection *Who's Irish?*, eight short stories, unlike her novels, "do not all deal with the Asian American subject or Asian American experiences" (S. Huang 102); they instead look into the American experiences of all ethnic groups and hyphenated Americans. Some pieces feature only mainstream American characters while others present only Chinese. Stories like "The White Umbrella," "In the American Society," and "The Water Faucet Vision" feature the same characters first seen in Jen's two novels. The title piece, "Who's Irish?" narrates the intergenerational and interracial conflicts that occur between a Chinese grandmother and her American-born (and Americanized) granddaughter and her Irish-American husband.

Both Jen's novels and her short stories have been critically acclaimed. Apart from reviews of her books, a good number of critical studies are available:

Feddersen, R. C. "From Story to Novel and Back Again: Gish Jen's Developing Art of Short Fiction." In Noel Harold Kaylor Jr., ed., *Creative and Critical Approaches to the Short Story* (Lewiston, NY: The Edwin Mellen Press, 1997), 349–58.

Gilbert, Matthew. "Gish Jen, All-American: The Cambridge Novelist Doesn't Like to Be Labeled—Except as a Bigmouth." *Boston Globe,* June 4, 1996, 53.

Huang, Shuchen Susan. "Gish Jen." In Guiyou Huang, ed., *Asian American Short Story Writers: An A-to-Z Guide* (Westport, CT: Greenwood Press, 2003), 101–8.

Lee, Margaret Juhae. "Talking with Gish Jen." *Newsday,* July 11, 1999, B11.

Lee, Rachel. "Gish Jen." In King-Kok Cheung, ed., *Words Matter: Conversations with Asian American Writers* (Honolulu: University of Hawai'i Press, 2000), 215–32.

Lin, Erika T. "Mona on the Phone: The Performative Body and Racial Identity in *Mona in the Promised Land.*" *MELUS* 28, no. 2 (Summer 2003): 47–57.

Matsukawa, Yuko. "A *MELUS* Interview: Gish Jen." *MELUS* 18, no. 4 (Winter 1993–1994): 111–20.

Pearlman, Mickey. "Gish Jen." In Pearlman, *Listen to Their Voices: Twenty Interviews with Women Who Write* (New York: Norton, 1993), 36–46.

Satz, Martha. "Writing About the Things That Are Dangerous: A Conversation with Gish Jen." *Southwest Review* 78, no. 1 (Winter 1993): 132–40.

Trudeau, Lawrence J. "Gish Jen." In Trudeau, ed., *Asian American Literature: Reviews and Criticism of Works by American Writers of Asian Descent* (Detroit: Gale, 1999), 176–86.

Cynthia Kadohata (1956–). A *sansei* Japanese American novelist, Kadohata was born in Chicago but traveled and lived with her family in the southern states of Arkansas and Georgia and the midwestern states of Illinois and Michigan before settling down in California. Kadohata attended various colleges, including Los Angeles City College and the University of Southern California, as well as writing programs at the University of Pittsburgh and Columbia University. While convalescing from an automobile accident in Boston, she started to write fiction, publishing her first novel, *The Floating World* in 1989 (New York: Ballantine). *In the Heart of the Valley of Love* appeared in 1997 (Los Angeles: University of California Press). Her short stories have also been published in magazines. Among the awards Kadohata has received is a grant from the National Endowment for the Arts.

The Floating World and *In the Heart of the Valley of Love* both exhibit signs of autobiography. The former, for example, centers on a twelve-year-old girl, Olivia, and her family, almost always on the move, reflecting Kadohata's own family travels when she was a small child. The latter novel narrates the disabling experience of a car accident sustained by a young woman named Francie, not unlike the trauma that Kadohata herself suffered in 1977. Both narratives have a woman protagonist who is Asian American, though Francie is also part African. While Olivia's world floats—her family's constant relocations do not provide her with any sense of stability—Francie's is set in Los Angeles in the future: 2052, not exactly a floating world but undoubtedly one of uncertainty and complexity. A futuristic novel, *In the Heart of the Valley of Love* not only tries to predict—as many such works do—the future of the world as seen through the eyes of the narrator, it also attempts to convey messages of the power and promise of love.

More reviews than full-length studies exist of Kadohata's novels. See:

Heeger, Susan. "Los Angeles: 2050." Rev. of *In the Heart of the Valley of Love. Los Angeles Times Book Review*, August 23, 1992, 1, 8.

Henry, Jim. "Cynthia Kadohata." In *Notable Asian Americans* (Detroit: Gale, 1995), 142–43.

Moore, Susanna. "On the Road with Charlie-O." Rev. of *The Floating World. Washington Post*, June 25, 1989, 5–7.

Pearlman, Mickey. "Cynthia Kadohata." In Pearlman, *Listen to Their Voices: Twenty Interviews with Women Who Write* (New York: Norton, 1993), 112–20.

Roth, John K. "Cynthia Kadohata." In Roth, ed., *American Diversity, American Identity* (New York: Holt, 1995), 603–6.

See, Lisa. "Cynthia Kadohata." *Publishers Weekly* (August 3, 1992): 48–49.

* * *

Nora Okja Keller (1965–). Born in Seoul, South Korea, to a Korean mother and a German father who was a computer engineer, Keller immigrated to Hawai'i at the age of three. She grew up on the island and attended the University of Hawai'i, where she first learned of the Japanese military's so-called "recreation centers" in 1993, at a lecture by a survivor comfort woman called Keum Ja Hwang in World War II. In 1995 Keller was awarded the Pushcart Prize for a short story, "Mother Tongue," which she later incorporated into *Comfort Woman* (New York: Viking, 1997), which was inspired by the 1993 lecture. For this novel Keller won the 1998 American Book Award and the 1999 Elliot Cades Award. She went on to publish her second novel, *Fox Girl*, in 2002 (New York: Viking); it was long-listed for the Orange Prize.

Comfort Woman is no doubt one of the most powerful and emotionally charged novels ever written on a neglected, and perhaps taboo topic from World War II—"comfort women" forced to serve the Japanese army as sex slaves. It is a widely read novel that has sparked renewed interest in this painful historical issue. Keller zooms in on a mother–daughter relationship in the aftermath of World War II. The novel recounts the story of Akiko, the mother and former comfort woman, and Beccah, the daughter, from their respective perspectives. *Fox Girl*, set in a military camp town in 1960s Korea, is a dark tale of the survival and transformation of two mixed-race teenage girls, Hyun Jin and Sookie, along with their teenage pimp, Lobetto—all products of the Korean War. These people, known as "throwaway children"—abandoned by the American GIs who fathered them—live in a forgotten world of poverty and despair, ostracized from the Korean society that values purity above life and forced to endure abuse and neglect.

Keller's two novels have been reviewed in a wide range of venues, including *Harper's Bazaar, Kirkus, Library Journal, The Nation, Publishers Weekly, Tribune Books,* and *Women's Review of Books,* though more substantive studies are still emerging. See:

Farley, Christopher John. "No Man's Land." *Time* (May 5, 1997): 101–2.

Funderberg, Lisa. Rev. of *Comfort Woman. New York Times Book Review,* August 31, 1997, 14.

Kakutani, Michiko. "Repairing Lives Torn by the Past." *The New York Times,* March 25, 1997, B8.

Rubin, Merle. "The Haunting." *Los Angeles Times Book Review,* December 14, 1997, 4.

Sato, Gayle K. "Nora Okja Keller's *Comfort Woman* and Chang-rae Lee's *A Gesture Life*: Gendered Narratives of the Home Front." *AALA Journal* (Japan) 7 (2001): 22–33.

Shapiro, Laura. "They Gotta Be Making This Up." *Newsweek* (April 28, 1997): 78.

Wilkinson, Joanne. Rev. of *Comfort Woman. Booklist* (March 15, 1997): 1226.

* * *

Richard E. Kim (1932–). Korean American novelist and memoirist Kim was born in Hamheung, North Korea, during the Japanese occupation, and also lived with his family in Manchuria for a few years to escape Japanese persecution due to his father's involvement in Korea's national independence movement. Kim attended schools in North Korea until 1945, when his family fled to South Korea to avoid communist rule. He studied economics at Seoul National University, then volunteered in the South Korean army; later he worked as a liaison officer between U.S. and South Korean forces until he was honorably discharged in 1954. The following year Kim enrolled at Middlebury College in Vermont to study political philosophy and history, and without getting a degree, he went on to obtain an M.A. in creative writing from Johns Hopkins University in 1960, an M.F.A. in creative writing from the University of Iowa in 1962, and finally another M.A. in Far Eastern studies from Harvard in 1963. During his time at Iowa, Kim started to write a novel, *The Martyred,* which was published in 1964 (New York: George Brazilier), followed in 1968 by *The Innocent* (Boston: Houghton Mifflin). His third book, *Lost Names: Scenes from a Korean Boyhood,* is a memoir and came out in 1970 (New York: Praeger). Kim also writes in Korean; in fact, his last two books were nonfiction written in Korean and published in South Korea: *In Search of Lost Years* (Seoul: Somundang, 1985) and *In Russia and China: In Search of Lost Koreans* (Seoul: Uryu Munhwasa, 1989).

Kim has received a Ford Foundation Foreign Fellowship, a National Endowment for the Arts Literary Fellowship, and a Guggenheim Foundation Fellowship. Pearl S. Buck, who lived in China and wrote extensively about China and Korea and won a Nobel prize for literature, predicted that "If this young man [Kim] continues to do as well as this [*Lost Names*], he will some day be worthy of the Nobel Prize" (qtd. in Jae-Nam Han 136). Kim has not won it yet, but according to Elaine Kim, "The book [*The Martyred*] remains the only work by an Asian American ever nominated for a Nobel Prize for literature" (161).

Unlike that of many other Asian American writers, Kim's narrative focus is almost entirely on twentieth-century Korea. This forms the foundation of his writing in both English and Korean, with Korean settings, Korean characters, and Korean historical events, though Japan as an invader and occupier also figures prominently in his novels and the memoir. *The Martyred* deals with the Korean War, *The Innocent* explores a military coup d'état, and *Lost Names* examines the national disaster and tragic consequences of the Japanese occupation. *The Martyred*, set in Pyongyang during the Korean War, looks into the North Korean communists' execution of twelve Christian ministers and the survival of two others, Mr. Hann and Mr. Shin, a mystery that the narrator, South Korean army officer Captain Lee, is in charge of investigating. The novel weaves violence, religion, loyalty, and betrayal into a tale of human suffering, martyrdom, and triumph. *The Innocent*, based on the 1961 historical military coup d'état in South Korea, examines the question of the morality of using force in overthrowing a civilian government. While the hawkish Colonel Min represents the use of force, Major Lee believes in peaceful means of changing government, but when violence helps achieve that end, Major Lee evolves from idealism to belief in violence. Violence also looms large in Kim's autobiographical work, *Lost Names*, which is devoted to childhood memories of Japanese-occupied Korea from 1909 to 1945, when the Koreans were forced to adopt Japanese names in place of their ancestral names. The work effectively portrays the brave resistance that the Koreans put up against Japanese domination, as well as the national pride that they displayed.

For more information, see:

Fuse, Montye P. "Richard E. Kim." In Guiyou Huang, ed., *Asian American Autobiographers: A Bio-Bibliographical Critical Sourcebook* (Westport, CT: Greenwood Press, 2001), 159–64.

French, Robert W. Rev. of *Lost Names*. *Massachusetts Review* 11, no. 4 (1970): 840–42.

Gallway, David D. "The Love Stance: Richard E. Kim's *The Martyred*." *Critique* 7 (1964–1965): 165–71.

Han, Jae-Nam. "Richard E. Kim." In Emmanuel S. Nelson, ed., *Asian American Novelists: A Bio-Bibliographical Critical Sourcebook* (Westport, CT: Greenwood Press, 2000), 132–37.

Kim, Elaine H. "Korean American Literature." In King-Kok Cheung, ed., *An Interethnic Companion to Asian American Literature* (New York: Cambridge University Press, 1997), 156–91.

Lee, James Kyung-Jin. "Best-selling Korean American: Revisiting Richard E. Kim." *Korean Culture* 19, no. 1 (Spring 1998): 30–39.

* * *

Ronyoung Kim (Gloria Kim, 1926–1987). Born in Los Angeles's Koreatown, Kim was raised in California, though she spent two years visiting relatives in North Korea. She became seriously interested in art and literature after her four children had already graduated from college. Eventually she received a bachelor's degree in Far Eastern art and culture from San Francisco State University. Her autobiographical novel, *Clay Walls*, written while taking writing classes and attending workshops, was published in 1986 (Sag Harbor, NY: Permanent). For this novel she was nominated for the Pulitzer Prize, just before she died of breast cancer in 1987.

Clay Walls is critically significant because it is one of the earliest Korean American novels; it is thus a pioneering work in Korean American literature. The book was translated into Korean in 1989, three years after its original publication in English. It has been compared to John Okada's *No-No Boy* and Louis Chu's *Eat a Bowl of Tea* in terms of their status in Japanese and Chinese American literature, respectively. Kim's novel portrays the life of a Korean American family—the mother, Haesu; the father, Chun; and their American-born daughter, Faye—from around 1920 to 1945, when World War II ended. Each of the three members is the focus of one of the book's three sections. And like many other novels about immigration, Kim's narrative depicts the hardships and struggles of the first-generation immigrants as well as the trepidations and triumphs of the American-born second generation. The metaphor of the novel's clay walls carries similar connotations as Robert Frost's poem, "Mending Wall": walls shield and protect, but they also separate and alienate. "For Chun [the husband], the clay walls stand for the familiar, the known, the shield that protects him from the alien and hostile world. For Haesu [the wife], however, they represent the oppressive forces emanating from her culture, especially toward Korean women. Chun wants to build walls around the house they bought; Haesu wants to annihilate walls altogether" (Yun, *Resource Guide*, 82).

For more information, see:

Kim, Elaine H. "Kim, Ronyoung." In Cathy N. Davidson and Linda Wagner-Martin, eds., *The Oxford Companion to Women's Writing in the United States* (New York: Oxford University Press, 1995), 457.

Lee, Kyung-won. "Whispers from *Clay Walls* Heard Around the World." *Newsreview* 10 (September 1988): 30–31.

Oh, Seiwoong. "Cross-Cultural Reading Versus Textual Accessibility in Multicultural Literature." *MELUS* 18, no. 2 (1993): 3–16.

Solberg, S.E. "*Clay Walls*: Korean-American Pioneers." *Korean Culture* (December 1986): 30–35.

Yun, Chung-Hei. "Beyond *Clay Walls*." In Shirley Geok-lin Lim and Amy Ling, eds., *Reading the Literatures of Asian America* (Philadelphia: Temple University Press, 1992), 79–95.

——. "*Clay Walls*, by Ronyoung Kim." In Sau-ling Cynthia Wong and Stephen H. Sumida, eds., *A Resource Guide to Asian American Literature* (New York: MLA, 2001), 78–85.

* * *

Maxine Hong Kingston (1940–). Born in Stockton, California, to Tom and Ying Lan Hong, first-generation Chinese immigrants from Toishan, Guangdong province, Kingston was educated in English at the University of California at Berkeley. She played a pioneering role in the establishment of an Asian American literary canon with her famous book, *The Woman Warrior: Memoirs of a Girlhood Among Ghosts* (New York: Knopf, 1976), the genre of which generated a great deal of discussion as well as criticism by both mainstream and Asian American, especially male, critics. The book is catalogued as an autobiography, but there are obvious elements of fantasy and fiction, admixed with folktales as well as historical and familial stories. Kingston followed the huge success of her first book with a sequel, *China Men*, in 1980 (New York: Knopf), another auto/biographical work with a narrative focus on the male side of her immigrant family that participated in the building of the transcontinental railroad. Both auto/biographical works have received major recognition: the National Book Critics Circle Award for nonfiction for *The Woman Warrior* in 1976 and the National Book Award for *China Men* in 1981, among other honors. In 1989, Kingston published her first novel, *Tripmaster Monkey: His Fake Book* (New York: Knopf), which won her the 1989 PEN USA West Award in Fiction. Knopf released Kingston's new work, *The Fifth Book of Peace*, in late 2003, categorized as memoir. Kingston has also published a prose work called *Hawai'i One Summer* (San Francisco: Meadow, 1987), a few poems, and a considerable number of articles in books, magazines, journals, and newspapers.

Kingston is primarily a prose writer, in the form of the novel, the memoir, or the essay. The popularity of her first book is evident in the MLA's publication of *Approaches to Teaching Kingston's* The Woman Warrior in 1991, an honor that few contemporary writers have received. However, *The Woman Warrior* defies genre categorization. Fiction and nonfiction in *The Woman Warrior* and *China Men* sometimes are hardly distinguishable—the novel and the autobiography seem to blend well in both works. In the former, the author attempts to record the life of a young Chinese American girl who lives in a ghostly world, stuck between reality and fantasy, and who tries but often fails to fend off the evils of racism and sexism in America. She dreams of becoming a fearless woman warrior like the celebrated Chinese legendary heroine Fa Mu Lan (Hua Mulan), who avenges her family by killing the baron and beheading the emperor. But this militaristic course of action is achievable only by a swordswoman in a fantasized land; the more realistic and realizable dream is to be another sort of warrior, like Ts'ai Yen, the ancient Chinese woman poet who expressed feelings of alienation and oppression through writing poems. Hence the narra-

tor becomes a woman warrior in the intellectual sense.

The male half of Kingston's auto/biographical narrative is presented in *China Men*, where male Chinese immigrants work Hawaii's sugarcane plantations, and sweat and bleed along the railroad tracks they help to lay across the U.S. continent. The book not only attempts to document her father's legal or illegal entry into the United States, in which case the author plays the role of the "family historian," in the words of Linda Ching Sledge (3), it also re-presents certain U.S. immigration laws in the larger contexts of U.S. history, Asian American history, and Kingston's own family history. While *China Men* is less concerned with the theme of sexism than *The Woman Warrior*, it probes deep into issues of racism as an institutionalized practice sanctioned by the government.

Kingston's novel, *Tripmaster Monkey*, departs considerably in theme and structure from her two previous works: it deals less with racism and sexism than with (self-)identity and the conceptualization of Asian America. The protagonist, Wittman Ah Sing, possesses 100 percent of the Asian American sensibility: American-born, Americanism-speaking, and rebellious, he is the embodiment of the perfect combination of Chinese and American cultures, resembling both the mischievous, obnoxious, and yet righteous Monkey King of China, the protagonist of the sixteenth-century Chinese novel *Journey to the West* (translated as *Monkey King* by Arthur Waley), and the garrulous, all-embracing, and free-spirited quintessential American poet, Walt Whitman—he even shares his name. Despite failures of all kinds, Wittman forges ahead in his quest for a place and identity in his community and society at large. Critics and readers have noted similar character traits between Kingston's Wittman and the writer

Frank Chin. Hence the parodic quality of the novel. *The Fifth Book of Peace*, Kingston's latest book, is divided into four sections, "Fire," "Paper," "Water," and "Earth." Kingston describes her new book as "nonfiction-fiction-nonfiction sandwich," and says, "Some might even toss around terms such as metafiction—because much of the book explores the act of the author's rewriting it" (Shea 32).

Kingston is beyond any doubt the most studied Asian American writer of the twentieth century. Studies of her works—books, articles, reviews, interviews, and dissertations—are legion. The following is a select list:

Baer, Elizabeth. "The Confrontation of East and West: *The Woman Warrior* as Postmodern Autobiography." *Redneck Review of Literature* 21 (1991): 26–29.

Cheung, King-Kok. "The Woman Warrior Versus the Chinaman Pacific: Must a Chinese American Critic Choose Between Feminism and Heroism?" In Marianne Hirsch and Evelyn Fox Keller, eds., *Conflicts in Feminism* (New York: Routledge, 1990), 234–51.

Chin, Frank. "This Is Not an Autobiography." *Genre* 18 (1985): 109–30.

——. "Come All Ye Asian American Writers of the Real and the Fake." in Jeffery Paul Chan, Frank Chin, Lawson Fusao Inada, and Shawn Wong, eds., *The Big Aiiieeeee!* (New York: Meridian, 1991), 1–92.

Chu, Patricia P. "'The Invisible World the Emmigrants Built': Cultural Self-Inscription and the Antiromantic Plots of *The Woman Warrior*." *Diaspora* 2, no. 1 (1992): 95–115.

——. "*The Woman Warrior: Memoirs of a Girlhood Among Ghosts*, by Maxine Hong Kingston." In Sau-ling Cynthia Wong and Stephen H. Sumida, eds., *A Resource Guide to Asian American Literature* (New York: MLA, 2001), 86–96.

Deeney, John J. "Of Monkeys and Butterflies: Transformation in M.H. Kingston's *Tripmaster Monkey* and D.H. Hwang's *M. Butterfly*." *MELUS* 18, no. 4 (1993): 21–40.

Fichtelberg, Joseph. "Poet and Patriarch in Maxine Hong Kingston's *China Men*." In Shirley Neuman, ed., *Autobiography and Questions of Gender* (Portland, OR: Frank Cass, 1991), 166–85.

Fishkin, Shelley Fisher. "Interview with Maxine Hong Kingston." *American Literary History* 3, no. 4 (Winter 1991): 782–91.

Goellnicht, Donald C. "Tang Ao in America: Male Subject Positions in *China Men*." In Shirley Geok-lin Lim and Amy Ling, eds., *Reading the Literatures of Asian America* (Philadelphia: Temple University Press, 1992), 191–212.

Huang, Guiyou. "Maxine Hong Kingston." In Emmanuel Nelson, ed., *Asian American Novelists: A Bio-Bibliographical Critical Sourcebook* (Westport, CT: Greenwood Press, 2000), 138–55.

Li, David Leiwei. "*China Men*: Maxine Hong Kingston and the American Canon." *American Literary History* 2, no. 3 (1990): 482–502.

Lim, Shirley Geok-lin. "The Tradition of Chinese American Women's Life Stories: Thematics of Race and Gender in Jade Snow Wong's *Fifth Chinese Daughter* and Maxine Hong Kingston's *The Woman Warrior*." In Margo Culley, ed., *American Women's Autobiography: Fea(s)ts of Memory* (Madison: University of Wisconsin Press, 1992), 252–67.

Lim, Shirley Geok-lin, ed. *Approaches to Teaching Kingston's* The Woman Warrior. New York: MLA, 1991.

Lin, Patricia. "Clashing Constructs of Reality: Reading Maxine Hong Kingston's *Tripmaster Monkey: His Fake Book* as Indigenous Ethnography." In Shirley Geok-lin Lim and Amy Ling, eds., *Reading the Literatures of Asian America* (Philadelphia: Temple University Press, 1992), 333–48.

Shea, Renee H. "The Story Revisited: A Profile of Maxine Hong Kingston." *Poets & Writers* 31, no. 5 (September/October 2003): 31–35.

Skandera-Trombley, Laura E., ed. *Critical Essays on Maxine Hong Kingston.* Boston: G. K. Hall, 1998.

Skenazy, Paul and Tera Martin, eds. *Conversations with Maxine Hong Kingston.* Jackson: University Press of Mississippi, 1998.

Sledge, Linda Ching. "Maxine Hong Kingston's *China Men*: The Family Historian as Epic Poet." *MELUS* 7, no. 4 (1980): 3–22.

Thomas, Brook. "*China Men, United States v. Wong Kim Ark*, and the Question of Citizenship." *American Quarterly* 50, no. 4 (December 1998): 689–717.

Wong, Sau-ling Cynthia. "Ethnic Dimensions of Postmodern Indeterminacy: Maxine Hong Kingston's *The Woman Warrior* as Avant-garde Autobiography." In Alfred Hornung and Ernestpeter Ruhe, eds, *Autobiographie and Avant-garde: Alain Robbe-Grillet, Serge Doubrovsky, Rachid Boudjedra, Maxine Hong Kingston, Raymond Federman, Ronald Sukenick* (Tübingen, Germany: G. Narr, 1992), 274–84.

* * *

Joy Kogawa (1935–). Probably the most renowned Canadian writer of Japanese ancestry, Kogawa was born Joy Nakayama in Vancouver, British Columbia, and married David Kogawa in 1957. Like thousands of American and Canadian Japanese living on the West Coast of North America during World War II, Kogawa was interned with her family at age six, a traumatic experience that inspired her autobiographical novel *Obasan*. After relocation, Kogawa attended the Women's Training College, the Conservatory of Music, the University of Alberta, and the University of Saskatchewan. She first became known as a poet, publishing *The Splintered Moon* in 1968 (Fredericton: University of New Brunswick Press), followed by *A Choice of Dreams* in 1974 (Toronto: McClelland and Stewart), *Jericho Road* in 1977 (Toronto: McClelland and Stewart), *Six Poems* in 1978 (Toronto: League of Canadian Poets), *Woman in the Woods* in 1985 (Oakville, ON: Mosaic Press), *A Song of Lilith* in 2001 (Vancouver: Polestar Book Publishers), and most recently, *A Garden of Anchors: Selected Poems* (Oakville, ON: Mosaic Press, 2003). Kogawa was already a successful poet when she started to write fiction, publishing her first, also her most acclaimed, prose work, *Obasan*, in 1981 (Harmondsworth, England: Penguin), followed by its American editions in 1982 and 1994. The novel was rewritten for children as *Naomi's Road*, published in 1986 (Toronto: Oxford University Press). *Itsuka*, a sequel to *Obasan*, appeared in 1992 (Toronto: Viking Press). Her most recent prose work, *The Rain Ascends* (Toronto: Knopf), came out in 1995.

Kogawa has received many awards for her literary achievements, including the Books in Canada First Novel award in 1981, the Authors Association Book of the Year award in 1982, the Before Columbus Foundation American Book Award in 1982, and the Periodical Distributions of Canada

Award for Best Paperback Fiction, in addition to a number of honorary degrees.

The title *Obasan* means both "aunt" and "woman." The title character is the aging aunt of Naomi Nakane, a thirty-six-year-old school teacher who struggles between two approaches to the consequences of Japanese Canadians' internment in World War II: the stoic reserve of her surrogate mother, Obasan, and the activist reparation efforts of her mother's sister, Aunt Emily. The former uses silence to deal with the tragedy while the latter resorts more to the power of words. Naomi confronts her family's tragic past—her father's death and her mother's disfigurement—while undergoing a journey of self-knowledge and discovery. Even though *Itsuka*, a sequel to *Obasan*, has been less favorably received, it shares the historical theme of internment and traces the circumstances of the death of Naomi's mother while Naomi completes her search and finds ways of healing. The novel ends on a note of optimism. Kogawa's third novel, *The Rain Ascends*, again told through the voice of a daughter, considers the intersections of the private and public worlds of a clergyman, Millicent Shelby's father. Millicent's moral dilemma about her father's sexual abuse constitutes the narrative focus of the novel.

Though Kogawa's production volume of poetry outweighs that of fiction, her novels, particularly *Obasan*, have received a great deal more critical attention. See:

Cheung, King-Kok. *Articulate Silences: Hisaye Yamamoto, Maxine Hong Kinston, Joy Kogawa*. Ithaca, NY: Cornell University Press, 1993.

——. "Attentive Silence in Joy Kogawa's *Obasan*." In Elaine Hedges and Shelley Fisher Fishkin, eds., *Listening to Silences: New Essays in Feminist Criticism* (New York: Oxford University Press, 1994), 113–29.

Chua, Cheng Lok. "Witnessing the Japanese Canadian Experience in World War II: Processual Structure, Symbolism, and Irony in Joy Kogawa's *Obasan*." In Shirley Geok-lin Lim and Amy Ling, eds., *Reading the Literatures of Asian America* (Philadelphia: Temple University Press, 1992), 97–108.

Davidson, Arnold. *Writing Against the Silence: Joy Kogawa's* Obasan. Toronto: ECW, 1993.

Fairbank, Carol. "Joy Kogawa's *Obasan*: A Study in Political Efficacy." *Journal of American and Canadian Studies* 5 (1990): 73–92.

Fujita, Gayle K. "'To Attend the Sound of Stone': The Sensibility of Silence in *Obasan*." *MELUS* 12, no. 3 (1985): 33–42.

Goellnicht, Donald C. "Father Land and/or Mother Tongue: The Divided Female Subject in Kogawa's *Obasan* and Hong Kingston's *The Woman Warrior*." In Janice Morgan, Colette T. Hall, and Carol Snyder, eds., *Redefining Autobiography in Twentieth-Century Women's Fiction* (New York: Garland, 1991), 119–34.

——. "Minority History as Metafiction: Joy Kogawa's *Obasan*." *Tulsa Studies in Women's Literature* 8 (Fall 1989): 287–306.

Gottlieb, Erika. "The Riddle of Concentric Worlds in *Obasan*." *Canadian Literature* 109 (Summer 1986): 34–53.

Harris, Mason. "Broken Generations in *Obasan*: Inner Conflict and the Destruction of Community." *Canadian Literature* 127 (Winter 1990): 41–57.

Jones, Manina. "The Avenues of Speech and Silence: Telling Difference in Joy Kogawa's *Obasan*." In Martin Kreiswirth and Mark A.

Cheetham, eds., *Theory Between the Disciplines: Authority/Vision/Politics* (Ann Arbor: University of Michgan Press, 1990), 213–29.

Kanefsky, Rachelle. "Debunking a Postmodern Conception of History: A Defence of Humanist Values in the Novels of Joy Kogawa." *Canadian Literature* 148 (Spring 1996): 11–36.

Lim, Shirley Geok-lin. "Japanese American Women's Life Stories: Maternity in Monica Sone's *Nisei Daughter* and Joy Kogawa's *Obasan*." *Feminist Studies* 16, no. 2 (Summer 1990): 289–312.

Lo, Marie. "*Obasan*, by Joy Kogawa." In Sau-ling Cynthia Wong and Stephen H. Sumida, eds., *A Resource Guide to Asian American Literature* (New York: MLA, 2001), 97–107.

Magnusson, A. Lynne. "Language and Longing in Joy Kogawa's *Obasan*." *Canadian Literature* 116 (Spring 1988): 58–66.

Merivale, Patricia. "Framed Voices: The Polyphonic Elegies of Hebert and Kogawa." *Canadian Literature* 116 (Spring 1988): 68–82.

Potter, Robin. "Moral—in Whose Sense? Joy Kogawa's *Obasan* and Julia Kristeva's *Powers of Horror*." *Studies in Canadian Literature* 15 (1990): 117–39.

Rose, Marilyn Russell. "Hawthorne's 'Customs House,' Said's *Orientalism* and Kogawa's *Obasan*: An Intertextual Reading of an Historical Fiction." *Dalhousie Review* 67, no. 2–3 (Summer–Fall 1987): 286–96.

——. "Politics Into Art: Kogawa's *Obasan* and the Rhetoric of Fiction." *Mosaic* 21 (1988): 215–26.

Snelling, Sonia. "'A Human Pyramid': An (Un)Balancing Act of Ancestry and History in Joy Kogawa's *Obasan*

and Michael Ondaatje's *Running in the Family*." *Journal of Commonwealth Literature* 32 (1997): 21–33.

St. Andrews, B. A. "Reclaiming a Canadian Heritage: Kogawa's *Obasan*." *International Fiction Review* 13 (1986): 29–31.

Tapping, Craig. "Joy Kogawa." In Guiyou Huang, ed., *Asian American Autobiographers: A Bio-Bibliographical Critical Sourcebook* (Westport, CT: Greenwood Press, 2001), 179–86.

Thiesmeyer, Lynn. "Joy Kogawa's *Obasan*: Unsilencing the Silence of America's Concentration Camps." *Journal of the Faculty of Humanities* [Japan Women's University] 41 (1991): 63–80.

Turner, Margaret E. "Power, Language and Gender: Writing 'History' in *Beloved* and *Obasan*." *Mosaic* 25 (Fall 1992): 81–97.

Ty, Eleanor. "Struggling with the Powerful (M)Other: Identity and Sexuality in Kogawa's *Obasan* and Kincaid's *Lucy*." *International Fiction Review* 20 (1993): 120–26.

Ueki, Teruyo. "*Obasan*: Revelations in a Paradoxical Scheme." *MELUS* 18, no. 4 (Winter 1993–1994): 5–20.

Williamson, Janice. "Biocritical Essay on Joy Kogawa." in *Sounding Differences: Conversations with Seventeen Canadian Women Writers* (Toronto: University of Toronto Press, 1993), 352–54.

Willis, Gary. "Speaking the Silence: Joy Kogawa's *Obasan*." *Studies in Canadian Literature* 12, no. 2 (1987): 239–49.

——. "Kogawa." In James P. Draper, ed., *Contemporary Literary Criticism*, vol. 78 (Detroit: Gale Research, 1994), 164–95.

Wong, Cynthia. "Joy Kogawa." In Emmanuel S. Nelson, ed., *Asian*

American Novelists: A Bio-Bibliographical Critical Sourcebook (Westport, CT: Greenwood Press, 2000), 161–67.

Zwicker, Heather. "Canadian Women of Color in the New World Order: Marlene Nourbese Philip, Joy Kogawa, and Beatrice Culleton Fight Their Way Home." In Mickey Pearlman, ed., *Canadian Women Writing Fiction* (Jackson: University Press of Mississippi, 1993), 142–54.

* * *

Lydia Kwa. See Kwa in "Poetry."

Jhumpa Lahiri. See Lahiri in "Short Fiction."

* * *

Wendy Law-Yone (1947–). The daughter of a famous Burmese journalist, Law-Yone was born in Mandalay and raised in Rangoon, the capital city of Burma. Marriage to an American citizen took her to the United States in 1967, and she became a U.S. citizen in 1968. Law-Yone also lived briefly in several Southeast Asian countries, including Thailand, Singapore, and Malaysia. Returning to the United States in 1973, she attended Eckerd College in Florida, but since 1975 she has resided in Washington, DC, where she works as an editor. She started to write fiction in the 1980s and published her first novel, *The Coffin Tree*, in 1983 (New York: Knopf), and her second, *Irrawaddy Tango* (New York: Knopf), in 1993. Law-Yone is a recipient of a National Endowment for the Arts fellowship and a Carnegie Endowment fellowship; *Irrawaddy Tango* was nominated for the Irish Times Literary Award in 1995.

Law-Yone is no doubt a unique novelist in the Asian American literary canon because she is the first Burmese American to publish a critically acclaimed novel, a work that deals with Southeast Asian experience from historical, political, cultural, and feminist perspectives. As Tamara C. Ho puts it, "*The Coffin Tree* is a novel in the form of a memoir being written by an unnamed woman recalling her childhood in Burma and her subsequent immigration to the United States" (108). The narrator is a twenty-year-old woman whose mother died giving birth to her and who lives with her half-brother Shan, first in Rangoon and then in New York. The title of the book refers to a story about the spirit of the coffin tree that Shan had kept before his sudden death, now a spiritual guide to the woman narrator in her struggle to survive trauma (personal and national) and instability. *Irrawaddy Tango* explores similar themes of alienation, immigration, the effects of colonialism, and the relationship of the First and Third Worlds.

There has been little creative and critical literature written by and about Burmese Americans, which only heightens the literary value of Law-Yone's work. While reviews of her novels are not rare, article-length studies are still limited. See:

Bow, Leslie. "Beyond Rangoon: An Interview with Wendy Law-Yone." *MELUS* 27, no. 4 (Winter 2002): 183–200.

Chua, Cheng Lok. "Asian Americans Imagining Burma: Chang-rae Lee's *A Gesture Life* and Wendy Law-Yone's *Irrawaddy Tango*." In Guiyou Huang, ed., *Asian American Literary Studies* (Edinburgh, Scotland: Edinburgh University Press, 2005), 64–76.

Har, Janie C. "Food, Sexuality, and the Pursuit of a Little Attention."

Hitting Critical Mass: A Journal of Asian American Cultural Criticism 1, no. 1 (Fall 1993): 83–92.

Ho, Tamara C. "*The Coffin Tree*, by Wendy Law-Yone." In Sau-ling Cynthia Wong and Stephen H. Sumida, eds., *A Resource Guide to Asian American Literature* (New York: MLA, 2001), 108–20.

Interview with Tamara Ho and Nancy Yoo. In King-Kok Cheung, ed., *Words Matter: Conversations with Asian American Writers* (Honolulu: University of Hawai'i Press, 2000), 283–302.

Lee, Rachel. "The Erasure of Places and Re-siting of Empire in Wendy Law-Yone's *The Coffin Tree*." *Cultural Critique* 35 (Winter 1996–97): 149–78.

* * *

Chang-rae Lee (1965–). Born in Seoul, South Korea, Lee moved to New York with his parents at the age of three. He attended Phillips Exeter Academy and went on to earn a B.A. in English from Yale University in 1987 and an M.F.A. in creative writing from the University of Oregon in 1993. He analyzed stocks on Wall Street for a year, but his true interest remained writing. Lee published his first novel, *Native Speaker,* in 1995 (New York: Putnam/Riverhead); he is believed to be the first Korean American to have a novel published by a major American publisher (Kish 175; Park 148). *A Gesture Life* (New York: Riverhead), his second novel, came out in 1999. Lee has also written short stories and articles for magazines and journals. He has received numerous awards and recognitions: he was a finalist for *Granta's* Best American Novelists Under 40 in 1996, one of *The New Yorker's* twenty best American writers under 40 in 1999, and a Guggenheim Foundation Fellow in 2000–2001. *Native Speaker* won the PEN/Hemingway Award for Best First Fiction, the American Book Award, the Barnes and Noble Discover Award, the QPB New Voices Award, and the Oregon Book Award, and was one of *Time* magazine's Best Books of 1995. *A Gesture Life* has also garnered several awards: the Anisfield-Wolf Prize, the Myers Outstanding Book Award, the NAIBA Book Award, the Asian American Literary Award for Fiction, *New York Times* Notable Book of the Year, and *Talk* magazine's Best Book of 1999, among others.

Lee's most acclaimed novel to date, *Native Speaker* refers to both the mother tongue of immigrants and the language of native-born Americans; like *A Gesture Life*, it narrates the Asian immigrant experience, telling the story of Henry Park, a Korean American spy-for-hire working for a company that specializes in ethnic and racial issues. When his role as a spy is exposed, Park is forced to confront personal and political issues concerning his identity and place in American culture and society. *A Gesture Life* continues the novelist's exploration of immigration and assimilation topics, through the character of Franklin "Doc" Hata, who goes through several stages of life involving the change of his occupation and identity, first as a native Korean, then a Japanese soldier, then an owner of a surgical supply store in America, and finally, a retiree reflecting on his dramatic past life.

Reviews of Lee's novels abound. Articles include:

"Chang-rae Lee." *Contemporary Literary Criticism* 91 (1995): 53–58.

"Chang-rae Lee." In Lawrence J. Trudeau, ed., *Asian American Literature: Reviews and Criticism of Works by American Writers of Asian Descent* (Detroit: Gale Research, 1999), 241–49.

"Chang-rae Lee." *Contemporary Authors New Revision Series* 89 (2000): 224–26.

Chua, Cheng Lok. "Asian Americans Imagining Burma: Chang-rae Lee's *A Gesture Life* and Wendy Law-Yone's *Irrawaddy Tango*." In Guiyou Huang, ed., *Asian American Literary Studies* (Edinburgh, Scotland: Edinburgh University Press, 2005), 64–76.

Engles, Timothy David. "'Visions of Me in the Whitest Raw Light': Assimilation and Toxic Whiteness in Chang-rae Lee's *Native Speaker*." *Hitting Critical Mass: A Journal of Asian American Cultural Criticism* 4, no. 2 (1997): 27–48.

Huh, Joonok. "'Strangest Corale': New York City in *East Goes West* and *Native Speaker*." In Will Wright and Steven Kaplan, eds., *The Image of the Twentieth Century in Literature, Media, and Society* (Pueblo, CO: Society for the Interdisciplinary Study of Social Imagery, University of Southern Colorado, 2000), 419–22.

Kich, Martin. "Chang-rae Lee." In Emmanuel S. Nelson, ed., *Asian American Novelists: A Bio-Bibliographical Critical Sourcebook* (Westport, CT: Greenwood Press, 2000), 175–79.

Millard, Kenneth. "Chang-rae Lee: *Native Speaker*." In *Contemporary American Fiction* (New York: Oxford University Press, 2000), 163–69, 185.

Pandiscio, Richard. "Great New Stories." *Interview* 25 (September 25, 1995): 136–39.

Park, Joonseong. "Chang-rae Lee." In Guiyou Huang, ed., *Asian American Short Story Writers: An A-to-Z Guide* (Westport, CT: Greenwood Press, 2003), 147–50.

Park, You-mei and Gayle Wald. "Native Daughters in the Promised Land: Gender, Race, and the Question of Separate Spheres." *American Literature* 70, no. 3 (1998): 607–33.

* * *

C. Y. Lee (1917–). Born in Hunan province, China, Chin-Yang (C. Y.) Lee went to high school in Beijing and attended college at Shandong University, but due to the eruption of the Sino-Japanese War in the north, he had to complete his bachelor's degree in 1942 at Southwest Allied University in Kunming, capital of the southern Chinese province of Yunnan. Lee immigrated to the United States in 1942; he earned an M.F.A. in drama from Yale University in 1947 and became a naturalized American citizen in 1949.

In his long writing career, Lee wrote at least ten novels: *The Flower Drum Song* (New York: Farrar, Straus, and Cudahy, 1957), *Lover's Point* (New York: Farrar, Straus, and Cudahy, 1958), *The Sawbwa and His Secretary* (New York: Farrar, Straus, and Cudahy, 1959), *Madame Goldenflower* (New York: Farrar, Straus, and Cudahy, 1960), *Cripple Mah and the New Order* (New York: Farrar, Straus, and Cudahy, 1961), *The Virgin Market* (New York: Farrar, Straus, and Cudahy, 1964), *The Land of the Golden Mountain* (New York: Farrar, Straus, and Cudahy, 1967), *China Saga* (New York: Weidenfeld and Nicolson, 1987), *The Second Son of Heaven* (New York: William Morrow, 1990), and *Gate of Rage: A Novel of One Family Trapped by the Events at Tiananmen Square* (New York: William Morrow, 1991). Of all these long narratives, *The Flower Drum Song* remains Lee's most read work. The title of the novel reflects the author's nostalgia about his home province in China, Hunan—the birthplace and main stage for the local dramatic genre called Flower Drum Song. The novel depicts life in North America's most famous Chinatown, in San Francisco, where Lee edited a Chinese-language newspaper and wrote columns for *Chinese World*. Chinatown is not merely a place where the East and the West meet, it is a site where the values of the old world of China and the new world of America compare, contrast, and clash, as is represented by the generational conflicts between the protagonist, Mr. Wang, and his American-born son.

Reviewers have noted the exoticism and focus on China in Lee's novels, which may partly explain his lack of popularity with American critics. Even though Lee has had a long writing career that has produced many books, studies of his work have been scarce and are mainly in the form of reviews. Four pieces are of interest:

Li, Luchen. "C. Y. Lee." In Emmanuel S. Nelson, ed., *Asian American Novelists: A Bio-Bibliographical Critical Sourcebook* (Westport, CT: Greenwood Press, 2000), 180–84.

See, Lisa. "C.-Y. Lee Interview." *Publishers Weekly* (August 14, 1987): 84–85.

Wakeman, John. *World Authors: 1950–1970* (New York: H. W. Wilson, 1975).

Zia, Helen and Susan B. Gall, eds. *Notable Asian Americans* (Detroit: Gale Research, 1995).

* * *

Don Lee. See Lee in "Short Fiction."

* * *

Gus Lee (1946–). Lee was born in San Francisco and grew up in a predominantly African American neighborhood. He enrolled at West Point, only to drop out; then he attended the University of California at Davis, receiving a B.A. in 1969 and a J.D. in 1976. Lee followed the law profession in various capacities and in different places until he retired to Colorado Springs in order to write full time.

Lee's law career provided much of the base material for his two recent novels, *Tiger's Tail* (New York: Knopf, 1996) and *No Physical Evidence* (New York: Columbine,

1998). His first two novels, *China Boy* (New York: Dutton, 1991) and *Honor and Duty* (New York: Knopf, 1994) also contain recognizable autobiographical elements. As John C. Hawley observes, "The topics of Lee's novels have tended to follow his career. *China Boy*…tells of his boyhood in San Francisco. *Honor and Duty* recounts his struggles at West Point. *Tiger's Tail* draws on Lee's assignment in postwar Korea as one of ten army attorneys in the Connelly Commission that investigated illegal practices. *No Physical Evidence* is set in the law courts of Sacramento" ("Gus Lee" 186). Lee's novels cultivate two prominent themes: the author's quest for identity as an Asian American in the mainstream society, and issues relevant to assimilation. Even though the protagonists have different names and characteristics, the four novels contain autobiographical details that flash back on Lee's life and career. All his protagonists are male—Kai Ting in *China Boy* and *Honor and Duty*; Jackson Hu-chin Kan in *Tiger's Tail*; and Joshua Jin in *No Physical Evidence*. In the first two books, the author's father and mother figure prominently in a family disrupted and broken by the death of a loving mother and the arrival of a stepmother after the father's remarriage. *Tiger's Tail* looks into the themes of male bonding, loyalty, and comradeship. *No Physical Evidence*, as the title indicates, is set in the courtroom, where the rule of law and friendships confront each other headlong.

Lee's novels have been greeted with a considerable amount of enthusiasm, particularly *China Boy* and *Honor and Duty*, though critics generally agree that the latter is his best book to date (Hawley, "Gus Lee," 189). Studies of Lee are still emerging, though the following pieces have laid the groundwork for further discussions:

Hawley, John C. "Gus Lee, Chang-Rae Lee, and Li-Young Lee: The Search for the Father in Asian American Literature." In Geoffrey Kain, ed., *Ideas of Home: Literature of Asian Migration* (East Lansing: Michigan State University Press, 1997), 183–95.

———. "Gus Lee." In Emmanuel S. Nelson, ed., *Asian American Novelists: A Bio-Bibliographical Critical Sourcebook* (Westport, CT: Greenwood Press, 2000), 185–91.

Nguyen, Viet Thanh. "The Remasculization of Chinese America: Race, Violence, and the Novel." *American Literary History* 12, no. 1 (2000): 130–57.

So, Christine. "Delivering the Punch Line: Racial Combat as Comedy in Gus Lee's *China Boy.*" *MELUS* 21, no. 4 (Winter 1996): 141–55.

Stone, Judy. "Gus Lee, A China Boy's Rites of Passage." *Publishers Weekly* (March 18, 1996): 47–48.

* * *

Marie G. Lee (1964–). A Korean American novelist born in Hibbing, Minnesota, Lee was raised in a small-town community of Scandinavians that had only one family of Asian descent, her own. As a child, Lee was an avid reader. She attended Brown University and earned an A.B. in economics in 1986. Lee taught one semester at Yale University in 1997 and spent the following year at Seoul Women's University as a Fulbright scholar. She published three novels before she turned thirty: *Finding My Voice* (New York: Houghton Mifflin, 1992), *If It Hadn't Been for Yoon Jun* (New York: Houghton Mifflin, 1993), and *Saying Goodbye* (New York: Houghton Mifflin, 1994). The next three novels came out within three years of one another: *Necessary Roughness* (New York: HarperCollins, 1997), *Night of the Chupacabras* (New York: Avon, 1998), and *F Is for Fabuloso* (New York: Avon, 1999).

If It Hadn't Been for Yoon Jun; Night of the Chupacabras; and *F Is for Fabuloso* were written for young readers. The title character of *If It Hadn't Been for Yoon Jun* is a Korean boy of the same age and grade as Alice Larson, a Korean girl adopted by a white couple and now a cheerleader in school. In their first interactions, Alice views Yoon Jun as foreign and different; after a series of events including one in which Yoon Jun saves Alice from an automobile accident, she is able to identify with him. *Night of the Chupacabras* also probes interracial issues, though this thriller focuses on mysterious killings of goats involving Mexicans and Koreans. *F Is for Fabuloso* examines immigration issues that face both the newcomers and America.

Lee's three young adult novels explore similar themes about being different and about peer and parental pressure. *Finding My Voice* and *Saying Goodbye* share the same protagonist, Ellen Sung, who has to cope with athletic competition, academic performance, relationships, and peer pressure. The former focuses on Ellen's life in high school and the latter deals with her experience in college at Harvard. In both works race has an important role in the growth of the protagonist. Growing pains also constitute a major theme in *Necessary Roughness*, which features a male Korean American, Chan Kim, trying to fit in in a small midwestern town, not unlike Marie Lee's own birthplace, while coping with the death of his sister and his difficult relationship with his father. In general, all Lee's novels maintain a focus on young adults and almost exclusively deal with issues relevant to family, school, race, and gender.

Despite her prolific oeuvre, Marie Lee is not a critically or popularly acclaimed novelist; she just turned forty, and a wider reception of her work is yet to come. Though reviews of her novels are not difficult to locate, there have been a few article-length studies:

Brock-Servais, Rhonda. "Marie G. Lee." In Emmanuel Nelson, ed., *Asian American Novelists: A Bio-Bibliographical Critical Sourcebook* (Westport, CT: Greenwood Press, 2000), 192–96.

Jones, J. Sydney. "Marie G. Lee." In Thomas McMahon, ed., *Authors and Artists for Young Adults*, vol. 25 (Detroit: Gale, 1998), 111–17.

Lee, Marie. "How I Grew." *ALAN Review* (Winter 1995): 8–11.

* * *

SKY Lee. See Lee in "Short Fiction."

* * *

Aimee E. Liu (1953–). Chinese American novelist and autobiographer Liu was born in Connecticut to a half-Chinese father and a Caucasian mother. Liu attended Yale in 1971 and graduated with a B.A. in fine art in 1975. From 1975 to 1978 she worked as a flight attendant for United Airlines. Other occupations she followed were an editor for business journals, a programmer for cable television, and associate producer for NBC's *TODAY* show. Liu served as the 2002 President of PEN USA. She published an autobiography, *Solitaire,* in 1979 (New York: Harper & Row), then she turned to writing fiction full time. Her first novel, *Face,* came out in 1994 (New York: Warner Books), followed by a second, *Cloud Mountain,* in 1998 (New York: Warner Books) and a third, *Flash House,* in 2003 (New York: Warner Books). In addition, she has coauthored several books in psychology, child care, and business management.

Face narrates the story of a photographer, Maibelle Chung, who is forced to deal with her interracial identity living in New York's Chinatown; the novel also delves into the complexity of racial and interracial relations between ethnic Chinese and the mainstream society. *Cloud Mountain,* based on the story of Liu's grandparents' interracial marriage and set in California and China, relates the love story of a white woman, Hope Newfield, and a Chinese man, Liang Po-Yu, as well as the extreme difficulties they must overcome in order to be married. *Flash House,* Liu's most recent fiction work, is a suspense novel about the Cold War set in India and Central Asia. *Solitaire,* Liu's only autobiographical book, offers a personal account of anorexia nervosa. Published when she was twenty-six, *Solitaire* explores two important personal issues: the physical condition and social ramifications of being an anorexic, and the racial and cultural identity of an interracial person. As a teenage girl Liu suffered anorexia nervosa because of a desire to fit in. As a one-quarter Chinese, she struggled with questions of belonging and the social effects of interracial marriages.

For more information, see:

Fuchs, Marcia G. Rev. of *Solitaire. Book Review Digest* 75 (1979): 777.

Hoffert, Barbara. Rev. of *Face. Library Journal* 119 (August 1994): 130.

Leebore, Patricia Harusame. Rev. of *Face. Belles Lettres* 10 (Spring 1995): 65–67.

Li, Luchen. "Aimee E. Liu." In Guiyou Huang, ed., *Asian American Autobiographers: A Bio-Bibliographical Critical Sourcebook* (Westport, CT: Greenwood Press, 2001), 227–31.

Rev. of *Cloud Mountain. Publishers Weekly* 244 (May 12, 1997): 57.

Rev. of *Cloud Mountain. Books* 12 (Summer 1998): 14.

Rev. of *Face. Publishers Weekly* (August 8, 1994): 386.

Seebolm, Caroline. Rev. of *Solitaire. New York Times Book Review,* July 29, 1979, 13.

* * *

Bette Bao Lord (1938–). Born in Shanghai, Bette Bao spent her first eight years in China. In 1946, her family moved to the United States for her father's diplomatic mission. Bette grew up in New York and New Jersey. She attended Tufts University in Boston and completed an M.A. at the Fletcher School of Law and Diplomacy, where she met her future husband, Winston Lord, a would-be U.S. ambassador to China. Her education at the school also paved the way for her to become a novelist as well as an international activist. Between 1964 and 1996, Lord published four novels: *Eighth Moon* (New York: Harper and Row, 1964), *Spring Moon* (New York: Harper and Row, 1981), *The Year of the Boar and Jackie Robinson* (New York: HarperCollins, 1984), and *The Middle Heart* (New York: Knopf, 1996); and a nonfiction book, *Legacies: A Chinese Mosaic* (New York: Knopf, 1990). In her active public life, Lord has served in a number of important and prestigious international organizations, including the National Commission on U.S.–China Relations; she has also been awarded honorary doctorates as well as major literary awards.

Eighth Moon depicts the relationships of three major characters: Steel Hope, Mountain Pine (a servant), and Firecrackers, a grave keeper's daughter. Jean Amato summarizes the novel adeptly: "In an idealistic, patriotic pact that begins during the Japanese occupation and survives fifty years of revolutionary chaos, loss, and triumph, the novel traces the social/political upheavals from the Cultural Revolution to Tiananmen Square that the characters face" (212). *Spring Moon*, named for its female protagonist, is an autobiographical novel that recounts her visits to China soon after the thawing of diplomatic ties with the United States, especially since 1972 when President Richard Nixon made his landmark visit to Beijing. *The Year of the Boar and Jackie Robinson* is a children's book that fictionalizes the author's own

experience during her first year of life in the United States.

Even though Bette Bao Lord is not a strange name to literary scholars or in the diplomatic circles within which she and her husband keep both professional and personal ties, and even though her novels have been reviewed in numerous venues, article or book-length studies are limited. Jean Amato's "Bette Bao Lord" in Emmanuel Nelson's *Asian American Novelists: A Bio-Bibliographical Critical Sourcebook* (Westport, CT: Greenwood Press, 2000), 211–13, contains useful information on the novelist's life and work. Mary Virginia Fox's *Bette Bao Lord: Novelist and Chinese Voice for Change* (Chicago: Children's Press, 1993) likewise offers insights into Lord's career and novels. Amy Ling's *Between Worlds: Women Writers of Chinese Ancestry* (New York: Pergamon Press, 1990) includes discussions of Lord's novels. Wei-hsiung Kitty Wu's doctoral dissertation, "Cultural Ideology and Aesthetic Choices: A Study of Three Works by Chinese American Women: Diana Chang, Bette Bao Lord, and Maxine H. Kingston" (University of Maryland, 1989) considers Lord's work in context and comparison with Chang's and Kingston's.

Anchee Min (1957–). Min was born in Shanghai during the fervent days of China's Great Leap Forward; at the young age of ten, she enthusiastically involved herself in the Cultural Revolution by becoming a Litter Red Guard in her school. Like millions of other "educated" city youths, Min went to a farm, Red Fire, to become a peasant in 1974; during this time she was chosen by the Shanghai Film Studio to play the lead female role in *Red Azalea*, which celebrates the life of Chairman Mao's wife, Jiang Qing. But after the 1976 fall of the infamous "Gang of Four," in which Madame Mao was a key figure, Min lost favor with the Communist Party for several years. She then immigrated to the United States. She took pains to study English and to learn to write in it as a second language, before she completed a B.F.A. and an M.F.A. at the Art Institute of Chicago. Min published *Red Azalea,* a memoir, in 1994 (New York: Pantheon); it won the Quality Paperback Club's nonfiction award. *Katherine* (New York: Riverhead Books), her first and only novel to date, appeared in 1995.

Katherine is titled for the protagonist of the novel, who is an American teacher of English in China in the early 1980s, when the open door policy was being implemented and foreign teachers were allowed to work in the erstwhile closed country. Katherine's experiences with her Chinese students highlight the moral, psychological, and traumatic effects of the Cultural Revolution on the younger generations of Chinese from a Westernized perspective, through the narrative voice of Zebra, a student, moderated by the distanced and Americanized author of the novel. Min attempts to understand the societywide consequences and victimizing effects of the ten-year-long Cultural Revolution, with which many Chinese were still trying to come to terms even years after it ended.

For more information, see:

Lin, An-Chi. "The Figurative Language of Anchee Min: Cross-Cultural Meaning and Schemata in the English Prose of a Non-Native Writer." M.A. thesis, University of California, 1996.

O'Hara, Delia. "Author Anchee Min's Book Weaves Her Story and History of China." *Chinatown News,* December 18, 1994, 16.

Somerson, Wendy. "Under the Mosquito Net: Space and Sexuality in *Red Azalea." College English* 24, no. 1 (February 1998): 98–115.

Wang, Shunzhu. "Anchee Min." In Emmanuel Nelson, ed., *Asian American Novelists: A Bio-Bibliographical Critical Sourcebook* (Westport, CT: Greenwood Press, 2000), 214–18.

Wilson, Kathleen. "Interview with Anchee Min." *Contemporary Literary Criticism,* vol. 86 (Detroit: Gale Research, 1994), 94–97.

Ward, Elizabeth. "Anchee Min's Quiet Stiletto Stabs at Modern China." *Japan Times,* March 12, 1996, 16.

* * *

Kyoko Mori (1957–). Mori was born in Kobe, Japan, and left to study at Rockford College in the United States, from which she received a bachelor's degree in 1979. She went on to earn a master's degree in 1981 and a doctoral degree in 1984, both at the University of Wisconsin, Milwaukee. Her doctoral dissertation, consisting of a group of stories, formed the base of her first novel, *Shizuko's Daughter* (New York: Holt, 1993). Her second novel, *One Bird,* came out in 1995 (New York: Holt). In 1990 Mori took a sabbatical leave in Japan that produced an autobiographical work, *The Dream of Water* (New York: Holt, 1995). Her Japanese travels also left significant marks on the nonfiction book, *Polite Lies: On Being a Woman Caught Between Cultures* (New York: Holt, 1998). Mori's most recent novel, *Stone Field, True Arrow* (New York: Metropolitan Books), appeared in 2000. She has also published a poetry collection, *Fallout* (Chicago: Ti Chucha, 1994).

Mori's first two novels were written for young readers. *Shizuko's Daughter* was chosen by *The New York Times* as the Best Young Children's Book. In fact, both novels tell the same story from different perspectives. Both focus on a female protagonist: Yuki in *Shizu-*

ko's Daughter and Megumi in *One Bird*; both suffer the loss of the mother, one to death and the other to departure, and therefore grow up with the pain of loss; and both struggle to define their self-identity in a patriarchal world. *Stone Field, True Arrow*, Mori's latest novel, makes a thematic departure. While it also features a female protagonist, the clothes weaver Maya Ishida, the novel probes topics of love, marriage, and choice of career, in the midst of sorrow. *The Dream of Water* and *Polite Lies* are both considered memoirs that record incidents and events that happened during Mori's seven-week visit to Japan during her 1990 sabbatical, and in the voice of a narrator coming of age and coming to terms with who she is and is not.

Mori's fiction is yet to attract more scholarly attention. Two article-length studies illuminate Mori's life and writing:

Brock-Servais, Rhonda. "Kyoko Mori." In Emmanuel S. Nelson, ed., *Asian American Novelists: A Bio-Bibliographical Critical Sourcebook* (Westport, CT: Greenwood Press, 2000), 229–33.

Shelton, Pamela. "Kyoko Mori." In Thomas McMahon, ed., *Authors and Artists for Young Adults* (Detroit: Gale, 1998), 181–86.

Reviews of her work include:

Barton, Emily. Rev. of *Polite Lies: On Being a Woman Caught Between Cultures*. *The New York Times*, March 8, 1998, late edition, section 7:19.

Blinkhorn, Lois. "Out of Tragedy, a Quiet Pursuit of Truth." *Milwaukee Journal Sentinel*, March 22, 1998, C1.

Corson, Bruce. "Fading Memory, Lingering Pain." *The Plain Dealer* [Cleveland], April 23, 1995, 12J.

Harris, Michael. Rev. of *Shizuko's Daughter*. *Los Angeles Times*, June 13, 1993, book review section 6.

Heller, Amanda. Rev. of *Polite Lies: On Being a Woman Caught Between Cultures*. *Boston Globe*, February 8, 1998, G2.

Prose, Francine. "Shizuko's Daughter." *The New York Times*, November 12, 1995, late edition, section 7:50.

Rosenberg, Liz. Rev. of *Shizuko's Daughter*. *The New York Times*, August 22, 1993, late edition, section 7:19.

Sandin, Jo. "Caught Between Cultures: In the Mid-West, a Japanese-American Finds Her Voice." *Milwaukee Journal Sentinel*, January 25, 1998, C11.

* * *

Shani Mootoo. See Mootoo in "Short Fiction."

* * *

Bharati Mukherjee (1940–). One of the most accomplished and prolific Indian American fiction writers, Mukherjee was born into an upper-middle-class Hindu Brahmin family in Calcutta, India. A truly diasporic writer, she was educated in both India and the West: she first went to school in England (where her father's business had taken the family) and then in Switzerland. Returning to India in 1951, she attended the Loretto Convent School, run by Irish nuns, in Calcutta, then Calcutta University, from which she received a B.A. in English in 1959. She received an M.A. in English and ancient Indian culture from Baroda University in 1961. Soon afterward she entered the Writers' Workshop at the University of Iowa, where she first met her Canadian husband, Clark Blaise, and earned an M.F.A. in creative writing. She completed her graduate education by obtaining a Ph.D. in English and comparative literature in 1969. Soon after their marriage in 1963, the couple moved to Montreal, Canada, and Mukherjee became a Canadian citizen in 1972. She taught at McGill University and became a full professor there in 1978. Disillusioned with Canada's treatment of immigrants, Mukherjee finally moved back to the United States with her family; she has lived and worked at different U.S. institutions and is now a distinguished professor of English at the University of California at Berkeley.

Mukherjee wrote her first two novels while in Canada: *The Tiger's Daughter* (Boston: Houghton Mifflin, 1972), and *Wife* (Boston: Houghton Mifflin, 1975). The decade between 1975 and 1985 saw the publication of only one nonfiction work, *Days and Nights in Calcutta* (Garden City, NY: Doubleday, 1977), coauthored with her husband and based upon their year-long stay in India in 1973. In the following years a burst of creative energy focused on short story writing resulted in two volumes, *Darkness* (New York: Penguin, 1985) and *The Middleman and Other Stories* (New York: Fawcett Crest, 1988). Between 1989 and 2002 Mukherjee produced a novel every four to five years: *Jasmine* (New York: Grove Weidenfeld, 1989), *The Holder of the World* (Toronto: HarperCollins, 1993), *Leave It to Me* (New York: Knopf, 1997), and *Desirable Daughters* (New York: Hyperion, 2002). In 1987 Mukherjee and Blaise published their coauthored investigative study of the tragic downing of Air India Flight 182, titled *The Sorrow and the Terror: The Haunting Legacy of the Air India Tragedy* (Markham, ON: Viking). Her two other nonfiction books, *Political Culture and Leadership in India: A Study of West Bengal* (New Delhi: Mittal Publications) and *Regionalism in Indian Perspective* (Calcutta: K. P. Bagchi), came out in 1991 and 1992, respectively.

Mukherjee's work has been recognized with a number of awards that include a grant from the National Endowment for the Arts in 1986 and a National Book Critics Circle Award for Fiction for *The Middleman and Other Stories* in 1988.

Mukherjee's fictions are concerned with several prominent themes: the Indian diaspora, immigration, displacement, Americanization/assimilation, adaptability, contrasts between and transition from the old world (Asia, specifically India) and the new world (specifically the United States). Despite her years of residence in Canada, Craig Tapping writes, "Mukherjee is not so widely known for her examinations of Canadian racism in different genres" (298), because, one might add, she wrote many of her works while living on the southern side of the U.S.–Canadian border. The protagonist of *The Tiger's Daughter*, Tara, experiences the contrast of the old and new world during a return visit to India after seven years of Westernized life in places like Vassar College and the University of Wisconsin at Madison. *Wife* narrates the story of an immigrant woman who moves from Calcutta to New York. Dimple Dasgupta follows her husband to the new world only to find herself trapped at home alone, while being bombarded with TV images of violence and snapshots of a life of freedom. As depression and desperation become overwhelming and the possibility of gaining freedom proves incompatible with traditional middle-class Indian values of submissiveness, the wife stabs her husband. *Jasmine*, perhaps Mukherjee's best-known novel, deals with transformation of identities. First in India and then in Florida, Queens, and Manhattan, the novel's protagonist, Jyoti, undergoes both hardships and transformations to achieve liberation and new identities, becoming Jasmine, Jassy, Jase, and finally Jane in the new land of America.

The Holder of the World spans two continents across three centuries, as the narrator, Beigh Masters, pursues his research on a seventeenth-century Puritan woman called

Hannah who ventured from New England to India and then back, only to be revealed as Hester Prynne, the protagonist of Nathaniel Hawthorne's romance *The Scarlet Letter*. The quest for self-invention and identity transformation constitutes the prime theme of *Leave It to Me*, the tale of Debbie DiMartino, an Indian girl who was adopted by an Italian American couple in Schenectady, New York. Debbie's quest to find her biological parents leads to a change of identity and the new name Devi Dee, but in the persona of the goddess of revenge, she leaves behind her a trail of violence. *Desirable Daughters*, Mukherjee's last novel to date, turns again to themes straddling the new world of California, which the protagonist/narrator Tara calls home, and the old world of India, where her sisters still live; it chronicles Tara's struggles to reconcile the ancient traditions of her past and the new challenges of her present life.

Mukherjee's short fiction is also very noteworthy. *Darkness*, consisting of twelve stories, offers a wide spectrum of Indian immigrant characters, and "has an important place in the new literatures of America for its portrayal of Indian immigrants, a group that had never been written about" (Kapai 205); *The Middleman and Other Stories*, composed of seven pieces, presents portraits of different groups of immigrants from countries other than India; it won the National Book Critics Circle Award for Fiction. As in her novels, in her short stories Mukherjee insists on the importance of assimilation and adaptability to the survival and success of the individual in the new culture.

Bharati Mukherjee is a well-studied figure among contemporary Asian American writers. Two book-length studies are Fakrul Alam, *Bharati Mukherjee* (New York: Twayne Publishers, 1996) and Emmanuel S. Nelson, ed., *Bharati Mukherjee: Critical Perspectives* (New York: Garland, 1993). Selected articles are:

Bannerji, Kaur Ranee. "Singing in the Seams: Bharati Mukherjee's Immigrants." In Michael Thomas, ed., *No Small World: Visions and Revisions of World Literature* (Urbana, IL: NCTE, 1996), 189–201.

Bowen, Deborah. "Spaces of Translation: Bharati Mukherjee's 'The Management of Grief." *ARIEL: A Review of International English Literature* 28, no. 3 (July 1997): 47–60.

Carb, Alison B. "An Interview with Bharati Mukherjee." *Massachusetts Review* 29, no. 4 (1988): 645–54.

Carchidi, Victoria. "'Orbiting': Bharati Mukherjee's Kaleidoscopic Vision." *MELUS* 20, no. 4 (Winter 1995): 91–101.

Chen, Tina and S. X. Goudie. "Holder of the Word: An Interview with Bharati Mukherjee." *Jouvert: A Journal of Postcolonial Studies* (1997) (http://social.class.ncsu.edu/jouvert/v1il/bharati.html).

Connell, Michael, Jessie Grierson, and Tom Grimes. "An Interview with Bharati Mukherjee." *Iowa Review* 20, no. 3 (1990): 7–30.

Davé, Shilpa. "The Doors to Home and History: Post-colonial Identities in Meena Alexander and Bharati Mukherjee." *Amerasia Journal* 19, no. 3 (1993): 103–13.

Desai, Shefali and Tony Barnstone. "A Usable Past: An Interview with Bharati Mukherjee." *Manoa* 10, no. 2 (1998): 130–47.

Doerkson, Teri Ann. "Bharati Mukherjee." In *Dictionary of Literary Biography*, vol. 218, *American Short Story Writers Since World War II*, second series (New York: The Gale Group, 1999), 228–34.

Drake, Jennifer. "Looting American Culture: Bharati Mukherjee's Immigrant Narratives." *Contem-*

porary Literature 40, no. 1 (Spring 1999): 60–84.

Fruchter, Barry. "Bharati Mukherjee." In Guiyou Huang, ed., *Asian American Autobiographers: A Bio-Bibliographical Critical Sourcebook* (Westport, CT: Greenwood Press, 2001), 257–72.

Knippling, Alpana Sharma. "Towards an Investigation of the Subaltern in Bharati Mukherjee's *The Middleman and Other Stories* and *Jasmine*." In Emmanuel S. Nelson, ed., *Bharati Mukherjee: Critical Perspectives* (New York: Garland, 1993), 143–59.

Koshy, Susan. "*Jasmine*, by Bharati Mukherjee." In Sau-ling Cynthia Wong and Stephen H. Sumida, eds., *A Resource Guide to Asian American Literature* (New York: MLA, 2001), 121–29.

Leong, Liew-Geok. "Bharati Mukherjee." In Robert L. Ross, ed., *International Literature in English: Essays on the Modern Writers* (New York: St. James Press, 1991), 487–500.

Low, Gail Ching-Liang. "In a Free State: Post Colonialism and Postmodernism in Bharati Mukherjee's Fiction." *Women: A Cultural Review* 4, no. 1 (Spring 1993): 8–17.

Nelson, Emmanuel S. "Kamalo Markandaya, Bharati Mukherjee, and the Immigrant Experience." *Toronto South Asian Review* 9, no. 2 (Winter 1991): 1–9.

Pati, Mitali R. "Love and the Indian Immigrant in Bharati Mukherjee's Short Fiction." In Emmanuel S. Nelson, ed., *Bharati Mukherjee*, 197–211.

Sant-Wade, Arvindra and Karen Marguerite Radell. "Refashioning the Self: Immigrant Women in Bharati Mukherjee's New World." *Studies in Short Fiction* 29, no. 1 (Winter 1992): 11–17.

Sengupta, C. "Asian Protagonist in Bharati Mukherjee's *The Middleman and Other Stories.*" *Language Forum* 18 (1992): 148–56.

Sharma, Maya Manju. "The Inner World of Bharati Mukherjee: From Expatriate to Immigrant." In Emmanuel S. Nelson, ed., *Bharati Mukherjee*, 3–22.

Srivaramkrishna, M. "Bharati Mukherjee." In Madhusudhan Prasad, ed., *Indian English Novelists* (New Delhi: Sterling, 1982), 71–86.

Tapping, Craig. "South Asia Writes North America: Prose Fictions and Autobiographies from the Indian Diaspora." In Shirley Geok-lin Lim and Amy Ling, eds., *Reading the Literatures of Asian America* (Philadelphia: Temple University Press, 1992), 285–301.

Venkateswaran, Pramila. "Bharati Mukherjee as an Autobiographer." in Emmanuel S. Nelson, ed., *Bharati Mukherjee*, 23–42.

* * *

Milton Murayama (1923–). *Nisei* Japanese Hawaiian novelist Murayama was born in Lahaina, Maui, and first attended the University of Hawai'i in 1941, but following Japan's bombing of Pearl Harbor he served in the Territorial Guard briefly, then worked for the Military Intelligence Service, where his Japanese language skills were used, from 1944 to 1946. He returned home in 1946 and resumed studies at the University of Hawai'i, from which he received a B.A. in English and philosophy in 1947; then he went on to obtain a master's degree in Japanese and Chinese from Columbia University in 1952. During his time at Columbia (1948–1952), Murayama completed a draft of his first novel, *All I Ask-*

ing for Is My Body, of which "I'll Crack Your Head *Kotsun*," a story he had published in *Arizona Quarterly* in 1959, was the first chapter. But Murayama encountered difficulty finding a publisher, so he and his wife published the novel on their own, under the imprint of Supa Press, in San Francisco in 1975. The book won Murayama the American Book Award of the Before Columbus Foundation in 1980. He also wrote a play, *Yoshitsune*, that was staged by the local Honolulu theater company Kumu Kahua in 1982. In 1991 Murayama won the Hawai'i Award for Literature. His second novel, *Five Years on a Rock*, appeared in 1994 (Honolulu: University of Hawai'i Press), and a third, *Plantation Boy* (Honolulu: University of Hawai'i Press), in 1998.

Although Murayama prefers to live on the mainland, he chooses to write about his native Hawai'i. All his three novels are set on a plantation in Hawai'i, all focus on the Oyama clan, and all deal with cross-cultural differences between the new world of Hawai'i and the traditions and values represented by Japan. *All I Asking for Is My Body*, narrated by Kiyoshi (Kiyo) Oyama, examines the problems of class and ethnicity in the Japanese and Filipino communities on the plantation. In *Five Years on a Rock*, the narrative focus shifts to Kiyoshi's mother, Sawa Oyama, who relates her experience in a marriage that started as a parental imposition, though in the end she decides to make the commitment. *Plantation Boy*'s narrator is Kiyoshi's older brother Toshio (Tosh), who pursues several career possibilities but decides to stay with his correspondence studies and make his dreams come true. All three novels share the same large setting and the same principal characters, and they show characteristics of a trilogy, with the same background and narrative focus; they are about the same clan on the same plantation, and the events and plots interlock.

For more information, see:

Hiura, Arnold. "Comments on Milton Murayama." In Eric Chock and Jody Manabe, eds., *Writers of Hawai'i: A Focus on Our Literary Heritage* (Honolulu: Bamboo Ridge Press, 1981), 65–70.

Luangphinith, Seri. "Milton Murayama." In Emmanuel S. Nelson, ed., *Asian American Novelists: A Bio-Bibliographical Critical Sourcebook* (Westport, CT: Greenwood Press, 2000), 251–56.

Sumida, Stephen H. "Japanese American Moral Dilemmas in John Okada's *No-No Boy* and Milton Murayama's *All I Asking for Is My Body*." In Gail Nomura, Russell Endo, Stephen Sumida, and Russell Leong, eds., *Frontiers of Asian American Studies: Writing, Research, and Commentary* (Pullman: Washington State University Press, 1989), 222–33.

———. "*All I Asking for Is My Body*, by Milton Murayama." In Sau-ling Cynthia Wong and Stephen H. Sumida, eds., *A Resource Guide to Asian American Literature* (New York: MLA, 2001), 130–39.

Wilson, Rob. "The Language of Confinement and Liberation in Milton Murayama's *All I Asking for Is My Body*." In Eric Chock and Jody Manabe, eds., *Writers of Hawai'i: A Focus on Our Literary Heritage* (Honolulu: Bamboo Ridge Press, 1981), 62–65.

N

Kirin Narayan (1959–). Born in Bombay into a bicultural and biracial family with a

German American mother and an Indian father (the couple had met while studying at the University of Colorado, Boulder), Narayan grew up in India under strong influences from the grandmothers on both sides of her family—both taught her, in different ways, to be creative and artistic. From a very young age Narayan decided that she wanted to be a writer, like Louisa May Alcott, the nineteenth-century American author of *Little Women*. Narayan sustained a strong interest in storytelling and in collecting and studying folktales, which led to the writing and publication of *Storytellers, Saints and Scoundrels: Folk Narrative in Hindu Religious Teaching* (Philadelphia: University of Pennsylvania Press, 1989). While living with her mother in a village in the foothills of the Himalayas, Narayan came to know a woman called Urmilaji, with whom she collaborated on a collection of retold stories and tales, published in 1997 as *Mondays on the Dark Side of the Moon* (New York: Oxford University Press).

In 1995 Narayan released a novel titled *Love, Stars, and All That* (New York: Washington Square Press). Like her other works, it exhibits the author's passion for storytelling and folktales. The story of Indian woman Gita Das follows her footsteps from one academic institution to another in the United States. Narayan looks into issues of sexual awakening, intellectual life as represented in the relationship between a professor and a graduate assistant, and racial and cultural identity politics.

Since Narayan has published only one novel so far, there are not yet any full-length studies of her work. The only article-length bio-critical study—and a short one at that—is Maya M. Sharma's "Kirin Narayan," in Emmanuel S. Nelson, ed., *Asian American Novelists: A Bio-Bibliographical Critical Sourcebook* (Westport, CT: Greenwood Press, 2000), 257–60. Reviews include:

Both, R. T. "A Searching of the Soul." *Milwaukee Journal*, January 30, 1994, E8.

Fine, Mary. "Novel Delves Deep Into Cuisine of Culture." *West Palm Beach Post*, May 1, 1994, J16.

Kendall, Elaine. "One Girl's Invention of an American Self." *Los Angeles Times*, March 4, 1994, E4.

Moraes, Dom. "Coming of Age." *India Today*, July 31, 1994, 95.

* * *

Fae Myenne Ng (1957–). Daughter of an immigrant family from Guangzhou, China, Ng was born in San Francisco's Chinatown, the setting of her first novel, *Bone* (New York: Hyperion, 1993). Her parents supported their daughter and son by working manual jobs. As a child Ng attended both American and Chinese schools; she obtained a B.A. in English from the University of California at Berkeley and an M.F.A. from Columbia University. She lives in Brooklyn, New York, where she is writing her second novel. Ng's literary efforts have garnered her a number of prestigious awards, including the National Endowment for the Arts Award, the D. H. Lawrence Fellowship, the San Francisco Foundation's Joseph Henry Jackson Award, and a Fellowship in Literature from the American Academy of Arts and Letters. Ng has also published short stories that are widely anthologized.

Bone, narrated by Leila, the oldest of three daughters of the Leong family, explores the lure and failure of the American dream of gold and success. The narrative focus of the novel is made explicit in the opening paragraphs: "We were a family of three daughters. By Chinese standards, that wasn't lucky. In Chinatown, everyone knew our story. Outsiders jerked their chins, looked at us, shook their heads. We heard things." "A failed family. That Dulcie Fu. And you know which one: bald Leon. Nothings but daughters" (3).

Gender issues and family history figure prominently in the stories of an immigrant family that tries to fit in and survive in an alienating society. Leon Leong, Leila's stepfather, came to the United States as a paper son to his sponsor, on the condition that when the old man died, Leon would return his bones to China; however, his "paper father" is buried in the immigrant country that he refused to call home. Family secrets, hidden shames, pains and sorrows, loyalty and love all find expression in the novel that offers insights into the life of an immigrant family.

Even though Ng has published only one novel thus far, the book has received a great deal of critical acclaim. Studies of *Bone* include many reviews, interviews, journal articles, and book chapters. See:

Bromstrom, Jennifer. Interview. *Contemporary Literary Criticism* 81 (1993): 87–88.

Chuang, Jay. "Bone in *Bone*." *Hitting Critical Mass: A Journal of Asian American Cultural Criticism* 2, no. 1 (1994): 53–57.

Goellnicht, Donald C. "Of Bones and Suicide: Sky Lee's *Disappearing Moon Café* and Fae Myenne Ng's *Bone*." *Modern Fiction Studies* 46, no. 2 (Summer 2000): 301–30.

Ho, Wendy. "The Heart Never Travels: Fathers in the Mother-Daughter Stories of Maxine Hong Kingston, Amy Tan, and Fae Myenne Ng." In *In Her Mother's House: The Politics of Asian American Mother-Daughter Writing* (Walnut Creek, CA: AltaMira Press, 1999), 195–231.

Huang, Su-ching. "Fae Myenne Ng." In Guiyou Huang, ed., *Asian American Short Story Writers: An A-to-Z Guide* (Westport, CT: Greenwood Press, 2003), 215–23.

Kim, Thomas W. "'For a Paper Son, Paper Is Blood': Subjectivation and Authenticity in Fae Myenne Ng's *Bone*." *MELUS* 24, no. 4 (Winter 1999): 45–56.

Lee, A. Robert. "Imagined Cities of China: Timothy Mo's London, Sky Lee's Vancouver, Fae Myenne Ng's San Francisco and Gish Jen's New York." *Wasafiri* 22 (Autumn 1995): 25–30.

Sze, Julie. "Have You Heard? Gossip, Silence, and Community in *Bone*." *Hitting Critical Mass: A Journal of Asian American Cultural Criticism* 2, no. 1 (1994): 59–69.

Waller, Nicole. "Past and Repast: Food as Historiography in Fae Myenne Ng's *Bone* and Frank Chin's *Donald Duk*." *Amerikastudien/American Studies* 40, no. 3 (1996): 485–502.

Yen, Xiaoping. "Fae Myenne Ng." In Emmanuel S. Nelson, ed., *Asian American Novelists: A Bio-Bibliographical Critical Sourcebook* (Westport, CT: Greenwood Press, 2000), 261–66.

* * *

Hualing Nieh (1925–). Born in Hubei province and educated in English at the National Central University, Nanjing, China, Nieh moved with her family to Taiwan in 1949, when the communists took control of the mainland. Nieh worked in Taiwan as a magazine editor, college instructor, novelist, short story writer, and translator until 1964, when, at the invitation of Paul Engle (whom she had first met in Taipei in 1963 at a reception in honor of the American poet), she made a trans-Pacific move to the University of Iowa, where she earned an M.F.A. in creative writing. Iowa was a career and life turning point, for it was there in 1967 that, with her future husband, Paul Engle, she cofounded and codirected the International Writing Program. Because of their outstanding contributions to world literary culture and international cooperation, the couple was nominated for the Nobel Peace Prize in 1976; in 1982, Nieh was given the Award for Distinguished Service to the Arts from the governors of the fifty states of America; in addition, she received a number of honorary doctorates. Nieh retired from the University of Iowa in 1988.

One of the most prolific and versatile Asian American literary writers working mainly in Chinese but publishing in English and other languages, Nieh is best known for her novel *Mulberry and Peach: Two Women of China* (first published in Chinese in Hong Kong: Youlian Chubanshe, 1976; translated into English by Jane Parish Yang and Linda Lappin, Boston: Beacon Press, 1988). She is also acclaimed for numerous collections of short stories, nonfiction, and volumes of translations. During her sojourn in Taiwan, Nieh published a novella, *Creeper* (Taipei: Free China Magazine, 1953); a novel, *The Lost Golden Bell* (Taipei: Xuesheng Chubanshe, 1960); two collections of short fiction, *The Emerald Cat* (Taipei: Minghua Shuju, 1959) and *A Little White Flower* (Taipei: Book World, 1963); and a collection of stories in English, *The Purse* (Hong Kong: Heritage, 1959). After relocating to the United States, she published *Far Away, a River* (novel) in China (Chengdu: Sichuan People's Publishing House, 1984); *The Several Blessings of Wang Danian* (short story collection) (Hong Kong: Haiyang Wenyishe, 1980); *Stories from Taiwan* (Beijing: Beijing Chubanshe, 1980); *Where Are You, Shanshan?* (short story collection) (Beijing: Xinhua Shudian, 1994); and most recently, *Tales from the Deer Garden* (Shanghai: Shanghai Literature Press, 1996).

The Lost Golden Bell, Nieh's first novel in Chinese, features a young female protagonist, Lingzi (Golden Bell), who remembers her life in the small hometown that she left five years before. *Mulberry and Peach*, the first novel Nieh wrote after her move to Iowa, remains her most interesting and most studied work. The protagonist Mulberry (Sangqing in Chinese) suffers severe schizophrenia that causes a split personality; Mulberry narrates her own stories that took place in mainland China, Taiwan, and the United States as if they happened to someone else called Peach (Taohong in Chinese). Through Mulberry's eventful life, the novel explores twentieth-century Chinese political history as well as the turmoil and trauma it inflicted on its people. *Far Away, a River* is about the daughter, Lotus, of an interracial relationship between a Chinese woman student and an American reporter, set against the historical background from the Sino-Japanese War in the late 1930s to the Cultural Revolution in the 1960s and 1970s.

Studies of Hualing Nieh's work are available in both Chinese and English. Most of the reviews in English are of *Mulberry and Peach*. The English-language sources include:

Nazareth, Peter. "An Interview with Chinese Author Hua-ling Nieh." *World Literature Today* 55, no. 1 (1981): 221–38.

Pai, Hsien-yung. "The Wandering Chinese: The Theme of Exile in Taiwan Fiction." *The Iowa Review* 7, no. 2–3 (1976): 205–12.

Wong, Sau-ling Cynthia. "The Stakes of Textual Border-Crossing: Hualing Nieh's *Mulberry and Peach* in Sinocentric, Asian-American, and Feminist Critical Practices." In Kandice Chuh and Karen Shimakawa, eds., *Orientations: Mapping Studies in the Asian Diaspora* (Durham: Duke University Press, 2001), 130–35.

Xiao, Hailing. "Hualing Nieh." In Emmanuel Nelson, ed., *Asian American Novelists: A Bio-Bibliographical Critical Sourcebook* (Westport, CT: Greenwood Press, 2000), 271–76.

Yu, Shiao-ling. "The Themes of Exile and Identity Crisis in Nieh Hualing's Fiction." In Hsin-sheng C. Kao, ed., *Nativism Overseas: Contemporary Chinese Women Writers* (Albany: State University of New York Press, 1993), 127–56.

John Okada (1923–1971). The oldest of three sons, Okada was born to *issei* Japanese parents in Seattle, Washington, the setting for his only novel, *No-No Boy*. Okada attended the University of Washington and received a bachelor's degree in English and library science. For his master's degree in English he attended Columbia University, where he met his future wife Dorothy, with whom he had a daughter and a son. During World War II he and his family, like many other Japanese Americans living on the West Coast, were evacuated and interned at Minidoka, Idaho. But unlike his principal character, Ichiro, in *No-No Boy,* who refused military service, Okada volunteered to serve in the U.S. Air Force; he was discharged in 1946. In an afterword to Okada's novel, Frank Chin writes, "John Okada was not No-No boy. He served in WWII hanging out of an airplane over Japanese-held islands asking their occupants in their own language to give up" (256).

The internment and his military service marked major turning points in Okada's life, incorporated into *No-No Boy*, which he started to write while working as a librarian, first in Seattle and then in Detroit, in the early 1950s; he completed the novel in 1955 and published it in 1957. Regrettably, as noted by Lawson Fusao Inada, Frank Chin, and many Asian American critics today, before Okada died of a heart attack in February 1971 in Los Angeles, he was very close to completing a draft of a second novel about the immigrant experience of *issei* Japanese in America. After his death, his wife Dorothy offered all of his manuscripts, notes, and letters to the Japanese American Research Project at UCLA, but the organization refused even to look at them; as a result, Dorothy burned them all. Between its initial Charles Tuttle publication in 1957 and its Combined Asian American Research Project (CARP) publication in 1976, *No-No Boy* experienced almost total oblivion, but today it is recognized as an Asian American classic.

No-No Boy, the first Japanese American novel to explore the relationship of the individual and his ethnic community as well as his country from the perspective of racial politics, is about the confusion, loss, and quest for self-identity under extreme circumstances: a war that involves Ichiro's country of citizenship, the United States, and the country of his ancestry, Japan. While the war itself was not racially motivated, the government's decision to evacuate and intern its citizens of Japanese descent was (Italian and German Americans, whose ancestral countries were also at war with the United States, were not interned); national loyalty thus became a racialized and politicized issue for Japanese Americans like Ichiro. The so-called "identity" crisis is delineated powerfully. Lawson Fusao Inada, who, along with Frank Chin, was instrumental to *No-No Boy*'s publication by CARP, warmly writes: "Whoever reads this book will be a bigger person for it. Whoever reads this book will never be the same. Whoever reads this book will see, and be, with greater strength and clarity. And in this way does the world begin to change" (vi).

No book-length studies of *No-No Boy* exist, but there are many articles. Lawson

Fusao Inada's introduction (iii–vi) and Frank Chin's afterword (253–60) in *No-No Boy* (Seattle: University of Washington Press, 1979) are both early responses to the recovery and reading of the novel. Gayle K. Fujita's "Momotaro's Exile: John Okada's *No-No Boy*," in Shirley Geok-lin Lim and Amy Ling, eds., *Reading the Literatures of Asian America* (Philadelphia: Temple University Press, 1992), 239–58, is an insightful reading of the binary opposition of "dual identity" in Ichiro. Other useful essays include:

Chen, Fu-jen. "John Okada." In Emmanuel S. Nelson, ed., *Asian American Novelists: A Bio-Bibliographical Critical Sourcebook* (Westport, CT: Greenwood Press, 2000), 281–88.

Gribben, Bryn. "The Mother That Won't Reflect Back: Situating Psychoanalysis and the Japanese Mother in *No-No Boy*." *MELUS* 28, no. 2 (Summer 2003): 31–46.

Ling, Jinqi. "Race, Power, and Cultural Politics in John Okada's *No-No Boy*." *American Literature* 67, no. 2 (1995): 359–81.

——. "*No-No Boy*, by John Okada." In Sau-ling Cynthia Wong and Stephen H. Sumida, eds., *A Resource Guide to Asian American Literature* (New York: MLA, 2001), 140–50.

McDonald, Dorothy Ritsuko. "After Imprisonment: Ichiro's Search for Redemption in *No-No Boy*." *MELUS* 6, no. 3 (1979): 19–26.

Sumida, Stephen H. "Japanese American Moral Dilemmas in John Okada's *No-No Boy* and Milton Murayama's *All I Asking for Is My Body*." In Gail M. Nomura et al., eds., *Frontiers of Asian American Studies* (Pullman: Washington State University Press, 1989), 222–33.

Yeh, William. "To Belong or Not to Belong: The Liminality of John Okada's *No-No Boy*." *Amerasia Journal* 19, no. 1 (1993): 121–33.

Yogi, Stan. "'You Had to Be One or the Other': Opposition and Reconciliation in John Okada's *No-No Boy*." *MELUS* 21, no. 2 (1996): 63–77.

* * *

Michael Ondaatje (1943–). Sri Lankan Canadian novelist and poet Ondaatje was born into an English-speaking family in Colombo, Ceylon (now Sri Lanka). He went to school in Colombo, and at about age ten he went to join his mother in London, where he attended Dulwich College, before moving to Canada to be with his brother Christopher and to study English literature at Bishop's University in Lennoxville, Quebec. By 1965 he had married and had a daughter. The family relocated to Toronto, where he enrolled at the University of Toronto, again studying English. In the late 1960s Ondaatje moved again, this time to Queen's University in Kingston, Ontario, where he completed his M.A. It was during the 1960s that he started to write poetry and win prizes for his creative work; he embarked upon a highly productive career, first as a poet and then as an internationally acclaimed novelist.

Starting in 1967, Ondaatje's poetry collections came out in quick succession: *The Dainty Monsters* (Toronto: Coach House Press, 1967), *The Man with Seven Toes* (Toronto: Coach House Press, 1969), *The Collected Works of Billy the Kid: Left Handed Poems* (Toronto: Anansi, 1970), *Rat Jelly* (Toronto: Coach House Press, 1973), *Elimination Dance* (Ilderton, ON: Nairn Coldstream, 1978), *There's a Trick with a Knife I'm Learning to Do: Poems, 1963–1978* (New York: Norton, 1979), *Secular Love* (Toronto: Coach House Press, 1984), *The Cinnamon Peeler: Selected Poems* (London:

Pan, 1989), and *Handwriting* (London: Bloomsbury, 1998). Ondaatje started to publish novels after he had established himself as a poet in Canada: *Coming Through Slaughter* (Toronto: Anansi, 1976), *In the Skin of a Lion* (New York: Knopf, 1987), *The English Patient* (New York: Knopf, 1992), and *Anil Ghost* (New York: Knopf, 2000). Three of his works were adapted into plays or screenplays: *The Collected Works of Billy the Kid*, *In the Skin of a Lion*, and most famous of all, *The English Patient*, which became an internationally known film. A professor, first at the University of Western Ontario and then at Glendon College at York University, Ondaatje has also written and published critical works: *Leonard Cohen* (Toronto: McClelland and Stewart, 1970), *Claude Glass* (Toronto: Coach House Press, 1979), and *An H in the Heart: A Reader* (Toronto: McClelland and Stewart, 1994). In addition, he has edited a number of critical works and creatively oriented books. Another work that has garnered Ondaatje critical fame is his autobiography, *Running in the Family* (Toronto: McClelland and Stewart, 1982; New York: Norton, 1982).

Ondaatje remains a private and quiet person and seldom grants interviews, but his literary achievements have made him one of the most visible Asian North American writers. When he was in college he won several prizes for his poetry, which appeared in various anthologies, and for *The English Patient* he received the Booker Prize, becoming the first Canadian to be honored with this prestigious award; the novel also became a best-seller after its adaptation into a movie in 1996. Other major national and international awards include the Books in Canada First Novel Award, the Canadian Governor General's Award, the Trillium Book Award, and the du Maurier Award for Poetry.

Although Ondaatje first became known as a poet, his poetry has been outshined by his fiction. His poems touch upon familiar themes such as daily experience (*The Dainty Monsters*), personal experience (*The Man with Seven Toes*), animals (*The Broken Ark*), and his first marriage (*Secular Love*); one collection recounts the author's childhood obsession with the American West and incorporates poetry and prose about a legendary figure based on a historical personality (*The Collected Works of Billy the Kid*). The novel *Coming Through Slaughter* narrates the story of another historical figure, Buddy Bolden, a Louisiana jazz musician who descended into madness. Two principal characters woven into the plot of *The English Patient*, Hana and Carravaggio, first appeared in Ondaatje's second novel, *In the Skin of a Lion*, which looks into immigrant communities and their contributions to Canadian history and culture. *The English Patient*, by far Ondaatje's most accessible and best-known work, is set in northern Italy and relates the story of a plane-crash survivor and a Canadian nurse who takes care of him, among other traumatized characters of different national origins (Indian, Italian, and Canadian). The complexity of the novel's story lines is further deepened by the mystery of the identity of the English patient, whose activities during World War II evoke suspicion about his possibly being a Nazi spy.

Ondaatje is undoubtedly a well-studied writer. His work has received "hundreds of very favorable reviews" (Fitzpatrick 295), and as Cynthia Wong notes, "Criticism appearing in Canada outnumbers that in America and Europe by a considerable margin, and it is therefore not surprising that studies of Ondaatje's works focus on technical literary aspects, such as their formal construction, narrative strategy, thematic concerns, or subject matter" (292). What follows is a selected bibliography of studies of this prolific writer:

Barbour, Douglas. *Michael Ondaatje.* New York: Twayne, 1993.

Bjerring, Nancy. "Deconstructing the 'Desert of Facts': Detection and Antidetection in *Coming Through Slaughter*." *English Studies in Canada* 16 (1990): 325–38.

Bok, Christian. "Destructive Creation: The Politicization of Violence in the Works of Michael Ondaatje." *Canadian Literature* 132 (1992): 109–24.

Butterfield, Martha. "The One Lighted Room: *In the Skin of a Lion*." *Canadian Literature* 119 (1988): 162–67.

Clarke, George. "Michael Ondaatje and the Production of Myth." *Studies in Canadian Literature* 16 (1991): 1–21.

Fitzpatrick, Elizabeth. "(Philip) Michael Ondaatje." In Guiyou Huang, ed., *Asian American Autobiographers: A Bio-Bibliographical Critical Sourcebook* (Westport, CT: Greenwood Press, 2001), 291–98.

Greenstein, Michael. "Ondaatje's Metamorphoses: *In the Skin of a Lion*." *Canadian Literature* 126 (1990): 116–30.

Heble, Ajay. "Michael Ondaatje and the Problem of History." *CLIO* 19 (1990): 97–110.

Heighton, Stephen. "Approaching 'That Perfect Edge': Kinetic Techniques in the Poetry and Fiction of Michael Ondaatje." *Studies in Canadian Literature* 13 (1988): 223–43.

Hutcheon, Linda. "*Running in the Family*: The Postmodern Challenge." In Hutcheon, ed., *The Canadian Postmodern* (Toronto: Oxford University Press, 1988), 81–106.

Jewinski, Ed. *Michael Ondaatje: Express Yourself Beautifully*. Toronto: ECW, 1994.

Kamboureli, Smaro. "The Poetics of Geography in Michael Ondaatje's *Coming Through Slaughter*." *Descant* 14 (1983): 112–26.

Kertzer, J. M. "On Death and Dying: *The Collected Works of Billy the Kid*." *English Studies* 1 (1975): 88–96.

MacFarland, Susan. "Picking up the Pieces: *Coming Through Slaughter*: As Paragram." *Open Letter* 6 (1989): 72–83.

Maxwell, Barry. "Surrealistic Aspects of Michael Ondaatje's *Coming Through Slaughter*." *CLIO* 19, no. 2 (Winter 1990): 97–110.

Mukherjee, Arun. "The Poetry of Michael Ondaatje and Cyril Dabydeen: Two Responses to Otherness." *Journal of Commonwealth Literature* 20, no. 1 (1995): 49–67.

Mundwiler, Leslie. *Michael Ondaatje: Word, Image, Imagination*. Vancouver: Talon-books, 1984.

Ray, Sangeeta. "Memory, Identity, Patriarchy: Projecting a Past in the Memoirs of Sara Suleri and Michael Ondaatje." *Modern Fiction Studies* 39, no. 1 (1993): 37–58.

Rooke, Constance. "Dog in a Grey Room: The Happy Ending of *Coming Through Slaughter*." In Sam Solecki, ed., *Spider Blues* (Montreal: Vehicule Press, 1985), 268–92.

Scobie, Stephen. "*Coming Through Slaughter*: Fictional Magnets and Spider Webs." *Essays on Canadian Writing* 12 (1978): 5–23.

Smythe, Karen E., ed. "Special Issue on Michael Ondaatje." *Essays on Canadian Writing* 53 (Summer 1994).

Solecki, Sam. "Making and Destroying: Michael Ondaatje's *Coming Through Slaughter* and Extremist Art." *Essays on Canadian Writing* 12 (1978): 24–47.

——. "Michael Ondaatje." *Descant* 14 (1983): 77–88.

Solecki, Sam, ed. *Spider Blues: Essays on Michael Ondaatje*. Montreal: Vehicule Press, 1985.

Van Wart, Alice. "The Evolution of Form in Michael Ondaatje's *The Collected Works of Billy the Kid* and *Coming Through Slaughter*." *Canadian Poetry* 17 (1985): 1–28.

Verhoeven, W. M. "(De)Facing the Self: Michael Ondaatje and (Auto) Biography." In Th. D'haen and H. Bertens, eds., *Postmodern Fiction in Canada* (Amsterdam: Rodopi, 1992), 181–200.

Waldman, Nell Kozak. *Michael Ondaatje and His Works*. Toronto: ECW Press, 1992.

Wilson, Ann. "*Coming Through Slaughter*: Storyville Twice Told." *Descant* 14 (1983): 99–111.

Wong, Cynthia F. "Michael Ondaatje." In Emmanuel S. Nelson, ed., *Asian American Novelists: A Bio-Bibliographical Critical Sourcebook* (Westport, CT: Greenwood Press, 2000), 288–93.

Gary Pak. See Pak in "Short Fiction."

Ninotchka Rosca (1946–). Filipina American journalist, activist, and novelist Rosca was born in Manila, the Philippines, and completed her undergraduate education in comparative literature and a graduate concentration on Khmer civilization, both at the University of the Philippines. As managing editor of the magazine *Graphic* that reported on hard-core politics and for her involvement in political organizations,

Rosca was arrested and detained for six months in 1972 under the martial law declared by the Ferdinand Marcos regime. In 1976 Rosca moved to the United States to study writing at the University of Iowa's International Writing Program. Unable to return to her homeland while Marcos was still in power, Rosca started an academic career teaching Tagalog at the University of Hawai'i at Manoa. She had begun to write fiction before her expatriation to the United States. Her first collection of short stories, *Bitter Country and Other Stories*, appeared in 1970 (Quezon City, Philippines: Malaya Books), but her second volume, *The Monsoon Collection* (Santa Lucia: University of Queensland Press, 1983), did not come out until after she had moved to New York. Her first novel, *State of War*, was published in 1988 (New York: Norton); the second, *Twice Blessed*, in 1992, again by Norton. *Endgame: The Fall of Marcos* (New York: Franklin Watts, 1987) was the product of her career as a journalist writing nonfiction.

Rosca has received several awards and fellowships, including a fellowship in the International Writing Program at the University of Iowa in 1977, two fellowships from the New York Foundation for the Arts in 1986–1987 and 1991, respectively, and the 1993 American Book Award for *Twice Blessed*.

Rosca's two novels were both written and published after her political imprisonment, i.e., during her expatriation in the United States, and they fictionalize Philippine politics under Ferdinand Marcos. In both works, the personal, the political, and the national are interconnected to reflect and resist the tyrannical rule of a corrupt regime. *State of War* focuses on the lives of three characters (Adrian Banyaga, Eliza Hansen, and Anna Villaverde) and their fates in relation to national politics and history. *Twice Blessed*, again concerned with Philippine politics, is a political satire that focuses on the central figures of martial law, the Marcoses, symbolically portrayed in the twin figures of Hector Basbas and Katerina Basbas Gloriosa, who embody total corruption and ruthlessness.

While reviews of Rosca's novels, short story collections, and nonfiction are numerous, there are just a few article-length studies of her works:

Casper, Leonard. "Minoring in History: Rosca as Ninotchka." *Amerasia Journal* 16, no. 1 (1990): 201–10.

——. "Social Realism in the Stories of Edilberto Tiempo and Ninotchka Rosca." *Solidarity* 8, no. 1 (1973): 68–74.

Hidalgo, Cristina P. "Now That Dear Kerima, Carmen, Gilda, and Ninotchka Have Come, Can Our Simone de Beauvoir Be Far Behind?" *Manila Review* 1, no. 1 (1976): 104–13.

Leonard, Shannon T. "Ninotchka Rosca." In Emmanuel S. Nelson, ed., *Asian American Novelists: A Bio-Bibliographical Critical Sourcebook* (Westport, CT: Greenwood Press, 2000), 308–12.

Nguyen, Viet Thanh. "The Postcolonial State of Desire: Homosexuality and Transvestitism in Ninotchka Rosca's *State of War*." *Critical Mass: A Journal of Asian American Cultural Criticism* (special issue on U.S. Filipino Literature and Culture) 2, no. 2 (1995): 67–93.

S

Bienvenido N. Santos (1911–1996). Among the most prolific of Filipino American fiction writers, Santos was born in Tondo, a slum section of Manila, the Philippines.

After losing both parents to diseases in his teens, Santos managed to obtain a baccalaureate degree in education at the University of the Philippines in 1931. He started to write short stories in 1930. In 1941 he enrolled in the University of Illinois on a government scholarship and then studied creative writing at Columbia and English at Harvard, but World War II disrupted his plans when he was called to work for the Philippine government in Washington, D.C. He also toured the United States and gave lectures on his home country at the request of the U.S. Department of Education. In 1946 Santos returned to the Philippines and was reunited with his wife and daughters. In 1955 he published *You Lovely People* (Manila: Benipayo Press), a collection of short stories written in memory of the Pinoys he met on his U.S. tours in World War II. *Brother, My Brother: A Collection of Short Stories* appeared in 1960 (Manila: Benipayo Press); *The Day the Dancers Came: Selected Prose Writings* (Manila: Bookmark) in 1967; *Scent of Apples: A Collection of Stories* (Seattle: University of Washington Press) in 1979; and *Dwell in the Wilderness: Selected Short Stories (1931–1941)* (Quezon City: New Day) in 1981.

Santos's career as a novelist took off in 1965, with the publications of *Villa Magdalena* (Manila: Erewhon) and *The Volcano* (Quezon City: Phoenix Publishing House). The novel *The Praying Man* was first serialized in the Manila magazine *Solidarity* and published in book form in 1982 (Quezon City: New Day). The following year saw the appearance of *The Man Who (Thought He) Looked Like Robert Taylor* (Quezon City: New Day), and *What the Hell for You Left Your Heart in San Francisco?* came out in 1987 (Quezon City: New Day). Santos's literary talents are also evident in other genres. *The Wounded Stag: A Collection of Poetry* (Manila: Capital Publishing House, 1956) and *Distances in Time: Selected Poems* (Quezon City: Ateneo de Manila University Press, 1983) are two collections of poetry, while *The Bishop's Pet* is a one-act play he published in 1966 (Manila: Philippine Free Press). *Memory's Fictions: A Personal History* (Quezon City: New Day, 1993) and *Postscript to a Saintly Life* (Pasig City, Philippines: Anvil, 1994) are generally considered autobiographical works. In addition, he published letters and some essays.

Santos's versatility and productivity garnered him a good number of prestigious awards. In 1958 a Rockefeller creative writing fellowship enabled him to study at the Writers Workshop at the University of Iowa. *Villa Magdalena* and *The Volcano* were written while he was on a Guggenheim Fellowship. In 1965 he received the Republic Cultural Heritage Award in Literature in the Philippines, and the following year an Exchange Fulbright Professorship returned him to Iowa. He was also a recipient of the National Achievement Award for Literature in Fiction, the National Endowment for the Arts Award in Creative Writing, and the Southeast Asia Writer's Award, in addition to numerous honorary degrees from both Philippine and American universities.

Despite the versatility and prolificacy of Santos's oeuvre, his literary achievements lie mainly in fiction—novels and short stories. Anita Mannur puts Santos's novels into two categories: "On one hand are the novels that specifically engage the Philippines. Included in this category are his first two novels, *Villa Magdalena* and *Volcano*, as well as the novel that earned him notoriety, *The Praying Man*. The second category includes works such as *The Man Who (Thought He) Looked Like Robert Taylor*, *What the Hell for You Left Your Heart in San Francisco?*, *Memory's Fictions*, and *You Lovely People*, all of which deal specifically with the Filipino experience in the United States. A unifying theme in many of these works is the sense of alienation and ambivalence felt by many Filipinos as they move between the Philippines and the United States in search of a place to call home" (318). The themes apparent in his novels are also explored in his short stories. *Dwell in the Wilderness*, for example, deals with feelings of belonging, as does *You Lovely People*, which also examines the topic of displacement. *Scent of Apples*, Santos's only book published in the United States, again looks into themes of dislocation and alienation and the difficulty Filipino exiles and expatriates have in holding on to their identity.

For more information, see:

Bresnahan, Roger. "The Midwestern Fiction of Bienvenido N. Santos." *Society for the Study of Midwestern Literature Newsletter* 13, no. 2 (Summer 1983): 28–37.

Campomanes, Oscar V. "Filipinos in the United States and Their Literature of Exile." In Shirley Geok-lin Lim and Amy Ling, eds., *Reading the Literatures of Asian America* (Philadelphia: Temple University Press, 1992), 49–78.

Carpio, Rustica C. "Bienvenido Santos and *Brother, My Brother*." *Solidarity* 5, no. 12 (1970): 58–64.

Casper, Leonard. "Greater Shouting and Greater Silences: The Novels of Bienvenido Santos." *Solidarity* 3, no. 10 (1968): 76–84.

——. "Paperboat Novels: The Later Bienvenido Santos." *Amerasia Journal* 13, no. 1 (1986–1987): 163–70.

Cheung, King-Kok. "Bienvenido Santos: Filipino Old-Timers in Literature." *Markham Review* 15 (1986): 49–53.

Cruz, Isagani and David Jonathan Bayot. *Reading Bienvenido Santos*. Manila: De La Salle University Press, 1994.

Grow, L. M. "The Poet and the Garden: The Green World of Bienvenido N. Santos." *WLWE: World*

Literature Written in English 29, no. 1 (1984): 136–45.

Huot, Nikolas. "Bienvenido N. Santos." In Guiyou Huang, ed., *Asian American Short Story Writers: An A-to-Z Guide* (Westport, CT: Greenwood Press, 2003), 273–79.

Mannur, Anita. "Bienvenido N. Santos." In Emmanuel S. Nelson, ed., *Asian American Novelists: A Bio-Bibliographical Critical Sourcebook* (Westport, CT: Greenwood Press, 2000), 317–22.

Puente, Lorenzo. "Split-Level Christianity in *The Praying Man*." *Philippine Studies* 40, no. 1 (1992): 111–20.

Reyes, Soledad S. "Death-in-Life in Santos's *Villa Magdalena*." In Joseph A. Galdon, ed., *Essays on the Philippine Novel in English* (Quezon City: Ateneo de Manila University Press, 1979), 125–49.

Rico, Victoria S. "*You Lovely People*: The Texture of Alienation." *Philippine Studies* 42, no. 1 (1994): 91–104.

——. "Themes in the Poetry of Bienvenido Santos." *Philippine Studies* 42, no. 4 (1994): 452–74.

Valdez, Maria Stella. "The Myth and the Matrix in Bienvenido N. Santos' 'Scent of Apples': Searching for Harmony Among Incongruities." *DLSU Dialogue* 25, no. 1 (1991): 73–86.

Vidal, Lourdes H. "Echoes and Reflections in *Villa Magdalena*." *Philippine Studies* 35, no. 3 (1987): 377–82.

* * *

Shyam Selvadurai (1965–). Sri Lankan Canadian novelist Selvadurai was born in Colombo, Sri Lanka, and moved to Canada with his parents in 1983, after the anti-Tamil riots. He completed a degree in theater and television studies at York University in Toronto, and published his first novel, *Funny Boy*, in 1994 (Toronto: McClelland and Stewart), followed by a second, *Cinnamon Gardens*, in 1999 (New York: Hyperion). For *Funny Boy* Selvadurai was awarded the United States Lambda Literary Award for Best Gay Male Novel, and the 1994 Smithbooks/Books in Canada First Novel Award.

Funny Boy has the appearance of an autobiography because the protagonist, Arjie, and the novelist share some similar aspects of personal background: both are gay and have to deal with issues of homosexuality; both left their home country of Sri Lanka; and both have Tamil ancestral roots. Divided into six sections and spanning a time period of six years, from 1977 to 1983, the year the Selvadurais left Sri Lanka, *Funny Boy* focuses on Arjie's evolution from an awareness of different sexual interests than other boys to gay activities to coming to terms with his sexual orientation. *Cinnamon Gardens* continues to explore gay issues but also deals with the institution of marriage, the pursuit of happiness, and the struggles to be overcome in order to achieve personal expectations. Annalukshmi and her uncle Balendran are both lonely; she faces a forced marriage while her uncle—married and a father—confronts his same-sex desire when his former lover Richard shows up after years of absence.

There are many reviews of Selvadurai's fiction, though not a great deal of substantial study has emerged. See:

Adams, Timothy Dow. "Coming of Age." *Canadian Literature* 149 (Summer 1996): 112–13.

Christensen, Peter G. "Shyam Selvadurai." In Emmanuel S. Nelson, ed., *Asian American Novelists: A Bio-Bibliographical Critical Sourcebook* (Westport, CT: Greenwood Press, 2000), 332–38.

Foster, Cecil Foster. "A Love Beyond Bigotry." *Canadian Forum* 73, no. 836 (January–February 1995): 40–41.

Rev. of *Funny Boy. Kirkus Reviews* 64 (January 1, 1996): 21.

Rev. of *Funny Boy. Publishers Weekly* 242, no. 45 (November 6, 1995): 80.

St. John, Janet. Rev. of *Funny Boy. Booklist* 92, no. 9–10 (January 1, 15, 1996): 792.

* * *

Vikram Seth (1952–). An Indian American novelist and poet, Seth was born in Calcutta and moved to New Delhi at age four, then to Britain in his mid-teens, where he studied at Oxford University's Corpus Christi College. He did graduate work in economic demography at Stanford University in the United States and wrote a dissertation on village economies of China; the academic experience also took him to that country and enabled him to master the Chinese language. Seth's acquaintances with Donald Davie and Timothy Steele, two poets, steered him toward a career as a poet and then a novelist. In fact, his first novel, *The Golden Gate*, is subtitled *A Novel in Verse* (New York: Random House, 1986); his second, *A Suitable Boy: A Novel* (New York: Harper Collins) came out in 1993; the travel narrative, *From Heaven Lake: Travels Through Sinkiang and Tibet* (London: Chatto and Windus, 1985) is a result of a hitchhiking journey he took in northwest China and the neighboring countries of Nepal and India. Seth's Chinese experience—linguistic, cultural, and geographical—also facilitated his translation of *Three Chinese Poets: Translations of Poems by Wang Wei, Li Bai and Du Fu* (New York: HarperCollins, 1992). His own poetry collections include *Mappings* (Calcutta: Writers Workshop, 1980), *The Humble Administrator's Garden* (Manchester: Carcenet, 1985), *All You Who Sleep Tonight* (New York: Knopf, 1990), *Beastly Tales from Here and There* (New Delhi: Viking, 1992), and *The Poems, 1981–1994* (New York: Penguin, 1995). Seth won the Thomas Cook Travel Award for *From Heaven Lake* and a Guggenheim Fellowship, among other awards.

The Golden Gate, as the title indicates, is a San Francisco novel that "translates the ironic social commentary Pushkin disguised as exoticism into an immediately familiar vocabulary…that falls comfortably into the insistent rhythms of the tetrameter" and that portrays "San Franciscan life and its avoidance of the twin banes of Asian American literature, immigrant angst and generational conflict" (Guneratne 341). *A Suitable Boy*, Seth's prose novel set in the early 1950s, while less critically acclaimed, has been a much larger financial success. It recounts the story of a Hindu family trying to find an appropriate husband for their daughter, Lata. The poems in *All You Who Sleep Tonight* represent Seth's multilingual talents and the breadth of his international themes. *Beastly Tales from Here and There* falls into the genre of the beast fable but retells and re-creates the fables in verse.

There are many reviews of Seth's fiction and poetry; the most comprehensive study is Shyam Agarwalla, *Vikram Seth's "A Suitable Boy": Search for an Indian Identity* (New Delhi: Prestige Books, 1995). See also:

Guneratne, Anthony R. "Vikram Seth." In Emmanuel S. Nelson, ed., *Asian American Novelists: A Bio-Bibliographical Critical Sourcebook* (Westport, CT: Greenwood Press, 2000), 339–44.

Paranjape, Makarand. "*The Golden Gate* and the Quest of Self-Realisation." *ACLAS Bulletin* (8th series) 1 (1989): 58–73.

Ragen, Brian Abel. "Vikram Seth." In *Dictionary of Literary Biography* (Detroit: Gale Research, 1992), 281–85.

Vijayasree, C. "Vikram Seth." In Emmanuel S. Nelson, ed., *Writers of the Indian Diaspora: A Bio-*

Bibliographical Critical Sourcebook (Westport, CT: Greenwood Press, 1993), 401–6.

Wachtel, Eleanor. Interview with Vikram Seth. *The Malahat Review* 107 (Summer 1994): 85–102.

Walker, J. H. "Trunks of the Banyan Tree: History, Politics and Fiction." *Island* 63 (Winter 1995): 18–26.

* * *

Bapsi Sidhwa (1938–). Born in Karachi, then part of India and present-day Pakistan, and raised in Lahore, in the Punjab, Sidhwa did not go to a school for education until age fourteen, due to health problems. But even as a young child she enjoyed reading, and as she grew, she became more interested in women's issues and even represented Pakistan at the 1975 Asian Women's Congress. Sidhwa published her first novel, *The Crow Eaters*, in 1978 (Lahore: Ilmi Print Press; reissued in the United States in 1987 and 1992 [Minneapolis: Milkweed Editions]); *The Bride* followed in 1983 (New York: St. Martin's Press). Her third novel, first released in England as *Ice-Candy Man* (London: Heineman, 1988), was published in the United States under the title *Cracking India* (Minneapolis: Milkweed Editions) in 1992. *An American Brat* came out in 1993 (New Delhi: Penguin India). For her achievements, Sidhwa received a National Endowment for the Arts Grant Award for Creative Writing in 1987, the Sitara-I-Imtiaz award for the arts from Pakistan in 1991, the Liberatur Prize from Germany, and a Writer's Grant award from the Lila Wallace–Reader's Digest Fund in 1993.

The Crow Eaters is about the novelist's own ethnic community, Parsees, and explores gender issues in relation to the pervasive patriarchy. *The Bride*, based on a true story, expresses Sidhwa's concern with the repercussions of arranged marriage. *Cracking India* (a.k.a. *Ice-Candy Man*), perhaps Sidhwa's best-known work, is a novel of partition narrated by a young girl who witnessed the violence caused by this historical separation of Pakistan from India. *An American Brat* continues the story of *The Crow Eaters* by following the footsteps of Feroza, the latter novel's protagonist and a member of the younger generation of the Junglewalla family, who encounters difficulties of various magnitudes when Pakistani and American values clash while he is living in the United States.

For more information, see:

Abnoux, Cynthia. "A Study of the Stepfather and the Stranger in the Pakistani Novel: *The Bride* by Bapsi Sidhwa." *Commonwealth Essays and Studies* 13, no. 1 (Autumn 1990): 68–72.

Afzal-Khan, Fawzia. "Bapsi Sidhwa." *International Literature in English* (New York: Garland, 1991), 271–81.

Bharucha, Nilufer E. "From Behind a Fine Veil: A Feminist Reading of Three Parsi Novels." *Indian Literature* 39, no. 5 (September–October 1996): 132–41.

Montenegro, David. "Bapsi Sidhwa: An Interview." *Massachusetts Review* 31, no. 4 (Winter 1990): 513–33.

Montenegro, David, ed. *Points of Departure: International Writers on Writing and Politics: Interviews with Bapsi Sidhwa et al.* Ann Arbor: University of Michigan Press, 1991.

Powers, Janet M. "Bapsi Sidhwa." In Emmanuel Nelson, ed., *Asian American Novelists: A Bio-Bibliographical Critical Sourcebook* (Westport, CT: Greenwood Press, 2000), 350–56.

Ross, Robert. "The Emerging Myth: Partition in the Indian and Pakistani Novel." *Association for Commonwealth Literature: Indian Literature and Language Studies Bulletin 7* (1986): 63–69.

Zaman, Niaz. "Images of Purdah in Bapsi Sidhwa's Novels." In Jasbir Jain and Amina Amin, eds., *Erasure of Purdah in the Subcontinental Novel in English* (New Delhi: Sterling, 1995), 156–73.

T

Amy Tan (1952–). One of the most acclaimed Asian American fiction writers, partly due to the adaptation of her novel *The Joy Luck Club* into a movie of the same title (for which she was coproducer and coscreenwriter), Tan was born in Oakland, California, to Chinese parents John and Daisy Tan. The life stories of her parents provided the sources for *The Joy Luck Club* and *The Kitchen God's Wife*, Tan's first two novels. Tan studied at San Jose State University, from which she obtained both her bachelor's and master's degrees in linguistics. Tan worked in the areas surrounding Oakland, first as a language development consultant for the Alameda County Association for Retarded Citizens, then as a language specialist in programs serving children with developmental disabilities, before she started a freelance writing business and wrote short stories, which eventually made their way into *The Joy Luck Club* (New York: G. P. Putnam's, 1989), a collection of sixteen interlocked stories narrating the Chinese and American lives of four Chinese mothers and their respective daughters. Two years later, Tan published *The Kitchen God's Wife* (New York: G. P. Putnam's, 1991), again based upon the life stories of her mother and father. In 1995, *The Hundred Secret Senses* (New York: G. P. Putnam's) was released. Most recently, she produced *The Bonesetter's Daughter* (New York: G. P. Putnam's, 2001), a *New York Times* best-seller. Tan has also published two children's books, *The Moon Lady* (New York: Macmillan, 1992) and *The Chinese Siamese Cat* (New York: Macmillan, 1994); the latter has been adapted into *Sagwa*, a PBS series for children.

Tan's four major novels recurrently deal with the same subject matter, though often from different perspectives. *The Joy Luck Club*, arguably Tan's most famous book to date, portrays cultural and societal differences through the dramatization of generational conflicts caused by social conditions, race relations, and cultural misunderstanding. Through the tensions and reconciliations of mother-daughter relationships, Tan shows what it is to be a woman—wife, mother, daughter, sister—in cross-cultural Americanizing situations. While at least half of the stories in the book are set in the United States, Tan's second novel, *The Kitchen God's Wife*, is Chinese-heavy in both setting and characters. While the narrative again revolves around a Chinese mother (Winnie) and her daughter (Pearl), it devotes a considerable amount of space to depicting Confucian, chauvinistic men—male characters who dominate and even abuse their wives—with the exception of Jimmy Louie, an American Chinese stationed in China during World War II who later becomes a minister and marries Pearl's mother, Winnie. This aspect of the novel echoes Nathaniel Hawthorne's romance *The Scarlet Letter*. *The Hundred Secret Senses* again examines cultural conflicts and tensions of assimilation/Americanization as seen in the strained relationship of two sisters, the Chinese-born Kwan and the American-born Olivia. *The Bonesetter's Daughter*, Tan's most recent fictional endeavor, thematically deviates little from its predecessors. The novel offers insights into Chinese American family relationships, mother-daughter bonds, cultural complexity and self-identity, and stories of Chinese immigrants, as portrayed through the relationship of LuLing Young and her daughter Ruth.

Tan is among the most discussed of all contemporary Asian American writers. Reviews, articles and essays, book chapters, and books are legion, and most of them deal with her first book, *The Joy Luck Club*. See:

Adams, Bella. "Representing History in Amy Tan's *The Kitchen God's Wife*." *MELUS* 28, no. 2 (Summer 2003): 9–30.

Bow, Leslie. "*The Joy Luck Club*, by Amy Tan." In Sau-ling Cynthia Wong and Stephen H. Sumida, eds., *A Resource Guide to Asian American Literature* (New York: MLA, 2001), 159–71.

Braendlin, Bonnie. "Mother/Daughter Dialog(ic)s in, Around, and About Amy Tan's *The Joy Luck Club*." In Nancy Owen Nelson, ed., *Private Voices, Public Lives: Women Speak on the Literary Life* (Denton: University of North Texas Press, 1995), 111–24.

Caesar, Judith. "Patriarchy, Imperialism, and Knowledge in *The Kitchen God's Wife*." *North Dakota Quarterly* 62, no. 4 (Fall 1994): 164–74.

Feldman, Gayle. "*The Joy Luck Club*: Chinese Magic, American Blessings, and a Publishing Fairy Tale." *Publishers Weekly* (July 7, 1989): 24.

Foster, M. Marie Booth. "Voice, Mind, Self: Mother-Daughter Relationships in Amy Tan's *The Joy Luck Club* and *The Kitchen God's Wife*." In Elizabeth Brown-Guillory, ed., *Women of Color: Mother-Daughter Relationships in 20th-Century Literature* (Austin: University of Texas Press, 1996), 208–27.

Gately, Patricia, ed. *The World of Amy Tan*. Special issue of *Paintbrush* 22 (Autumn 1995).

Hawley, John C. "Assimilation and Resistance in Female Fiction of Immigration: Bharati Mukherjee, Amy Tan, and Christine Bell." In Leslie Barry et al., eds., *Rediscovering America 1492–1992: National, Cultural, and Disciplinary Boundaries Re-Examined* (Baton Rouge: Louisiana State University Press, 1992), 226–34.

Heung, Marina. "Daughter-Text/Mother-Text: Matrilineage in Amy Tan's *Joy Luck Club*." *Feminist Studies* 19 (Fall 1993): 597–616.

Ho, Wendy. "Swan-Feather Mothers and Coca-Cola Daughters: Teaching Amy Tan's *The Joy Luck Club*." In John R. Maitino and David R. Peck, eds., *Teaching American Ethnic Literatures: Nineteen Essays* (Albuquerque: University of New Mexico Press, 1996), 327–45.

Huang, Guiyou. "Long a Mystery and Forever a Memory: God vs. Goddess in the Ethnic Novel." In Huang, ed., *Asian American Literary Studies* (Edinburgh, Scotland: Edinburgh University Press, 2005), 132–51.

Huntley, D., ed. *Amy Tan: A Critical Companion*. Westport, CT: Greenwood Press, 1998.

Schueller, Malini Johar. "Theorizing Ethnicity and Subjectivity: Maxine Hong Kingston's *Tripmaster Monkey* and Amy Tan's *The Joy Luck Club*." *Genders* 15 (Winter 1992): 72–85.

Shear, Walter. "Generation Differences and the Diaspora in *The Joy Luck Club*." *Critique: Studies in Contemporary Fiction* 34, no. 3 (Spring 1993): 193–99.

Shen, Gloria. "Born of a Stranger: Mother-Daughter Relationships and Storytelling in Amy Tan's *The Joy Luck Club*." In Anne E. Brown and

Maryanne E. Gooze, eds., *International Women's Writing: New Landscapes of Identity* (Westport, CT: Greenwood Press, 1995), 233–44.

Smorada, Claudia Kovach. "Side-Stepping Death: Ethnic Identity, Contradiction, and the Mother(land) in Amy Tan's Novels." *Fu Jen Studies: Literature and Linguistics* 24 (1991): 31–45.

Souris, Stephen. "'Only Two Kinds of Daughters': Inter-Monologue Dialogicity in *The Joy Luck Club*." *MELUS* 19, no. 2 (Summer 1994): 99–123.

Wong, Sau-ling Cynthia. "'Sugar Sisterhood': Situating the Amy Tan Phenomenon." In David Palumbo-Liu, ed., *The Ethnic Canon: Histories, Institutions, and Interventions* (Minneapolis: University of Minnesota Press, 1995), 174–210.

Xu, Ben. "Memory and the Ethnic Self: Reading Amy Tan's *The Joy Luck Club*." *MELUS* 19, no. 1 (1995): 3–18.

Xu, Wenying. "Amy Tan." In Emmanuel S. Nelson, ed., *Asian American Novelists: A Bio-Bibliographical Critical Sourcebook* (Westport, CT: Greenwood Press, 2000), 365–73.

* * *

Linda Ty-Casper (1931–). Filipina American novelist and short story writer Ty-Casper was born in Manila, the Philippines; she received an A.A. in 1951 and a law degree in 1955, both from the University of the Philippines. In 1956 she married Leonard Casper and they relocated to Boston. She earned an advanced law degree from Harvard but developed a keen interest in fiction writing. Ty-Casper has published ten novels and three collections of short stories. *The Peninsulars*, her first novel, came out in 1964 (Manila: Bookmark); *The Three-Cornered Sun* appeared in 1979 (Quezon City, Philippines: New Day); and *Dread Empire* was published in 1980 (Hong Kong: Heinemann Asia). The rest of the novels appeared within a few years of one another: *Hazards of Distance* (Quezon City: New Day, 1981), *Awaiting Trespass* (New York and London: Readers International, 1985), *Fortress in the Plaza* (Quezon City: New Day, 1985), *Wings of Stone* (London: Readers International, 1986), *Ten Thousand Seeds* (Quezon City: Ateneo de Manila University Press, 1987), *A Small Party in a Garden* (Quezon City: New Day, 1988), and *DreamEden* (Quezon City: Ateneo de Manila University Press, 1996). In addition to short stories published in various anthologies, Ty-Casper's short fiction has been published in collections including *The Transparent Sun and Other Stories* (Manila: Alberto Florentino, 1963), *The Secret Runner and Other Stories* (Manila: Alberto Florentino, 1974), and *Common Continent: Selected Stories* (Quezon City: Ateneo de Manila University Press, 1991).

Ty-Casper has won a number of awards and honors, including a Siliman University fellowship in 1963, a Radcliffe Institute fellowship in 1974–1975, a Djerassi writing fellowship in 1984, and the Filipino-American Women's Network's literature award in 1985. She was also a writer-in-residence at the University of the Philippines Creative Writing Center in the early 1980s.

Despite Ty-Casper's productivity, not many of her novels are easily obtainable, as she has published in the Philippines, Hong Kong, and the United States. *Awaiting Trespass*, *Wings of Stone*, and *DreamEden*, however, are familiar texts. The genre of *Awaiting Trespass* is a *passion*, that, like the passion of Jesus Christ, deals with the suffering and agonies of ordinary people under the tyrannical rule of martial law implemented by the Marcos regime. *Wings of Stone*, again dealing with the effects of martial law, narrates the story of Johnny Manalo, whose departure for the United States and return to the

Philippines thirteen years later shows how severe the repercussions of tyrannical rule can be. *DreamEden*, one of Ty-Casper's latest and better-known novels, looks at the post-Marcos era in the Philippines, especially since Corazon Aquino's assumption of power in 1986. Though readers still get snapshots of political oppression and poverty, the novel is ultimately more optimistic. As Shannon T. Leonard puts it: "Whereas the novel refuses to forecast the Philippines' future, readers take comfort in the successful achievement of Ty-Casper's overarching literary goal—to bring history into the realm of the imagination and therewith delineate versions of the nation's people's tales, in order to comprehend and chart Philippine collective and individual identities" (378).

While there are a considerable number of reviews of Ty-Casper's novels and short stories, serious scholarship on her work has been minimal, partly because most of her works are Philippine-published, and partly because of "Asian American criticism's heavy concentration on American nativity and narratives of Asian immigration and settlement within the boundaries of the United States' fifty states" (Leonard 379). Nonetheless, Harold Bloom includes a chapter on Ty-Casper in his *Asian American Women Writers* (Philadelphia: Chelsea House, 1997), 98–109. Her husband, Leonard Casper, discusses her work about martial law in *The Opposing Thumb: Decoding Literature of the Marcos Regime* (Quezon City: Giraffe Books, 1995). See also:

Leonard, Shannon T. "Linda Ty-Casper." In Emmanuel S. Nelson, ed., *Asian American Novelists: A Bio-Bibliographical Critical Sourcebook* (Westport, CT: Greenwood Press, 2000), 374–81.

Lim, Jaime An. "*The Three-Cornered Sun*: Portraits of the Revolutionary." *Philippine Studies* 40, no. 2 (1992): 255–66.

Martinez-Sicat, Maria Teresa. "The Exceptional Son in Linda Ty-Casper's *The Three-Cornered Sun*." In Martinez-Sicat, *Imagining the Nation in Four Philippine Novels* (Quezon City: University of the Philippines Press, 1994), 70–91.

Scott, Suzanne and Lynne M. Constantine. "Belles Lettres Interview" with Linda Ty-Casper. *Belles Lettres* 2, no. 5 (1987): 5, 15.

Holly Uyemoto (1970–). A published writer at the age of nineteen, Uyemoto is a young Japanese American novelist whose writing career is still on the rise. Born in Ithaca, New York, Uyemoto has lived in Kansas and California with her family. She was so determined to be a writer that she dropped out of high school and started to write at fifteen; the result was a novel called *Rebel Without a Clue* (New York: Crown, 1989). Encouraged by the publication of the novel and with strong support from her parents, Uyemoto completed her second novel, *Go*, in 1995 (New York: Dutton). Uyemoto loves things Japanese and even majored in Japanese history at Wellesley College in the late 1990s.

Rebel Without a Clue, narrated by Christian Delon, a recent high school graduate from a dysfunctional family, is about the coming of age of two young men, Christian and his close friend Thomas Bainbridge, an AIDS victim. Christian and Thomas live in an upscale neighborhood with affluent homes and expensive cars, as well as money to buy drugs, but the dysfunctionality of both their families deprives them of parental love and care and as a result, they turn to each other for a surrogate family. As Thomas comes ever closer to his own mortality and

Christian gains a greater sense of morality, their parting as friends becomes inevitable. While *Rebel Without a Clue* unmistakably displays signs of the author's youth, *Go* seems more mature and has been better appreciated by reviewers. Written more under the influence of histories such as Ronald Takaki's *Strangers from a Different Shore* than of literary writers, and named for a board game popular in Japan and China, *Go* recounts the story of a twenty-year-old Japanese American college student, Wilhemina (Wil), who has to deal with personal problems such as abortion, emotional instability, and a difficult relationship with her mother, as well as historical issues such as the Japanese American internment during World War II and its consequences on Japanese families. Wil is an only child and has a strong desire to be a different individual; in this regard, Uyemoto admits in an interview with Scott Shepard, *Go* is autobiographical.

Reviews of Uyemoto's novels are easily found but critical studies are yet to emerge. One bio-critical essay and one interview, however, shed light on her fiction:

Massa, Suzanne Hotte. "Holly Uyemoto." In Emmanuel S. Nelson, ed., *Asian American Novelists: A Bio-Bibliographical Critical Sourcebook* (Westport, CT: Greenwood Press, 2000), 382–86.

Shepard, Scott. "An Interview with Holly Uyemoto." *Hitting Critical Mass: A Journal of Asian American Cultural Criticism* 4, no. 2 (Summer 1997) (http://socrates.berkeley.edu/~critmass/v4n2/shepardprint.html).

Reviews include:

Abe, Patricia. Rev. of *Go*. *Ms*. 5 (January–February 1995): 71.

Estes, Sally. Rev. of *Rebel Without a Clue*. *Booklist* 86 (September 15, 1989): 146.

Hanes, Margaret. Rev. of *Go*. *Library Journal* 120 (January 1995): 139.

Monks, Merri. Rev. of *Go*. "Adult Books for Young Adults." *Booklist* 91 (February 1, 1995): 996.

Rees, Douglas. Rev. of *Rebel Without a Clue*. *Wilson Library Bulletin* 64 (March 1990): 12.

Sullivan, Mary Ellen. Rev. of *Go*. *Booklist* 91 (February 1, 1995): 991–92.

Shawn Hsu Wong (1949–). Born in Oakland and raised in Berkeley, California, among other places, Wong first enrolled at San Francisco State University as a premed student, but he developed an enthusiasm for writing under the particular influence of his writing mentor, Kay Boyle. Wong changed his major to English and completed his undergraduate studies at the University of California at Berkeley. His love of writing, however, took him back to San Francisco State, where he completed a master's degree in creative writing in 1974. His master's thesis laid the groundwork for *Homebase: A Novel*, which he published in 1979 (New York: I. Reed Books); it won the 1980 Pacific Northwest Booksellers' Award and the Washington State Governor's Writers Day Award. Wong also received a National Endowment for the Arts creative writing fellowship in 1981. His second novel, *American Knees*, was published in 1995 (New York: Simon & Schuster). Wong's literary career is also marked by his participation in the creation, with Frank Chin, Jeffery Paul Chan, and Lawson Fusao Inada, of CARP— the Combined Asian American Resources Project, dedicated to the discovery and study of Asian American literary and cultural works—as well as his involvement in the editing and publication of two anthologies: the groundbreaking *Aiiieeeee!*, coedited with Frank Chin, Jeffery Paul Chan, and Lawson Fusao Inada (Washington, DC: Howard University Press, 1974), and *The Big Aiiieeeee!* (New York: Meridian, 1991), coedited with the same team. In 1996, Wong published his own singly edited anthology, *Asian American Literature: A Brief Introduction and Anthology* (New York: HarperCollins).

Homebase tells the story of a son's love for his parents. The narrator, Rainsford Chan, named for the town where his great-grandfather lived, is a fourth-generation Chinese American who undertakes a quest to find both himself and the history of his family. He achieves both goals through narrating historical events that defined the life of early Asian American communities, such as the building of the Pacific Railroad and the Chinese Exclusion Act. Through the literal and figurative journey, Rainsford finally comes to terms with his ethnic identity and accepts his bicultural heritage. *American Knees*, set in the two major California metropolises, Los Angeles and San Francisco, again examines issues of identity and racial stereotyping. Raymond Ding, working as an assistant director of minority affairs at a community college, is forced to deal with the sting of racism contained in racial slurs that he hears on campus. "American Knees" is an affirmative response to the derogative question, "What are you?"

While Wong enjoys a well-deserved reputation as a pioneering editor and writer in Asian American literary communities, his novels have not been given due critical acclaim. Thus far notices of his works are mostly reviews. A few studies are noteworthy:

Chen, Chi-Ping. "Shawn Wong." In Emmanuel S. Nelson, ed., *Asian American Novelists: A Bio-Bibliographical Critical Sourcebook* (Westport, CT: Greenwood Press, 2000), 391–97.

Kim, Elaine. "Shawn Hsu Wong." In Kim, *Asian American Literature: An Introduction to the Writings and Their Social Context* (Philadelphia: Temple University Press, 1982), 194–97.

Lee, A. Robert. "Decolonizing America: The Ethnicity of Ernest Gaines, Jose Antonio Villarreal, Leslie Marmon Silko and Shawn Wong." In C. C. Barfoot and Theo D'haen, eds., *Shades of Empire in Colonial and Post Colonial Literatures* (Amsterdam: Rodopi, 1993), 269–82.

Sakurai, Patricia A. "The Politics of Possession: The Negotiation of Identity in *American in Disguise, Homebase,* and *Farewell to Manzanar.*" In Gary Y. Okihiro, Marilyn Alquizola, Dorothy Fujita Rony, and K. Scott Wong, eds., *Privileging Positions: The Sites of Asian American Studies* (Pullman: Washington State University Press, 1995), 157–70.

Lois-Ann Yamanaka (1961–). *Sansei* Japanese Hawaiian novelist and poet Yamanaka was born in Ho'olchua, Molokai, Hawai'i, and raised in the Hilo, Kau, and Kona districts of the island. She grew up speaking pidgin, the Hawaiian Creole English. Yamanaka attended the University of Hawai'i at Manoa, from which she received both her bachelor's and master's degrees in education, in 1983 and 1987, respectively. She became a teacher in the public school system, but a strong desire prompted her to start to write at age twenty-seven. Her first major literary effort was a collection of poetry, *Saturday Night at the Pahala Theatre* (Honolulu: Bamboo Ridge Press, 1993), which won the Pushcart Prize XVIII in 1993 and the Asian American Studies National Book Award in 1994. Her next book, *Wild Meat and the Bully Burgers*, consisting of a series of short narratives, appeared in 1996 (New York: Farrar, Straus & Giroux), followed by the novel *Blu's Hanging* in 1997 (New York: Farrar, Straus & Giroux). The year 1999 saw the publication of two other novels, *Heads by Harry* (New York: Farrar, Straus & Giroux) and *Name Me Nobody* (New York: Hyperion). Her most recent novel, *Father of the Four Passages*, came out in 2001 (New York: Farrar, Straus & Giroux).

Yamanaka is a controversial writer, partly because of her use of Hawaiian Creole English and partly because of her unflattering depictions of Filipino Americans, especially in some poems and most obviously in *Blu's Hanging*. Nonetheless, her literary contributions have been widely recognized with prizes and awards, including a National Endowment for the Humanities grant in 1990, the Elliot Cades Award for Literature in 1993, a Carnegie Foundation grant in 1994, a National Endowment for the Arts creative writing fellowship in 1994, the Pushcart Prize XIX for the short story "Yarn Wig" in 1994, the Rona Jaffe Award for Women Writers in 1996, the Lannon Literary Award and the Asian American Literary Award in 1998, and the American Book Award for *Heads by Harry* in 2000, among others.

Wild Meat and the Bully Burgers, like *Blu's Hanging* and *Heads by Harry*—Yamanaka's other early novels—is loosely based upon her adolescent years, and as has been frequently noted by critics, was inspired by Sandra Cisneros's novel, *The House on Mango Street*, which loosely strings together a series of short vignettes focusing on the lives of Chicano/a adolescents. *Wild Meat*, also using vignettes, follows the life of a Japanese American girl, Lovey Nariyoshi, who lives in a poor Hilo community. The girl's growing consciousness of her female, non-Caucasian identity contributes to her desire to be different from who she is, not unlike the young girl Pecola Breedlove in Toni Morrison's *The Bluest Eye*, who prays for white skin and blue eyes and ultimately, for love and acceptance. *Blu's Hanging* features a young Japanese American girl of thirteen, Ivah Ogata, who is forced to cope not only with the death of her mother and her father's shame of leprosy but also with parental responsibilities for her two siblings, her sister Maisie and her brother Blu, who is molested by their Filipino neighbor Uncle Paulo. The image of Uncle Paulo as a sexual predator, among other things, triggered the 1998 controversy regarding the awarding and then rescinding of the Association for Asian American Studies Literature Award to Yamanaka. *Heads by Harry* also has a female protagonist, Toni Yagyuu, a college student who faces another set of problems: sexuality, self-esteem, and racism. Rather than falling victim to male sexual abuse, as happens to characters in *Wild Meat* and *Blu's Hanging*, Toni uses her sexuality as a means of self-empowerment and struggles to survive. "Taken as a whole, Yamanaka's works are both female bildungsroman and cultural documents" (Chen 400). Another way to approach these three novels is to read them as a trilogy, as Kyoko Amano points out: "*Heads by Harry*, along with *Wild Meat and the Bully Burgers* and *Blu's Hanging*, is a part of the Hilo trilogy, novels set in Hilo on the Big Island" (319).

Name Me Nobody is a young adult novel that deals with issues of adolescence—love, acceptance, race, and identity—from the point of view of a teenager. *Father of the Four Passages*, Yamanaka's first novel not written in pidgin, explores the themes of motherhood, drug abuse, and familial relationships from a mother's perspective. *Saturday Night at the Pahala Theatre*, Yamanaka's only poetry collection to date, written in pidgin, is a series of "verse novellas" that focus on the life experience of working-class Hawaiian teenagers.

For more information, see:

Amano, Kyoko. "Lois-Ann Yamanaka." In Guiyou Huang, ed., *Asian American Short Story Writers: An A-to-Z Guide* (Westport, CT: Greenwood Press, 2003), 317–25.

Chen, Chi-Ping. "Lois-Ann Yamanaka." In Emmanuel S. Nelson, ed., *Asian American Novelists: A Bio-Bibliographical Critical Sourcebook* (Westport, CT: Greenwood Press, 2000), 398–402.

James, Jaime. "This Hawaii Is Not for Tourists." *Atlantic Monthly* 238, no. 2 (February 1999): 90–94.

Moran, Edward. "Lois-Ann Yamanaka." *Current Biography Yearbook* 60, no. 6 (June 1999): 57–59.

Morgan, Peter E. "Lois-Ann Yamanaka." In Guiyou Huang, ed., *Asian American Poets: A Bio-Bibliographical Critical Sourcebook* (Westport, CT: Greenwood Press, 2002), 337–41.

Shea, Renee H. "Pidgin Politics and Paradise Revised." *Poets and Writers* 26, no. 5 (1998): 32–39.

Shim, Rosalee. "Power in the Eye of the Beholder: A Close Reading of Lois-Ann Yamanaka's *Saturday Night at the Pahala Theatre*." *Hitting Critical Mass: A Journal of Asian American Cultural Criticism* 3, no. 1 (Winter 1995): 85–91.

Soong, Micheline M. "*Yosegire Buton*, the 'Crazy' Patchwork Quilt: An Alternative Narrative Strategy of Three Local Japanese Women Writers of Hawai'i." Ph.D. diss., UCLA, 1999.

Wilson, Rob. "Bloody Mary Meets Lois-Ann Yamanaka: Imagining Asia/Pacific—from *South Pacific* to *Bamboo Ridge*." In Shirley Geok-lin Lim, Larry E. Smith, and Wimal Dissanayake, eds., *Transnational Asia Pacific: Gender, Culture, and the Public Sphere* (Urbana: University of Illinois Press, 1999), 92–110.

* * *

Karen Tei Yamashita (1951–). Yamashita is a *sansei* novelist born in Oakland, California; her family moved to Los Angeles when she was a young child. She attended Carlton College in Minnesota, majoring in English and Japanese literature; she also spent a year and half of her college time in Japan's Waseda University. Yamashita started to learn Portuguese after graduation from Carlton. A Thomas J. Watson Fellowship afforded her an opportunity to conduct research on Japanese immigration to Brazil, where she lived between 1974 and 1984, and where she also met and married her Brazilian husband, Ronaldo Lopes de Oliveira. A very important result of her decade-long experience with Brazil was the development of an interest in creative writing: she started to write short stories while in Sao Paolo and won several writing contests. She won a Rockefeller Playwright-in-Residence Fellowship at East/West Players in Los Angeles in 1977. Yamashita and her family returned to Los Angeles in 1984; she worked at a local public television station while writing prose and poetry as well as doing translations. She published a novel, *Through the Arc of the Rain Forest,* in 1990 (Minneapolis: Coffee House Press), followed by *Brazil-Maru* in 1992 (Minneapolis: Coffee House Press) and *Tropic of Orange* in 1997 (Minneapolis: Coffee House Press). She also wrote a number of short stories, a few poems, and several plays. *Circle K Cycles* (Minneapolis: Coffee House Press), a collection of pieces in miscellaneous genres, came out in 2001. Among Yamashita's dramatic works are *Omen: An American Kabuki* (produced in Los Angeles in 1978), *Hiroshima Tropical* (produced in Los Angeles in 1984), a screenplay, *Kusei: An Endangered Species* (coauthored with Karen Mayeda for Visual Communications, 1986), *Hannah Kusoh: An American Butoh* (produced in Los Angeles in 1995), *Tokyo Carmen vs. L.A. Carmen* (produced in Los Angeles in 1990), *GiLAwrecks* (produced in Seattle in 1992), and *Noh Bozos* (produced in Los Angeles in 1993).

Yamashita won first place in the 1975 *Amerasia Journal* Short Story Contest for "The Bath," first prize for "Tucano" in *Rafu Shimpo*'s 1975 short story contest, and the 1979 American-Japanese National Literary Award for her short story "Asaka-No-Miya." *Through the Arc of the Rain Forest* won a 1991 American Book Award and the 1992 Janet Heidinger Kafka Award; *The Village Voice* chose *Brazil-Maru* as one of the twenty-five best books of 1992.

Despite her versatility in several literary genres, Yamashita is primarily known as a novelist, and not exactly an Asian American one at that, if her work is defined in terms of content or geography: unlike other Asian American novels, hers do not contain a significant ethnic component; if anything, her writing is more Japanese South American than Japanese American. The breadth and contents of her novels are adeptly summed up by Douglas Sugano: "Her works concern social dynamics, with the assumption that subtle political, environmental, and technological shifts can alter whole cultures. Her novels combine anthropology, science fiction, the picaresque, and magic realism. In brief, Yamashita delights in the combinational possibilities that change our lives" (404).

Through the Arc of the Rain Forest uses an unconventional narrator, a little ball that hangs around the principal character, Kazumasa Ishimaru's, forehead, telling the stories of a diverse range of characters with special talents. *Brazil-Maru* takes a different narrative format: each section of the book starts with a quote from Rousseau and adopts a different narrator who focuses on the rise and decline of a colony called Esperanca established by Japanese Christians in Brazil, from the 1920s to the mid-1970s. Yamashita's interest in the permeability of borders—political, social, cultural, racial, and geographical—also surfaces in her third novel, *Tropic of Orange*, though the scene is now Los Angeles, Yamashita's own city. The racially and culturally diverse metropolis serves as a large canvas on which borders, redefined through the interactions of human relationships, are dissolved.

Yamashita's short fiction has also garnered critical acclaim, though she has not published a collection of purely short stories. *Circle K Cycles* includes a number of short stories but also journal entries, photos, and illustrations; it thus defies genre classification. Nonetheless, the collection reflects Yamashita's thematic interests, such as geographical boundaries, global migration, human relations, and so on. This collection of miscellaneous types of writing and print media is itself a specimen of the collapsibility or permeability of boundaries, as the novelist has demonstrated in her novels, essays, short stories, poems, and pictures.

Reviews of Yamashita's *Through the Arc of the Rain Forest* and *Tropic of Orange* can be found in various journals and magazines. Articles include:

Field, Robin E. "Karen Tei Yamashita." In Guiyou Huang, ed., *Asian American Short Story Writers: An A-to-Z*

Guide (Westport, CT: Greenwood Press, 2003), 327–32.

Murashige, Kenneth. "Karen Tei Yamashita: An Interview." *Amerasia Journal* 20, no. 3 (1994): 49–59.

Murphy, Patrick D. "Commodification, Resistance, Inhabitation, and Identity in the Novels of Linda Hogan, Edna Escamill, and Karen Tei Yamashita." *Phoebe* 9 (1997): 1–10.

Sugano, Douglas. "Karen Tei Yamashita." In Emmanuel S. Nelson, ed., *Asian American Novelists: A Bio-Bibliographical Critical Sourcebook* (Westport, CT: Greenwood Press, 2000), 403–8.

5. Poetry

Ai (1947–). Japanese/African American poet Florence Ai Ogawa was born in Albany, Texas. Raised in Tucson, Arizona, Ai lived in Los Angeles for three years, where she started to write poetry. In her mid-teens she returned to Tucson to finish high school. She enrolled at the University of Arizona and earned a B.A. in English and Oriental Studies; in 1971 she completed an M.F.A. at the University of California at Irvine. Throughout her educational period, Ai changed her surname several times until she officially took her biological father's Japanese name, Ogawa, and Ai for her pen name. The word "Ai" in Japanese (and Chinese) is the same character meaning love. In 1973 Ai published her first book of poetry, *Cruelty* (Boston: Houghton Mifflin). In the two decades from 1979 to 1999, six more collections ensued: *Killing Floor* (Boston: Houghton Mifflin, 1979), *Sin* (Boston: Houghton Mifflin, 1986), *Cruelty/Killing Floor* (New York: Thunder's Mouth Press, 1987), *Fate: New Poems* (Boston: Houghton Mifflin, 1991), *Greed* (New York: Norton, 1993), and *Vice: New and Selected Poems* (New York: Norton, 1999).

Ai has received fellowships from the Guggenheim and the Bunting Foundation in 1975, the National Endowment for the Arts in 1978, and the Ingram-Merrill Foundation in 1983, and a grant from the St. Botolph Foundation. For *Vice*, she won the National Book Award for Poetry in 1999.

Ai's poems often take the form of dramatic monologue, spoken by a wide range of personae and characters. In *Cruelty*, for example, the speakers are usually anonymous women—ordinary people who are often dealt cruel blows and made victims of disillusion and desperation by unfortunate circumstances. In her second volume, *Killing Floor*, however, most of the speakers are famous historical personalities—usually males like Leon Trotsky and Emiliano Zapata, with occasional exceptions like Marilyn Monroe—recounting sad events of life as well as successes of survival. *Sin* employs both (in)famous and anonymous characters for dramatic monologues exploring themes such as power and sex. Poems in *Fate* and *Greed* continue to probe vices and evils of society, returning to the use of well-known historical figures such as J. Edgar Hoover and Elvis Presley, among others. *Vice* collects eighteen new pieces and fifty-eight previously published monologues; once again, these depict or touch upon violence and immorality in American society.

Ai has also published a couple of essays and a short story. The essays provide insights on the author's views of race and discuss some of the themes in her poetry: "On Being 1/2 Japanese, 1/8 Choctaw, 1/4 Black, and 1/6 Irish," *Ms.* 6 (June 1974): 58; and "Movies, Mom, Poetry, Sex, and Death: A Self-Interview," *Onthebus* 3–4, no. 2–1 (1991): 240–48. Because of Ai's complex ethnic backgrounds, literary scholarship on both the Asian American and African American sides claims her, as is evident in reviews and studies of her poetry. See:

Ackerson, Duane. "Ai." In Pamela L. Shelton, ed., *Contemporary Women Poets* (Detroit: St. James Press, 1998), 8–9.

Dooley, Dale A. "Ai." In Carol Hurd Green and Mary Grimley Mason, eds., *American Women Writers*, vol. 5 (New York: Continuum, 1994), 7–9.

Erb, Lisa. "An Interview with Ai: Dancing with the Madness." *Mānoa: A Pacific Journal of International Writing* 2, no. 2 (Fall 1990): 22–40.

Huot, Nikolas. "Ai." In Guiyou Huang, ed., *Asian American Poets: A Bio-Bibliographical Critical Sourcebook* (Westport, CT: Greenwood Press, 2002), 15–20.

Ingram, Claudia. "Writing the Crises: The Development of Abjection in Ai's Dramatic Monologues." *LIT: Literature Interpretation Theory* 8, no. 2 (October 1997): 172–91.

Kilcup, Karen L. "Dialogue of the Self: Toward a Theory of (Re)Reading Ai." *Journal of Gender Studies* 7, no. 1 (1998): 5–20.

Lee, A. Robert. "Ai." In William Andrews, Frances Smith Foster, and Trudier Harris, eds., *The Oxford Companion to African American Literature* (New York: Oxford University Press, 1997), 10.

Moore, Lenard D. Rev. of *Vice. Black Issues Book Review* 2, no. 2 (March/April 2000): 44–45.

Redmond, Eugene. "Five Black Poets: History, Consciousness, Love, and Harshness." *Parnassus: Poetry in Review* 3, no. 2 (1975): 153–72.

Wilson, Rob. "The Will to Transcendence in Contemporary American Poet Ai." *Canadian Review of American Studies* 17, no. 4 (1986): 437–48.

* * *

Meena Alexander (1951–). An Indian American poet, memoirist, and novelist, Alexander was born in Allahabad, India and grew up in different places in India and in different countries of the world. Alexander began college at the University of Khartoum in Sudan at the young age of thirteen and finished her B.A. in 1969, when she also started to write poems; she went on to graduate school at the University of Nottingham in England at age eighteen and received her Ph.D. in 1973. When she returned to India, she taught at different universities, including the University of Delhi, Jawaharlal Nehru University in Delhi, and the University of Hyderabad. In 1978 she was a visiting fellow at the Centre de Recherches en Litterature et Civilization Nord-Americaines, Sorbonne. The following year, after she had met and married an American of Jewish descent in India, the couple left Hyderabad for New York, where she has been teaching at Hunter College and Columbia University.

Alexander began her writing career as a poet and has remained primarily a poet. Her first collection, *The Bird's Bright Ring*, appeared in 1976 (Calcutta: Writers Workshop); *I Root My Name* (Calcutta: United Writers), *In the Middle Earth* (New Delhi: Enact), and *Without Place* (Calcutta: Writers Workshop) all followed in 1977. In the following two decades, she published *Stone Roots* (New Delhi: Arnold-Heinemann, 1980), *House of a Thousand Doors* (Washington, DC: Three Continents Press, 1988), *The Storm: A Poem in Five Parts* (New York: Red Dust Press, 1989), *Night-Scene, the Garden* (New York: Red Dust Press, 1992), *River and Bridge* (Toronto: TSAR, 1996), and *Illiterate Heart* (Evanston, IL: Triquarterly, 2002). In 1991 Alexander published her first novel,

Nampally Road (San Francisco: Mercury House), followed by a memoir, *Fault Lines* (New York: Feminist Press) in 1992. Her second novel, *Manhattan Music*, came out in 1997. *The Shock of Arrival: Reflections on Postcolonial Experience* (Boston: South End Press, 1996) literally represents all the genres that Alexander works with—essays, poems, imaginary dialogues, anecdotes, and autobiographical pieces. As an academic she has written two scholarly books, *The Poetic Self: Towards a Phenomenology of Romanticism* (New Delhi: Arnold-Heinemann, 1979), and *Women in Romanticism: Mary Wollstonecraft, Dorothy Wordsworth, and Mary Shelley* (Savage, MD: Barnes & Noble Books, 1989).

Alexander's multicultural experience, coupled with her diasporic migration within and among three continents—Asia, Europe, and North America—is evident in many of her poems from virtually all her collections. As an immigrant, a feminist, a woman of color, a postcolonial, and an academic as well as a creative writer—a poet and a novelist—she works across genres and across cultures. As Purvi Shah puts it, "Poetry serves as a form for voicing what has been left out of the annals of history, providing Alexander with a chance to place the self in a larger social, national, or historical context" (23). In her ten collections of poems, Alexander delves into issues of self-creation and identity formation from the position of a marginalized member of society. Themes of dislocation and sense of exile, belonging and home, locale and memory, the past and the present, all come together in the poet's efforts to express her life experiences through the power of language. In her two novels, *Nampally Road* and *Manhattan Music*, similar themes persist, though the narratives focus on women's diasporic experiences that reflect her own journey from locale to locale. The first novel deals with the dislocation and displacement of an English professor, Mira Kannabeen, who has returned from England to Hyderabad, where Alexander herself taught. Even though the second novel shifts its setting to the contemporary United States, it continues the author's explorations of memory, dislocation, and intercultural and racial problems.

Alexander is a versatile and prolific writer. Studies of her poetry and novels are not difficult to find. See:

Ali, Zainab and Dharini Rasiah. "Interview with Meena Alexander." In King-Kok Cheung, ed., *Words Matter: Conversations with Asian American Writers* (Honolulu: University of Hawai'i Press, 2000), 69–91.

Bahri, Deepika and Mary Vasudeva. "Observing Ourselves Among Others: Interview with Meena Alexander." In Bahri and Vasudeva, eds., *Between the Lines: South Asians and Postcoloniality* (Philadephia: Temple University Press, 1996), 35–53.

Davé, Shilpa. "The Doors to Home and History: Post-Colonial Identities in Meena Alexander and Bharati Mukherjee." *Amerasia Journal* 19, no. 3 (1993): 103–13.

——. "*Nampally Road*, by Meena Alexander." In Sau-ling Cynthia Wong and Stephen H. Sumida, eds., *A Resource Guide to Asian American Literature* (New York: MLA, 2001), 13–20.

Duncan, Erika. "A Portrait of Meena Alexander." *World Literature Today* 73, no. 1 (Winter 1999): 23–28.

Kumar, Manjushree. "Journey Through Time, Meena Alexander's *Fault Lines*." In R. K. Dhawan, ed., *Indian Women Novelists* (New Delhi: Prestige Books, 1995), 208–21.

"Meena Alexander: Poet, Novelist, and Memorist." In Amy Ling, ed., *Yellow Light: The Flowering of Asian American Arts* (Philadelphia: Temple University Press, 1999), 83–91.

Moka-Dias, Brunda. "Meena Alexander." In Emmanuel S. Nelson, ed., *Asian American Novelists: A Bio-Bibliographical Critical Sourcebook* (Westport, CT: Greenwood Press, 2000), 1–7.

Perry, John Oliver. "Contemporary Indian Poetry in English." *World Literature Today* 68, no. 2 (Spring 1994): 261–71.

———. "Exiled by a Woman's Body: Substantial Phenomenon in the Poetry of Meena Alexander." *Journal of South Asian Literature* 12 (1986): 1–10.

Ramraj, Ruby S. "Meena Alexander." In Guiyou Huang, ed., *Asian American Autobiographers: A Bio-Bibliographical Critical Sourcebook* (Westport, CT: Greenwood Press, 2001), 17–26.

Rustomji-Kerns, Roshni. "In a Field of Dreams: A Conversation with Meena Alexander." *Weber Studies* 15, no. 1 (Winter 1998): 18–27.

Shah, Purvi. "Meena Alexander." In Guiyou Huang, ed., *Asian American Poets: A Bio-Bibliographical Critical Sourcebook* (Westport, CT: Greenwood Press, 2002), 21–29.

Tharu, Susie. "A Conversation with Meena Alexander." *Chandrabhaga* 7 (Summer 1982): 69–74.

* * *

Agha Shahid Ali (1949–2001). Indian American poet Ali was born in New Delhi, India, and grew up in a family where poetry was always present. He started to write poetry at age ten. Ali was educated in India, first at the University of Kashmir and then at the University of Delhi; he completed a doctoral degree in English at Pennsylvania State University in 1984, writing his dissertation on the modernist poet T. S. Eliot. In his short life of fifty-two years, Ali published eight collections of poems: *Bone-Sculpture* (Calcutta: Writers Workshop, 1972), *In Memory of Begum Akhtar and Other Poems* (Calcutta: Writers Workshop, 1979), *The Half-Inch Himalayas* (Middletown, CT: Wesleyan University Press, 1987), *A Walk Through the Yellow Pages* (Tucson, AZ: SUN/Gemini Press, 1987), *A Nostalgist's Map of America* (New York: Norton, 1991), *The Belovéd Witness: Selected Poems* (New York: Viking Penguin, 1992), *The Country Without a Post Office* (New York: Norton, 1997), and *Rooms Are Never Finished* (New York: Norton, 2001). Ali also translated the poetry of Faiz Ahmed Faiz, published in *The Rebel's Silhouette: Selected Poems by Faiz Ahmed Faiz* (Amherst: University of Massachusetts Press, 1995). A year before he died of a brain tumor, Ali published his edition of a volume of *ghazals* called *Ravishing DisUnities: Real Ghazals in English* (Middletown, CT: Wesleyan University Press, 2000).

Ali received awards and prizes including fellowships from the Guggenheim Foundation and the Ingram-Merrill Foundation and grants from the Pennsylvania Council on the Arts and the New York Foundation for the Arts.

Of Ali's works, the books that have been reviewed or studied are *A Nostalgist's Map of America*, *The Country Without a Post Office*, and *The Half-Inch Himalayas*. The latter collection was his first book published in the United States, in the respected Wesleyan New Poets series, and it deals with themes of exile and home: as Ali labeled himself a Kashmir exile, the loss of Kashmir as a homeland finds its way into many of his poems. Ali's familiarity with Urdu poets such as Faiz Ahmed Faiz and his knowledge of American poets such as Emily Dickinson and Eliot shine through in *A Nostalgist's Map of America*, in which Kashmir and America illuminate each other in the poet's explorations of themes of hope and loss. The title of *The Country Without a Post Office* spreads again a heavy sense of loss as well as chaos: breakdown of communication due to the violence that broke out in Kashmir, and chaos caused by displacement from home and country.

For all the collections Ali produced and all the awards he won, his poetry has not received a great deal of critical notice, though a few reviews and articles are available. The inaugural issue of *Catamaran: A Journal of South Asian American Writing* 1, no. 2 (2004) is on the work of Ali. See also:

King, Bruce. Rev. of *The Country Without a Post Office. World Literature Today* 71, no. 3 (1997): 590–91.

Katrak, Ketu H. "South Asian American Writers: Geography and Memory." *Amerasia Journal* 22, no. 3 (1996): 121–38.

Needham, Lawrence. "'The Sorrows of a Broken Time': Agha Shahid Ali and the Poetry of Loss and Recovery." In Emmanuel S. Nelson, ed., *Reworlding: The Literature of the Indian Diaspora* (Westport, CT: Greenwood Press, 1992), 63–76.

Perry, John Oliver. Rev. of *A Nostalgist's Map of America. World Literature Today* 66, no. 4 (1992): 779–80.

See, Dianne. Rev. of *A Nostalgist's Map of America. Amerasia Journal* 21, no. 1–2 (1995): 176–78.

Shah, Purvi. "Agha Shahid Ali." In Guiyou Huang, ed., *Asian American Poets: A Bio-Bibliographical Critical Sourcebook* (Westport, CT: Greenwood Press, 2002), 31–35.

B

Himani Bannerji. See Bannerji in "Fiction."

* * *

Mei-Mei Berssenbrugge (1947–). Born in Beijing, China, to a Chinese mother and a Dutch American father, Berssenbrugge was raised in a suburban town in Massachusetts. She earned a B.A. from Reed College in Oregon and an M.F.A. from Columbia University in New York. Since 1974 she has published ten collections of poems: *Summits Move with the Tide* (Greenfield Center, NY: Greenfield Review Press, 1974), *Random Possession* (New York: I. Reed Books, 1979), *The Heat Bird* (Providence, RI: Burning Deck Books, 1983), *Empathy* (Barrytown, NY: Station Hill Press, 1989), *Mizu* (Tucson, AZ: Chax Press, 1990), *Sphericity* (Berkeley: Kelsey St. Press, 1993), *Endocrinology: Poetry, Art* (Berkeley: Kelsey St. Press, 1997), *Four-Year-Old-Girl* (Berkeley: Kelsey St. Press, 1998), *Audience* (Brooklyn, NY: Belladonna Books/Boog Literature, 2000), and most recently, *Nest* (Berkeley: Kelsey St. Press, 2003). Berssenbrugge has been recognized as an outstanding poet with a good number of awards, including two American Book Awards, a PEN West Award, the 1997 Asian American Literary Award, the 1999 Western States Book Award, and two National Endowment for the Arts Fellowships.

Summits Move with the Tide collects thirty-two poems and a single-act play. The poems address a range of topics, from personal feelings to events to different locales the poet has resided in or visited, such as Nepal, China, New Mexico, New York City, and so on. *Random Possession* consists of seventeen poems that deal with disparate topics such as death, love, and gender relationships. *The Heat Bird*, one of Berssenbrugge's more widely read volumes, is a unique collection that contains fewer poems—only four—and has a specific locus: New Mexico, where the poet lived for over a quarter of a century. Fifteen of the eighteen pieces in *Empathy* were written by Berssenbrugge herself, and three were the products of collaboration with artists

Theodora Yoshikami and Richard Tuttle; some poems deal with nature and others with culture. *Mizu,* a collaboration with choreographer Theodora Yoshikami and musician Jason Hwang, was written for performance and tells the imaginative story of a boy's adventure under the sea. The collection in *Sphericity* consists of six poems and is an examination of the power and limits of words as seen in the way the poet uses them. *Endocrinology* (in collaboration with artist Kiki Smith) is a postillness work: because of exposure to a pesticide Berssenbrugge fell sick, a life-changing event that contributed to the writing of this collection that considers the functions of the human body, love, and mortality, among other subjects. The eleven poems gathered in *Four-Year-Old-Girl* attempt to describe human presence in the phenomenal world and express perceptions of human experience.

For more information, see:

Altieri, Charles. "Intimacy and Experiment in Mei-Mei Berssenbrugge's *Empathy.*" In Laura Hinton and Cynthia Hogue, eds., *We Who Love to Be Astonished: Experimental Women's Writing and Performance Poetics* (Tuscaloosa: University of Alabama Press, 2002).

Fraser, Kathleen. "Overheard." *Poetics Journal* 4 (May 1984): 98–105.

Newman, Denise. "The Concretion of Emotion: An Analytic Lyric of Mei-Mei Berssenbrugge's *Empathy.*" *Talisman* 9 (Fall 1992): 119–24.

Rasula, Jed. "Ten Different Fruits on One Different Tree: Experiment as a Claim of the Book." *Chicago Review* 43, no. 4 (Fall 1997): 28–39.

Simpson, Megan. *Poetic Epistemologies: Gender and Knowing in Women's Language-Oriented Writing.* Albany: State University of New York Press, 2000.

Tabios, Eileen. *Black Lightning: Poetry-in-Progress.* New York: Asian American Writers' Workshop, 1998.

Yen, Xiaoping. "Mei-Mei Berssenbrugge." In Guiyou Huang, ed., *Asian American Poets: A Bio-Bibliographical Critical Sourcebook* (Westport, CT: Greenwood Press, 2002), 45–51.

Zhou Xiaojing. "Blurring the Borders Between Formal and Social Aesthetics: An Interview with Mei-Mei Berssenbrugge." *MELUS* 27, no. 1 (Spring 2002): 199–212.

C

Virginia R. Cerenio (1955–). A second-generation Filipina American poet, Cerenio was born and raised in California. She graduated from San Francisco State University with a B.A. in English and then an M.A. in education. Cerenio is known for her political activism and for being a founding member of BAYPAW—the Bay Area Philipino American Writers. She has published poems in many noted Asian American anthologies, including Joseph Bruchac's *Breaking Silence*, Shirley Lim et al.'s *The Forbidden Stitch*, and Nick Carbo's *Returning a Borrowed Tongue*. The majority of her individually published poems are collected in a volume called *Trespassing Innocence* (San Francisco: Kearny Street Workshop Press, 1989) that deals with familiar social and cultural aspects of immigration and immigrants: their history and cultural heritage, as well as problems and obstacles they face living in an adopted land. Cerenio shows special concern and sympathy for the downtrodden, the poor, and the marginalized people such as Filipino immigrant old-timers, known as *manongs*; her own activism is also manifest in the poems that explore political issues in both the United States and the Philippines.

Cerenio is known to some as a "Flip poet"—an American-born and/or raised Filipino writer active in the Third World student movement and the International Hotel protests in the 1960s and 1970s—and her poetry has received some critical notice. See:

Campomanes, Oscar. "Filipinos in the United States and Their Literature of Exile." In Shirley Geok-lin Lim and Amy Ling, eds., *Reading the Literatures of Asian America* (Philadelphia: Temple University Press, 1992), 49–78.

de Jesús, Melinda L. "Virginia R. Cerenio." In Guiyou Huang, ed., *Asian American Poets: A Bio-Bibliographical Critical Sourcebook* (Westport, CT: Greenwood Press, 2002), 53–57.

Interview. In Organization of Pan Asian American Women, ed., *Asian Pacific American Mothers and Daughters: Visions and Fierce Dreams* (Washington, DC: Organization of Pan Asian American Women, Inc., 1983), 8–17.

Gier, Jean Vengua. "'… To Have Come from Someplace': *October Light*, *America Is in the Heart*, and 'Flip' Writing After the Third World Strikes." *Hitting Critical Mass* 2, no. 2 (Spring 1995): 1–33.

* * *

G. S. Sharat Chandra (1938–2000). A truly international and diasporic poet and short story writer, Chandra was born in Nanjangud, Karnatak, India, and raised in an affluent family with a prominent lawyer father. Chandra received his first two college degrees in India: a bachelor of arts in English in 1953 and a bachelor of law in 1958, both from the University of Mysore. As a law career held less appeal for him than creative writing, in 1962 Chandra left India ostensibly to study English and law in the United States, first earning an M.S. in English at the State University of New York at Oswego in 1964, then an LL.M. from the Osgoode Law School in Toronto in 1966, but he did not obtain the degree he wanted to help him launch his writing career, an M.F.A. in poetry, from the University of Iowa until 1968, the year that he published his first two of nine collections of poems: *Bharata Natyam Dancer and Other Poems* (Calcutta: Writers Workshop, 1968), and *Will This Forest* (Milwaukee: Morgan Press, 1968). Seven other collections were to follow in the next quarter century, with publishers across three continents—Europe, North America, and the Indian Subcontinent: *Reasons for Staying* (Toronto: Coach House Press, 1970), *April in Nanjangud* (London: Alan Ross, 1971), *Once or Twice* (Sutton, England: Hippopotamus Press, 1974), *The Ghost of Meaning* (Lewiston, ID: Confluence Press, 1978), *Heirloom* (London and Delhi: Oxford University Press, 1982), *Family of Mirrors* (Kansas City, MO: BkMk Press, 1993), and *Immigrants of Loss* (Sutton, England: Hippopotamus Press, 1993). Two years before his death from a sudden brain hemorrhage, Chandra published his only short story collection, *Sari of the Gods* (Minneapolis, MN: Coffee House, 1998).

Family of Mirrors was nominated for the Editors' Choice Pushcart Award in 1990 and the Pulitzer Prize in poetry in 1993; *Immigrants of Loss* won the most prestigious awards: the Commonwealth Poetry Prize and the T. S. Eliot Poetry Prize, both in 1993. As this list of nominations and prizes has already implied, of the many volumes of Chandra's poems, *Family of Mirrors* and *Immigrants of Loss* were greeted with the most popular and critical acclaim. While *Bharata Natyam Dancer and Other Poems* was published for an Indian audience, its poems reappeared in *April in Nanjangud*, his longest collection, which deals with memories of India and awareness of loneliness, among other subjects. *Once or Twice*, a very small book, probes the politics of immigration to America. *Heirloom* collects a good number of previously printed poems from *April in Nanjangud* and *Once or Twice*, as well as new pieces on the topic of death. *Family of Mirrors*, Chandra's "most idiosyncratic and most potentially enduring work" (Lawrence 61), is composed of five sections that, to varying degrees, revolve around family matters such as love, childhood, home, and displacement, themes that also dominate his final collection, *Immigrants of Loss*, in which the poet critically examines the consequences of immigration, including displacement and loss, as forecasted in the title of the book. Chandra's only story collection, *Sari of the Gods*, consists of nineteen short stories grouped into three sections. The titles of the sections—"Here," "There," "Neither Here Nor There"—signify not only the physical spaces that the self can occupy but also the dilemma of belonging or not belonging in a racially divided and culturally diverse but not necessarily tolerant society. All together, Chandra's poetry and short fiction represent the Indian American experience and a poet's views of South Asian diasporas.

For more information, see:

Brown, Neil. "Present Absences: G. S. Sharat Chandra's *Family of Mirrors*." *Poet and Critic* 25, no. 1 (Spring 1994): 42–45.

Das, Kamar. "Indian English Poetry by an Expatriate Indian: A Note on G. S. Sharat Chandra's *Heirloom*." *Literary Half-Yearly* 32, no. 1 (January 1991): 34–42.

Lawrence, Keith. "G. S. Sharat Chandra." In Guiyou Huang, ed., *Asian American Poets: A Bio-Bibliographical Critical Sourcebook* (Westport, CT: Greenwood Press, 2002), 59–63.

Miller, Philip. "*Immigrants of Loss*: The Pleasures of Mixed Prosodies." *Literary Review* 40, no. 2 (1999): 336–38.

Sturr, Robert D. "G. S. Sharat Chandra." In Guiyou Huang, ed., *Asian American Short Story Writers: An A-to-Z-Guide* (Westport, CT: Greenwood Press, 2003), 39–44.

Vasudeva, Mary and Deepika Bahri. "'Swallowing for Twenty Years / The American Mind and Body': An Interview with G. S. Sharat Chandra." *Journal of Commonwealth and Postcolonial Studies* 5, no. 1 (Fall 1997): 9–17.

* * *

Diana Chang. See Chang in "Fiction."

* * *

Marilyn Mei Ling Chin (1955–). Born in Hong Kong and raised in Portland, Oregon, the Chinese American poet Chin studied at the University of Massachusetts at Amherst and received a bachelor's degree in Chinese language and literature in 1977, then went on to obtain an M.F.A. in creative writing from the University of Iowa in 1981. Chin also studied Chinese in Taiwan for a year and spent another year at Stanford University as a Stegner Fellow. Her concentrated study of Chinese classics, her translations of Japanese (Gozo Yoshimasu) and Chinese (Ai Qing) poetry, and the years at Iowa prepared Chin for a thriving poetic career. Gozo Yoshimasu's *Devil's Wind: A Thousand Steps and More*, cotranslated with the author, was published in 1980 (Oakland, MI: Oakland University Press); *Selected Poems of Ai Qing*, cotranslated with Peng Wenlan and

Eugene Eoyang, appeared in 1982 (Bloomington: Indiana University Press). Her own first collection of poetry, *Dwarf Bamboo*, was published in 1987 (Greenfield Center, NY: Greenfield Review Press), followed by a second collection in 1994, *The Phoenix Gone, the Terrace Empty* (Minneapolis, MN: Milkweed Editions), and a third, *Rhapsody in Plain Yellow* (New York: Norton), in 2003.

Chin has received a number of awards and prizes: the Bay Area Book Review Award for *Dwarf Bamboo*, the PEN Josephine Miles Award for *The Phoenix Gone, the Terrace Empty*; three Pushcart Prize awards, a Mary Roberts Rinehart Award, the Centrum Fellowship, the MacDowell Colony Fellowship, a Virginia Center for the Creative Arts Fellowship, a Senior Fulbright Fellowship to Taiwan, and two National Endowments for the Arts grants.

The titles of Chin's first two books suggest how deeply she delves into the troves of classical Chinese poetry: *Dwarf Bamboo* references a poem written by a Tang dynasty Chinese poet, Po Chu-yi (Bai Jüyi), who wrote numerous poems about his favorite cold-climate plant, bamboo, and *The Phoenix Gone, the Terrace Empty* alludes to the work of another poet of the Tang dynasty, Li Po (Li Bai). *Dwarf Bamboo* consists of two sections. The first, "Parent Node," covers themes of Chinese history and civilization, and Chinese American issues such as gender identity and cultural heritage. The second, "American Soil," shifts the focus to more American themes, including assimilation, Chinese women's American experience, and the American dream lived by Chinese Americans—their hardships and triumphs. *The Phoenix Gone, the Terrace Empty* has been more favorably reviewed than Chin's first volume. While the title apparently signals a sense of double loss and deprivation suggested by "gone" and "empty," Chin seems to use this evocation of loss and void to inscribe not merely nostalgia but also the effects of assimilation (a.k.a. Americanization), as well as racial and cultural stereotyping. The title poem, "The Phoenix Gone, the Terrace Empty"—one of Chin's longest poems to date—is both a feminist and a woman's poem that narrates the pain of an imperial consort with bound feet; it also describes the lives of the speaker's parents in China and the United States, and the life of their daughter. Chin's third book, *Rhapsody in Plain Yellow*, was greeted warmly as well. This is a collection where the East fuses with the West, and the Chinese ancient past greets the American present. Chin looks into the effects of the fusion of the old and the new world and of the conflicts caused by fear and racial tensions; mother–daughter relations, choices in life, the self and the surrounding world combine to create a resonant chorus of poems.

For more information, see:

Altieri, Charles. "Images of Form vs. Images of Content in Contemporary Asian American Poetry." *Qui Parle* 9, no. 1 (Fall–Winter 1995): 71–91.

Marquart, Lisa. "The Zen of Irony and Wit: Poet Marilyn Chin Strikes a Balance Between East and West." *Daily Aztec* 2 (March 1994): 9.

Moyers, Bill. "Marilyn Chin." In *The Language of Life: A Festival of Poets* (New York: Doubleday, 1995), 67–79.

Tabios, Eileen. "Marilyn Chin's Feminist Muse Addresses Women, 'The Grand Victims of History'." In Tabios, *Black Lightning: Poetry-in-Progress* (New York: Asian American Writers' Workshop, 1998), 280–312.

Uba, George. "Versions of Identity in Post-activist Asian American Poetry." In Shirley Geok-lin Lim and Amy Ling, eds., *Reading the Literatures of Asian America* (Philadelphia: Temple University Press, 1992), 33–48.

Wang, Dorothy Joan. "Necessary Figures: Metaphor, Irony, and Parody in the Poetry of Li-Young Lee, Marilyn Chin, and John Yau." Ph.D. diss., University of California, Berkeley, 1998.

Zhou Xiaojing. "Breaking from Tradition: Experimental Poems by Four Contemporary Asian American Women Poets." *Revista Canaria de Estudios Ingleses* 37 (November 1998): 199–218.

——. "Marilyn Mei Ling Chin." In Guiyou Huang, ed., *Asian American Poets: A Bio-Bibliographical Critical Sourcebook* (Westport, CT: Greenwood Press, 2002), 71–82.

* * *

Eric Edward Chock (1950–). Chinese Hawaiian poet and editor Chock was born in Hawai'i. He received a bachelor's degree in sociology from the University of Pennsylvania in 1971 and completed a master's degree at the University of Hawai'i in 1977. Chock is known for a number of literary projects in which he was centrally involved: he and Stephen Sumida organized the 1978 Talk Story Writers Conference in Hawai'i; Chock conceived and, with Darrell Lum, founded *Bamboo Ridge*, a literary journal that publishes local Hawaiian writers, and Bamboo Ridge Press, which publishes the journal as well as collected works of Hawaiian and Asian American authors. He was also the Poets in the Schools Coordinator/Master for the Hawai'i Department of Education's Artists in the Schools program for many years. Chock's contributions to Hawaiian and Asian American literature have been in both editorial work and creative writing. On his Web site (http://socrates.uhwo.hawaii. edu/Humanities/chock/default.html),

Chock identifies himself as "poet, editor, and literary promoter."

Indeed, his edited works include *Talk Story: An Anthology of Hawaii's Local Writers* (Honolulu: Petronium/Talk Story, 1978), *Ten Thousand Wishes* (Honolulu: Bamboo Ridge Press, 1978), *Small Kid Time Hawaii* (Honolulu: Bamboo Ridge Press, 1981), *The Best of Bamboo Ridge*, edited with Darrell Lum (Honolulu: Bamboo Ridge Press, 1986), *Paké: Writings by Chinese in Hawaii*, edited with Darrell Lum (Honolulu: Bamboo Ridge Press, 1989), *Growing up Local: An Anthology of Prose and Poetry from Hawai'i*, edited with James Harstad, Darrell Lum, and Bill Teter (Honolulu: Bamboo Ridge Press, 1998), and *Best of Honolulu Fiction*, edited with Darrell Lum (Honolulu: Bamboo Ridge Press, 1999). His only published collection of poems to date, *Last Days Here*, came out in 1990 (Honolulu: Bamboo Ridge Press), and he has had scattered poems printed in various anthologies. Chock's literary achievements have been recognized with prestigious awards, including the Cades Award for Literature, the Hawai'i Alliance for Arts Education's Arts Educator of the Year Award, the 1996 Hawai'i Award for Literature, and the Pushcart Prize XVI.

Last Days Here, like some other works by Hawaiian writers associated with Bamboo Ridge (both the journal and the publishing company), such as Lois-Ann Yamanaka, was written in Hawai'i Creole English, or pidgin, which has been employed by some local writers as a way to articulate literary, cultural, and even geographical identities as distinct from the mainland. The thematic concerns of the poems range from the Asian immigrant experience in Hawai'i to observations on Chinese traditions to outdoor activities such as fishing, which occupies a very conspicuous place in the collection, as ten poems were written on "the Meaning of Fishing" alone. Like other Chinese Hawaiian and Asian American writers, Chock also probes into cultural and generational conflicts commonly seen in immigrant families; however, the focus of his poetry stays on the local cultures of Hawai'i.

For more information, see:

Fujikane, Candace. "Between Nationalisms: Hawaii's Local Nation and Its Troubled Racial Paradise." *Hitting Critical Mass: A Journal of Asian American Cultural Criticism* 1, no. 2 (Spring 1994): 1–5.

Yen, Rhoda J. "Eric Chock." In Guiyou Huang, ed., *Asian American Poets: A Bio-Bibliographical Critical Sourcebook* (Westport, CT: Greenwood Press, 2002), 83–87.

* * *

Rienzi Crusz (1925–). Sri Lankan Canadian poet Crusz was born in Galle, Ceylon (present-day Sri Lanka) and received his high school and college education in Colombo. After graduating from the University of Colombo with a degree in history and teaching briefly at a high school, Crusz went to study library science at the University of London. He immigrated to Canada in 1965 and obtained a B.L.S. from the University of Toronto and then an M.A. from the University of Waterloo. Crusz started to publish poems in his forties, shortly after his arrival in Canada. In 1974 his first collection appeared, titled *Flesh and Thorn* (Stratford, ON: Pasdeloup Press), followed by eight other collections in quick succession: *Elephant and Ice* (Erin, ON: Porcupine's Quill, 1980), *Singing Against the Wind* (Erin, ON: Porcupine's Quill, 1985), *A Time for Loving* (Toronto: TSAR Publications, 1986), *Still Close to the Raven* (Toronto: TSAR Publications, 1989), *The Rain Doesn't Know Me Anymore* (Toronto: TSAR Publications, 1992), *Beatitudes of Ice* (Toronto: TSAR Publications, 1995), *Insurgent Rain: Selected Poems, 1974–1996* (Toronto: TSAR Publica-

tions, 1997), and *Lord of the Mountain: The Sardiel Poems* (Toronto: TSAR Publications, 1999). In 1994 Crusz was awarded the Kitchener-Waterloo Prize for his poetic achievements.

The more powerful and emotional poems Crusz has published are found in his first collection, *Flesh and Thorn;* even the title evokes images of pain and suffering. Many pieces are personal or autobiographical, as Crusz uses poetry as an important venue to express the anger and betrayal that he felt after his first wife walked out on him and their children. The subsequent books continue to explore this personal theme, though a good deal of his later poetry turns to cross-cultural issues such as immigration and diaspora, hyphenated identity, notably in *Elephant and Ice* and *Singing Against the Wind.*

All of Crusz's poetry books were published in Canada and not surprisingly, the majority of studies of his work are also Canadian. See:

Blackburn, Di Gan. "Rienzi Crusz." In Guiyou Huang, ed., *Asian American Poets: A Bio-Bibliographical Critical Sourcebook* (Westport, CT: Greenwood Press, 2002), 89–91.

Kanaganayakam, Chelva. *Dark Antonyms and Paradise: The Poetry of Rienzi Crusz.* Toronto: TSAR Publications, 1997.

———. "A Passionate Dance: The Poetry of Rienzi Crusz." In Nurjehan Aziz, ed., *Floating the Borders: New Contexts in Canadian Criticism* (Toronto: TSAR Publications, 1999), 37–50.

Mukherjee, Arun. "Songs of an Immigrant: The Poetry of Rienzi Crusz." *Currents* 4 (1986–87): 19–21.

Parameswaran, Uma. "Rienzi Crusz." In Emmanuel S. Nelson, ed., *Writers of the Indian Diaspora: A Bio-Bibliographical Critical Sourcebook*

(Westport, CT: Greenwood Press, 1993), 59–63.

——. "The Singing Metaphor: The Poetry of Rienzi Crusz." *Canadian Literature* 132 (1992): 146–54.

Sugunasiri, Suwanda H.J. "'Sri Lankan' Canadian Poets: The Bourgeoisie That Fled the Revolution." *Canadian Literature* 132 (1992): 60–79.

Chitra Banerjee Divakaruni. See Divakaruni in "Fiction."

Benny Feria. See Feria in "Autobiographies/ Memoirs."

Jessica Tarahata Hagedorn. See Hagedorn in "Fiction."

* * *

Kimiko Hahn (1955–). Born in New York to a Japanese Hawaiian mother and a Caucasian father, Hahn grew up in the suburbs of New York City. In the 1970s she was engaged in Asian American political activism and developed an interest in Japanese language and literature. She earned a B.A. in English and East Asian Studies from the University of Iowa and an M.A. in Japanese literature from Columbia University. Hahn started to publish poetry and prose works in the late 1980s. She coauthored *We Stand Our Ground: Three Women, Their Vision, Their Poems* with Gale Jackson and Susan Sherman (New York: Ikon, 1988), and in the following decade, published five books of her own poetry: *Air Pocket* (Brooklyn, NY: Hanging Loose Press, 1989), *Earshot* (Brooklyn, NY: Hanging Loose Press, 1992), *The Unbearable Heart* (New York: Kaya Productions, 1995), *Mosquito and Ant* (New York: Norton, 1999), and *Volatile* (Brooklyn, NY: Hanging Loose Press, 1999). *Earshot* won Hahn the Theodore Roethke Memorial Poetry Prize and the Asian American Studies Literature Award. *The Unbearable Heart* garnered her an American Book Award; in addition, she received a Lila Wallace–Reader's Digest Writers' Award as well as fellowships from the National Endowment for the Arts and the New York Foundation for the Arts.

Hahn's poetry reflects her political and ethnic leanings as well as her concerns about women's issues in relation to racial and class structures in the American social landscape. *Air Pocket* deals with subjects that are important to her and to her community, such as love and social justice; she incorporates elements from Japanese literature and history to articulate her perceptions. Hahn's Marxist leanings also find expression in poems that examine the relationship between oppression and domination. The incorporation of Japanese literary texts or allusions to them continues in Hahn's second volume, *Earshot*, though Western literary and cultural traditions are not trundled aside. Themes such as women's desire and relationships with men make up a significant portion of the collection. *The Unbearable Heart* likewise focuses on women's experience, but it is often more personal, for Hahn recounts her own experience of the loss of her mother in an automobile accident and links women's issues to larger frames of reference rooted in both the Eastern and Western social, historical, and cultural traditions. Hahn seems to espouse the belief that poetry can fulfill the social function of representation, in this case, of social justice and women's experience, evident in both *Volatile* and *Mosquito and Ant*. If poetry does not solve social problems—be it the plight of Korean comfort women during World War II or Cambodian women's suffering under dictatorship—it can at least raise them to enhance society's awareness, as in *Volatile*. *Mosquito and Ant* seeks to establish a tradition of women's writing by intertextualizing ancient works like the Chinese *Nüshu*—women's book— and the Japanese *The Pillow Book*, to demonstrate both women's accomplishments and the power of language through poetry writing.

For more information, see:

Brouwer, Joel. Rev. of *Mosquito and Ant. Progressive* 63, no. 12 (December 1999): 43.

Chang, Juliana. Rev. of *Earshot. Amerasia Journal* 21, no. 1–2 (1995): 188–92.

Ethelbert, E. Rev. of *Earshot. American Poetry Review* 21, no. 6 (Nov./Dec. 1992): 33.

Millard, Elizabeth. Rev. of *The Unbearable Heart. Booklist* 92, no. 9–10 (January 1996): 778.

Tabios, Eileen. Interview, "Kimiko Hahn: Expressing Self and Desire, Even If One Must Writhe." In Tabios, *Black Lightning: Poetry-in-Progress* (New York: Asian American Writers' Workshop, 1998), 24–68.

Zhou Xiaojing. "Kimiko Hahn." In Guiyou Huang, ed., *Asian American Poets: A Bio-Bibliographical Critical Sourcebook* (Westport, CT: Greenwood Press, 2002), 113–19.

———. "Breaking from Tradition: Experimental Poems by Four Contemporary Asian American Women Poets."

Revista Canaria de Estudios Ingleses 37 (November 1998): 199–218.

* * *

Yukihide Maeshima Hartman (1939–). Born and raised in Tokyo, Japan, Hartman lost his father in World War II; after his mother remarried an American civilian attached to the occupying U.S. military, he adopted his stepfather's surname and, in 1958, moved with him and his mother to Pearl River, New York. Hartman's education comprised interrupted attendance at Fairleigh Dickinson University, the University of South Carolina, and the New School for Social Research in the early 1960s, with two years of leave when he served in the U.S. Army. At the New School he studied with the Filipino American poet José Garcia Villa. In 1977 Hartman became involved with the St. Mark's Poetry Project, where he studied with other established poets. Along with Michael Slater, he coedited *Fresh Paint: An Anthology of Younger Poets* (New York: Ailanthus Press, 1977). Between 1970 and 1997 Hartman published a total of seven books of poetry: *A One of Me: 27 Poems* (New York: Grasp Press, 1970), *Hot Footsteps* (New York: Telephone Books, 1976), *Red Rice* (Putnam Valley, NY: Swollen Magpie Press, 1980), *Ping* (New York: Kulchur Foundation, 1984), *New Poems* (Montreal: Empyreal, 1991), *A Coloring Book* (Brooklyn, NY: Hanging Loose Press, 1996), and *Triangle* (New York: Situation Press, 1997). In addition, his poems have been anthologized in both mainstream and Asian American poetry anthologies. Hartman was included in *The Pushcart Prize III: Best of the Small Presses, 1978–79*; he was a fellow at the MacDowell Colony three times; and he received the Fund for Poetry Prize in 1991.

Hartman's poetry often looks inward, hovering between the inner world of the poet and the outside world of nature; the interrelationships of the two are explored through descriptions of nature, love, beauty, and so on. These themes are found in collections such as *Ping*. Hartman's poetry is full of positive forces: he seems able to find the positive in the negative and in the end almost always manages to see beauty, peace, and joy in the ordinary, be it food, relationships, or just daily life, as in poems from *Red Rice*. *A Coloring Book* deals with a different set of issues, including occasional pieces on being Japanese American and the bifurcation of the East and the West, and the poet's attempt to find a foothold in between. The yearning for peacefulness and quiet echoes in *A One of Me*, and topics of tensions and conflicts can be found in *Hot Footsteps*, mostly on the psychological level.

Studies of Hartman's poetry are yet to emerge. For more information, see:

Kraus, Joe. "Yukihide Maeshima Hartman." In Guiyou Huang, ed., *Asian American Poets: A Bio-Bibliographical Critical Sourcebook* (Westport, CT: Greenwood Press, 2002), 121–24.

Kushner, Bill. Rev. of *A Coloring Book*. *Poetry Project Newsletter* 162 (Oct–Nov. 1996).

Slater, Michael. "Vision Is Dizziness: The Technology of Yuki Hartman." Rev. of *Hot Footsteps*. *Poetry Project Newsletter* (February 1, 1977): 42.

* * *

Garrett Hongo (1951–). A Japanese American poet and memoirist, Hongo was born in the village of Volcano, Hawai'i, the place that was to give the title to his memoir. At age six Hongo's family moved to Los Angeles, where he experienced urban life that he had not been exposed to in Hawai'i. He attended Pomona College and received a B.A. in English in 1973. He spent the following year in Japan on a Thomas J. Watson Fellowship. His continued interest in Japanese culture took him to the University of Michigan as a graduate student in Japanese language and literature for a year, but he did not stay to complete the program. Hongo lived a couple of years in Seattle, where he met Frank Chin and Lawson Fusao Inada and took part in their efforts to create an Asian American literary movement and found a theater group named the Asian Exclusion Act that staged the productions of his play *Nisei Bar & Grill* (Seattle: Ethnic Cultural Center, June 1976), Frank Chin's *The Year of the Dragon*, and Wakako Yamauchi's *And the Soul Shall Dance*.

Hongo returned to school and obtained an M.F.A. from the University of California at Irvine in 1980. He first developed an interest in writing in high school and started to publish after college: with Alan Chong Lau and Lawson Fusao Inada, Hongo collaborated on a volume of poetry titled *The Buddha Bandits down Highway 99* (Mountain View, CA: Buddhahead Press, 1978). His own single-author collection, *Yellow Light*, came out in 1982 (Middletown, CT: Wesleyan University Press), followed by *The River of Heaven* (New York: Knopf, 1988). Hongo has also edited three anthologies: *The Open Boat: Poems from Asian America* (New York: Anchor/Doubleday, 1993), *Songs My Mother Taught Me: Stories, Plays, and Memoir* by Wakako Yamauchi (New York: Feminist Press, 1994), and *Under Western Eyes: Personal Essays from Asian America* (New York: Anchor, 1995). Most recently, he put out *Volcano: A Memoir of Hawaii* (New York: Knopf, 1995).

Hongo has received numerous awards and fellowships: the Discovery/The Nation Award, the Lamont Poetry Prize, the Oregon Book Award in Non-Fiction, the Hopwood Prize, a Guggenheim Fellowship, a Rockefeller Foundation Residency Fellowship, two National Endowment for the Arts Fellowships; and, in 1989, a nomination for the Pulitzer Prize.

A good amount of Hongo's poetry concerns the history and culture of Asian Americans, especially the silence of Asians in the United States. *Yellow Light* particularizes the Asian American experience through describing his own family history and the Japanese American community. Concern for the welfare of these people leads the poet to critique America's racism. Hongo's second collection, *The River of Heaven*, while continuing themes from his previous book, focuses on the idea of home and homeland, as opposed to the homelessness of diasporan Asian peoples. The two-section volume looks back at the poet's experiences in two different geographical cultures—section one in Hawai'i and section two on the mainland, both places connected to real and imagined characters associated with the two locations, imbued with a heavy sense of nostalgia. Cultural and ethnic heritages, landscapes, summoning the dead—his father and grandfather in particular—and giving them voice, all find articulate expression in Hongo's poems. His memoir, *Volcano*, supplements these thematic concerns by reifying his personal and familial history. As Leilani Nishime writes, "Although only *Volcano* fits easily into the genre of autobiography, almost all of Hongo's work, especially his poetry, is, in some way, autobiographical" (117). As his poetry has demonstrated, Hongo maintains an interest in cultural and ethnic heritage, and thus his quest for an understanding and knowledge of the self is clear throughout his memoir; as his family's history is not separable from its community's, the internment of Japanese Americans (his family excluded, because then they lived in Hawai'i) remains a significant recurring subject in his autobiographical writing.

Hongo is a widely studied poet. Besides a considerable number of reviews of his poetry and memoir, there have appeared many articles and even a slim monograph by Laurie Filipelli, titled *Garrett Hongo* (Boise, ID: Boise State University Press, 1997). See:

Colley, Sharon. "An Interview with Garrett Hongo." *Forkroads: A Journal of Ethnic American Literature* 4 (Summer 1996): 47–63.

Drake, Barbara. "Garrett Kaoru Hongo." In *Dictionary of Literary Biography: American Poets Since World War Two*, vol. 120 (Detroit: Gale, 1992), 133–36.

Evans, Alice. "A Vicious Kind of Tenderness: An Interview with Garrett Hongo." *Poets and Writers Magazine* 20, no. 5 (Sept./Oct. 1992): 36–46.

Jarman, Mark. "The Volcano Inside." *Southern Review* 32, no. 2 (1996): 337–43.

"Hongo, Garrett, Poet." Interview. In Amy Ling, ed., *Yellow Light: The Flowering of Asian American Arts* (Philadelphia: Temple University Press, 1999), 103–10.

Kamada, Roy. "Heterogeneity, Hybridity, and Multiplicity in *Volcano*: Garrett Hongo's Interventionist Poetics and the Intersection of Asian-American Identity." In Somdatta Mandal, ed., *The Diasporic Imagination: Identifying Asian-American Representations in America*, 2 vols. (New Delhi: Prestige Books, 2000), 183–97.

——. "Garrett Hongo." In Guiyou Huang, ed., *Asian American Poets: A Bio-Bibliographical Critical Sourcebook* (Westport, CT: Greenwood Press, 2002), 133–44.

Lee, A. Robert. "Ethnicities: The American Self-Tellings of Leslie Marmon Silko, Richard Rodriguez, Darryl Pickney, and Garrett Hongo." In Hans Bak and Hans Krabbendam, eds., *Writing Lives: American Biography and Autobiography* (Amsterdam,

Netherlands: VU University Press, 1998), 122–35.

Moyers, Bill. "Garrett Kaoru Hongo." In *The Language of Life: A Festival of Poets* (New York: Doubleday, 1995), 201–15.

Nishime, Leilani. "Garrett Hongo." In Guiyou Huang, ed., *Asian American Autobiographers: A Bio-Bibliographical Critical Sourcebook* (Westport, CT: Greenwood Press, 2001), 115–19.

Tabios, Eileen. "Garrett Hongo: Feeling Knowing, Knowing Feeling." *Asian Pacific American Journal* 5, no. 1 (1996): 139–71.

I

Lawson Fusao Inada (1938–). An influential Japanese American poet and editor, Inada is a *sansei* born in Fresno, California four years before his family was evacuated and relocated to three different internment camps— Fresno Assembly Center, California; Jerome, Arkansas; and Amache, Colorado—during World War II. Returning to Fresno after the war, Inada lived there for fifteen years. He graduated from California State University at Fresno in 1959; from 1960 to 1962 he attended the University of Iowa for graduate studies on a scholarship, but he did not complete his graduate education until 1966, when he obtained an M.F.A. from the University of Oregon. Inada published his first poems in 1970 in *3 Northwest Poets*, a collection written with Albert Drake and Douglas Lawder (Madison, WI: Quixote Press), followed by his own collection, *Before the War: Poems as They Happened,* in 1971 (New York: Morrow); *The Buddha Bandits down Highway 99*, written with Garrett Hongo and Alan Chong Lau, came out in 1978 (Moun-

tain View, CA: Buddhahead Press). His two most recent books of poetry appeared in the 1990s: *Legends from Camp* (Minneapolis: Coffee House Press, 1992), and *Drawing the Line* (Minneapolis: Coffee House Press, 1997). In addition, Inada has published dozens of scattered poems in anthologies, magazines, newspapers, and journals. He is also known as one of the four editors of the influential anthology *Aiiieeeee!* (Washington, DC: Howard University Press, 1974) and *The Big Aiiieeeee!* (New York: Meridian Books, 1991). Inada's poetic achievements have been recognized with awards: a 1994 American Book Award for *Legends from Camp* and the Hazel Hill Award for Poetry for *Drawing the Line.*

Even though Inada was a child during World War II and the consequential internment of Japanese Americans on the West Coast, those traumatizing events remain focal targets of examination and interpretation throughout his poetic efforts. The titles of his first two books reflect these thematic interests: *Before the War* and *Legends from Camp.* The connection between Inada's poetry writing and the historical reality of the Japanese American internment is constantly explored and re-explored. In the former collection, many poems depict objects that are related to, and later, reflexive of the concentration camps where internees found ways to pass time and survive the government-imposed exile. Other poems deal with more positive and productive themes, such as love relations and yearning for the birth of a child, which, as a metaphor of generational continuity and survival, appears to be a form of resistance and an outcry against the internment. The latter collection consists of five sections—"Camp," "Fresno," "Jazz," "Oregon," and "Performance"—that delineate ideas of home, art, and jazz, and many pieces seem to be autobiographical of the poet's movement from locale to locale and of the artistic influences under which he has worked. Thus, geography, family history, war politics, and personal life all merge to mount a powerful critique of institutionalized racism and the Japanese American internment. Internment continues to be a central subject in Inada's third volume, *Drawing the Line*, conveniently illustrated with the title poem that is dedicated to Yosh Kuromiya, who provided a drawing of Heart Mountain—a relocation center in Wyoming—for the cover of the book. In Inada's poems, we learn that Yosh was interned there but returned to the camp many years after the war as a way to recuperate from the historical trauma. The poetry of internment therefore turns into a therapeutic, performative art that liberates, heals, and transforms.

Inada as "poet laureate of Asian America" and "Japanese America's poet" (Sato, *Asian American Poets*, 150) has received a good deal of critical attention. See:

Chang, Juliana. "Time, Jazz, and the Racial Subject: Lawson Inada's Jazz Poetics." In Ellen Goldner and Safiya Henderson-Holmes, eds., *Racing and (E)Racing Language: Living with the Colors of Our Words* (Syracuse, NY: Syracuse University Press, 2001), 134–54.

——. "Reading Asian American Poetry." *MELUS* 21, no. 1 (Spring 1996): 81–98.

Endo, Ellen. "Is Anyone Out There Really Listening? An Interview with Lawson Inada, Poet." *Rafu Shimpo Supplement,* December 21, 1974, 16.

"Inada, Lawson Fusao 1938–." In Ann Evory, ed., *Contemporary Authors: A Bio-Bibliographical Guide to Current Authors and Their Works,* vols. 33–36 (Detroit: Gale, 1973), 432–33.

Lim, Shirley Geok-lin. "Reconstructing Asian-American Poetry: A Case for Ethnopoetics." *MELUS* 14, no. 2 (Summer 1987): 51–63.

Lu, James. "Enacting Asian American Transformations: An Inter-Ethnic Perspective." *MELUS* 23, no. 4 (Winter 1998): 85–99.

Mura, David. "The Margins at the Center, the Center at the Margins: Acknowledging the Diversity of Asian American Poetry." In Wendy L. Ng, Soo-Young Chin, James S. Moy, and Gary Y. Okihiro, eds., *Reviewing Asian America: Locating Diversity* (Pullman: Washington State University Press, 1995), 171–83.

Salisbury, Ralph. "Dialogue with Lawson Fusao Inada." *Northwest Review* 20, no. 2–3 (1982): 60–75.

Sato, Gayle K. "Lawson Fusao Inada." In Teruyo Ueki and Gayle K. Sato, eds., *Reading Japanese American Literature: The Legacy of Three Generations* [Nikkei Amerika Bungaku: Sansedai No Kiseki O Yomu] (Osaka, Japan: Sogensha, 1999), 168–75.

——. "Lawson Inada's Poetics of Relocation: Weathering, Nesting, Leaving the Bough." *Amerasia Journal* 26, no. 3 (2000–2001): 139–60.

——. "Lawson Fusao Inada." In Guiyou Huang, ed., *Asian American Poets: A Bio-Bibliographical Critical Sourcebook* (Westport, CT: Greenwood Press, 2002), 145–57.

Uba, George. "The Representation of Asian American Poetry in *The Heath Anthology of American Literature.*" In Wendy L. Ng, Soo-Young Chin, James S. Moy, and Gary Y. Okihiro, eds., *Reviewing Asian America: Locating Diversity* (Pullman: Washington State University Press, 1995), 185–93.

Yogi, Stan. "Yearning for the Past: The Dynamics of Memory in Sansei Internment Poetry." In Amritjit Singh, Joseph T. Skerrett Jr., and Robert E. Hogan, eds., *Memory and Cultural Politics: New Approaches* to American Ethnic Literatures (Boston: Northeastern University Press, 1996), 245–65.

Lonny Kaneko (1939–). *Sansei* Japanese American poet and short story writer Kaneko was born in Seattle, Washington, and after World War II broke out, when he was only three years old, he was relocated, along with his parents, first to Camp Harmony in Puyallup, Washington and then to Minidoka, Idaho. His only chapbook of poetry, *Coming Home from Camp* (Waldron Island, WA: Brooding Heron Press, 1986), though written and published nearly half a century after the internment, is concerned mainly with these traumatic years. Kaneko studied poetry writing with Theodore Roethke and started to write his own poems in 1960; he completed an M.A. in English at the University of Washington in 1963, with a thesis titled "Catchcan of Chicken Feathers in an Old Roost," a collection of poems. However, most of his scattered poems were published in the 1970s and 1980s. In the 1990s he produced a few more poems as well as several short stories, of which "The Shoyu Kid" became well known.

Kaneko won the Coeur d'Alene Festival of Arts poetry contest in 1973 and *Amerasia Journal*'s short story contest in 1975; his coauthored (with Amy Sanbo) play, *Lady Is Dying* (San Francisco: Asian American Theatre Company, October 1977), won the Henry Broderick Playwright Prize at the Pacific Northwest Writers Conference in 1977. He also received a fellowship from the National Endowment for the Arts in 1981.

Coming Home from Camp is a thirteen-poem chapbook, and like many other works by *sansei* poets who have had similar camp experience, this book emphasizes the internment and its aftermath for the internees and their descendants. But the collected poems do not just deal with the years of concentration camp life, they also look at the idea of home after leaving the camps. Home in the sense of an owned house was not available to his family when Kaneko was writing these poems, approximately four decades after the internment had ended. The poems are a commentary on the Kanekos' economic status and call for the renewal of landscapes and communities. Kaneko's "The Shoyu Kid," a haunting story about the internment life of an adolescent, Shoyu, who was a detainee and suffered sexual molestation by a soldier at the relocation center, was anthologized in *The Big Aiiieeeee!*.

Kaneko's poetry is generally discussed in Elaine Kim's *Asian American Literature* (Philadelphia: Temple University Press, 1982), David Palumbo-Liu's *Asian/American* (Stanford, CA: Stanford University Press, 1999), and Sau-ling Cynthia Wong's *Reading Asian American Literature* (Princeton, NJ: Princeton University Press, 1993). Three more specialized articles are:

Amano, Kyoko. "Lonny Kaneko." In Guiyou Huang, ed., *Asian American Short Story Writers: An A-to-Z Guide* (Westport, CT: Greenwood Press, 2003), 115–18.

Eng, David L. "Primal Glances: Race and Psychoanalysis in Lonny Kaneko's 'The Shoyu Kid'." *Hitting Critical Mass: A Journal of Asian American Cultural Criticism* 1, no. 2 (1994): 63–83.

Nimura, Tamiko. "Lonny Kaneko." In Guiyou Huang, ed., *Asian American Poets: A Bio-Bibliographical Critical Sourcebook* (Westport, CT: Greenwood Press, 2002), 159–63.

* * *

Myung Mi Kim (1957–). Born in Seoul, South Korea, Kim moved to the United States with her family when she was nine. She attended Oberlin College in Ohio with double majors in music and chemistry, intending to become a doctor; then she earned an M.A. in creative writing from Johns Hopkins University. Kim also took coursework in clinical social work at New York University, but after she earned an M.F.A. in creative writing from the University of Iowa in 1986, she started to publish seriously as a poet, in anthologies and literary magazines. From 1991 to 2002 she produced five books of poetry: *Under Flag* (Berkeley, CA: Kelsey St. Press, 1991), *The Bounty* (Minneapolis, MN: Chax Press, 1996), *Dura* (Los Angeles: Sun & Moon Press, 1998), *Spelt*, with Susan Gevirtz (San Francisco: A+bend Press, 1999), and most recently, *Commons* (Berkeley and Los Angeles: University of California Press, 2002). The accolades Kim has received include two Fund for Poetry Awards, two Gertrude Stein Awards for Innovative North American Poetry, and a Multicultural Publishers Book Award.

In *Under Flag*, Kim writes about painful subjects such as the eroding effect of war on the wholeness of human existence. She adopts the perspectives of females and the occupied, focusing on the connection between language and power as methods of representation. In *The Bounty* and *Dura* Kim utilizes Hangul (Korean alphabet) and romanized Korean as a means to study the politics of translation and instruction. Throughout *Dura*, Kim portrays Korean immigrant women at the century's end and explores ways to make inclusive her personal relationship to issues of immigration and cultural severing. Poems in *Commons* capture the cultural and linguistic displacement of immigration. Composed of a series of aphoristic phrases or individual words scattered across the page, the three longish poems in the collection explore the relationships between languages, using Korean and English as paradigms and finding a lyric play between the two.

For more information, see:

Knowlton, Edgar C., Jr. Rev. of *Dura*. *World Literature Today* 73, no. 2 (1999): 389.

Lee, James Kyung-Jin. "'What was given, given over?': Competing Subjectivities in Myung Mi Kim's 'Into Such Assembly.'" M.A. thesis, UCLA, 1995.

——. Interview with Myung Mi Kim. In King-Kok Cheung, ed., *Words Matter: Conversations with Asian American Writers* (Honolulu: University of Hawai'i Press, 2000), 92–104.

——. "Myung Mi Kim." In Guiyou Huang, ed., *Asian American Poets: A Bio-Bibliographical Critical Sourcebook* (Westport, CT: Greenwood Press, 2002), 165–71.

Menon, Vikas. Rev. of *Dura*. *Ten Magazine* 5, no. 1 (Spring 1999): 18.

Park, Jane. "Remembering Memory: An Analysis of Myung Mi Kim's *Under Flag*." Ph.D. diss., Brown University, 1995.

* * *

Joy Kogawa. See Kogawa in "Fiction."

* * *

Juliet Sanae Kono (1943–). Born and raised in Hilo, Hawai'i, and of Japanese ancestry, Kono has lived most of her life in Honolulu. She earned a B.A. and M.A. in English from the University of Hawai'i at Manoa; in her college years she was involved with the Bamboo Ridge group and its publishing branch, Bamboo Ridge Press. In 1998 Kono studied in Japan for six months on a fellowship awarded by the Japan–United States Friendship Commission. She published her first volume of poetry, *Hilo Rains* (Honolulu:

Bamboo Ridge Press) in 1988; a second collection, titled *Tsunami Years* (Honolulu: Bamboo Ridge Press), appeared in 1995. In between, she coedited, with another celebrated Hawaiian poet, Cathy Song, a collection called *Sister Stew: Fiction and Poetry by Women* (Honolulu: Bamboo Ridge Press, 1991). Kono's work has been recognized with several awards: the Elliot Cades Award for Literature in 1991, the James Clavell Award in 1991, and the Ka Palapala Po'okela for Excellence in Writing Literature in 1996.

Geography and meteorology provide much of Kono's material: both titles of her books refer to climatic phenomena in the locales she is familiar with in Hawai'i, and her depictions of these natural forces are closely intertwined with her portrayal of characters and events that have affected her personal life: growing up on a sugarcane plantation, memories of her grandparents, hardships for Japanese immigrant workers, natural disasters like tsunamis, and human-caused threats like internment camps all find expression in *Hilo Rains*. *Tsunami Years* is also autobiographical. The dominant voice is that of a woman in her fifties (Kono was in her early fifties when she wrote and published this book) who is a care provider for her ill mother-in-law, has to cope with the death of her son, and contemplates the devastating consequences of tsunamis; thus death, along with its multitude of causes, is the central topic of exploration.

Despite the awards Kono has garnered, her poetry has not received wide notice, certainly not on the mainland, except for some brief mentions in general studies. The few available studies and reviews include:

Huot, Nikolas. "Juliet Sanae Kono." In Guiyou Huang, ed., *Asian American Poets: A Bio-Bibliographical Critical Sourcebook* (Westport, CT: Greenwood Press, 2002), 173–77.

Roddy, Kevin M. Rev. of *Sister Stew*. *Library Journal* 117, no. 12 (July 1992): 85.

Usui, Masami. "A Conflict with Tsunami in Juliet S. Kono's Poetry." *Studies in American Literature* 35 (February 1999): 157–74.

* * *

Alex Kuo. See Kuo in "Short Fiction."

* * *

Lydia Kwa (1959–). Born and raised in Singapore, Kwa arrived in Canada in 1980 to study psychology at the University of Toronto and later completed a doctoral degree at Queen's University. The training she received in creative writing was a result of attending writing workshops while at Queen's. During the same time period, she came out as a lesbian. Kwa started to publish poetry in the late 1980s, in magazines and anthologies, but it was not until 1994 that her first, and so far only, collection of poems, *The Colours of Heroines* (Toronto: Women's Press), was published; a novel titled *This Place Called Absence* followed in 1999 (Winnipeg, Manitoba: Turnstone Press).

At once a poet and a novelist, Kwa cannot be said to be better known as one than as the other, for both her books—the poetry collection and the novel—seem to have garnered similar critical acclaim in terms of the number of reviews of and articles about them. Both books claim Vancouver, where Kwa has lived since 1993, as the setting. Kwa's professional interest in parent-child relationships permeates her prose and poetry. And the factors that affect relationships of all kinds, such as power, constitute the focus of examination in some poems. Kwa also draws comparisons and builds bridges between the new world of Canada and the old world of Singapore, following the traces of Asian, especially Chinese, diaspora in the Western world. Kwa's *This Place Called*

Absence, one of few Asian/lesbian themed novels, narrates the life of Wu Lan, whose emptiness deepens after her father commits suicide. Depressed and despondent, Wu Lan seeks solace in reading the arcane journals of two prostitutes who lived in Singapore around 1900, which chronicle barbaric brothel life and illicit lesbian love.

For more information, see:

Bates, Judy Fong. "*This Place Called Absence*." *Quill & Quire* 66, no. 6 (July 2000): 49–50.

Khoo, Gaik Cheng. "*The Colours of Heroines* by Lydia Kwa." *Calyx* 17, no. 3 (1998): 117–18.

———. "Lydia Kwa." In Guiyou Huang, ed., *Asian American Poets: A Bio-Bibliographical Critical Sourcebook* (Westport, CT: Greenwood Press, 2002), 179–83.

Koh, Karlyn. "Speculations and (Dis)identification: Notes on Asian Canadian Women Writers." *New Scholars–New Visions in Canadian Studies* 1, no. 1 (Summer 1996): 1–30.

Lu, T. "*The Colours of Heroines*." *Fireweed* 48 (Summer 1995): 68–69.

Younka, Reina. "*This Place Called Absence*." *Prairie Fire* 22, no. 2 (2001): 118–19.

Alan Chong Lau (1948–). Born in Oroville, California, the Chinese American poet received a B.A. in art from the University of California at Santa Cruz in 1976. Two years after graduation, he coauthored a series of prose poems with Garrett Hongo and Lawson Fusao Inada, titled *The Buddha Bandits down Highway 99* (Mountain View, CA: Buddhahead Press, 1978), and he published his own poetry collection, *Songs for Jadina*, in 1980 (Greenfield Center, NY: Greenfield Review Press); however, his third book of poetry, *Blues and Greens: A Produce Worker's Journal* (Honolulu: University of Hawai'i Press), did not appear until two decades later, in 2000. Lau has spent many years as a produce worker. He won the 1981 American Book Award for *Songs for Jadina*.

Lau's pieces in *The Buddha Bandits down Highway 99* illustrate small town life for Chinese Americans, as well as his family's experience of running a Chinese restaurant in the California town of Paradise, themes that are tied to his ethnic and cultural heritages. *Songs for Jadina* continues to explore these cultural traditions and the poet's family history. Though this second collection makes the father the central figure that embodies his search for identity, Lau traces his ancestral roots generations back, to the time of Chinese immigration through the infamous Angel Island Immigration Station, used by the government to detain Chinese immigrants in the early decades of the twentieth century. *Blues and Greens*, on the other hand, literally chronicles the poet's experience as a produce worker; the speaker often plays the role of the observer while working in an Asian grocery store, interacting with the customers and proudly selling his vegetables and fruits.

For more information, see:

Dempster, Brian Komei. "Alan Chong Lau." In Guiyou Huang, ed., *Asian American Poets: A Bio-Bibliographical Critical Sourcebook* (Westport, CT: Greenwood Press, 2002), 185–87.

Desoto, Hisaye Yamamoto. Rev. of *Songs for Jadina*. *MELUS* 10, no. 4 (Winter 1983): 78–83.

Hamill, Sam. "Alan Lau and Colleen McElroy: Local Poets Against the

Grain." *Weekly* (October 7, 1981): 32.

Kaneko, Lonny. "A Journey Into Place, Race, and Spirit." *Amerasia Journal* 6, no. 2 (1979): 91–95.

Lim, Genny. Rev. of *Songs for Jadina*. *East/West* 20 (May 1981): 9.

Roche, Judith. Rev. of *Songs for Jadina*. *Seattle Voice* (June 1981): 23.

Wallenstein, Barry. Rev. of *Songs for Jadina*. *American Book Review* 4, no. 6 (Sept./Oct. 1982): 17.

Yee, Cordell. Rev. of *The Buddha Bandits down Highway 99*. *East/West* 22 (August 1979): 11.

* * *

Evelyn Lau (1971–). A Chinese Canadian poet and fiction writer, Lau was born in Vancouver, British Columbia. Parental pressure and other circumstances forced her out of her parents' home and into the street, where she worked as a prostitute to support herself at the age of fourteen. That experience provided the base material for her autobiography *Runaway: Diary of a Street Kid*, published in 1989 (Toronto: Harper-Collins), when she was merely eighteen; a collection of poetry titled *You Are Not Who You Claim* followed the next year (Victoria, BC: Porcépic Books, 1990). Her second collection, *Oedipal Dreams*, came out in 1992 (Victoria, BC: Beach Holme), and a third, *In the House of Slaves*, was published in 1994 (Toronto: Coach House Press). Lau published her first book of short stories, *Fresh Girls and Other Stories*, in 1993 (Toronto: HarperCollins), and a second collection, *Choose Me: A Novella and Stories*, came out in 1999 (Toronto: Doubleday). *Other Women*, a novel, appeared in 1995 (Toronto: Random House). Most recently, she compiled some autobiographical essays in *Inside Out: Reflections on a Life So Far*, published in 2001 (Toronto: Doubleday). Lau was awarded the Air Canada/Canadian Authors Association's Award for the Most Promising Writer Under 30 and the Milton Acorn People's Poetry Award, both for her first poetry collection, *You Are Not Who You Claim*.

Although Lau writes both poetry and prose, her fame as a poet surpasses that as a fiction writer. The three volumes of poems she has published so far all represent an attempt to expose to her readers a world with which she was only too familiar. *You Are Not Who You Claim*, written when she was only nineteen—just a year after she got off the street—includes poems that deal with sexual behaviors and the attendant struggles involving power or lack thereof. In the brutal world of prostitution and drug abuse, violence is never far away. *Oedipal Dreams*, consisting of five sections, does not depart from the major thematic concerns found in her first collection; in fact, Lau continues to probe into the shady world of prostitution, though now she focuses more on the physical and psychological effects of sex-related violence. The speakers in the poems reflect on their life experiences characterized by brutality and lack of stability; they also express a strong desire for security and love. Disillusionment with the harsh realities of their world prompts them to seek the ultimate solution to the never-ending problems: suicide. *In the House of Slaves* starts where *Oedipal Dreams* ended: the topic of sadomasochism and power differentials in sexual relationships. The dominatrix, though called "mistress," does not exactly possess power in such relationships because she follows orders rather than giving them; she is therefore a subservient slave.

Lau's short fiction has also garnered a considerable amount of critical acclaim. Her stories in *Fresh Girls and Other Stories* deal with very much the same themes and are populated with prostitutes and dominatrixes, and the so-called "fresh girls" are really young women who lead the unfulfilling life of prostitutes, for whom love and happiness remain dreams. In a thematic shift from her earlier works, *Choose Me: A Novella and Stories* disengages from sex-related issues and examines the choices her women characters make, as well as the eventual consequences for these women who yearn for sincere and real relationships and attempt to gain independent identities, only to be disappointed or defeated. Finally, brief mention should be made of Lau's autobiography, *Runaway: Diary of a Street Kid*, the work that took her off the street and put her on the Canadian best-seller list for over thirty weeks.

Evelyn Lau's books have reaped a considerable number of reviews in both Canada and the United States. What follows are significant article-length studies of her work:

Condé, Mary. "An Interview with Evelyn Lau." *Études Canadiennes/ Canadian Studies* 21, no. 38 (June 1995): 105–11.

Dean, Misao. "Reading Evelyn Right." *Canadian Forum* 73, no. 837 (1995): 22–26.

Huot, Nikolas. "Evelyn Lau." In Guiyou Huang, ed., *Asian American Poets: A Bio-Bibliographical Critical Sourcebook* (Westport, CT: Greenwood Press, 2002), 195–200.

——. "Evelyn Lau." In Guiyou Huang, ed., *Asian American Short Story Writers: An A-to-Z Guide* (Westport, CT: Greenwood Press, 2003), 141–46.

Wong, Rita. "Market Forces and Powerful Desires: Reading Evelyn Lau's Cultural Labour." *Essays on Canadian Writing* 73 (Spring 2001): 122–40.

* * *

Li-Young Lee (1957–). Indonesian-Chinese American poet Lee represents the most typical Asian diasporic experience in a global sense. He was born in Jakarta, Indonesia, to Chinese parents who had left the mainland to escape communism. The overwhelmingly dominant figure in Lee's life was his father, who served as private physician to two very powerful political figures in the Asian/Pacific region of the twentieth century—Chairman Mao Zedong of China and President Sukarno of Indonesia—though in the latter country he was imprisoned for allegedly conspiring with the CIA. After a few years living in Indonesia, Lee's father took the family on travels throughout Indonesia, Southeast Asia, Hong Kong, Macau, and Japan to avoid race-based persecution. In 1964 they finally arrived and settled in Pennsylvania, the United States, where Lee's father became a Presbyterian minister. His profound love of philosophy and literature, especially classical Chinese poetry, produced a lasting impact on the young boy. Lee's life took an upward turn when he attended the University of Pittsburgh, where he met Gerald Stern and read his *Lucky Life*, a collection of poems that inspired Lee to write his own. Between 1979 and 1981 he studied creative writing at the University of Arizona and the State University of New York at Brockport. Lee has also taught at various universities, including Northwestern University and the University of Iowa.

Lee's major works to date consist of a memoir, *The Winged Seed* (New York: Simon & Schuster, 1995), and two books of poetry, *Rose* (Rochester, NY: BOA Editions, 1986) and *The City in Which I Love You* (Rochester, NY: BOA Editions, 1990). He has won notable literary awards, in addition to several grants from prestigious organizations. *Rose* won New York University's Delmore Schwartz Memorial Poetry Award, and *The City in Which I Love You* was the 1990 Lamont Poetry Selection of the Academy of American Poets. Lee's memoir, *The Winged Seed*, received the American Book Award from the Before Columbus Foundation in 1995. In 2003 he was awarded the 69th Academy of American Poets Fellowship.

Lee is one of only two Asian American poets included in the fifth edition of *The Norton Anthology of American Literature*, the other being the Korean/Chinese American poet Cathy Song. Lee's collection *Rose*, consisting of twenty poems, largely deals with personal issues such as family, loss, and the past, all of which are represented by the departed father figure. "The Gift," "The Weight of Sweetness," "Eating Alone," "Eating Together," "Mnemonic," and "Visions and Interpretations," all are about his father; other poems, such as "Dreaming of Hair," "Early in the Morning," "Irises," "Braiding," and "My Sleeping Loved Ones," portray the characteristics of human hair and its connective function that binds the family together. Memory and mortality, the past and the present, the individual and the family all find sensitive expression. *The City in Which I Love You* continues to focus on the poet's father's memory, though Lee also considers political issues such as citizenship ("For a New Citizen of These United States") and racism ("The Cleaving"). *The Winged Seed* deserves mention because this memoir delineates Lee's growth as a poet and person, and provides material useful for understanding his work as well as his career.

Many reviews of Lee's works are available. Gerald Stern's foreword to *Rose* (8–10) is a must read. See also:

Engles, Tim. "Lee's *Persimmons*." *Explicator* 54, no. 3 (Spring 1996): 191–92.

Hawley, John. "Gus Lee, Chang-Rae Lee, and Li-Young Lee: The Search for the Father in Asian American Literature." In Geoffrey Kaim, ed., *Ideas of Home: Literature of Asian Migration* (East Lansing: Michigan State University Press, 1997), 183–94.

Hesford, Walter. "*The City in Which I Love You*: Li-Young Lee's Excellent Song." *Christianity and Literature* 46, no. 1 (Autumn 1996): 37–60.

Huang, Yibing. "*The Winged Seed*." *Amerasia Journal* 24, no. 2 (Summer 1998): 189–91.

Kitchen, Judith. "*The City in Which I Love You*." *Georgia Review* 45, no. 1 (Spring 1991): 160–63.

——. "*Rose*." *Georgia Review* 42, no. 2 (Summer 1988): 419–22.

Lee, James. "Li-Young Lee." *Bomb* 51 (Spring 1995): 10–13.

Marshall, Tod. "To Witness the Invisible: A Talk with Li-Young Lee." *Kenyon Review* 22, no. 1 (Winter 2000): 129–47.

McGovern, Martin. "*Rose*." *Kenyon Review* 9, no. 4 (1987): 134–35.

Mitchell, Roger. "*Rose*." *Prairie Schooner* 63 (Fall 1989): 129–39.

Moyers, Bill. "Li-Young Lee." In *The Language of Life: A Festival of Poets* (New York: Doubleday, 1995), 257–69.

Nelson, Marilyn. "*The City in Which I Love You*." *Kenyon Review* 13 (Fall 1991): 214–26.

Nobles, Edward. "*Rose*." *Southern Humanities Review* 22 (Spring 1988): 200–201.

Pinsker, Sanford. "*Rose*." *Literary Review* 32 (Winter 1989): 256–62.

Rector, Liam. "*Rose*." *Hudson Review* 41 (Summer 1988): 399–400.

Shefler, Laura. "Strength of the Spirit." *Pitt Magazine* 13, no. 5 (December 1998): 30–35.

Xu, Wenying. "Li-Young Lee." In Guiyou Huang, ed., *Asian American Poets: A Bio-Bibliographical Critical Sourcebook* (Westport, CT: Greenwood Press, 2002), 205–11.

Zhou Xiaojing. "Inheritance and Invention in Li-Young Lee's Poetry." *MELUS* 21, no. 1 (Spring 1996): 113–32.

———. "Li-Young Lee." In Guiyou Huang, ed., *Asian American Autobiographers: A Bio-Bibliographical Critical Sourcebook* (Westport, CT: Greenwood Press, 2001), 193–98.

* * *

Shirley Geok-lin Lim (1944–). Born in Malacca, Malaysia, to parents of Chinese heritage, Lim grew up under British colonial rule and endured starvation, desperation, and abandonment by her mother. In her early teens she decided to be a poet; indeed, she became a poet, short story writer, novelist, memoirist, critic, editor, and academic. Lim excelled in her education at the University of Malaya, winning the great accolade of "First Class Honors" from the British; she also won scholarships to study in the United States, where she obtained an M.A. in 1971 and a Ph.D. in 1973, both from Brandeis University. She started to publish poetry: *Crossing the Peninsula and Other Poems* (Kuala Lumpur: Heinemann Writing in Asian Series, 1980), *No Man's Grove and Other Poems* (Singapore: National University of Singapore English Department Press, 1985), *Modern Secrets: New and Selected Poems* (Sydney: Dangaroo Press, 1989), *Monsoon History: Selected Poems* (London: Skoob Pacifica, 1994), and *What the Fortune Teller Didn't Say* (Albuquerque, NM: West End Press, 1998). One of the most prolific and versatile Asian American writers, Lim has also published three collections of short stories: *Another Country and Other Stories* (Singapore: Times Books International, 1982), *Life's Mysteries: The Best of Shirley Lim* (Singapore: Times Books International, 1995), and *Two Dreams* (New York: Feminist Press, 1997). Her memoir, published in the United States as *Among the White Moon Faces: An Asian-American Memoir of Homelands* (New York: Feminist Press, 1996), was released in Singapore as *Among the White Moon Faces: Memoirs of a Nonya Feminist* (Singapore: Times Books International, 1996). Most recently, Lim published a novel, *Joss and Gold* (New York: Feminist Press, 2001).

Lim's scholarly work also makes up a long list of monographs and essays, including *Nationalism and Literature: English-Language Writing from the Philippines and Singapore* (Quezon City: New Day Publishers, 1993), *Writing the Southeast/Asia in English: Against the Grain* (London: Skoob Pacifica, 1994), *Transnational Asia Pacific: Gender, Culture, and the Public Sphere* (Urbana-Champaign: University of Illinois Press, 1999), and *Power, Race, and Gender in Academe: Strangers in the Tower?*, coedited with María Herrera-Sobek (New York: MLA, 2000). Lim's edited works are numerous as well: *The Forbidden Stitch: An Asian American Women's Anthology* (Corvallis, OR: Calyx Books, 1989), *Approaches to Teaching Kingston's* The Woman Warrior (New York: MLA, 1991), *Reading the Literatures of Asian America*, coedited with Amy Ling (Philadelphia: Temple University Press, 1992), *One World of Literature: An Anthology of Contemporary Global Literature* (Boston: Houghton Mifflin, 1992), *Asian-American Literature: An Anthology* (Lincolnwood, IL: NTC/Contemporary Press, 1999), and *Tilting the Continent: An Anthology of Southeast Asian American Writing*, coedited with Cheng Lok Chua (St. Paul, MN: New Rivers Press, 2000).

The awards and prizes that Lim has won include the Commonwealth Poetry Prize in 1980, the American Book Award/Before Columbus Award in 1990, the American Book Award in 1997, two National Endowment for the Humanities fellowships, and two Mellon fellowships, among others.

Lim is difficult to categorize—she seems to have achieved equally in poetry and fiction, and her accomplishments in autobiography and editorial work are just as impressive. However, Lim has a solid claim as a poet. As a postcolonial, feminist, immigrant, Southeast Asian American writer, Lim has created work that demonstrates rich complexities. As Nina Morgan puts it, "Lim's is a poetry of precision. Tight lines, concrete yet lyrical images, and raw emotion characterize Lim's confrontations with the past and the places she has occupied in relation to her parents, her Asian heritage, and her Western world. With a hard-won feminist perspective, Lim's poetry indicts political and cultural forms of oppression while simultaneously maintaining a personal voice that nevertheless effects a transnational, transcultural perspective" (*Asian American Poets* 215). The collection that typifies these poetic characteristics is *What the Fortune Teller Didn't Say*. Descriptions of postcolonial Malaysian and Southeast Asian diasporan experiences can be found in *Monsoon History*. Exile, gender, and identity are common themes in her other poetry collections, as well as in her short stories. *Two Dreams*, Lim's better-known collection of short fiction, examines these and other issues— including class, sexuality, immigration, and ethnicity—by focusing on the life experiences of a young woman. Lim's memoir, *Among the White Moon Faces*, while dealing with political and social issues in Malaysian life, traces the author's childhood in her family's Westernized house under British colonial rule. Lim's only novel to date, *Joss and Gold*, tells the haunting story of an unlikely family—a fiercely independent mother, an estranged father, and their daughter—attempting to bridge Malaysia and America and come to terms with their past.

Studies of Lim's work are truly international, just like her publications. In addition to many reviews and interviews available in numerous venues, these critical sources are useful:

Eng, Ooi Boo. "Singapore/Malaysian Poetry: At Least Something and Less and More." *Southeast Asian Review of English* 2 (August 1981): 44–62.

Means, Laurel. "The 'Orient-ation' of Eden: Christian/Buddhist Dialogues in the Poetry of Shirley Geok-lin Lim." *Christianity and Literature* 43, no. 2 (Winter 1994): 189–203.

Morgan, Nina. "Locating Shirley Geok-lin Lim, an Interview." In Somdatta Mandal, ed., *The Diasporic Imagination: Asian American Writing* (New Delhi: Prestige Press, 2000), 99–110.

———. "Shirley Geok-lin Lim." In Guiyou Huang, ed., *Asian American Autobiographers: A Bio-Bibliographical Critical Sourcebook* (Westport, CT: Greenwood Press, 2001), 215–20.

———. "Shirley Geok-lin Lim." In Guiyou Huang, ed., *Asian American Poets: A Bio-Bibliographical Critical Sourcebook* (Westport, CT: Greenwood Press, 2002), 213–18.

Park, John H. "Shirley Geok-lin Lim." In Guiyou Huang, ed., *Asian American Short Story Writers: An A-to-Z Guide* (Westport, CT: Greenwood Press, 2003): 166–72.

Singh, Kirpal. "An Interview with Shirley Geok-lin Lim." *ARIEL: A Review of International English Literature* 30, no. 4 (October 1999): 135–41.

Wang, Jennie. "Interview with Shirley Geok-lin Lim." In Farhat Iftekharuddin and Mary Rohrberger, eds., *Speaking of the Short Story: Interviews with Contemporary Writers* (Jackson: University Press of Mississippi, 1997), 153–65.

Yu, Larry. "New and Selected Stories, by Shirley Geok-lin Lim." *MELUS* 24, no. 4 (Winter 1999): 173–76.

Pat Matsueda (1952–). Daughter of a Japanese American father and a Japanese mother, Matsueda was born in Fukuoka, Japan, and at seven, after her parents' divorce, she immigrated to Honolulu, Hawai'i with her mother and sister. At the University of Hawai'i she majored first in environmental studies, then switched to English literature with a concentration in visual arts. While starting to write poems, Matsueda was involved in editorial work, first as editor of the *Hawaii Literary Arts Council Newsletter*, then as founding editor of a literary periodical called *The Paper*, and finally as managing editor of *Mānoa: A Pacific Journal for International Writing*, a position she has held since 1992. Between these jobs she published poems in anthologies and magazines, producing her first collection, *X*, in 1983 (Honolulu: Communica Press), followed by *The Fish Catcher* in 1985 (Honolulu: Petronium). In 1988 Matsueda won Hawaii's Elliot Cades Award.

Matsueda's poetry illustrates "the spiritual journey of the exile who is no longer sure where home is. Borders preoccupy Matsueda's work: between innocence and knowledge, dream and reality, illness and wellness, Japan and America" (Leong 230). The distinctions of these dichotomies, however, are not always clear-cut, but they are presented from an existential perspective: life brings challenges and opportunities, and balance has to be kept in order to survive. Matsueda's interest in art is also evident in her poems: the process of artistic creation and the relationship between art and artist are important topics.

Matsueda's autobiographical article, "Old Neighborhoods," in *Hawaii Herald* (January 2, 1981):6, is a useful source for understanding her work. See also:

Carter, Jared. "Poetry Chapbooks: Back to the Basics." *Georgia Review* 40, no. 2 (Summer 1986): 532–47.

Leong, Lavonne. "Pat Matsueda." In Guiyou Huang, ed., *Asian American Poets: A Bio-Bibliographical Critical Sourcebook* (Westport, CT: Greenwood Press, 2002), 229–32.

* * *

Janice Mirikitani (1941–). *Sansei* poet and activist Mirikitani was born in Stockton, California and was soon incarcerated, along with her family, in the concentration camp in Rohwer, Arkansas, in 1942. The internment and her sexual molestation by family relatives were two big traumas that would haunt her poetry. In the early 1960s Mirikitani received a B.A. from UCLA and in 1963, teaching credentials from the University of California at Berkeley. Later she pursued graduate studies in creative writing at San Francisco State University, where she was involved in the Asian American Political Alliance that became part of the Third World liberation movement. She helped create a collective called Third World Communications and became editor of the first Asian American literary magazine, *Aion*.

Mirikitani started to write and edit in 1972, publishing an edited collection called *Third World Women* (San Francisco: Third World Communications). Her first book of poetry, *Awake in the River*, came out in 1978 (San Francisco: Isthmus Press); a second collection, *Shedding Silence: Poetry and Prose*, in 1987 (Berkeley, CA: Celestial Arts); and a third volume, *We, the Dangerous: New and Selected Poems*, in 1995 (London: Virago). The anthologies that she has edited or coedited are also noteworthy: *Time to Greez! Incantations from the Third World* (San Francisco: Glide Publications/Third World Communications, 1975), *Ayumi: A Japanese American Anthology* (San Francisco: Japanese American Anthology Committee,

1980), *I Have Something to Say About This Big Trouble: Children of the Tenderloin Speak Out* (San Francisco: Glide Word Press, 1989), and *Watch Out! We're Talking* (San Francisco: Glide Word Press, 1993).

Mirikitani has received awards for both her poetry and her activism, from such organizations as the California State Assembly and San Francisco State University; in 2000 San Francisco named her the second poet laureate of the city.

The recurring themes throughout Mirikitani's work are the Japanese American internment, *nisei* silence about this historical trauma, her sexual abuse by relatives and friends, protest against racial inequality, and women of color—subjects that fit well in the political activism of the 1960s and 1970s, of which she was a major literary voice. The *nisei* parents' reluctance to speak about or confront their wartime incarceration only hardens the *sansei* child/poet's determination to break that silence, as is evident in many poems in *Awake in the River*. The power of the word is used to help awaken ethnic and political consciousness. *Shedding Silence* continues this vital theme of breaking silence about the government's mistreatment of Japanese Americans during World War II as well as the dismantling of stereotypes of Asian American women. The strength and skills needed to shake free of demeaning stereotypes are key to survival in a racially divided society. Mirikitani's political activism is manifest in *We, the Dangerous*, where the poet's concerns about women's issues, sex-related violence, and devastating effects of wars—from World War II to the Vietnam War to the Gulf War in the early 1990s—all find unambiguous expression.

An article useful for understanding Mirikitani's life and work is "Rebirth: Janice's Story," in a book by her husband, Cecil Williams (with Rebecca Laird), *No Hiding Place: Empowerment and Recovery for Our Troubled Communities* (San Francisco: HarperSanFrancisco, 1992), 64–76. See also:

Crawford, John. "Notes Toward a New Multicultural Criticism: Three Works by Women of Color." In Marie Harris and Kathleen Aguero, eds., *A Gift of Tongues: Critical Challenges in Contemporary American Poetry* (Athens: University of Georgia Press, 1987), 155–95.

Interview with Grace Kyungwon Hong. In King-Kok Cheung, ed., *Words Matter: Conversations with Asian American Writers* (Honolulu: University of Hawai'i Press, 2000), 123–39.

Lashgari, Deirdre. "Disrupting the Deadly Stillness: Janice Mirikitani's Poetics of Violence." In Lashgari, ed., *Violence, Silence, and Anger: Women's Writing as Transgression* (Charlottesville: University Press of Virginia, 1995), 291–304.

Nimura, Tamiko. "Janice Mirikitani." In Guiyou Huang, ed., *Asian American Poets: A Bio-Bibliographical Critical Sourcebook* (Westport, CT: Greenwood Press, 2002), 233–42.

Salvina, Christina Kim. "Exploring Asian American Literary Style: Janice Mirikitani and Ronyoung Kim." M.A. thesis, San Jose State University, 1994.

Usui, Masami. "'No Hiding Place, New Speaking Space': Janice Mirikitani's Poetry of Incest and Abuse." *South Asian Literature* 32 (1996): 56–65.

Yamamoto, Traise. "Embodied Language: The Poetics of Mitsuye Yamada, Janice Mirikitani, and Kimiko Hahn." In Yamamoto, *Masking Selves, Making Subjects: Japanese American Women, Identity, and the Body* (Berkeley: University of California Press, 1999), 198–261.

Yogi, Stan. "Yearning for the Past: The Dynamics of Memory in Sansei Internment Poetry." In Amritjit Singh, Joseph T. Skerrett Jr., and Robert E. Hogan, eds., *Memory and Cultural Politics: New Approaches to American Ethnic Literatures* (Boston: Northeastern University Press, 1996), 245–65.

* * *

David Alan Mura (1952–). *Sansei* Japanese American poet and memoirist Mura was born David Alan Uyemura at Great Lakes, Illinois; his father changed the family name to Mura when David was seven. In 1970 Mura went to Grinnell College, Iowa, where he majored in political science and English; he graduated in 1974 with a B.A. He started graduate studies in English at the University of Minnesota but did not stay to finish. In 1984 he spent a year in Japan on a U.S./Japan Creative Artist Fellowship. He finally received an M.F.A. from Vermont College in 1991. Mura started his prolific writing and artistic career in the mid-1980s, publishing his first book of prose, *A Male Grief: Notes on Pornography and Addiction* in 1987 (Minneapolis, MN: Milkweed Editions), followed by a poetry collection, *After We Lost Our Way* (New York: Dutton, 1989), and his first memoir, *Turning Japanese: Memoirs of a Sansei* (Boston: Atlantic Monthly Press, 1991). His second volume of poetry, titled *The Colors of Desire,* came out in 1995 (New York: Anchor/Doubleday), followed by a second memoir, *Where the Body Meets Memory: An Odyssey of Race, Sexuality, and Identity,* in 1996 (New York: Anchor/Doubleday). Most recently, he published *Song for Uncle Tom, Tonto, and Mr. Moto: Poetry and Identity,* a volume in the Poets on Poetry series (Ann Arbor: University of Michigan Press, 2002). Mura has also engaged in other forms of art, including performance, theater, and films; in addition, he has authored a great number of articles and essays.

Mura's list of awards and prizes includes the 1987 Milkweed Prize for Creative Nonfiction, a 1987 Discovery/The Nation Award, the 1989 National Poetry Series Contest, a 1990 Pushcart Prize, the 1991 Josephine Miles Book Award, the 1995 Carl Sandburg Literary Award, and a 1995 Lila Wallace–Reader's Digest Writers' Award, as well as numerous fellowships from prestigious foundations.

After We Lost Our Way is concerned with the poet's family history, the history of the Japanese American community, and the identity of the individual. The connections of individuals and their identities in Mura's poems are always linked to the larger historical context of the era, for example, the repercussions of the Japanese American incarceration in World War II on individual victims and their descendants. Poems in *The Colors of Desire,* while continuing with themes set forth in the previous volume, look more closely at life before World War II, with a focus on Mura's own self as the inheritor of legacies such as racism, consequences of the internment, and implications for personal identity. Mura's prose memoirs do not depart greatly from his poetry in terms of themes; again, those important on a personal level—history, racial issues, sex and pornography, and the general silence about the Japanese American internment—are just as significant on the political level. *Turning Japanese* is based on Mura's yearlong stay in Japan and consists of essays and stories—personal and otherwise—that deal with the issue of ethnic identity from multiple perspectives: the author's own, other Japanese and Japanese Americans', and Euro-Americans'. In *Where the Body Meets Memory,* Mura traces the history of his family by making connections between his *nisei* parents who were interned and his grandparents, and between them and the larger history of Japanese Americans, linking the past and the present; he also draws clear connections between sexual desire and consciousness of the racialized body, indicting internalized racism as the cause of the consciousness of racial inferiority.

For more information, see:

Nishime, Leilani Linda. "David Mura." In Guiyou Huang, ed., *Asian American Poets: A Bio-Bibliographical Critical Sourcebook* (Westport, CT: Greenwood Press, 2002), 243–54.

Tabios, Eileen. "How History Stains the Colors of Desire." In Tabios, *Black Lightning: Poetry-in-Progress* (New York: Asian American Writers' Workshop, 1998), 333–78.

Taylor, Gordon O. "'The Country I Had Thought Was My Home': David Mura's *Turning Japanese* and Japanese-American Narrative Since World War II." *Connotations: A Journal for Critical Debate* 6, no. 3 (1996): 283–309.

Yogi, Stan. "Yearning for the Past: The Dynamics of Memory in Sansei Internment Poetry." In Amritjit Singh, Joseph T. Skerrett Jr., and Robert E. Hogan, eds., *Memory and Cultural Politics: New Approaches to American Ethnic Literatures* (Boston: Northeastern University Press, 1996), 245–65.

Zhou Xiaojing. "A Poetics of Identity: David Mura's Poetry." *MELUS* 23, no. 3 (Fall 1998): 145–66.

——. "Race, Sexuality, and Representation in David Mura's *The Colors of Desire.*" *JAAS: Journal of the Association of Asian American Studies* 1, no. 3 (October 1998): 245–67.

——. "David Mura." In Guiyou Huang, ed., *Asian American Autobiographers: A Bio-Bibliographical Critical Sourcebook* (Westport, CT: Greenwood Press, 2001), 273–80.

N

Tran Thi Nga (1927–). The Chinese-born Vietnamese American poet is truly diasporic: while she calls Vietnam home, she has lived in Burma, China, and Wales. She studied at Swansea University, Wales, and in 1975 she immigrated from Saigon to the United States, along with the other staff who were working for *Time* magazine. In the United States she reencountered her former boss's wife, Wendy Larsen from Saigon, with whom she collaborated on a collection of poems titled *Shallow Graves: Two Women and Vietnam* (New York: Random House, 1986).

The title of Larsen and Nga's book refers to the belief that the souls of those buried in shallow graves are doomed to wander. Larsen portrays her experience as an American poet and teacher based in Saigon; for example, her apprehensive first walk to work in the war-torn city and a discussion in a Vietnamese classroom. Nga recounts her life as a Vietnamese social worker and mother of four. The one-page prose poems depict major events and emotions, the cruelty of families separated and a country divided. Nga's poems provide personal details about the horror of famine during the Japanese occupation of Vietnam; other issues that she examines concern gender roles as defined by Confucianism, Vietnam War traumas, and the effects of imperialism and assimilation that she personally experienced in the West, especially the United States.

For more information, see:

Des Pres, Terrence. "Sisters to Antigone." *Parnassus* 14, no. 1 (1987): 187–200.

Gotera, Vince. "Reconciliation and Women's Poetry." In Robert M. Slabey, ed., *The United States and Vietnam from War to Peace* (Jefferson, NC: McFarland, 1996), 150–60.

Janette, Michele. "Tran Thi Nga." In Guiyou Huang, ed., *Asian American Poets: A Bio-Bibliographical Critical Sourcebook* (Westport, CT: Greenwood Press, 2002), 255–57.

Uba, George. "Friend and Foe: De-collaborating Wendy Larsen and Tran Thi Nga's *Shallow Graves*." *Journal of American Culture* 16, no. 3 (Fall 1993): 63–70.

Michael Ondaatje. See Ondaatje in "Fiction."

Uma Parameswaran (1938–). Indian Canadian poet, playwright, short fiction writer, and critic Parameswaran was born in Madras and raised in Jabalpur, India. She received a B.A. from Jabalpur University and an M.A. in English from Nagpur University. A Fulbright Fellowship enabled her to pursue an M.A. in creative writing at Indiana University before she earned a Ph.D. in English from Michigan State University in 1972. She has taught and resided in Canada since 1966, where she was centrally involved in founding PALI (performing arts and literatures of India) and, perhaps more visibly, in developing what she termed SACLIT (South Asian Canadian literature). Parameswaran published her first collection of poetry, *Trishanku*, in 1988 (Toronto: TSAR); a second collection, *The Door I*

Shut Behind Me (New Delhi: Affiliated East West Press, 1990), consists of selected fiction, poetry, and drama; a third is called *Trishanku and Other Writings* (New Delhi: Prestige Press, 1998); and a recent collection of poems, *Sisters at the Well*, came out in 2002 (New Delhi: Indialog Publications). All her dramatic works—*Rootless but Green Are the Boulevard Trees; Dear Deedi; My Sister; Meera: A Dance Drama; Sita's Promise;* and *Sons Must Die*—are collected in *Sons Must Die and Other Plays* (New Delhi: Prestige Books, 1998). *What Was Always Hers* (Fredericton, New Brunswick: Broken Jaw Press, 1999) is a collection of short stories.

Parameswaran's multigenre works often share themes and even characters, but she is primarily recognized as a poet and a critic. Like many other immigrant writers, she shows a strong thematic interest in the experience of immigrants, particularly South Asians in Canada, with an emphasis on issues of assimilation and racial politics. The title *Trishanku* refers to a mythic king in Hindu literature. This collection is generally considered her major poetic achievement. Written in different voices, it is a long narrative poem about the life of an Indian Canadian family in Winnipeg, Manitoba. *Sisters at the Well*, her recent collection, starts with two poems on the Air India crash of 1985, but it also includes a number of earlier pieces. Her plays take up themes of cultural and intergenerational conflicts, most notably in *Rootless but Green Are the Boulevard Trees*, Parameswaran's best-known drama. Set in Winnipeg, Canada, the play dramatizes the clashes of cultures, generations, and values within an Indian immigrant family living in Canada, symbolized by the boulevard trees that are themselves transplanted.

For more information, see:

Blackburn, Di Gan. "Uma Parameswaran." In Guiyou Huang, ed., *Asian American Poets: A Bio-*

Bibliographical Critical Sourcebook (Westport, CT: Greenwood Press, 2002), 267–70.

James, Jancy. "Remythologizing as Expatriate Vision and Art: An Intertextual Reading of Uma Parameswaran's *Sita's Promise* and *Meera*." In Jasbir Jain, ed., *Writers of the Indian Diaspora: Theory and Practice* (Jaipur, India: Rawat, 1998), 199–208.

McGifford, Diane. "Uma Parameswaran." In Emmanuel S. Nelson, ed., *Writers of the Indian Diaspora* (Westport, CT: Greenwood Press, 1993): 305–9.

Mittal, Bina. "Exploring the Immigrant Experience Through Theatre: Uma Parameswaran's *Rootless but Green Are the Boulevard Trees*." *Canadian Theatre Review* 94 (1998): 32–35.

Pandey, M. S. "The Trishanku Motif in the Poetry of Sujata Bhatt and Uma Parameswaran." In A. L. McLeod, ed., *The Literature of the Indian Diaspora: Essays in Criticism* (New Delhi: Sterling Publishers, 2000), 225–38.

Perry, John Oliver. Rev. of *Trishanku*. *World Literature Today* 63, no. 3 (1989): 536–37.

Rao, Susheela N. Rev. of *Sons Must Die and Other Plays*. *World Literature Today* 73, no. 2 (1999): 344.

Singh, Rashna B. "Uma Parameswaran." In Miles Xian Liu, ed., *Asian American Playwrights: A Bio-Bibliographical Critical Sourcebook* (Westport, CT: Greenwood Press, 2002), 278–82.

S

Albert Saijo (1926–). Born in Los Angeles, Japanese American poet Saijo was a young man of sixteen when he was interned with his family at the Heart Mountain Relocation Center in Wyoming. After high school he served three years in the U.S. Army. In the late 1940s Saijo earned a B.A. in international politics, with a minor in Chinese, from the University of Southern California. He started work on a master's degree, only to abandon it soon after. In 1972, he published *The Backpacker* (San Francisco: 101 Productions), a primer on backpacking based on his years of experience in the High Sierra. Saijo's life in the San Francisco Bay area afforded him an opportunity not only to meet Jack Kerouac and other Beat poets but also to drive through the country with Kerouac and Lew Welch, with both of whom he coauthored *Trip Trap: Haiku Along the Road from San Francisco to New York* (Bolinas, CA: Grey Fox Press, 1973). At seventy-one, Saijo published a collection of his own poems titled *Outspeaks: A Rhapsody* (Honolulu: Bamboo Ridge Press, 1997). For his poetry he won a Pushcart Prize and the 1998 Small Press Book Award.

Written in capital letters, the poems in *Outspeaks* cover a wide range of subjects, including religion, war, and the environment. While original methods—use of capitals and syntactical unconventionalities—shine throughout the poems, Saijo hearkens back to mainstream literary, especially poetic sources including Emerson, Whitman, and Blake; his use of dashes is even reminiscent of Emily Dickson's style of structuring her poems. As an ethnic poet, Saijo also explores issues pertinent to racial and cultural heritages, such as identity and colonialism.

For more information, see:

Adams, Wanda. "An Outspoken Way with Words and Ideas." Rev. of *Outspeaks: A Rhapsody. Honolulu Advertiser*, September 28, 1997, F5+.

Kam, Nadine. "Running on Rhapsody: Albert Saijo, the World's 'Oldest

Asian Hippie' and Inspiration for Kerouac's Baso, Raps About Writing and Life in the '60s." *Honolulu Star-Bulletin,* June 6, 1997, D-1.

Leong, James. "A Zen Pastry Shop." Rev. of *Outspeaks: A Rhapsody. Pacific Reader* (Spring/Summer 1997): poetry section.

Leong, Lavonne. "Albert Saijo." In Guiyou Huang, ed., *Asian American Poets: A Bio-Bibliographical Critical Sourcebook* (Westport, CT: Greenwood Press, 2002), 271–73.

Spahr, Juliana. Rev. of *Outspeaks: A Rhapsody. Tinfish* 6 (March 1998): 52–54.

* * *

Vikram Seth. See Seth in "Fiction."

* * *

Cathy Song (1955–). Born in Wahiawa, on the island of Oahu, to a Korean father and a Chinese mother, Song was raised in Hawai'i and attended the University of Hawai'i before she transferred to Wellesley College on the mainland, from which she received a B.A. in English in 1977; she went on to obtain an M.F.A. from Boston College in 1981. Song started to publish poems in the late 1970s. Her first collection, *Picture Bride,* which won the Yale Series of Younger Poets Award in 1982, was published in 1983 (New Haven: Yale University Press). *Frameless Windows, Squares of Light: Poems* followed in 1988 (New York: Norton); *School Figures* came out in 1994 (Pittsburgh: University of Pittsburgh Press); and most recently, *The Land of Bliss* was published in 2001 (Pittsburgh: University of Pittsburgh Press). Song won the Hawai'i Award for Literature in 1993, and the Shelley Memorial Award from the Poetry Society of America.

As Gayle K. Sato has pointed out, Song's poetry "has always been autobiographical, more explicitly so with each successive book, and clearly reflects the shaping—often the enabling—influences of region, ethnicity, gender, and class on her three central subjects: art, family, and women's experience" (*Asian American Poets* 275). This observation applies to all her books of poetry. *Picture Bride,* which has won Song the most critical and popular acclaim, starts with a poem about her Korean grandmother and continues with pieces about her grandfather and father, but female figures appear frequently in many other poems that explore issues concerning her own family's history, life in Hawai'i, and women's experiences as daughter, sister, or mother. Women's experience spills over into her second collection, *Frameless Windows, Squares of Light,* even though male presence is also quite visible. The male figures—fathers, grandfathers, husbands, and sons—are not there to exactly explore male issues but rather serve to show how marriage, dominated by men in a patriarchal culture, becomes an institution of oppression for women. In these first two volumes Song depicts both male and female characters from her family, but not until her third book, *School Figures,* does she start to write about her mother and the misfortunes, deprivation, and losses that she suffered as a child. Other poems, including the title piece, deal with positive themes such as affirmation of life and the pursuit of beauty that embodies the poet's dedication to artistic creativity. Art and its relationship to the artist also hold a significant place in Song's poetry, with focus on two particular artists: the American Georgia O'Keeffe and the Japanese Kitagawa Utamaro. In her fourth book, *The Land of Bliss,* Song intertwines the harsh reality of her aging parents, especially her mother, who was frequently hospitalized for depression, with memories of her grandparents. The past and the present likewise meet in these poems to articulate Song's thematic concern with her ancestral heritage.

Song is a well-studied poet; in fact, she is more widely anthologized than most others within the Asian American subgroups. See:

"Cathy Song 1955– ." In Lawrence J. Trudeau, ed., *Asian American Literature: Reviews and Criticism of Works by American Writers of Asian Descent* (Detroit: Gale Research, 1999), 421–51.

Chang, Juliana. "Reading Asian American Poetry." *MELUS* 21, no. 1 (1996): 81–98.

Choo, David. "Cathy's Song: Interview with Cathy Song." *Honolulu Weekly*, June 15, 1994, 6–8.

Fujita-Sato, Gayle K. "Third World as Place and Paradigm in Cathy Song's *Picture Bride.*" *MELUS* 15, no. 1 (Spring 1988): 49–72.

Gall, Susan. "Cathy-Lynn Song." In Helen Zia and Susan B. Gall, eds., *Notable Asian Americans* (Detroit: Gale Research, 1995), 353–55.

Green, Ann-Elizabeth. "Song, Cathy." In Pamela L. Shelton, ed., *Contemporary Women Poets* (Detroit: St. James Press, 1998), 322–24.

Hugo, Richard. Foreword to *Picture Bride* (New Haven: Yale University Press, 1983), ix–xiv.

Sato, Gayle K. "Cathy Song." In Guiyou Huang, ed., *Asian American Poets: A Bio-Bibliographical Critical Sourcebook* (Westport, CT: Greenwood Press, 2002), 275–88.

Schultz, Susan M. "Cathy Song." In Joseph Conte, ed., *Dictionary of Literary Biography*, vol. 169, *American Poets Since World War II: Fifth Series* (Detroit: Gale Research, 1996), 267–74.

Usui, Masami. "Women Disclosed: Cathy Song's Poetry and Kitagawa Utamaro's Ukiyoe." *Ningen Bunka Kenkyu* [Studies in Culture and the Humanities, Japan] 4 (1995): 1–19.

Wallace, Patricia. "Divided Loyalties: Literal and Literary in the Poetry of Lorna Dee Cervantes, Cathy Song, and Rita Dove." *MELUS* 18, no. 3 (Fall 1993): 3–19.

* * *

Arthur Sze (1950–). Chinese American poet and translator Sze was born in New York City and grew up in Garden City, Long Island. From 1968 to 1970 he was enrolled at MIT, but he completed his college education at the University of California at Berkeley in 1972, having studied poetry writing, philosophy, and classical Chinese literature. Intensive training in these fields helped shape Sze as a poet and prepared him as a translator; his first two collections contain both original poems and translations from the Chinese: *Willow Wind* (Berkeley, CA: Rainbow Zenith Press, 1972) and *Two Ravens* (Guadalupita, NM: Tooth of Time Books, 1976). *The Silk Dragon: Translations from the Chinese* (Port Townsend, WA: Copper Canyon Press, 2001), as the subtitle foretells, are all English renditions of Chinese poems. Four other books are his own poetry: *Dazzled* (Point Reyes, CA: Floating Island Publications, 1982), *River River* (Providence, RI: Lost Roads Publishers, 1987), *Archipelago* (Port Townsend, WA: Copper Canyon Press, 1995), and *The Redshifting Web: Poems, 1970–1998* (Port Townsend, WA: Copper Canyon Press, 1998). While Sze immerses himself in Chinese culture and literature mainly through books, his poetic vision has been shaped considerably by his residential/existential experience with New Mexico, where he has lived since 1972, and his poetry shows indelible marks of the cultural, artistic, and natural landscapes of China and New Mexico.

The number and variety of awards that Sze has won gauge the level of his success as not just an Asian American poet but also an American poet. His honors include the Lannan Literary Award for Poetry in 1995, the American Book Award in 1996, the Institute of American Indian Arts Foundation Award of Excellence in 1998, the Asian American Literary Award in Poetry in 1999, and a Lila Wallace–Reader's Digest Writers' Award for 1998–2000, in addition to a number of prestigious fellowships.

The subjects in Sze's poetry range from travel experiences to scientific and philosophical observations to cultural and ethnic issues. *Dazzled*, Sze's first collection consisting of only his own poems, probes into human events, natural phenomena, and relationships. *River River* offers glimpses of the interconnectedness of the world as well as humans' relation to it and their ability to understand the relationship through imagination. *Archipelago*, Sze's most acclaimed collection, contains poetic expressions of desire and passion as well as powerful descriptions of images and thoughts, once again illustrating the interdependence of worldly things as perceived by the poet. The unity and infinity of the world in motion constitutes a major theme in *The Redshifting Web*, with the web being the dominant, encompassing metaphor for the living dynamism of the universe; the collection demonstrates the poet's effective appropriation of both Chinese and American poetic and cultural heritages.

Despite Sze's large volume of production, like many other Asian American poets, he has received a good deal of reviews but only a few article-length studies. These include:

Barnstone, Tony. "Revelation Waiting to Happen: A Conversation with Arthur Sze on Translating Chinese Poetry." *Translation Review* 59 (August 2000): 4–19.

Bradley, John. "*The Redshifting Web: Poems 1970–1998*." *XCP: Cross-Cultural Poetics* 4 (April 1999): 144–46.

Fujita, Gayle. "The Imagination and Contemporary Life in the Poetry of Arthur Sze: A Review of *Dazzled*." *Literary Arts Hawaii* 80–81 (Summer 1986): 8–11.

Merrill, Christopher. "*Archipelago*." *El Palacio* 100, no. 3 (Summer 1995): 59–62.

Petoskey, Barbara. "The Unmelted Pot." Rev. of *River River*. *High Plains Literary Review* 3, no. 2 (September 1988): 112–14.

Tabios, Eileen. "Arthur Sze: Mixing Memory and Desire." In Tabios, *Black Lightning: Poetry-in-Progress* (New York: Asian American Writers' Workshop, 1998): 3–21.

Zhou Xiaojing. "Arthur Sze." In Guiyou Huang, ed., *Asian American Poets: A Bio-Bibliographical Critical Sourcebook* (Westport, CT: Greenwood Press, 2002), 293–303.

Nellie Wong (1934–). The path of Nellie Wong's life, work, and literary career epitomizes the hardships, racist and sexist discrimination, and patriarchal oppression experienced by immigrants. Wong was born in Oakland, California, to Chinese parents, but her biological father was not named Wong because the harsh restrictions imposed by the 1924 National Origins Act would not allow his wife to enter the country; as a result, the year before she gave birth to Nellie, she entered the United States posing as her husband's sister; later, she had to fake a marriage certificate to a man named Wong, and hence Nellie received that surname. Wong went to Oakland High School, then worked for Bethlehem Steel Corporation for almost two decades before she returned to California and attended Oakland Adult Learning School, where she studied fiction writing. In the 1970s she enrolled at San Francisco State University, where she continued to take courses in writing and

English, while developing a lifelong interest in Asian American and feminist issues. At thirty-three, she published a collection of poetry, *Dreams in Harrison Railroad Park* (San Francisco: Kelsey St. Press, 1977), followed nearly ten years later by a second volume, *The Death of a Long Steam Lady* (Los Angeles: West End Press, 1986), and more than another decade later, a third collection, *Stolen Moments* (Goshen, CT: Chicory Blue Press, 1997). In addition, Wong has published several autobiographical essays and a short story called "Broad Shoulders," included in the anthology *Making Waves: An Anthology of Writings by and About Asian American Women*, edited by Asian Women United of California (Boston: Beacon Press, 1989).

Wong started to write and publish poetry in the mid-1970s, soon after the appearance of Frank Chin et al.'s *Aiiieeeee!* (1974) and Maxine Hong Kingston's *The Woman Warrior* (1976). *Dreams in Harrison Railroad Park*, published in 1977, engages political and social issues that are still the focus of Asian American literary/cultural discourses today—ethnic and cultural heritages, assimilation, racism and sexism, and in her personal case, memories of growing up in a Chinese family, love for her parents, and concerns as a working woman. Poems in *The Death of a Long Steam Lady*, divided into four sections, portray characters ranging from herself to her parents to Miss Chinatown U.S.A. to the Long Steam Lady, the protagonist mentioned in the collection's title, whose real name the narrator did not know and will never learn because now she is dead. Wong's most recent book, *Stolen Moments*, written and published when she was in her early sixties, speaks out on a series of social, and often feminist, issues concerning the conditions of the oppressed, the working class, immigrants, and the poet's determination to articulate expressions of resistance against oppression.

In 1981, Women Make Movies released a film called *Mitsuye and Nellie: Asian American Poets* (San Francisco: Light-Saraf Films), in which Wong read some of her poetry and discussed her family's immigration history. This film, and her autobiographical essay, "In Search of the Self as Hero: Confetti of Voices on New Year's Night (A Letter to Myself)," in Cherríe Moraga and Gloria Anzaldúa, eds., *This Bridge Called My Back: Writings by Radical Women of Color* (Watertown, MA: Persephone Press, 1981), are excellent sources on her life and work. Other bibliographical pieces that touch on or review Wong's works include:

Leong, Russell. "Poetry Within Earshot." *Amerasia Journal* 15, no. 1 (1989): 165–93.

Smith, Ernest J. "Nellie Wong." In Guiyou Huang, ed., *Asian American Poets: A Bio-Bibliographical Critical Sourcebook* (Westport, CT: Greenwood Press, 2002), 313–18.

Uba, George. "Versions of Identity in Post-activist Asian American Poetry." In Shirley Geok-lin Lim and Amy Ling, eds., *Reading the Literatures of Asian America* (Philadelphia: Temple University Press, 1992), 33–48.

Yee, Marian. Rev. of *Dreams in Harrison Railroad Park. Calyx* 11 (1988): 245–47.

* * *

Merle Woo. See Woo in "Drama."

Mitsuye (May) Yamada (1923–). Born in Fukuoka, Japan, to U.S. resident parents, Yamada moved to Seattle with her parents at age three and a half. At eleven she went back to Japan to study for some time, then returned to the United States to finish high school. During World War II, while her father was arrested for alleged spying, she and the rest of her family were interned at the Minidoka Relocation Center in Idaho. She left to study at the University of Cincinnati in 1944, though she completed her B.A. in 1947 at New York University; Yamada also earned an M.A. from the University of Chicago in 1953. During her incarceration at Minidoka from 1942 to 1944, Yamada wrote a considerable number of poems that would not be published until 1976, in *Camp Notes and Other Poems* (San Lorenzo, CA: Shameless Hussy Press), and in 1988 she published her second book, *Desert Run: Poems and Stories* (Latham, NY: Kitchen Table/Women of Color Press). Yamada also edited, with Sarie Sachie Hylkema, an anthology titled *Sowing Ti Leaves: Writings by Multi-cultural Women* (Irvine, CA: MCWW, 1990). In addition, she has contributed poems and essays to anthologies and periodicals.

Like other *nisei* writers who were interned at a young age, Yamada makes the Japanese American internment a recurring theme in her poetry, examining this historical issue from the perspective of a woman and a Japanese American in both her books. Their titles—*Camp Notes* and *Desert Run*—reflect the internment experience by pinpointing the nature (camp) and location (desert) of the incarceration. A number of poems in *Camp Notes* were written between 1942 and 1944 and describe the internees' relocation from Seattle to Idaho. *Desert Run*, published forty-four years after the internment, continues to revolve around those traumatizing years, though now the stories are often told from female or feminist perspectives. In both collections, geography plays a significant role in the poet's portrayal and critique of the Japanese American experience as intern-ment victims and the psychological impact on especially *nisei* Japanese Americans.

Mitsuye and Nellie: Asian American Poets, a 1981 film made by Women Make Movies (San Francisco: Light-Saraf Films), features Yamada (along with Nellie Wong) reading her poems and discussing her life. For more information, see:

Blackburn, Di Gan. "Mitsuye Yamada." In Guiyou Huang, ed., *Asian American Poets: A Bio-Bibliographical Critical Sourcebook* (Westport, CT: Greenwood Press, 2002), 331–36.

Jaskoski, Helen. "A *MELUS* Interview with Mitsuye Yamada." *MELUS* 15, no. 1 (1988): 97–108.

Patterson, Anita Haya. "Resistance to Images of the Internment: Mitsuye Yamada's *Camp Notes*." *MELUS* 23, no. 3 (1998): 103–27.

Schweik, Susan. "A Needle with Mama's Voice: Mitsuye Yamada's *Camp Notes* and the American Canon of American Poetry." In Helen M. Cooper, Adrienne Auslander Munich, and Susan Merrill Squier, eds., *Arms and the Woman: War, Gender, and Literary Representation* (Chapel Hill: University of North Carolina Press, 1989), 225–43.

Usui, Masami. "A Language of Her Own in Mitsuye Yamada's Poetry and Stories." *Studies in Culture and the Humanities: Bulletin of the Faculty of Integrated Arts and Sciences* (Hiroshima University) 5, no. 3 (1996): 1–17.

Yamamoto, Traise. "Embodied Language: The Poetics of Mitsuye Yamada, Janice Mirikitani, and Kimiko Hahn." In Yamamoto, *Masking Selves, Making Subjects: Japanese American Women, Identity, and the Body* (Berkeley: University of California Press, 1999), 198–261.

* * *

Lois-Ann Yamanaka. See Yamanaka in "Fiction."

* * *

John Yau (1950–). Perhaps Asian America's most prolific poet in the last quarter of the twentieth century, Yau was born in Lynn, Massachusetts, to a Eurasian father and a Chinese mother, both immigrants from Shanghai, China. Yau earned a B.A. from Bard College and an M.F.A. from Brooklyn College. While working in various vocations—critic, curator, editor, and academic—Yau has managed to publish, since 1976, at least seventeen collections of poetry, three short story collections, three critical books, numerous monographs, and four edited or coedited volumes.

Yau's poetry collections include *Crossing Canal Street* (Binghamton, NY: Bellevue Press, 1976), *The Reading of an Ever-Changing Tale* (Clinton, NY: Nobodaddy Press, 1977), *Sometimes* (New York: Sheep Meadow Press, 1979), *The Sleepless Night of Eugene Delacroix* (Brooklyn, NY: Release Press, 1980), *Broken off by the Music* (Providence, RI: Burning Deck, 1981), *Notarikon*, with drawings by Jake Berthot (New York: Jordan Davies, 1981), *Corpse and Mirror* (New York: Holt, Rinehart, and Winston, 1983), *Dragon's Blood* (Colombes, France: Collectif Génération, 1989), *Radiant Silhouette: New and Selected Work, 1974–1988* (Santa Rosa, CA: Black Sparrow Press, 1989), *Big City Primer: Reading New York City at the End of the Twentieth Century*, with photographs by Bill Barrette (New York: Timken Publishers, 1991), *Edificio Sayonara* (Santa Rosa, CA: Black Sparrow Press, 1992), *Postcards from Trakl* (New York: ULAE, 1994), *Berlin Diptychon*, with photographs by Bill Barrette (New York: Timken Publishers, 1995), *Forbidden Entries* (Santa Rosa, CA: Black Sparrow Press, 1996), *I Was a Poet in the House of Frankenstein* (Brooklyn, NY: Poetry New York, 1999), and *Borrowed Love Poems* (New

York: Penguin Poets, 2002). Yau's story collections include *Hawaiian Cowboys* (Santa Rosa, CA: Black Sparrow Press, 1994), *My Symptoms* (Santa Rosa, CA: Black Sparrow Press, 1998), and *My Heart Is That Eternal Rose Tattoo* (Santa Rosa, CA: Black Sparrow Press, 2001).

Yau's stellar achievements in poetry have been recognized with numerous awards, including fellowships from the National Endowment for the Arts, the Ingram-Merrill Foundation, and the New York Foundation for the Arts and awards from the General Electric Foundation and the Academy of American Poets, among numerous others.

Yau's versatility in so many fields is self-evident, but nowhere does he stand out more distinctly than in the arena of poetry, having published seventeen volumes in less than three decades, from 1976 to date. The better-known and more studied books are *Corpse and Mirror*, *Radiant Silhouette*, *Edificio Sayonara*, and *Forbidden Entries*. And of all Yau's poems, the most acclaimed is perhaps his serial poem, "Genghis Chan: Private Eye," which was first printed in his 1989 collection, *Dragon's Blood*, reprinted in *Radiant Silhouette*, and further expanded in two later volumes, *Edificio Sayonara* and *Forbidden Entries*. Readers familiar with both Chinese history of the Yuan dynasty and American popular culture of the early twentieth century will quickly recognize the name of Genghis Chan in Yau's serial poem as a collapsing of Genghis Khan, the historical Mongol ruler of China (1155–1227), and Charlie Chan, the fictional Chinese American detective that Earl Derr Biggers created for Hollywood films. Thus the character embodies two cultures, two histories, and two nations, forming the site for racial politicking, cultural stereotyping, and identity constructing. Genghis Khan represents the fearless conquering forces, as Gary Okihiro writes: "Their [Genghis Khan's military] cavalry tactics and weapons maximized their striking force, and with their horses and light baggage they were able to cover long distances quickly. The Mongols devastated the nations they conquered, but they also unified vast areas and brought together diverse groups of people" (*The Columbia Guide to Asian American History* 5). Charlie Chan, on the other hand, embodies the stereotypes and stigmas of Chinese Americans, particularly of males: smart, subservient, effeminate. Yau's serial poems on Genghis Chan and many other pieces delve into such opposing characteristics to explore the cultural and historical constructions of Asian ethnic identities and to undermine the dominant mainstream ideology of race.

Yau's short fiction deals with similar issues and themes; indeed, often, the formal distinctions between his poetry and prose are not very marked because of the heavy use of prose in his poems or the fluid interplay of the two genres. Nevertheless, his first story collection, *Hawaiian Cowboys*, reminiscent of the author's biography, examines the complications and implications of racial borderlines and the struggles of mixed-race people to combat or just resist ethnic stereotyping; thus "the turbulent politics of self-representation always remains at the foreground of Yau's short fiction" (Lee 338). Yau's second collection, *My Symptoms*, shifts the focus away from the self and to the Other, both sexual and racial: the recurring figure of a white woman; but the later collection is more experimental in form and shows no attempt to markedly distinguish between short story and prose poetry. Yau's third and most recent story collection, *My Heart Is That Eternal Rose Tattoo*, contains exhilarating stories, and again, many can be easily labeled prose poems.

John Yau's critical and popular acclaim is evident in a special symposium published in *Talisman: A Journal of Contemporary Poetry and Poetics*, volume 5 (1990), with contributions from Bruce Campbell, David Chaloner, William Corbett, Joseph Donahue, Edward Halsey Foster, Peter Gizzi, Kris Hemensley, Albert Mobilio, and Priscilla Wald. Other studies include:

Chang, Juliana Chu. "Word and Flesh: Materiality, Violence and Asian American Poetics." Ph.D. diss., University of California, Berkeley, 1996.

Lee, Sue-Im. "John Yau." In Guiyou Huang, ed., *Asian American Short Story Writers: An A-to-Z Guide* (Westport, CT: Greenwood Press, 2003), 337–43.

Wald, Priscilla. "'Chaos Goes Uncourted': John Yau's Dis(-)Orienting Poetics." In Carol Colatrella and Joseph Alkana, eds., *Cohesion and Dissent in America* (Albany: State University of New York Press, 1994), 133–58.

Wang, Dorothy Joan. "Necessary Figures: Metaphor, Irony and Parody in the Poetry of Li-Young Lee, Marilyn Chin, and John Yau." Ph.D. diss., University of California, Berkeley, 1999.

Yu, Timothy. "Form and Identity in Language Poetry and Asian American Poetry." *Contemporary Literature* 41, no. 3 (Fall 2000): 422–62.

Zhou Xiaojing. "John Yau." In Guiyou Huang, ed., *Asian American Poets: A Bio-Bibliographical Critical Sourcebook* (Westport, CT: Greenwood Press, 2002), 343–56.

6. Short Fiction

B

Peter Bacho (1950–). Filipino American short story writer and novelist Bacho was born to immigrant parents in Seattle, Washington, where he was raised in a predominantly African American and Filipino neighborhood. He earned a bachelor's degree from Seattle University in 1971 and a law degree from the University of Washington in 1974. Bacho worked as a lawyer for a number of years before he started an academic career in the late 1980s. In 1991 he published a novel, *Cebu* (Seattle: University of Washington Press); in 1997 his short story collection, *Dark Blue Suit and Other Stories* (Seattle: University of Washington Press), came out; his second novel, *Nelson's Run*, was published in 2002 (Holliston, MA: Willowgate Press). Bacho also produced a collection of essays that deals with boxing and prominent boxers, titled *Boxing in Black and White* (New York: Henry Holt and Co., 1999). He has won several major literary awards: the American Book Award for *Cebu* and the Washington State Governor's Writers Award and the Murray Morgan Award for *Dark Blue Suit and Other Stories*.

Dark Blue Suit and Other Stories presents twelve stories that mostly deal with the Manongs—respected first-generation Filipino immigrants who came to the United States in the early decades of the twentieth century,

like Bacho's father (he arrived in 1923). The stories are narrated by a second-generation Filipino called Buddy, who holds a keen interest in the life of Filipinos in Seattle, as well as in the problems and issues (cultural and racial) confronting not only the first generation of Filipino immigrants but also their children, American-born Filipinos like himself. The title story, "Dark Blue Suit," is partly autobiographical and shows how Buddy's father, dressed in a dark blue suit, selects men for work in the Alaskan canneries. *Cebu*, Bacho's first novel, explores the classic struggle between spirit and flesh in the character of a young Filipino American priest, Ben Lucero, who leaves his Seattle parish to attend his mother's burial in her homeland city of Cebu, the Philippines, where he undergoes not only a sexual maturation but also a spiritual crisis. *Nelson's Run*, a political and sexual satire, is again set in the Philippines, on the war-stricken island of Samar, where the eponymous young protagonist escapes work and long-term relationships in search of pleasure, only to be caught in a guerrilla war as well as a sexual triangle, finding himself torn between conflicting paths and two attractive tango dancers. Gender roles, colonialism, and corruption are also examined in this novel.

For more information, see:

Davis, Rocío G. "Peter Bacho." In Guiyou Huang, ed., *Asian American*

Short Story Writers: An A-to-Z Guide (Westport, CT: Greenwood Press, 2003), 1–4.

Leonard, George J. and Diane Rosenblum. "A Reader's Guide to *Cebu* and *Dark Blue Suit* Based on Interviews with Its Author, Peter Bacho." In George Leonard, ed., *The Asian Pacific American Heritage: A Companion to Literature and Arts* (New York: Garland Press, 1999), 481–95.

Tepper, Anderson. "Dark Blue Suit and Other Stories," *New York Times Book Review,* October 26, 1997, 24.

* * *

Cecilia Manguerra Brainard. See Brainard in "Fiction."

Jeffery Paul Chan (1942–). A third-generation Chinese American short story writer, essayist, and critic, Chan was born in Stockton and grew up in Richmond, California. He first attended the University of California at Berkeley before he spent some time tutoring English and studying Spanish culture at the University of Barcelona in Spain. He completed a B.A. in English before he enrolled in the creative writing program at San Francisco State University. Chan is known for his work as a fiction writer, but he is equally, if not better recognized for his activist involvement in the Asian American literary movement in the 1970s: he played a central role in and served as founding director of the Combined Asian American Resources Project, Inc. (CARP); he also founded and served as the first chair of the Asian American Studies Department at San Francisco State. In 1974, Chan served as second editor, along with Frank Chin, Lawson

Fusao Inada, and Shawn Wong, of the breakthrough anthology *Aiiieeeee!,* and as the first editor for *The Big Aiiieeeee!* in 1991. Thus, while Chan has achieved high standing in the establishment and promotion of the then emerging field of Asian American Studies, his contributions to the Asian American community cross boundaries of literature, culture, politics, and community building.

It is difficult to simplistically categorize Chan as a short story writer, essayist, or editor, for he is accomplished in all three areas—he has contributed to the recovery, publication, and study of Asian American literary writing. His essays on race and related topics are influential. One in particular, "Racist Love," coauthored with Frank Chin, appeared in Richard Kostelanetz's *Seeing Through the Shuck* (New York: Ballantine, 1972), 65–79, and remains an oft-quoted piece. Chan has not published a separate collection of short stories; in fact, he has published only a few pieces, including "Auntie Tsia Lays Dying," *Aion* 1, no. 2 (1971): 82–87; "The Chinese in Haifa," in Chin et al., eds., *Aiiieeeee!* (Washington, DC: Howard University Press, 1974), 11–29; "Jack Rabbit," *Yardbird* 3 (1974): 217–38; "Sing Song Plain Song," *Amerasia Journal* 3, no. 2 (1976): 23–37; and "Cheap Labor," *Amerasia Journal* 9, no. 2 (1982): 99–116.

Of these short narratives, "Auntie Tsia Lays Dying" and "The Chinese in Haifa" are well anthologized and are familiar to readers. These two stories, like others Chan has written, utilize a male perspective to explore issues relevant to Chinese Americans, such as immigration, memories of homeland, and interracial relationships. "Auntie Tsia Lays Dying" tells the story of a dying old woman through the male narrator's memories of her life in China, making it a story about not only death but also loss and alienation from the homeland. "The Chinese in Haifa," on the other hand, examines an interracial, illicit relationship between a Chinese man and a Jewish woman, both married (the former separated from his wife), while the subplot considers the implications and consequences of whether or not to pass on one's ethnic cultural heritage as embodied in the learning of the Chinese language.

Chan's creative output unfortunately has not received much critical attention. One source, however, provides both biographical and critical analysis of his stories: Fu-jen Chen, "Jeffery Paul Chan," in Guiyou Huang, ed., *Asian American Short Story Writers: An A-to-Z Guide* (Westport, CT: Greenwood Press, 2003), 31–37.

* * *

G. S. Sharat Chandra. See Chandra in "Poetry."

Chitra Banerjee Divakaruni. See Divakaruni in "Fiction."

Gish Jen. See Jen in "Fiction."

Lonny Kaneko. See Kaneko in "Poetry."

* * *

Alex Kuo (1939–). A Chinese American short story writer, novelist, and poet, Kuo was born in Boston, Massachusetts, where his father taught psychology at Harvard. From 1942 to 1945 he lived in mainland China. He received his elementary and high school education in Hong Kong; then he went to the University of London, from which he received a General Certificate of Education. Returning to the United States, Kuo obtained a B.A. in writing from Knox College, Illinois, in 1961, as well as an M.F.A. in creative writing from the University of Iowa. Between 1975 and 2000, he published approximately two dozen short stories and four volumes of poetry: *The Window Tree* (Peterborough, NH: Windy Row Press, 1971), believed to be the first collection of poetry published by an Asian American; *New Letters from Hiroshima and Other Poems* (New York: Greenfield Review, 1974); *Changing the River* (Berkeley: Ishmael Reed, 1986); and *This Fierce Geography* (Boise, ID: Limberlost, 1999). In recent years he has turned his creative energy to prose writing: in 1998 he published his first novel, *Chinese Opera* (Hong Kong: Asia 2000), and in 2001 *Lipstick and Other Stories*, a collection including some previously published pieces, came out (Hong Kong: Asia 2000).

Lipstick and Other Stories consists of thirty-one stories—sixteen previously published and fifteen new. The book is subdivided into three sections: the first, including all previously published stories, generally recounts childhood stories from Kuo's years in wartime China; the second deals more with contemporary China; the third combines themes from the previous two but also explores cross-cultural issues related to China and the United States, alongside other international themes. Other subjects that inform Kuo's short fiction are his sustained concerns about modern and contemporary Chinese history. His stories published in the last decade often are set in significant or important historical periods, such as World War II, the Chinese Communist victory in 1949, the Proletarian Cultural Revolution of the

1960s–1970s, and the 1989 students' prodemocracy movement in Beijing. A distinctive characteristic of Kuo's writing is the absence of a clear-cut line between poetry and prose in many of his stories. His only novel, *Chinese Opera*, again takes up the themes of contemporary Chinese history and cross-culturalism between the United States and China. Set in Beijing in 1989, the year of massive student protests against government corruption and demand for political reform, *Chinese Opera* depicts the experience of an American couple—a Native American singer, Sissy George, and a Chinese American pianist, Sonny Ling—teaching in Beijing, and examines the complications of relationships between native and foreign-born nationals, and between cultural and ethnic boundaries.

For more information, see:

Grinnell, Jim. "Telling Truth in Art and Freedom of Expression: An Interview with Alex Kuo." *Bloomsbury Review* 22, no. 1 (Nov.–Dec. 1999): 17.

Huntington, Rebecca. Rev. of *Chinese Opera*. *Seattle Times*, September 20, 1998, B5.

Robert, Abel. "Telling the Stories of the Disappeared." Rev. of *Lipstick and Other Stories*, *Willow Springs* 50 (June 2002): 37–39.

Sugano, Douglas. "Alex Kuo." In Emmanuel Nelson, ed., *Asian American Novelists: A Bio-Bibliographical Critical Sourcebook* (Westport, CT: Greenwood Press, 2000), 168–71.

——. "Alex Kuo." In Guiyou Huang, ed., *Asian American Short Story Writers: An A-to-Z Guide* (Westport, CT: Greenwood Press, 2003), 119–23.

Webster, Dan. Rev. of *Chinese Opera*. *Spokane-Review*, September 20, 1998, E7 and E8.

Jhumpa Lahiri (1967–). Lahiri is an Indian diasporic writer: born in London to parents of Bengali ancestry, she was raised in Rhode Island, the United States, where her family immigrated when she was two. She has also traveled to Calcutta, India many times. Lahiri earned a B.A. from Barnard College and an M.F.A. from Boston University, before she went on to obtain two other M.A. degrees, one in English literature and one in Comparative Studies in Literature, and eventually a Ph.D. in Renaissance Studies in 1997, all at Boston University. Lahiri started to write fiction when she was a child. Before she published a collection, she had placed a number of short stories in reputable journals and magazines such as *Harvard Review* and *The New Yorker*. Her only collection of stories to date, *Interpreter of Maladies*, a best-seller, was published in 1999 (Boston: Houghton Mifflin), the same year *The New Yorker* named her one of the twenty best American fiction writers under forty. Lahiri's first novel, *The Namesake*, was published at the end of 2003 (Boston: Houghton Mifflin). In 2000, she was awarded the Pulitzer Prize in fiction for her story collection.

Interpreter of Maladies consists of nine stories, some set in America and others in India. They are often told from the perspective of second-generation Indian Americans. The American and South Asian settings reflect the geography of Lahiri's characters: Indian-born Indians, American-born Indians, Indian immigrants, and Caucasian Americans. The settings and the characters set up cultural clashes involving gender, ethnicity, and race, though race and ethnicity play a less visible role in Lahiri's fiction than in the work of some other diasporic or multicultural writers. The themes of displacement, dynamics of relationships, and communication difficulties are prevalent in her stories, and are most forcefully depicted in the title piece, also her most celebrated, "Interpreter of Maladies." This narrative tells the story of the Dases, who are touring their ancestral land of India under the guidance of a native Indian, Mr. Kapasi, whose other job is interpreting maladies for folks in his community. Even though the setting is an Indian tourist town, the United States as a "home" for the Indian American family forms a contrasting narrative background. The irony about Mr. Kapasi's interpretation of things arises from his misreading and misjudgment of Mrs. Das's marital situation; hence his expectations and preconceptions about Americans, or Indian Americans in this case, are dashed. The misinterpretation is therefore a result of the failure to understand the culture of the Other, even though this Other looks like the self in terms of skin color.

The Namesake, Lahiri's novel, "follows the Ganguli family from their tradition-bound life in India through their gradual transformation into Americans. The story centers on Gogol, a boy who grows up trying to shed his parents' ways and carve a life for himself from the world in which he feels comfortable" (Solan 37). To write the novel, Lahiri did research on the Russian novelist Nikolay Gogol and used the name of a friend of her cousin's in India, actually called Gogol. But her thematic concern is really with Indian immigrants; Lahiri "focuses on the particular psychological conflicts of an atypical subset of immigrants" (Solan 36), the highly educated professionals from India who have to battle to retain their identity in a new culture.

Lahiri's short story collection came out five years ago and has not been the subject of many substantial studies, but notices about her winning the Pulitzer Prize and reviews of her book abound. The novel *Namesake* appeared even more recently, and studies of it are of course yet to come. See:

Flynn, Gillian. "Passage to India: First-time Author Jhumpa Lahiri Nabs a Pulitzer." *Entertainment Weekly,* April 28, 2000, 100.

Guinn, Jeff. "Pulitzer Committee Uncovers a Treasure." *Plain Dealer,* April 24, 2000, 3E.

Huang, Shuchen Susan. "Jhumpa Lahiri." In Guiyou Huang, ed., *Asian American Short Story Writers: An A-to-Z Guide* (Westport, CT: Greenwood Press, 2003), 125–33.

Kipen, David. "Interpreting Indian Culture with Stories." *San Francisco Chronicle,* June 24, 1999, 10.

Noor, Ronny. Rev. of *Interpreter of Maladies. World Literature Today* 74, no. 2 (Spring 2000): 365–66.

Quinn, Mary Ellen. Rev. of *Interpreter of Maladies. Booklist* (April 15, 1999): 1514.

Shah, Purvi. Rev. of *Interpreter of Maladies. Amerasia* 27, no. 2 (2001): 183–86.

Solan, Matthew. "Catching up with Jhumpa Lahiri." *Poets & Writers* 31, no. 5 (September/October 2003): 36–38.

Taylor, Robert. "A Quietly Powerful 'Interpreter.'" *Boston Globe,* July 14, 1999, F8.

Uviller, Daphne. "Talking with Jhumpa Lahiri Through the Looking Glass." *Newsday,* July 25, 1999, B11.

Vibhuti, Patel. "The Maladies of Belonging." Interview. *Newsweek* (September 20, 1999): 80.

* * *

Andrew Lam (1963–). Born into an affluent family in Saigon, Vietnam, Lam grew up with privileges afforded by his father's position as a general. When Saigon fell into the hands of the North Vietnamese Army in April 1975, all of twelve-year-old Lam's family but his father fled to the United States and settled in the San Francisco Bay area, where his father joined them several months later. Lam attended the University of California at Berkeley and graduated with a degree in biochemistry. He went on to pursue his interest in creative writing at San Francisco State University, where he published his first short story, "Dark Wood and Shadows," in the student magazine *Transfer* 57 (Fall 1989): 24–35. Lam's most noted piece, "Grandma's Tales," appeared in *Amerasia Journal* 20, no. 3 (1994): 65–70. Other stories include "On the Perfume," *Manoa* 6, no. 2 (1994): 132–41; "She in a Dance of Frenzy," in Wayne Karlin, Le Minh Khue, and Truong Vu, eds., *The Other Side of Heaven: Postwar Fiction by Vietnamese and American Writers* (Willimantic, CT: Curbstone, 1995), 322–26; "Requiems in Blue," *Vietnam Review* 2 (Spring/Summer 1997): 449–53; "Slingshot," *Zyzzyva* (Winter 1998): 151–63; "Show and Tell," in Barbara Tran, Monique T.D. Truong, and Luu Truong Khoi, eds., *Watermark: Vietnamese American Poetry and Prose* (New York: Asian American Writers' Workshop, 1998), 111–21; "The Shard, the Tissue, an Affair," *Manoa* 12, no. 2 (2000): 64–67; and "Fire," in Jane Winston and Leakthina Ollier, eds., *Of Vietnam: Identities in Dialogue* (New York: Palgrave, 2001), 130–41. In addition, he coedited, with De Tran and Hai Dai Nguyen, the first Vietnamese American collection on literature and art, titled *Once Upon a Dream: The Vietnamese-American Experience* (San Jose, CA: San Jose Mercury News, 1995). Lam has been honored with the Storke Excellence in International Journalism Award and a Rockefeller Fellowship. He has also worked as a reporter for the *San Jose Mercury News*.

Even though Lam has yet to produce a collection of short stories, his published fiction is noteworthy for its reflections on his personal experience in wartime Vietnam ("Dark Wood and Shadows" and "On the Perfume"), and Vietnamese immigrants' acclimation to a new life in the United States—including the difficulty of learning a new language ("Show and Tell" and "Slingshot"). "Grandma's Tales" is not the typical grandmother story of life lessons but rather is about the death and reincarnation of a grandmother who becomes a source of strength for the narrator in his Vietnamese American surroundings. Bicultural, witty, and sometimes humorous, Lam's work has been favorably noted for its Vietnamese perspectives on the war and its aftermath, often different from mainstream American narratives of the same war.

For more information, see:

Hanig, Ross. "Author Andrew Lam Gives Personalized Book Reading." *California Aggie* (March 15, 1999): 1+.

Karlin, Wayne. "Hot Damn Vietnam: Twenty-Five Years Later, a Literature of War and Remembrance." *Los Angeles Times Book Review,* April 23, 2000, 1.

Lieberman, Kim-An. "Andrew Lam." In Guiyou Huang, ed., *Asian American Short Story Writers: An A-to-Z Guide* (Westport, CT: Greenwood Press, 2003), 135–39.

Nguyen, Phuong Madison. "Andrew Lam: Beyond the Fountain Pen." In Nguyen Thi Diem Huyen and Nguyen Thi Thuy, eds., *New Horizon/Chan Troi Moi: 25 Vietnamese Americans in 25 Years, 1975–2000* (San Jose, CA: New Horizon, 2000), 55–59.

* * *

Evelyn Lau. See Lau in "Poetry."

* * *

Don Lee (1959–). The son of a U.S. State Department officer of Korean descent, Lee spent his childhood mostly in Tokyo and Seoul. Back in the United States, he attended the University of California at Los Angeles, studying engineering for two years before he switched majors and graduated with a B.A. in English in 1982; in 1986 he earned an M.F.A. in creative writing and literature at Emerson College, Boston, where he remained as an adjunct faculty member until 1988, when he assumed the editorship of *Ploughshares*, the literary journal that is housed at Emerson College. Lee's stories have appeared in *GQ*, *New England Review*, *American Short Fiction*, and *Glimmer Train*. He published *Yellow*, his first and so far only collection of short stories, in 2001 (New York: Norton). Lee's first novel, *Country of Origin*, was published by Norton in 2004. *Yellow* won the 2002 Sue Kaufman Prize in First Fiction from the American Academy of Arts and Letters, as well as the Members' Choice Award from the Asian American Writers' Workshop. Lee's story "The Possible Husband" won an O. Henry Award; another piece, "The Price of Eggs in China," garnered him a Pushcart Prize. In addition, Lee has received fellowships from the Massachusetts Cultural Council and the St. Botolph Club Foundation.

Set in the fictional California town of Rosarita Bay, *Yellow* examines what it means to be "yellow" in America, and explores postimmigration issues such as identity, race, and relationships involving Chinese, Korean, Japanese, and Caucasian Americans across and within racial lines. Lee's eight stories deal mostly with Korean American males who have experienced the traumas of war, separation, and abandonment, and who are entangled in relationships that affect the racial dynamics surrounding them. The title story, "Yellow," is a fine example that probes the impact of racism on Asian-white relationships. The main plot of Lee's novel, *Country of Origin*, is set in Tokyo in 1980 and revolves around the case

of a missing young American woman, Lisa Countryman, whom a half-Korean, half-white Foreign Service Officer and a Japanese cop are assigned to find. And like the story "Yellow," the novel takes up interracial and international relationships as well.

The majority of the studies of Lee are reviews of *Yellow*. See:

Barber, Peggy. Rev. of *Yellow*. *Booklist* 97, no. 15 (April 2001): 1447.

Liu, Dana. "On Being Yellow: Don Lee." Rev. of *Yellow*, 10 7, no. 1–2 (2001): 33.

Oh, Seiwoong. "Don Lee." In Guiyou Huang, ed., *Asian American Short Story Writers: An A-to-Z Guide* (Westport, CT: Greenwood Press, 2003), 151–54.

Roca, Elizabeth. "Short Stories." Rev. of *Yellow*. *Washington Post*, April 8, 2001, BW 13.

Zaleski, Jeff. Rev. of *Yellow*. *Publishers Weekly* 248, no. 14 (April 2001): 38.

* * *

SKY Lee (1952–). Chinese Canadian short story writer and novelist Lee was born Sharon Lee in Port Alberni, British Columbia. She earned a B.A. in fine arts from the University of British Columbia and a diploma in nursing from Douglas College. Lee has worked as a nurse all her life while writing fiction: she coauthored, with Paul Yee, a collection of juvenile fiction titled *Teach Me to Fly Skyfighter and Other Stories* (Toronto: Lorimer, 1983). In 1991 her novel, *Disappearing Moon Café*, came out (Vancouver: Douglas and McIntyre); her short story collection, *Bellydancer: Stories*, followed in 1994 (Vancouver: Press Gang). For *Disappearing Moon Café*, Lee received the City of Vancouver Book Award and was short-listed for the Governor General's Award.

Bellydancer consists of fifteen stories that portray a considerable range of characters, from belly dancers to bag ladies and lesbians, who experience poverty, tragedy, and survival firsthand. The title story actually includes three separate narratives respectively subtitled "level one," "level two," and "level three." Belly dance is an erotic dance of creation originally performed at the bedside of women in labor. The belly dancing stories revolve around the character Seni and examine the politics of relationships involving men, women, and lesbians in the struggle for the ownership of women's bodies. Lee's novel *Disappearing Moon Café* probes the complex issues of ethnic communities and assimilation politics. The main plot of the novel follows the experience of four generations of a Chinese Canadian family living in Vancouver, the Wongs, and again the narrative focus remains on women, their relationships, and their lifestyles.

There have appeared a number of reviews of *Disappearing Moon Café* and some reviews of *Bellydancer* in both Canada and the United States. More substantial studies include:

Chao, Lien. "As Agents and as Perspective: Female Characters in *Disappearing Moon Café*." In Coomi S. Vevaina and Barbara Godard, eds., *Intersexions: Issues of Race and Gender in Canadian Women's Writing* (New Delhi: Creative, 1996), 219–30.

Conde, Mary. "Visible Immigrants in Three Canadian Women's Fictions of the Nineties." *Etudes Canadiennes/Canadian Studies* 19 (June 1993): 91–100.

Darias-Beautell, Eva. "Displacement, Self-Mockery, and Carnival in the Canadian Postmodern." *World Literature Today* 70 (Spring 1996): 316+.

Guilbert, Naomi. "Interview with Sharon Lee." In Momoye Sugiman, ed., *Jin Guo: Voices of Chinese Canadian Women* (New York: Women's Press, 1993), 91–98.

Huggan, Graham. "The Latitudes of Romance: Representations of Chinese Canada in Bowering's *To All Appearances a Lady* and Lee's *Disappearing Moon Café*." *Canadian Literature* (Spring 1994): 34–48.

Kish, Martin. "SKY Lee." In Emmanuel S. Nelson, ed., *Asian American Novelists: A Bio-Bibliographical Critical Sourcebook* (Westport, CT: Greenwood Press, 2000), 197–203.

Larson, Jesse. "*Disappearing Moon Café*, by SKY Lee." In Erica Bauermeister, ed., *500 Great Books by Women: A Reader's Guide* (New York: Penguin, 1994), 162–63.

Milnes, Stephen. "SKY Lee." In *Contemporary Novelists*, 6th ed. (Detroit: St. James Press, 1996), 601–2.

* * *

Monfoon Leong (1916–1964). Chinese American short story writer Leong was born in San Diego, the first of six siblings. During World War II he trained as a ferry pilot in the U.S. Army Air Force; afterward he attended San Jose State College, where he developed an interest in writing. He completed his bachelor's degree in English at Standford University in 1951, and two years later, he obtained a master's degree in American Studies at the University of Minnesota; the following year he received his teaching credentials from the University of California at Berkeley. Leong wrote and taught in the San Francisco Bay area until he was killed in a car accident while on a tour in Yogoslavia in 1964. His short story collection, *Number One Son*, was published posthumously (San Francisco: East/West Publishing Company, 1975).

The title *Number One Son* has an autobiographical significance because it reflects the author's own position in his family. His father died when Leong was only fourteen, making him the head of the household, as is historically the case with Chinese families in China and some immigrant families abroad. As such Leong came to know the Chinese community firsthand, and that experience was fully incorporated into his stories. As a result, Chinatown as a community and as a setting often appears in his writing, along with characters and themes he knew growing up: the principal characters in his narratives are all Chinese—members of the older generation who hold on to traditional Chinese customs and values and American-born Chinese who experience generational and cultural conflicts. In these stories, Leong shows a deep understanding of his ethnic culture as well as of the social and racial inequity prevalent in his time and society.

Leong's short fiction has not been given much critical attention, though he is briefly discussed in works including King-Kok Cheung, ed., *An Interethnic Companion to Asian American Literature* (New York: Cambridge University Press, 1997), and Elaine H. Kim, *Asian American Literature: An Introduction to the Writings and Their Social Context* (Philadelphia: Temple University Press, 1982). A bio-critical essay by Amy W.S. Lee, "Monfoon Leong," appears in Guiyou Huang, ed., *Asian American Short Story Writers: An A-to-Z Guide* (Westport, CT: Greenwood Press, 2003), 155–57.

* * *

Russell Leong (1950–). Chinese American short story writer, poet, and editor, Leong was born in San Francisco's Chinatown. He attended San Francisco State College and received a B.A. in 1972; he chose to spend the following two years at the National Taiwan University in Taipei, pursuing graduate studies. Leong earned an M.F.A. from the University of California at Los Angeles in 1990. His training in writing consisted of taking the

first classes in Asian American literature from Jeffery Paul Chan at San Francisco State and participating in the Kearny Street Workshop, the well-known workshop that included writers and artists of different ethnic Asian groups. Leong started to publish short stories in 1972, in anthologies such as Kai-yu Hsu and Helen Palubinskas's *Asian-American Authors* (Boston: Houghton Mifflin, 1972), in Frank Chin et al.'s *Aiiieeeee!* under the pseudonym Wallace Lin (Washington, DC: Howard University Press, 1974), and in Jessica Hagedorn's *Charlie Chan Is Dead* (New York: Penguin, 1993). His book of poetry, *The Country of Dreams and Dust: Poems*, came out in 1993 (Albuquerque, NM: West End Press), followed by a short story collection, *Phoenix Eyes and Other Stories* (Seattle: University of Washington Press) in 2000. Many readers also know Leong for his role as longtime editor of *Amerasia*, since 1977. In addition, he has edited and coedited a number of books and anthologies in literature, criticism, and media arts.

Leong was awarded the PEN Oakland Josephine Miles Literature Award in 1994 for *The Country of Dreams and Dust*, and the American Book Award from the Before Columbus Foundation in 2001 for *Phoenix Eyes and Other Stories*.

The issues and themes that Leong explores in *Phoenix Eyes and Other Stories* range widely, but often deal with Asian Americans, particularly single Asian gay males. The characters that populate the fourteen narratives are Chinese, Vietnamese, and Buddhist monks, among others. Whether located in Southern California, China, Japan, or Thailand, they experience displacement or fragmented identity—often related to their sexual orientation, religion, and ethnic heritage. The role of religion, often Buddhist transcendence, occupies a prominent position in Leong's fiction, in pieces such as "Where Do People Live Who Never Die?," the title story "The Phoenix Eyes," and "Samsara," to mention only three. Leong's depictions of human experiences—dislocation, identity crisis, religious beliefs, and gay issues—provide insights into a broad spectrum of the Asian American experience with force and poignancy.

For more information, see:

Chang, Leonard. "Rising Phoenix: Arresting New Works from Three West Coast Asian American Writers." *San Francisco Chronicle,* March 18, 2001, 16.

Davis, Robert Murray. "Phoenix Eyes and Other Stories." *World Literature Today* 1 (April 2001): 341.

Ito, Robert B. Interview with Russell Leong. In King-Kok Cheung, ed., *Words Matter: Conversations with Asian American Writers* (Honolulu: University of Hawai'i Press, and Los Angeles: UCLA Asian American Studies Center, 2000), 233–51.

Liu, Cynthia. "Looking Through the Eyes of Russell Leong." *International Examiner* 27, no. 16 (September 5, 2000): 13+.

Papinchak, Bob. "Story Collections Draw Portraits of Their Different Worlds." *Seattle Times,* August 20, 2000, M8.

Tian, Jie. "Russell Leong." In Guiyou Huang, ed., *Asian American Short Story Writers: An A-to-Z Guide* (Westport, CT: Greenwood Press, 2003), 159–66.

* * *

Shirley Geok-lin Lim. See Lim in "Poetry."

* * *

Darrell H.Y. Lum (1950–). Chinese Hawaiian short story writer and editor Lum was born in Honolulu. He went to McKinley High School and studied creative writing at the University of Hawai'i at Manoa. After graduation in 1972, he went on to earn an M.A. in Educational Communications and Technology in 1976 and then a Ph.D. in Educational Foundations in 1997, both at Manoa. Lum published his first book of short fiction and drama in 1980, titled *Sun: Short Stories and Drama* (Honolulu: Bamboo Ridge Press); a decade later, he produced a second collection, *Pass on, No Pass Back* (Honolulu: Bamboo Ridge Press, 1990), in addition to pieces published separately in Asian American and Hawaiian anthologies, including Jessica Hagedorn's *Charlie Chan Is Dead.* Lum is also noted for his children's books, including *The Golden Slipper: A Vietnamese Legend* (New York: Troll Associates, 1994), *Hot-Pepper-Kid and Iron-Mouth-Chicken Capture Fire and Wind* (New York: Macmillan/McGraw-Hill, 1997), *The Rice Mystery* (New York: Macmillan/McGraw-Hill, 1998), and *Riding the Bullet* (New York: Macmillan/McGraw-Hill, 1999).

Lum has made contributions in drama as well: his numerous plays have been anthologized in Eric Chock et al., eds., *Talk Story: An Anthology of Hawaii's Local Writers* (Honolulu: Petronium and Talk Story, 1978); in Dennis Kawaharada, ed., *Bamboo Shoots* (Honolulu: Bamboo Ridge Press, 1982); and in Dennis Carroll, ed., *Kumu Kahua Plays* (Honolulu: University of Hawai'i Press, 1983). Lum's perhaps most celebrated role is as a literary editor; he is often associated with Eric Chock, another Hawaiian writer and editor, and with Bamboo Ridge, both the magazine and the press. The anthologies he has coedited include *Talk Story: An Anthology of Hawaii's Local Writers,* with Eric Chock, Dave Robb, Frank Stewart, Gail Miyrasaki, and Kathy Uchida (Honolulu: Petronium and Talk Story, 1978); *The Best of Bamboo Ridge: The Hawai'i Writers' Quarterly,* with Eric Chock (Honolulu: Bamboo Ridge Press, 1986); *Paké: Writings by Chinese in Hawaii,* with Eric Chock (Honolulu: Bamboo Ridge Press, 1989); *Growing up Local: An Anthology of Poetry and Prose from Hawaiʻi*, with Eric Chock, James R. Harstad, and Bill Teter (Honolulu: Bamboo Ridge Press, 1999), *The Best of Honolulu Fiction: Stories from the Honolulu Magazine Fiction Contest*, with Eric Chock (Honolulu: Bamboo Ridge Press, 1999), and *The Quietest Singing*, with Joseph Stanton and Estelle Enoki (Honolulu: Bamboo Ridge Press, 2000). These edited works and Lum's role in the foundation of Bamboo Ridge have significantly contributed to the establishment and development of local literature in Hawaiʻi.

Lum has received numerous literary awards, including the Elliot Cades Award in 1991, the Association for Asian American Studies' Outstanding Book Award in 1992, and the Hawaiʻi Award for Literature in 1996; he also received a National Endowment for the Arts Fellowship in 1989.

Lum's short stories are generally concerned with three large subjects: Hawaiʻi, local, and Hawaiʻi Pidgin English. Hawaiʻi encompasses the land and its people, particularly racial and cultural issues on the island and beyond; "local" refers to the people who grew up in Hawaiʻi, excluding those who are natives; Hawaiʻi Pidgin English, or Creole, is the dialect that many Hawaiian residents and descendants of immigrant plantation laborers speak, and that many local writers, including Lum himself, use in their prose and poetry. Lum's stories in the two collections often deal with daily life on the island, examined in the larger political and social contexts of racial hierarchy and class differences; his characters are usually average and often marginalized members of society, giving him the opportunity to examine inequities of several kinds, not only in Hawaiʻi but also in American society at large.

For more information, see:

Okawa, Gail Y. "Resistance and Reclamation: Hawaii 'Pidgin English' and Autoethnography in the Short Stories of Darrell H.Y. Lum." In Julie Brown, ed., *Ethnicity and the American Short Story* (New York: Garland, 1997), 177–96.

"Response." Interview. In Amy Ling, ed., *Yellow Light: The Flowering of Asian American Arts* (Philadelphia: Temple University Press, 1999), 93–98.

Sato, Gayle K. Fujita. "The Island Influence on Chinese American Writers: Wing Tek Lum, Darrell H.Y. Lum, and Eric Chock." *Amerasia Journal* 16, no. 2 (1990): 17–33.

Speirs, Kenneth J. "Darrell H.Y. Lum." In Guiyou Huang, ed., *Asian American Short Story Writers: An A-to-Z Guide* (Westport, CT: Greenwood Press, 2003), 177–82.

Watanabe, Sylvia. "A Conversation with Darrell Lum and Eric Chock." In Sylvia Watanabe and Carol Bruchac, eds., *Into the Fire: Asian American Prose* (Greenfield Center, NY: Greenfield Review Press, 1996), 85–98.

Shani Mootoo (1958–). Indian Canadian short story writer, novelist, poet, and multimedia artist Mootoo has truly seen the world: born in Ireland to parents of Indian origin and raised in Trinidad, she immigrated to Canada at age nineteen. Mootoo is known in both literary and artistic circles in Canada and the United States: she started her career as a visual artist and has exhibited her photos and videos in North America and at international film festivals. She has engaged in three literary genres: short story, novel, and poetry. Her first book is a collection of short stories, *Out on Main Street and*

Other Stories (Vancouver: Press Gang Publishers, 1993); the second is a novel, *Cereus Blooms at Night* (Vancouver: Press Gang Publishers, 1996); and the third is a collection of poems, *The Predicament of Or* (Vancouver: Press Gang Publishers, 2000). Her novel won the Chapters/Books in Canada First Novel Award and was short-listed for the Giller Prize and the Ethel Wilson Fiction Prize.

The stories in *Out on Main Street and Other Stories* center on issues of identity, in particular the identity of women characters of South Asian descent. Mootoo's personal experiences of child sex abuse and her diasporic experiences as a lesbian of color are woven into her narratives. One of the most intriguing pieces is the title story "Out on Main Street," narrated by an Indo-Trinidadian butch lesbian who recounts the experience of shopping with her partner in an Indian area of Vancouver, where they are met with contempt because of their sexual orientation. Mootoo's novel, *Cereus Blooms at Night*, set in the imaginary city of Paradise and narrated by a male nurse, Tyler, explores the complexity of gendered relationships. Tyler is assigned to care for Mala, the central character, who went mad from years of sexual abuse by her father. In the end Tyler accepts his own sexuality and falls in love with the ambiguously gendered "son" of Mala's first lover, while Mala comes to grips with her life and starts anew. Mootoo's poetry collection, *The Predicament of Or*, deals with the interconnectedness of identity and language and presents pastoral seascapes as well as love stories; there are also poems that examine the place of the individuals in the world.

For more information, see:

Barak, Judith Misrahib. "Beginners' Luck Among Caribbean-Canadian Writers: Nalo Hopkinson, Andre Alexis and Shani Mootoo." *Commonwealth Essays and Studies* 22, no. 1 (Autumn 1999): 89–96.

Chakraborty, Chandrima. "Shani Mootoo." In Guiyou Huang, ed., *Asian American Short Story Writers: An A-to-Z Guide* (Westport, CT: Greenwood Press, 2003), 189–94.

Dhaliwal, Sarinder. "Shani Mootoo: Shifting Perceptions, Changing Practices." *Fuse Magazine* 22, no. 2 (Spring 1999): 18–25.

Ghosh, Dipti. "Baigan Aloo Tabanka Bachanal: Writer, Artist, Filmmaker Shani Mootoo in Her Own Words." *Trikone Magazine* 9, no. 4 (1994): 5–6.

Gillese, T. Virginia. "Isolation as Existence." Rev. of Kristjana Gunnars's *The Guest House and Other Stories* and Shani Mootoo's *Out on Main Street and Other Stories*. *Canadian Literature* 145 (Summer 1995): 131–32.

Saul, Joanne. "Home Free?" Rev. of Shani Mootoo's *Cereus Blooms at Night* and Constance Rooke's *Writing Home: A PEN Canada Anthology*. *Canadian Literature* 164 (Spring 2000): 166–67.

Smyth, Heather. "Sexual Citizenship and Caribbean-Canadian Fiction: Dionne Brand's *In Another Place, Not Here* and Shani Mootoo's *Cereus Blooms at Night*." *A Review of International English Literature* 30, no. 2 (April 1999): 141–60.

* * *

Toshio Mori (1910–1980). *Nisei* Japanese American short story writer and novelist Mori was born in San Leandro, California. He attended public schools and received a high school diploma; the rest of the education that he needed to become a writer he acquired by reading extensively American and world writers, including short story writers Guy de Maupassant, Anton Chekhov, Katherine Mansfield, and Sherwood Anderson, the last of whose influence is apparent in Mori's own short fiction. Mori worked at a plant nursery during the day and wrote at night. By 1941 he had completed his first collection of short stories, *Yokohama, California*, and it was accepted for publication, but the Pacific War involving Japan and the United States and its attendant anti-Japanese sentiment seem to have contributed to a substantial delay in the novel's release.

In the interim, Mori and his family were interned at Topaz Camp in Millard County, Utah, where he stayed for three years, during which time he and several other writers and artists started the camp magazine *Trek*. When he returned to California, *Yokohama, California* was finally published in 1949 (Caldwell, OH: Caxton Printers), only to meet an indifferent audience who seemed to have little interest in a work about Japanese Americans. The collection did not garner real critical attention until 1985, five years after the author's death, when the University of Washington Press released its second edition. Mori's second short story collection, *The Chauvinist and Other Stories*, was published in 1979 (Los Angeles: Asian American Studies Center, UCLA) and his only novel, *Woman from Hiroshima* (San Jose, CA: Isthmus Press), just before his death in 1980. *Unfinished Message: Selected Works of Toshio Mori* (Berkeley, CA: Heydey Books), posthumously published in 2000, includes a short novel called *The Brothers Murata*.

Woman from Hiroshima, Mori's only novel, explores themes that are prevalent in his stories: generational and cultural differences and the fortunes as well as frustrations of assimilation in the Japanese American community. Unfortunately, the book has received scant critical notice and is now out of print. *The Chauvinist and Other Stories* has been met with a similar lack of interest and likewise went out of print. Mori thus remains known primarily as a short story writer, particularly for *Yokohama, California*. All but two stories in the collection are set in his California hometown and were written before his evacuation; the two set in Topaz Camp were written during his incarceration there. The collection is a real Japanese American book, for "Mori chronicles a particular set of people in a particular time and place, Japanese Americans in his hometown of California in the late 1930s and early 1940s" (Barnhart 196). Several pieces—"The Woman Who Makes Swell Donuts," "Seventh Street Philosopher," "Slant-Eyed Americans," and "Toshio Mori"—have become familiar to readers. "The Chauvinist," the title story of *The Chauvinist and Other Stories*, is anthologized in *Charlie Chan Is Dead*, edited by Jessica Hagedorn.

For more information, see:

Barnhart, Sarah Catlin. "Toshio Mori." In Guiyou Huang, ed., *Asian American Short Story Writers: An A-to-Z Guide* (Westport, CT: Greenwood Press, 2003), 195–202.

Bedrosian, Margaret. "Toshio Mori's California Koans." *MELUS* 15, no. 2 (1988): 47–55.

Horikoshi, Peter. "Interview with Toshio Mori." In Emma Gee et al., eds., *Counterpoint: Perspectives on Asian America* (Los Angeles: Asian American Studies Center, 1976), 472–79.

Inada, Lawson Fusao. "Standing on Seventh Street." Introduction to *Yokohama, California*, by Toshio Mori (Seattle: University of Washington Press, 1985), v–xxvii.

——. Introduction to *Unfinished Message: Selected Works by Toshio Mori* (Berkeley, CA: Heydey Books, 2000), 1–10.

Leong, Russell. "Toshio Mori: An Interview." *Amerasia Journal* 7, no. 1 (1980): 89–108.

Mayer, David R. "The Short Stories of Toshio Mori." *Fu Jen Studies: Literature and Linguistics* 21 (1988): 73–87.

———. "Akegarasu and Emerson: Kindred Spirits of Toshio Mori's 'Seventh Street Philosopher.'" *Amerasia Journal* 16, no. 2 (1990): 1–10.

———. "Toshio Mori: Chronicler of Japanese-American Oakland." In *Door Stoops and Window Sills: Perspectives on the American Neighborhood Novel* (Nagoya: Nanzan University, 1992), 55–77.

———. "Toshio Mori and Loneliness." *Nanzan Review of American Studies* 15 (1993): 20–32.

———. "Toshio Mori's Neighborhood Settings: Inner and Outer Oakland." *Fu Jen Studies: Literature and Linguistics* 23 (1993): 100–15.

———. "The Philosopher in Search of a Voice: Toshio Mori's Japanese-Influenced Narrator." *AALA Journal* 2 (1995): 12–24.

Palomino, Harue. "Japanese Americans in Books or in Reality? Three Writers for Young Adults Who Tell a Different Story." In Betty Bacon, ed., *How Much Truth Do We Tell Children? The Politics of Children's Literature* (Minneapolis, MN: Marxist Educational Press, 1988), 125–34.

Palumbo-Liu, David. "Toshio Mori and the Attachments of Spirit: A Response to David R. Mayer." *Amerasia Journal* 17, no. 3 (1991): 41–47.

Saroyan, William. Introduction to *Yokohama, California*, by Toshio Mori (Caldwell, OH: Caxton Printers, 1949), 1–4.

Sato, Gayle K. "(Self) Indulgent Listening: Reading Cultural Difference in *Yokohama, California*." *The Japanese Journal of American Studies* 11 (2000): 129–46.

Yamamoto, Hisaye. Introduction to *The Chauvinist and Other Stories*, by Toshio Mori (Los Angeles: Asian American Studies Center, UCLA, 1979), 1–14.

* * *

Bharati Mukherjee. See Mukherjee in "Fiction."

N

Susan Nunes (1943–). A short story writer and author of children's books, Nunes was born in Hilo, Hawai'i, to parents of Japanese and Portuguese ancestry. She spent her childhood and adolescent years in Hilo and Honolulu. Nunes worked as a writer and editor at the University of Hawai'i until 1991, when she and her family relocated to Berkeley, California. In 1982 she published a short fiction collection, *A Small Obligation and Other Stories of Hilo* (Honolulu: Bamboo Ridge Press); since then she has published numerous other narrative pieces in magazines and anthologies. Nunes is nationally known as a writer of children's books, having published *Coyote Dreams* (New York: Atheneum, 1988), *Tiddalik the Frog* (New York: Atheneum, 1989), *To Find the Way* (Honolulu: University of Hawai'i Press, 1992), and *The Last Dragon* (New York: Clarion Books, 1995). In addition, she has coauthored a couple of scholarly books: *Language Functions*, with Edith Kleinjans (Honolulu: Hawai'i State Department of Education, 1983) and *Pathways*, with Leon Burton (Boston: Addison Wesley Publishing, 1984). The children's book *To Find the Way* won Nunes the 1994 Ka Palapala Po'okela Award.

A Small Obligation and Other Stories reflects personal issues that the writer is familiar with as a child of interracial marriage—cultural and ethnic identity, family relationships, and the individual's search for a home amid displacement. The world that Nunes explores is often hostile and peopled with mixed-race characters, notably of Japanese and Portuguese origins, like Nunes herself. Even though each of the pieces in the collection can stand alone, Nunes has the same protagonist, Amy, throughout the book, occasionally using her as a narrator. In "The Grandmother" Amy experiences the difficulty of being the product of an interracial union, and in "The Yardman" the reader is shown the complexity of Amy's identity as seen through her interactions with her grandparents and Mr. Naito, a loner who lives in their basement.

For more information, see:

D'Amore, Alice. "Susan Nunes." In Guiyou Huang, ed., *Asian American Short Story Writers: An A-to-Z Guide* (Westport, CT: Greenwood Press, 2003), 237–41.

Sato, Gayle K. "Susan Nunes." In Teruyo Veki and Gayle K. Sato, eds., *Reading Japanese American Literature: The Legacy of Three Generations* (Osaka, Japan: Sogensha, 1997), 266–71.

Usui, Masami. "The Global/Local Past Encounters the Local/Global Futures: The Japanese Local Literature in Hawaii." *AALA Journal 6* (2000): 79–92.

P

Gary Pak (1952–). A third-generation Korean Hawaiian short story writer and novelist, Pak was born in Honolulu, and since age three he has lived in the town of Kane'ohe, on the northeastern side of Oahu. Pak was educated at the prestigious private 'Iolani School in Honolulu, then at Boston

University, from which he received a B.A. in social psychology in 1974. But only after his children had been born and he had started to seriously write fiction did Pak resume his education, completing an M.A. in English in 1990 and a Ph.D. in English in 1997, both at the University of Hawai'i at Manoa. His collection of short stories, *The Watcher of Waipuna and Other Stories* (Honolulu: Bamboo Ridge Press, 1992), dating back to his M.A. thesis, "Kanewai," was completed during his doctoral studies. His Ph.D. dissertation, titled "'*E ala mai kakou e na kini na mamo*' ('We, the multitudes of descendants, are waking up'): 19th Century Hawaiian Historiography and the Historical Novel of Hawaii," was completed the same year that he published his novel, *A Ricepaper Airplane* (Honolulu: University of Hawai'i Press, 1997). Pak's story collection won the Association for Asian American Studies National Book Award for Literature in 1993.

The Watcher of Waipuna and Other Stories includes eight stories that reflect the author's involvement in the local community's struggles about urban development of agricultural lands. The bond between the land and the community is a very prominent theme throughout Pak's stories, most notably in pieces such as "The Valley of the Dead Air" and "The Watcher of Waipuna." Pak also gives voice to the socially marginalized in stories like "The Trial of Goro Fukushima" and "A Toast to Rosita." Together the stories present a multicultural and interethnic picture of Hawaiian life and landscape. Pak's novel, *A Ricepaper Plane*, is a heroic story of loss, love, and rebirth that focuses on a sugar plantation in the 1920s. A dying man named Kim Sung Wha, a patriot and revolutionary, dreams of building an airplane from rice paper, bamboo, and the scrap parts of a broken-down bicycle to carry him back to his Korean homeland and his family. Kim's dream, like the material of the plane he wants to build, is fragile and destined to fail, but his visions for the return remain strong and long lasting.

For more information, see:

Bott, Robin L. "Hawaiian-Style Mixed Stew." Rev. of *The Watcher of Waipuna and Other Stories, American Book Review* 16, no. 2 (1994): 18.

Cobb-Keller, Nora. "'Waipuna' a Village World Full of Magic, Dreams." Rev. of *The Watcher of Waipuna and Other Stories. Honolulu Advertiser* September 20, 1992, G6.

Fujikane, Candace. "Between Nationalisms: Hawaii's Local Nation and Its Troubled Racial Paradise." *Hitting Critical Mass: A Journal of Asian American Cultural Criticism* 1, no. 2 (1994): 23–57.

Gima, Charlene. "Writing the Pacific: Imagining Communities of Difference in the Fiction of Jessica Hagedorn, Keri Hulme, Rodney Morales, and Gary Pak." Ph.D. diss., Cornell University, 1997.

Kwon, Brenda Lee. "Gary Pak." Interview. In King-Kok Cheung, ed., *Words Matter: Conversations with Asian American Writers* (Honolulu: University of Hawai'i Press, 2000), 303–19.

McPherson, Michael. Rev. of *The Watcher of Waipuna and Other Stories*, by Gary Pak. *Manoa: A Pacific Journal of International Writing* 6, no. 1 (1994): 181–83.

Muromoto, Wayne. "Gary Pak and *The Watcher of Waipuna and Other Stories*: Recording an Oral Tradition." Rev. of *The Watcher of Waipuna and Other Stories. Hawaii Herald,* May 21, 1993, A10–11.

Oishi, Michael. "Gary Pak." In Guiyou Huang, ed., *Asian American Short Story Writers: An A-to-Z Guide* (Westport, CT: Greenwood Press, 2003), 243–49.

Takami, David. "Spinning a World of Colliding Cultures, Places." Rev. of *The Watcher of Waipuna and Other Stories. International Examiner Literary Supplement,* April 7, 1993, 6.

Young, Morris. Rev. of *The Watcher of Waipuna and Other Stories. Amerasia Journal* 20, no. 3 (1994): 108–10.

* * *

Ty Pak (1938–). A Korean American short story writer, Pak was born in Korea and lived there until 1965. His twenty-seven years in his home country spanned World War II, during which the Koreans fought the Japanese and freed themselves in 1945, and the Korean War in the early 1950s, which involved the two Koreas, the United States, and China, and in which his father was killed. Pak graduated from Seoul National University with a law degree in 1960 and moved to the United States in 1965. He earned a Ph.D. in English from Bowling Green State University in 1969. Pak's first book-length publication was a collection of short stories titled *Guilt Payment* (Honolulu: Bamboo Ridge Press, 1983); a second collection, *Moonbay,* came out in 1999 (New York: Woodhouse); the same year saw the publication of his novel *Cry Korea Cry* (New York: Woodhouse, 1999). Pak is primarily considered a short story writer.

Pak lived and taught in Hawai'i for seventeen years, from 1970 to 1987, and since then the islands have provided the setting for a number of his stories. While Pak writes immigration stories, his narratives focus more on Korean American characters who have made it in their immigrant society than on those who experience hardships and difficulties of all kinds. However, like other immigrant writers, Pak engages the past by utilizing memory and history. *Guilt Payment,* consisting of thirteen stories, mostly depicts the lives of Koreans in Hawai'i and how their traumatic past in their home country affects and shapes their life in the new world. Stories like "Guilt Payment," "Possession Sickness," and "Steady Hands," among other pieces, feature male protagonists whose current life is haunted by what happened or what they did during the wars and who must cope with reconciling the past and the present.

Stories in *Moonbay*, while continuing some of the themes explored in the previous book, introduce new settings and topics. The settings are less Hawaiian; in fact, they are quite international: Korea, Vietnam, the Soviet Union, and the United States are all involved in narratives that deal with wars, history, and contemporary events, such as the Los Angeles riots. The title story, "Moonbay," is about a boat captain who is murdered because of his mistaken identity. The navigator Daro Jo and the interim captain Moonbay Sin are look-alikes; the former joins a mutiny in which Moonbay is killed. Daro Jo is jailed in El Salvador but is rescued because he is taken for the interim captain. *Cry Korea Cry*, Pak's only novel to date, narrates the story of an interracial Korean War orphan who names himself Moo Moo (which literally means "Nothing Nothing") and whose personal life is inseparably linked to modern Korean history: the Japanese occupation, the Korean War, the division of the north and the south, and the devastating effects of these traumatic events on Koreans and Korean Americans.

For more information, see:

Cheung, King-Kok. "Fictional Representation of the Los Angeles Riots: 'The Court Interpreter' by Ty Pak." *Journal of American Studies* (Seoul) 33, no. 2 (Winter 2001): 183–200.

Harstad, James. Introduction to *Guilt Payment*, by Ty Pak (Honolulu: University of Hawai'i Press, 1983), 1–3.

Kim, Elaine. "Korean American Literature." In King-Kok Cheung, ed., *An Interethnic Companion to Asian American Literature* (New York: Cambridge University Press, 1997), 156–91.

Kwon, Brenda Lee. "Beyond Keeamoku: Koreans, Nationalism, and Local Culture in Hawai'i." Ph.D. diss., UCLA, 1997.

Oh, Seiwoong. "Ty Pak." In Guiyou Huang, ed., *Asian American Short Story Writers: An A-to-Z Guide* (Westport, CT: Greenwood Press, 2003), 251–55.

Ninotchka Rosca. See Rosca in "Fiction."

Patsy Sumie Saiki (1915–). *Nisei* Japanese Hawaiian short story writer Saiki was born on the island of Hawai'i. She started McKinley High School on Oahu in 1931 and earned a bachelor's degree in education from the University of Hawai'i in 1954 and a master's degree in 1959. In her sophomore year she received a Charles Eugene Banks award for her short story writing. A *Wall Street Journal* Fellowship sent her to study at the University of Wisconsin for a brief period; she completed her doctoral degree in curriculum design at Teachers' College of Columbia University in 1967. While working as an educator and administrator, Saiki continued writing, and in 1977 she published her first book of stories, *Sachie, A Daughter of Hawai'i* (Honolulu: Kisaku), followed by *Ganbare!*

An Example of Japanese Spirit (Honolulu: Kisaku) in 1981, *Japanese Women in Hawaii: The First 100 Years* (Honolulu: Kisaku) in 1985, and finally, *Early Japanese Immigrants in Hawaii* (Honolulu: Japanese Cultural Center of Hawai'i) in 1993. Except for *Sachie,* which has been considered both as a novel and as a collection of short stories, all the books are short story collections. In addition to two *Wall Street Journal* fellowships, Saiki has been recognized with the Japanese Imperial Order of the Precious Crown in 1996.

Saiki's parents were Japanese immigrants from Hiroshima and worked in Hawaii's sugar plantations, an experience that she wrote about extensively. *Sachie* deals with the subject matter of survival amid problems arising from cultural and racial issues. The title character, Sachie Himeno, thirteen years of age, is also the narrator who tries to make sense of the often violent life on the plantation and who copes with generational conflicts with her own parents. Racial, cultural, and generational issues are played out against the large backdrop of Hawaiian society, where cultural elements from Japan, the mainland United States, and Hawai'i compete, mix, and shape one another. *Japanese Women in Hawaii* focuses on individual experiences of early immigrant women from Japan in the first hundred years, as the subtitle indicates. *Early Japanese Immigrants in Hawai'i,* set in the same locale, narrates the angst, among other challenges, of immigration to a new land, and celebrates the triumph of human courage.

Studies of Saiki's work are sparse, but several critical sources are useful. See:

Enomoto, Catherine Kekoa. "Author Continues Circle of Compassion, Creativity." *Star Bulletin,* September 26, 1997, C6.

Lee, Amy W.S. "Patsy Sumie Saiki." In Guiyou Huang, ed., *Asian American Short Story Writers: An A-to-Z Guide* (Westport, CT: Greenwood Press, 2003), 268–72.

Luangphinith, Seri. "Patsy Sumie Saiki." In Emmanuel S. Nelson, ed., *Asian American Novelists: A Bio-Bibliographical Critical Sourcebook* (Westport, CT: Greenwood Press, 2000), 313–16.

Sumida, Stephen H. "Sense of Place, History, and the Concept of the 'Local' in Hawaii's Asian/Pacific Literatures." In Shirley Geok-lin Lim and Amy Ling, eds., *Reading the Literatures of Asian America* (Philadelphia: Temple University Press, 1992), 215–37.

* * *

Bienvenido N. Santos. See Santos in "Fiction."

Kathleen Tyau (1947–). Born in California to a Chinese mother and a part-Hawaiian father, Tyau was raised in Waikiki and Pearl City, Oahu; she returned to the mainland to attend Lewis and Clark College in Oregon and has made her home there since. She has published two books of short fiction: *A Little Too Much Is Enough* (New York: Farrar, Straus & Giroux, 1995) and *Makai* (New York: Farrar, Straus & Giroux, 1999). Tyau was awarded the 1996 Best Book of the Year by the Pacific Northwest Booksellers Association for her first book. *A Little Too Much Is Enough* was a finalist for the Oregon Book Award in fiction and a finalist for the Barnes and Noble Best New Writers Award. *Makai* made the final list for the 2000 Oregon Book Award.

A Little Too Much Is Enough was marketed as a novel, though a number of its forty chapters were previously published as independent stories, and the majority of the other chapters are self-contained episodes that can be read as short narratives. Though the book is not exactly autobiographical, the woman protagonist, Mahealani Suzanne Wong, left Hawai'i to go to college on the mainland, not unlike Tyau. Like Sandra Cisneros's *House on Mango Street*, Tyau's work narrates working-class women's experience through the perspectives of young girls (in Cisneros's book of vignettes, Esperanza's big dream is to leave Mango Street and her poverty-stricken homeland to search for more prosperous economic opportunities and an improved personal life). The narrator in *Makai*, Alice Lum, is an aging mother, and unlike Mahi Wong in the previous book who left home, she stayed because of family needs. Both books focus on women's experiences in public and in private, and are therefore examinations of the social meanings of women's positions.

The majority of studies of Tyau's work are reviews of her two books. See:

Cline, David. "A Wartime Friendship Hits the Rocks on the Maui Coast." Rev. of *Makai*. *San Francisco Chronicle*, June 27, 1999, 8.

D'Erasmo, Stacey. "Wild Palms." Rev. of *A Little Too Much Is Enough*. *Village Voice* (July 25, 1995): 86.

Gray, Julie. Rev. of *Makai*. *New York Times Book Review*, August 29, 1999, 21.

Heller, Amanda. "Short Takes." Rev. of *A Little Too Much Is Enough*. *Booklist* 91 (July 1995): 1861–62.

Lu, Lynn. Rev. of *Makai*. *Ms.* 9, no. 4 (June–July 1999): 88.

Pennybacker, Mindy. "Decolonizing the Mind." Rev. of *Makai*. *The Nation* 269, no. 10 (October 1999): 31–35.

Ross, Patricia. Rev. of *A Little Too Much Is Enough*. *Library Journal* 120 (June 1995): 168.

Sato, Gayle K. "Kathleen Tyau." In Guiyou Huang, ed., *Asian American Short Story Writers: An A-to-Z Guide* (Westport, CT: Greenwood Press, 2003), 281–85.

See, Carolyn. "Heaven in Small Bites." Rev. of *A Little Too Much Is Enough*. *Washington Post*, July 28, 1995, B-2.

Stead, Deborah. "Books in Brief: Fiction." Rev. of *A Little Too Much Is Enough*. *New York Times Book Review*, October 15, 1995, 20.

Tswei, Suzanne. "All Roads Lead to Makai." Rev. of *Makai*. *Honolulu Star-Bulletin*, July 9, 1999, B-1.

* * *

Linda Ty-Casper. See Ty-Casper in "Fiction."

Sylvia Watanabe (1953–). Japanese Hawaiian short story writer Watanabe was born in Wailuku, Maui, and grew up in Kailua, Oahu. She earned a B.A. in art history from the University of Hawai'i in 1980 and an M.A. in English and creative writing from the State University of New York at Binghamton in 1985. Between finishing graduate studies and landing a permanent teaching position at Oberlin College, Ohio, in 1995, Watanabe wrote short stories and other prose works, publishing a collection titled *Talking to the Dead: Stories* in 1992 (New York: Doubleday). Watanabe has also edited two favorably received literary anthologies: *Home to Stay: Asian American Women's Fiction*, with Carol Bruchac (Greenfield Center, NY:

Greenfield Review Press, 1990), and *Into the Fire: Asian American Prose* (Greenfield Center, NY: Greenfield Review Press, 1996). Her story collection was chosen as one of *People Magazine*'s Ten Best Books in 1992; won the Josephine Miles Award from the Oakland Chapter of PEN in 1993; and was a finalist for the 1992–1993 PEN/Faulkner Award for Fiction. In addition, some of her individual stories have been recognized with honors such as the O. Henry Award, the Japanese American Citizens League National Literary Award, and the Pushcart Prize.

Hawai'i as Watanabe's birthplace provides not only the inspiration but also the setting for many of her stories; some are based upon her father's memories of Maui, where he grew up and where Watanabe was born. The geography of Hawai'i gives meaning to the plots and themes of her stories about the Japanese American community, notably first- and second-generation Japanese American women in Luhi, the coastal Hawaiian town that Watanabe invented for the setting of her fiction. The stories span about three decades, from the end of World War II to the 1970s, when Hawai'i underwent major economic and societal changes. These changes are reflected in the lives of women characters in terms of their career choices, dilemmas and difficulties, and relationship to each other and to the land. The title story, "Talking to the Dead," presents the challenges modernization poses to the traditional way of life in the character of Aunty Talking to the Dead, who must find a successor to continue her role as a practitioner of the old ways.

The majority of studies of Watanabe's work are reviews of *Talking to the Dead*. See:

Choo, Donna J. Rev. of *Talking to the Dead. Manoa: A Pacific Journal of International Writing* 5, no. 1 (Summer 1993): 248–50.

Cobb-Keller, Nora. "Maui-Born Writer Stitches a Quilt of the Islands." Rev. of *Talking to the Dead. Honolulu Star-Bulletin*, November 17, 1992, D-1+.

Harris, Michael. "In Brief: Fiction." Rev. of *Talking to the Dead. Los Angeles Times*, August 9, 1992, 6.

Johnson, Greg. Rev. of *Talking to the Dead. New York Times Book Review*, September 27, 1992, 18.

Lawrence, Keith. "Watanabe, Sylvia." In Abby H.P. Werlock, ed., *The Facts on File Companion to the American Short Story* (New York: Checkmark Books, 2000), 437.

Rochman, Hazel. "The Asian American Experience: Fiction." Rev. of *Talking to the Dead. Booklist* 89 (December 1992): 660–61.

Sato, Gayle K. "Sylvia A. Watanabe." In Guiyou Huang, ed., *Asian American Short Story Writers: An A-to-Z Guide* (Westport, CT: Greenwood Press, 2003), 295–301.

Zhou Xiaojing. "Sylvia A. Watanabe." In Blanche H. Gelfant and Lawrence Graver, eds., *Columbia Companion to the Twentieth-Century American Short Story* (New York: Columbia University Press, 2001), 556–60.

Hisaye Yamamoto (1921–). One of the most celebrated and sophisticated Japanese American short story writers, Yamamoto was born in Redondo Beach, California, to *issei* parents from Kumamoto, Japan. Yamamoto started writing in her early teens. She completed her high school education at Excelsior Union High, then enrolled at Compton Junior College and studied foreign languages. In 1953 Yamamoto was invited to study at Stanford University, but she declined the opportunity and instead went to work at Peter Maurin Farm, a Catholic Worker rehabilitation camp on Staten Island, New York. But the most influential time period in her life and on her fictional imagination is the Japanese American internment during World War II. In 1941, at age twenty, Yamamoto was evacuated, along with thousands of other Japanese Americans, to the Poston Relocation Center in Arizona, where she remained until 1945. Then she returned to California and worked as a reporter and journalist for the African American newspaper *Los Angeles Tribune* until 1948.

Yamamoto's camp experience and newspaper work provide much of the raw material for the stories that she started to publish in 1948, in magazines such as *Partisan Review*, *Kenyon Review*, and *Harper's Bazaar*, among numerous other periodicals. Her first collection of short fiction, *Seventeen Syllables: 5 Stories of Japanese American Life*, was edited by Robert Rolf and Norimitsu Ayuzawa and published in Japan (Tokyo: Kirihara Shoten) in 1985. A larger, U.S. collection, called *Seventeen Syllables and Other Stories*, came out three years later (Latham, NY: Kitchen Table/Women of Color Press, 1988). A critical edition, titled *Seventeen Syllables: Hisaye Yamamoto*, edited by King-Kok Cheung for the Women Writers: Texts and Contexts Series, appeared in 1994 (New Brunswick, NJ: Rutgers University Press). Yamamoto's work was recognized with the American Book Award for Lifetime Achievement from the Before Columbus Foundation in 1986.

Yamamoto may well be the most discussed Asian American short story writer of the twentieth century; she certainly wrote some of the finest and most famous short narratives about Japanese American farm life before World War II and pieces about the Japanese American internment experience during the war. While a number of her stories are concerned with interethnic and interracial relationships, her most enduring and fascinating pieces are those that deal with Japanese American women's (and young girls') life experiences on the farm and in the concentration camp, with men's experience (often that of patriarchal fathers) usually as a secondary or subordinate theme. There is little doubt that Yamamoto's most anthologized, read, taught, and critiqued stories are "Seventeen Syllables," "Yoneko's Earthquake," and "The Legend of Miss Sasagawara," though pieces like "Las Vegas Charley," "A Fire in Fontana," and "The Brown House" have also gained considerable attention.

The title story of all three somewhat different collections, "Seventeen Syllables" explores the domestic and farm life of a Japanese American couple as seen through the eyes of their teenage daughter, Rosie. The wife expresses her artistic talents by writing haiku and wins recognition with a prize (a painting) from a local Japanese American newspaper, while her husband, a traditional-minded farmer, attempts to assert his domestic authority and control his wife's breaking out of her traditional role as a mother and wife. "Yoneko's Earthquake" is also narrated through the half-comprehending and observing eyes of a *nisei* daughter, and it also examines the limitations and challenges of the traditional role assigned to the Japanese woman. The main character is thrust into the position of the main laborer in the fields because her husband was injured in an earthquake that caused him to lose his sexual potency. This affords their Filipino farmhand an opportunity to develop an affair with his female employer. The story raises questions about patriarchal authority represented by the husband, whose functions—both inside and outside the home—are being taken up by his wife. Another haunting story is "The Legend of Miss Sasagawara." Set in a Japanese

American concentration camp during World War II, a religiously devoted father and a neglected daughter are both interned, but the eponymous daughter suffers doubly from her father's neglect and the community's refusal to accept her, despite her artistic abilities, because of her strange behaviors.

Studies of Yamamoto's short fiction are legion. The following is a selected listing:

Cheng, Ming L. "The Unrepentant Fire: Tragic Limitations in Hisaye Yamamoto's 'Seventeen Syllables.'" *MELUS* 19, no. 4 (Winter 1994): 91–107.

Cheung, King-Kok. "Double-Telling: Intertextual Silence in Hisaye Yamamoto's Fiction." *American Literary History* 3, no. 2 (Summer 1991): 277–93.

———. "Thrice Muted Tale: Interplay of Art and Politics in Hisaye Yamamoto's 'The Legend of Miss Sasagawara.'" *MELUS* 17, no. 3 (Fall 1991–92): 109–25.

———. *Articulate Silences: Hisaye Yamamoto, Maxine Hong Kingston, Joy Kogawa.* Ithaca, NY: Cornell University Press, 1993.

———. "Interview with Hisaye Yamamoto." In Cheung, ed., *Seventeen Syllables: Hisaye Yamamoto* (New Brunswick, NJ: Rutgers University Press, 1994), 3–16.

———. "The Dream in Flames: Hisaye Yamamoto, Multiculturalism, and the Los Angeles Uprising." *Bucknell Review* 39, no. 1 (1995): 118–30.

———. "Reading Between the Syllables: Hisaye Yamamoto's *Seventeen Syllables and Other Stories.*" In John R. Maitino and David R. Peck, eds., *Teaching American Ethnic Literatures: Nineteen Essays* (Albuquerque, NM: University of New Mexico Press, 1996), 313–25.

Crow, Charles L. "A *MELUS* Interview: Hisaye Yamamoto." *MELUS* 14, no. 1 (1987): 73–84.

Goellnicht, Donald C. "Transplanted Discourse in Yamamoto's 'Seventeen Syllables.'" In Cheung, ed., *Seventeen Syllables: Hisaye Yamamoto*, 181–94.

Hong, Grace K. "'Something Forgotten Which Should Have Been Remembered': Private Property and Cross-Racial Solidarity in the Work of Hisaye Yamamoto." *American Literature* 71, no. 2 (June 1999): 291–310.

Huang, Guiyou. "The Asian American Short Story—The Cases of Sui Sin Far, Yamamoto, and Peñaranda." In Huang, ed., *Asian American Short Story Writers: An A-to-Z Guide* (Westport, CT: Greenwood Press, 2003), xiii–xxxii.

McDonald, Dorothy R. and Katherine Newman. "Relocation and Dislocation: The Writings of Hisaye Yamamoto and Wakako Yamauchi." *MELUS* 7, no. 3 (1980): 21–38.

Mullins, Maire. "Esther's Smile: Silence and Action in Hisaye Yamamoto's 'Wilshire Bus.'" *Studies in Short Fiction* 35, no. 1 (Winter 1998): 77–84.

Oh, Seiwoong. "Hisaye Yamamoto (DeSoto)." In Guiyou Huang, ed., *Asian American Short Story Writers: An A-to-Z Guide* (Westport, CT: Greenwood Press, 2003), 303–15.

Payne, Robert M. "Adapting (to) the Margins: Hot Summer Winds and the Stories of Hisaye Yamamoto." *East West Film Journal* 7, no. 2 (July 1993): 39–53.

Sugiyama, Naoko. "Issei Mothers' Silence, Nisei Daughters' Stories: The Short Fiction of Hisaye Yamamoto." *Comparative Literature Studies* 33, no. 1 (1996): 1–14.

Usui, Masami. "Prison, Psyche, and Poetry in Hisaye Yamamoto's Three Short Stories: 'Seventeen Syllables,' 'The Legend of Miss Sasagawara,' and 'The Eskimo Connection'." *Studies in Culture and the Humanities* 6 (1997): 1–29.

Yogi, Stan. "Legacies Revealed: Uncovering Buried Plots in the Stories of Hisaye Yamamoto." *Studies in American Fiction* 17, no. 2 (1989): 169–81.

——. "Rebels and Heroines: Subversive Narratives in the Stories of Wakako Yamauchi and Hisaye Yamamoto." In Shirley Geok-lin Lim and Amy Ling, eds., *Reading the Literatures of Asian America* (Philadelphia: Temple University Press, 1992), 131–50.

Part III

Literary Criticism
A Selected Bibliography

Ammons, Elizabeth. *Conflicting Stories: American Women Writers at the Turn Into the Twentieth Century*. New York: Oxford University Press, 1991.

Ammons, Elizabeth and Annette White-Parks, eds. *Tricksterism in Turn-of-the-Century American Literature: A Multicultural Perspective*. Hanover, NH: University Press of New England, 1994.

Bahri, Deepika and Mary Vasudeva, eds. *Between the Lines: South Asians and Postcoloniality*. Philadelphia: Temple University Press, 1996.

Baker Jr., Houston A., ed. *Three American Literatures: Essays in Chicano, Native American, and Asian-American Literature for Teachers of American Literature*. New York: MLA, 1982.

Bloom, Harold, ed. *Asian American Women Writers*. Philadelphia: Chelsea House, 1997.

Brogan, Jacqueline Vaught and Cordelia Chávez Candelaria, eds. *Women Poets of the Americas: Toward a Pan-American Gathering*. Notre Dame: University of Notre Dame Press, 1999.

Brown, Julie, ed. *Ethnicity and the American Short Story*. New York: Garland Press, 1997.

Bryer, Jackson R., ed. *The Playwright's Art: Conversations with Contemporary American Dramatists*. New Brunswick, NJ: Rutgers University Press, 1995.

Cao, Lan and Himilce Novas. *Everything You Need to Know About Asian-American History*. New York: Plume/Penguin, 1996.

Chan, Mimi. *Through Western Eyes: Images of Chinese Women in Anglo-American Literature*. Hong Kong: Joint Publishing Company, 1989.

Chan, Mimi and Roy Harris, eds. *Asian Voices in English*. Hong Kong: Hong Kong University Press, 1991.

Cheung, King-Kok. *Articulate Silences: Hisaye Yamamoto, Maxine Hong Kingston, Joy Kogawa*. Ithaca, NY: Cornell University Press, 1993.

Cheung, King-Kok, ed. *An Interethnic Companion to Asian American Literature*. New York: Cambridge University Press, 1997.

——. *Words Matter: Conversations with Asian American Writers*. Honolulu: University of Hawai'i Press, 2000.

Cheung, King-Kok and Stan Yogi, eds. *Asian American Literature: An Annotated Bibliography*. New York: MLA, 1988.

Cho, Song. *Rice: Explorations Into Gay Asian Culture and Politics*. Toronto: Queer Press, 1997.

Culley, Margo, ed. *American Women's Autobiography: Fea(s)ts of Memory*. Madison: University of Wisconsin Press, 1992.

Davis, Rocío G. *Transcultural Reinventions: Asian American and Asian Canadian Short Story Cycles*. Toronto: TSAR, 2001.

Davis, Rocío G. and Sämi Ludwig, eds. *Asian American Literature in the International Context: Readings on Fiction, Poetry, and Performance*. Hamburg: LIT Verlag, 2002.

DiGaetani, John L. *A Search for a Postmodern Theater: Interviews with Contemporary Playwrights*. Westport, CT: Greenwood Press, 1991.

Eakin, Paul John, ed. *American Autobiography: Retrospect and Prospect*. Madison: University of Wisconsin Press, 1991.

——. *Fictions in Autobiography: Studies in the Art of Self-Invention*. Princeton: Princeton University Press, 1985.

——. *How Our Lives Become Stories*. Ithaca, NY: Cornell University Press, 1999.

Eng, David L. and Alice Y. Horn, eds. *Q & A: Queer in Asian America*. Philadelphia: Temple University Press, 1998.

Foner, Philip and Daniel Rosenberg, eds. *Racism, Dissent, and Asian Americans from 1850 to the Present*. Westport, CT: Greenwood Press, 1993.

Gee, Emma, ed. *Counterpoint: Perspectives on Asian America*. Los Angeles: UCLA Asian American Studies Center, 1976.

Ghymn, Esther Mikyung. *Images of Asian American Women by Asian American Women Writers*. New York: Peter Lang, 1995.

——. *Asian American Studies: Identity, Images, and Issues—Past and Present*. New York: Peter Lang, 2000.

Gilmore, Leigh. *Autobiographics: A Feminist Theory of Women's Self-Representation*. Ithaca, NY: Cornell University Press, 1994.

Gregson, Ian. *Contemporary Poetry and Postmodernism: Dialogue and Estrangement*. New York: St. Martin's Press, 1996.

Grewal, Inderpal and Caren Kaplan, eds. *Scattered Hegemonies: Postmodernity and Transnational Feminist Practices*. Minneapolis: University of Minnesota Press, 1994.

Hart, Lynda, ed. *Making a Spectacle: Feminist Essays on Contemporary Women's Theatre*. Ann Arbor: University of Michigan Press, 1989.

Henke, Suzette. *Shattered Subjects: Trauma and Testimony in Women's Life-Writing*. New York: St. Martin's Press, 1998.

Hidalgo, Christina Pantoja. *Filipino Women Writing: Home and Exile in the Autobiographical Narratives of Ten Writers*. Manila, Philippines: Ateno de Manila University Press, 1994.

Hirabayashi, Lane Ryo, ed. *Teaching Asian America: Diversity and the Problem of Community*. Lanham, MD: Rowman, 1998.

Hsu, Ruth, Cynthia Franklin and Suzanne Kosanke, eds. *Re-placing America: Conversations and Contestations: Selected Essays*. Honolulu: University of Hawai'i and the East-West Center, 2000.

Huang, Guiyou, ed., *Asian American Autobiographers: A Bio-Bibliographical Critical Sourcebook*. Westport, CT: Greenwood Press, 2001.

——. *Asian American Poets: A Bio-Bibliographical Critical Sourcebook*. Westport, CT: Greenwood Press, 2002.

——. *Asian American Short Story Writers: An A-to-Z Guide*. Westport, CT: Greenwood Press, 2003.

——. *Asian American Literary Studies*. Edinburgh, Scotland: Edinburgh University Press, 2005.

Hune, Shirley, Hyung-chan Kim, Stephen S. Fugita, and Amy Ling, eds. *Asian Americans: Comparative and Global Perspectives*. Pullman: Washington State University Press, 1991.

Kafka, Phillipa. *(Un)doing the Missionary Position: Gender Asymmetry in Asian American Women's Writing*. Westport, CT: Greenwood Press, 1997.

Kaim, Geoffrey, ed. *Ideas of Home: Literature of Asian Migration.* East Lansing: Michigan State University Press, 1997.

Kamboureli, Smaro, ed. *Making a Difference: Canadian Multicultural Literature.* Toronto: Oxford University Press, 1996.

Kim, Elaine H. *Asian American Literature: An Introduction to the Writings and Their Social Context.* Philadelphia: Temple University Press, 1982.

Knippling, Alpana Sharma, ed. *New Immigrant Literatures in the United States: A Sourcebook to Our Multicultural Literary Heritage.* Westport, CT: Greenwood Press, 1996.

Kolin, Philip C. and Colby H. Kullman, eds. *Speaking on Stage: Interviews with Contemporary American Playwrights.* Tuscaloosa: University of Alabama Press, 1996.

Kondo, Dorinne. *About Face: Performing Race in Fashion and Theater.* New York: Routledge, 1997.

Kurahashi, Yuko. *Asian American Culture on Stage: The History of the East West Players.* New York: Garland Press, 1999.

Lai, Him Mark, Ruthanne Lum McCunn, and Judy Yung, eds. *Chinese America: History and Perspectives.* San Francisco: Chinese Historical Society of America, 1987.

Lee, Jid. *From the Promised Land to Home: Trajectories of Selfhood in Asian-American Women's Autobiography.* Las Colinas, TX: Ide House, 1998.

Lee, Joanne Faung Jean. *Asian American Actors: Oral Histories from Stage, Screen, and Television.* Jefferson, NC: McFarland, 2000.

Lee, Josephine. *Performing Asian America: Race and Ethnicity on the Contemporary Stage.* Philadelphia: Temple University Press, 1997.

Lee, Rachel C. *The Americas of Asian American Literature: Gendered Fictions of Nation and Transnation.* Princeton: Princeton University Press, 1999.

Leonard, George J., ed. *The Asian Pacific American Heritage: A Companion to Literature and Arts.* New York: Garland Press, 1999.

Li, David Leiwei. *Imagining the Nation: Asian American Literature and Cultural Consent.* Stanford: Stanford University Press, 1998.

Lim, Shirley Geok-lin and Amy Ling, eds. *Reading the Literatures of Asian America.* Philadelphia: Temple University Press, 1992.

Lim, Shirley Geok-lin, Larry E. Smith, and Wimal Dissanayake, eds. *Transnational Asia Pacific: Gender, Culture, and the Public Sphere.* Urbana: University of Illinois Press, 1999.

Ling, Amy. *Between Worlds: Women Writers of Chinese Ancestry.* New York: Pergamon Press, 1990.

Ling, Amy, ed. *Yellow Light: The Flowering of Asian American Arts.* Philadelphia: Temple University Press, 1999.

Ling, Jinqi. *Narrating Nationalism: Ideology and Form in Asian American Literature.* New York: Oxford University Press, 1998.

Liu, Miles Xian, ed. *Asian American Playwrights: A Bio-Bibliographical Critical Sourcebook.* Westport, CT: Greenwood Press, 2002.

Lowe, Lisa. *Immigrant Acts: Asian American Cultural Politics.* Durham: Duke University Press, 1996.

Ma, Sheng-mei. *Immigrant Subjectivities in Asian American and Asian Diaspora Literatures.* Albany: State University of New York Press, 1998.

Maitino, John R. and David R. Peck, eds. *Teaching American Ethnic Literatures: Nineteen Essays.* Albuquerque: University of New Mexico Press, 1996.

Maufort, Marc, ed. *Staging Difference: Cultural Pluralism in American Theatre and Drama.* New York: Peter Lang, 1995.

Morgan, Janice, Colette T. Hall, and Carol L. Snyder, eds. *Redefining Autobiography in Twentieth-Century Women's Fiction.* New York: Garland Press, 1991.

Moy, James S. *Marginal Sights: Staging the Chinese in America.* Iowa City: University of Iowa Press, 1993.

Moyers, Bill D. *The Language of Life: A Festival of Poets.* New York: Doubleday, 1995.

Mukherjee, Arun. *Towards an Aesthetic of Opposition: Essays on Literature Criticism and Cultural Imperialism.* Stratford, Ontario: Williams-Wallace, 1988.

Nelson, Emmanuel S., ed. *Reworlding: The Literature of the Indian Diaspora.* Westport, CT: Greenwood Press, 1992.

———. *Writers of the Indian Diaspora: A Bio-Bibliographical Critical Sourcebook.* Westport, CT: Greenwood Press, 1993.

———. *Asian American Novelists: A Bio-Bibliographical Critical Sourcebook.* Westport, CT: Greenwood Press, 2000.

———. *The Greenwood Encyclopedia of Multiethnic American Literature.* Westport, CT: Greenwood Press, 2005.

Neuman, Shirley C., ed. *Autobiography and Questions of Gender.* Portland, OR: Frank Cass, 1991.

Nomura, Gail, Russell Endo, Stephen H. Sumida, and Russell C. Leong, eds. *Frontiers of Asian American Studies.* Pullman: Washington State University Press, 1989.

Okihiro, Gary. *The Columbia Guide to Asian American History.* New York: Columbia University Press, 2001.

Olney, James. *Metaphor of Self: The Meaning of Autobiography.* Princeton: Princeton University Press, 1972.

Olney, James, ed. *Autobiography: Essays Theoretical and Critical.* Princeton: Princeton University Press, 1980.

———. *Studies in Autobiography.* New York: Oxford University Press, 1988.

———. *Memory and Narrative: The Weave of Life-Writing.* Chicago: University of Chicago Press, 1998.

Palumbo-Liu, David. *Asian/American: Historical Crossings of a Racial Frontier.* Stanford: Stanford University Press, 1999.

Palumbo-Liu, David, ed. *The Ethnic Canon: Histories, Institutions, and Interventions.* Minneapolis: University of Minnesota Press, 1995.

———. *Streams of Cultural Capital: Transnational Cultural Studies (Mestizo Spaces).* Stanford: Stanford University Press, 1998.

Partnow, Elaine T. and Lesley Anne Hyatt. *The Female Dramatist: Profiles of Women Playwrights from the Middle Ages to Contemporary Times.* New York: Facts on File, 1998.

Payne, James Robert, ed. *Multicultural Autobiography: American Lives.* Knoxville: University of Tennessee Press, 1992.

Peterson, Jane T. and Suzanne Bennett, eds. *Women Playwrights of Diversity.* Westport, CT: Greenwood Press, 1997.

Revilla, Linda A., Gail M. Nomura, Shawn Wong, and Shirley Hune, eds. *Bearing Dreams, Shaping Visions: Asian Pacific American Perspectives.* Pullman: Washington State University Press, 1993.

Roberson, Susan L., ed. *Women, America, and Movement: Narratives of Relocation.* Columbia: University of Missouri Press, 1998.

Ruoff, A. LaVonne Brown and Jerry W. Ward Jr., eds. *Redefining American Literature.* New York: MLA, 1990.

Said, Edward W. *Orientalism.* New York: Vintage, 1979.

Savran, David. *In Their Own Words: Contemporary American Playwrights.* New York City: Theatre Communications Group, 1988.

Simpson, Megan. *Poetic Epistemologies: Gender and Knowing in Women's Language-Oriented Writing.* Albany: State University of New York Press, 2000.

Singh, Amritjit, Joseph T. Skerrett Jr., and Robert E. Hogan, eds. *Memory and Cultural Politics: New Approaches to American Ethnic Literatures.* Boston: Northeastern University Press, 1996.

Smith, Sidonie. *A Poetics of Women's Autobiography: Marginality and the Fictions of Self-Representation.* Bloomington: Indiana University Press, 1987.

Sumida, Stephen H. *Literary Tradition of Hawai'i.* Seattle: University of Washington Press, 1991.

Tabios, Eileen. *Black Lightning: Poetry-in-Progress.* New York: Asian American Writers' Workshop, 1998.

Trinh, Minh-ha. *Woman, Native, Other.* Bloomington: Indiana University Press, 1989.

Trudeau, Lawrence J., ed. *Asian American Literature: Reviews and Criticism of Works by American Writers of Asian Descent.* Detroit: Gale Research, 1999.

Uno, Roberta and Lucy Mae San Pablo Burns, eds. *The Color of Theater: Race, Culture, and Contemporary Performance.* London: Continuum, 2002.

Vevaina, Coomi S. and Barbara Godard, eds. *Intersexions: Issues of Race and Gender in Canadian Women's Writing.* New Delhi, India: Creative, 1996.

Waxman, Barbara Frey, ed. *Multicultural Literatures Through Feminist/Poststructuralist Lenses.* Knoxville: University of Tennessee Press, 1993.

Whitlock, Gillian. *The Intimate Empire: Reading Women's Autobiography (Literature, Culture and Identity).* London: Cassell Academic, 2000.

Williams, Dave. *Misreading the Chinese Character: Images of the Chinese in Euroamerican Drama to 1925.* New York: Peter Lang, 2000.

Wilson, Robert Arden and Bill Hosokawa. *East to America: A History of the Japanese in the United States.* New York: William Morrow, 1980.

Wolcott, John R. and Michael L. Quinn. *Staging Diversity: Plays and Practice in American Theatre.* Dubuque, IA: Kendall/Hunt, 1992.

Wong, K. Scott and Sucheng Chan. *Claiming America: Constructing Chinese American Identities During the Exclusion Era.* Philadelphia: Temple University Press, 1998.

Wong, Sau-ling Cynthia. *Reading Asian American Literature: From Necessity to Extravagance.* Princeton: Princeton University Press, 1993.

Wong, Sau-ling Cynthia and Stephen H. Sumida, eds. *A Resource Guide to Asian American Literature.* New York: MLA, 2001.

Wu, Frank. *Yellow: Race in America Beyond Black and White.* New York: Basic Books, 2002.

Yamamoto, Traise. *Masking Selves, Making Subjects: Japanese American Women, Identity and the Body.* Berkeley: University of California Press, 1999.

Yu, Henry. *Thinking Orientals: Migration, Contact, and Exoticism in Modern America.* New York: Oxford University Press, 2001.

Part IV
Periodicals

Amerasia Journal
American Literature
American Studies International
American Theatre
Asian Pacific American Journal
Auto-Biography Studies
Bamboo Ridge: A Hawai'i Writers Journal
Canadian Theatre Review
Catamaran: A Journal of South Asian American Writing
Critical Arts: A Journal for Cultural Studies
Diaspora: A Journal of Transnational Studies
Disorient: An Asian Pacific American Literary Arts Journalzine
The Drama Review
Hitting Critical Mass: A Journal of Asian American Cultural Criticism
JAAS: Journal of Asian American Studies
Journal of Dramatic Theory and Criticism
Journal of Ethnic Studies
Manoa: A Pacific Journal of International Writing
MELUS: Journal of the Society for the Study of the Multi-Ethnic Literature of the United States
Modern Drama
Mosaic: A Journal for the Interdisciplinary Study of Literature
Multicultural Review
positions: east asia cultures critique
Public Culture
Race, Gender and Class: An Interdisciplinary Journal
South Asian Literature
South Asian Popular Culture
SPAN: Journal of the South Pacific Association for Literature and Language Studies
Theater

Index